European Communication Research and Education Association

This series consists of books arising from the interests of ECREA members. Books address themes relevant to ECREA's interests; make a major contribution to the theory, research, practice and/or policy literature; are European in scope; and represent a diversity of perspectives. Book proposals are refereed.

Series Editors
Nico Carpentier
François Heinderyckx

Series Advisory Board
Denis McQuail
Robert Picard
Jan Servaes

The aims of the ECREA are:

a) To provide a forum where researchers and others involved in communication and information research can meet and exchange information and documentation about their work. Its disciplinary focus will include media, (tele)communications and informatics research, including relevant approaches of human and social sciences;

b) To encourage the development of research and systematic study, especially on subjects and areas where such work is not well developed;

c) To stimulate academic and intellectual interest in media and communication research, and to promote communication and cooperation between members of the Association;

d) To co-ordinate the circulation of information on communications research in Europe, with a view to establishing a database of ongoing research;

e) To encourage, support, and where possible, publish, the work of young researchers in Europe;

f) To take into account the desirability of different languages and cultures in Europe;

g) To develop links with relevant national and international communication organisations and with professional communication researchers working for commercial organisations and regulatory institutions, both public and private;

h) To promote the interests of communication research within and among the Member States of the Council of Europe and the European Union;

i) To collect and disseminate information concerning the professional position of communication researchers in the European region; and

j) To develop, improve and promote communication and media education.

Reclaiming the Media
Communication Rights
and Democratic Media Roles

Edited by Bart Cammaerts
and Nico Carpentier

intellect
Bristol, UK
Chicago, USA

First Published in the UK in 2007 by
Intellect Books, PO Box 862, Bristol BS99 1DE, UK
First Published in the USA in 2007 by
Intellect Books, The University of Chicago Press, 1427
E. 60th Street, Chicago, IL 60637, USA

A catalogue record for this book is available from the British Library

ISBN 978-1-84150-163-5
Cover Design: Gabriel Solomons

Printed and bound by Gutenberg Press Ltd, Malta.

Contents

Foreword

We inevitably find ourselves in the position of trying to understand contemporary situations with the aid of analytic tools derived from the past, whether the issues at hand have to do with our personal everyday lives or with macro-societal issues. In any given set of circumstances, we mobilize those familiar sets of concepts, those frames of reference that we have at our disposal, and we continue in that manner – that is, until discrepancies between newer situations and older ways of thinking force us into critical reflection. With a decade or two of hindsight, we can note that this seems certainly to be the case in regard to a nexus of themes having to do with democracy, citizenship, the media and journalism. A lot of history has been taking place over a relatively short time span in these areas, and in the process, we have been witnessing a great deal of reflection and reformulation about how to understand the developments. This book is an important contribution in that process.

The overarching notion of democracy has, of course, always been problematic at some level, not least in regard to whether it has been fully achieved or remains basically a vision that requires continual struggle to be minimally attained and maintained. No doubt one's views on such matters were, and still are, in part shaped by where in the world – in what particular society – one happens to be, but sharing the same socio-political realities per se does not ensure any consensus on that matter. The ideas and ideals of democracy remain contested, and if at times we may experience this as both cumbersome and tiresome, we should keep in mind that such debate is at bottom in itself a sign of democratic vitality, not least in societies where there are legal and other barriers to such discussion. In terms of the political systems of Western liberal democracies, it has almost become a truism in many circles that it is not functioning as it has in the past. Observers record general declines in party loyalties, in voter turnouts, in engagement with issues, even in involvement with the associations and other institutions of civil society. The official arenas of democratic politics are seemingly caught in an 'energy crisis' (though certainly the polarized climate in the United States around the Bush administration must be seen as a very important exception), while at the same time an expansive vitality is seen in extra-parliamentarian contexts. Various groups, networks, movements and NGOs are renewing political engagement in ways that are beginning to transform the very character of the 'democratic system', broadening its ideological spectrum and manifesting new (as well as traditional) forms of civic agency.

These developments must be understood against a backdrop of dramatic socio-cultural change that is altering the conditions that have shaped Western liberal democracy. In the context of a globalizing late modernity, many of the institutional forces, life patterns, modes of relationships, consumption patterns, media milieus and their info-symbolic frameworks, and processes of identity formation – to just name a few key aspects – have in the past three decades undergone deep-seated permutations if we compare with circumstances in the first three post-war decades. While there may at times be tendencies to exaggerate the decline in old patterns and ignore the continuities that are still with us, important factors that shape the experience of society and its cultural dimensions, at the level of the individual and of institutions, have nonetheless been mutating before our eyes. In this dynamic interplay of powerful societal vectors, people's horizons of knowledge and expectation, their values, sense of belonging, perceived efficacy and overall social imaginaries unavoidably become modified.

These changes are of course connected to another obvious puzzle piece, namely the neo-liberal turn in global capitalism. We need not get involved here in discussions about which factors are the most fundamental and which are derivative of other forces; we need only to note their simultaneity and reciprocal interplay for understanding the changing situation of democracy. While there have always been tensions between the ideals of democracy and the mechanisms of capitalism, the neo-liberal era of the past quarter century has immeasurably changed the circumstances in which democracy operates. Not only do we witness very real retrenchments in the kinds of decisions that are handled by formal democratic systems with considerable power shifting to the corporate sector, but also there is a significant ideological transformation at work: democracy is increasingly being reconfigured, in conceptual and rhetorical terms, to make it compatible with a corporate view of societal development. Democratic will becomes increasingly reduced to market choice. In such circumstances, to placidly continue with our previous notions of democracy – to not see and meet the challenge inherent in this development – is to abdicate responsibility for its future.

While some of the discussions and polemics around democracy also touch upon citizenship, the notion of citizenship has, until relatively recently, loped along in a somewhat taken-for-granted manner. It has been a formal category framed by normative and legal discourses, not one that invited a pro-active view on social agency. It has used as an admonishment in civic classes and public contexts: people are at times encouraged to play their civic roles, though it can be said that the understanding of this role has, at least implicitly, been rather delimited. Also, such encouragements have rarely touched on, for example, what the socio-cultural realities of civic agency might mean in today's world. Various developments have prompted wide-ranging reflection on citizenship: the nation–state's relative decline in power – and the relative increase in corporate power – in an ever globalizing world; the increasing demands for rights and recognition from groups who have felt themselves to be marginalized in some way; growing insight that citizenship has cultural as well as civil, political and social dimensions; and not least, recent dramatic events such as the collapse of communism and 9/11, with the security measures and restrictions on civil liberties that followed in the wake of the war on terrorism; these and other factors have all contributed to put citizenship on contemporary political and intellectual agendas. Thus, we have today, on the one hand, growing sectors of (largely) extra-parliamentarian engagement that embody and enact expanded versions of citizenship, and on the other, a robust multi-disciplinary field of citizenship studies, that is struggling to understand its contemporary significance, potential and the dangers that it faces.

These developments in the practice and theory of citizenship manifest themselves concretely in civic participation. While 'engagement' might be expressed in thought, in a subjective state, participation suggests some kind of visible practice. Indeed, in the wake of the growing informal, extra-parliamentarian initiatives over the past two decades or so, we have come to understand that there are many ways of enacting civic agency, of manifesting political involvement. One of the recurring themes in much of the relevant literature is precisely that the very notion of what constitutes 'the political' is being rethought and consequently, the repertoires of participation are expanding, moving far beyond the traditional forms of voting or writing a letter to one's representative. For many citizens today, politics is something larger, something beyond the domain defined by elected politicians. Today, participation not just anchored in overarching worldviews and political beliefs, but also in more personal values, or in moral views that resonate in a meaningful way. Thus, one can participate in anti-sweatshop movements without having a vision of a socialist future for society. On the other hand, one can be against abortion or for certain dress codes in schools based on religious beliefs. There is no guarantee that participation based on broader value considerations will always lead to progressive decisions, but at least democracy is enhanced by such involvement.

At what point we may deem that participation should be seen as activism can not be resolved in the abstract, but certainly in concrete cases we can sense when participation has taken on such a focused, critical mass of energy aimed at attaining specific changes that we would want to label it activism. The urgency, militancy, associated with activism should not be viewed as something negative that signals a 'failure' of deliberative democracy in various public spheres. Assuming that activism does not promote or indirectly generate violence, it should be valued as a central feature of democracy, an integral part of a healthy civic culture. While deliberation and other forms of civic talk are crucial, we should recall that talk *per se* does not exhaust the practices of civic agency. There are many other ways of intervening in politics, other skills and competencies that are necessary for democratic progress, such as lobbying, mobilizing, bargaining, disruption and even civil disobedience.

In liberal democracies, the media generally, and journalism specifically, have always generated discussion and criticism, most of it framed by the prevailing liberal assumptions about media and democracy, but also by radical critics. However, the intense developments within the media industries over the past couple of decades – with such trends as globalized conglomeration and concentration, deregulation and commercialization, ever-growing abundance, hybridization of traditional journalistic genres and formats, digitalization and the rise of relatively inexpensive interactive media – have all contributed to a media landscape that has become acutely altered over the past decades. Since the media comprises much of the scene in which politics is played out, these changes of course impact on the dynamics of democracy. News, for example, has seemingly become too important to be left solely in the hands of journalists, and we see a growing cadre of spin-doctors and other media professionals trying to shape the journalistic practices and output. While even politically marginalized groups can engage in such activities, it is the economic and political elites whose efforts in this regard show the greater pay-off.

The perspective of the media helps us to readily weave together the other themes of democracy, citizenship, participation and activism. These themes, critically reframed in the light of recent history, in turn, provide us with ports of entry to further our analyzes of the media, as well as guiding democratic intervention into the media landscape itself. We have come to see that the ensemble of rights – and duties – that are embodied in citizenship must be situated in the context of our mediatized societies. Thus, the media's democratic role have to be continually updated to take into account the changes in the media landscape – issues around availability, access, diversity, pluralism, costs, etc. However, from the standpoint of citizenship, it becomes imperative that we define, assert and protect communication rights. Given the character of the modern media, democracy will not function properly if the media are not made accountable to citizens, if their communication rights are not taken into account in the development of media policy.

Certainly, media development today is largely driven by market forces, and people's subject positions vis-à-vis the media are for the most part defined as consumers and spectators. At the present juncture in history, there does not appear to be any immediate alternative hovering in the wings. Yet, as with all commercially based enterprise, there exist possibilities for public interest regulation. It is encouraging that the media have thus increasingly become the object, target, of democratic participation and activism. Developing long-term campaigns to mobilize opinion from various quarters to impact on media policies and regulation becomes a way for people to place demands to reclaim and defend a sufficient part of the media – both the mass media and the newer interactive channels – for civic purposes. In the process, they are defending and extending democracy.

The present collection of excellent contributions takes up and extends these, and other, central themes. This volume consists of contemporary efforts to highlight the inexorable linkages between democracy, citizenship, journalism, participation and activism. It helps us to think critically and constructively about reclaiming the media for democracy. I would like to express my appreciation to Bart Cammaerts and Nico Carpentier for taking this fine initiative.

Peter Dahlgren

Introduction

Reclaiming the media: communication rights and expanding democratic media roles

Bart Cammaerts and Nico Carpentier

Media and democracy

The importance of media in terms of democratic practices and fostering a democratic or civic culture can hardly be denied. However, the way in which these democratic roles are articulated varies strongly and is necessarily ideologically laden, as it is embedded in distinct theoretical traditions, on at least two levels.

First, there is a considerable variety in democratic theories, as the overview in Table 1 suggests (see also Held, 2006). Some models tend to restrict democracy to more centralized and elitist forms of societal decision-making, protected by a legal-procedural articulation of democracy and a narrow definition of the political (as the political system). Ironically, its extreme variation brings us outside democracy and leads us towards totalitarian models. Other democratic models cherish a more decentralized version of societal decision-making, supported by a more substantial and/or culturalist interpretation of democracy and a broad definition of the political as a dimension of the societal.

A second dimension in democratic theory focuses on the main structuring concept that lies behind the societal decision-making process and ranges from conflict to consensus. In the first case, the socio-political is seen as dominated by manifest and latent conflicts, possibly within the context of hegemonic projects. The confrontation between different societal groups leads to (heated) debates and claims of victory. In the second case, consensus is seen as the main societal organizing principle, focussing on the presence and achievement of societal harmony and unity. Here, processes of deliberation and dialogue support a harmonious polis and (if necessary) aim to stabilize the disruptions of this harmony.

Apart from the wide range of democratic theories, an evenly wide range of normative theories on the relationship of the media, society and democracy exists. The liberal perspective is well (and approvingly) described in the *Four Theories of the Press* written by Siebert, Peterson and Schramm (1956). Its strong focus on information is complemented by the presence of the watchdog function of the media. This position can be illustrated, amongst others, by policy documents referring to media development and its role in transitional democracies. For example, US-AID builds on this Anglo–Saxon liberal tradition of access to information. As such, they define the role of media in a democracy in a narrow sense.

Table 1:

Dimensions of democratic theory

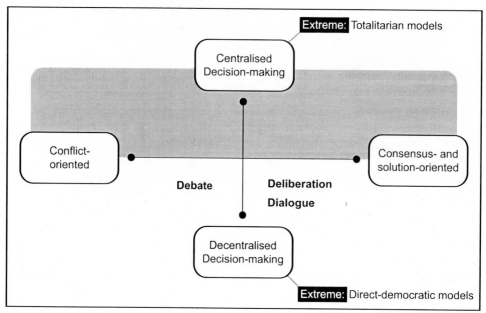

Access to information is essential to the health of democracy for at least two reasons. First, it ensures that citizens make responsible, informed choices rather than acting out of ignorance or misinformation. Second, information serves a "checking function" by ensuring that elected representatives uphold their oaths of office and carry out the wishes of those who elected them. (US-AID, 1999: 5)

The citizen is individualized, even atomized, and their ethical obligation to make informed choices in the marketplace of ideas is emphasized. In the earlier quotation, the watchdog function of the media is also explicitly mentioned, which is the second key component of the liberal model. This liberal perspective is closely linked to, and grounded in, a procedural-formal definition of what constitutes democracy, focussing on elections and the rational 'informed' choice of active citizens.

From a more critical perspective, Curran (2000: 148) provides us with a broader overview of the different roles that media could/should fulfil in (mature) democracies:

It should empower people by enabling them to explore where their interest lies; it should foster sectorial solidarities and assist the functioning of organisations necessary for the effective representation of collective interests; it should sustain vigilant scrutiny of government and centres of power; it should provide a source of protection and redress for the weak and unorganized interests; and it should create the conditions for real societal agreement or compromise based on an open working through of differences rather than a contrived consensus based on elite dominance.

Curran points to distinct but at the same time overlapping democratic media roles that re-enforce each other. His starting point goes beyond the procedural–formal democracy as he fosters the media's role in a civic or democratic culture. He nevertheless includes elements of the liberal model, by referring to the media's role in scrutinizing the powers that be and in exposing their dysfunctions. He also refers to the (evenly traditional) social responsibility model by stressing the moral obligation of media organizations to represent the social 'correctly', and to address misrepresentations and stereotypes of weak and disadvantaged groups in society. Curran transcends these more traditional approaches with his strong emphasis on the empowerment of citizens. This also questions the notion of citizenship as a collection of merely individual freedoms and also clearly supports collective rights and solidarities. His reference to the media's need to support deliberative processes that respect difference, and the need to avoid hegemonic practices, also introduces a more critical angle to Curran's normative account of media roles.

Curran's (1997) emphasis on the notion of difference already creates a bridge between the critical approaches and the challenges posed by post-structuralist and post-modern approaches. In his article 'Rethinking the Public Sphere', Curran attempts to articulate a radical democratic (normative) theory of the media, which he distinguishes from the more traditional liberal, Marxist and communist theories. In this model, the public sphere becomes a public arena of contest, filled with a diversity of representations. Or as Kellner (1992: 57) remarks, the media should not be defined as hypodermic needles, but as 'a crucial site of hegemony'. This implies that media play an important role as sites for both democratic deliberation and antagonistic or agonistic conflict (Mouffe, 1993), and as sites that combine the disciplining of societal voices with the resistant challenges of hegemony.

From these perspectives, media themselves become one of the key players in the democratic game. They are not seen as just passively expressing or reflecting social phenomena, or as sites where discourses merely circulate, but as specific machineries and 'systems of dispersion' (Foucault, 1984: 37–38) that produce, reproduce and transform social phenomena. This shaping and signifying social phenomena also includes the concept of democracy itself, as media constantly provide us with definitions of for instance democracy, participation and representation, normalizing some definitions and discrediting others. Power then again becomes an important analytical concept; it allows us to understand how the media position themselves as a social center (Couldry, 2002) and include or exclude people from the processes of naming (Melucci, 1996) and framing.

Communication rights

Part of this struggle is linked to the relationship between citizens, media organizations and states. Capitalist tendencies in both media landscapes and media policies have reduced the capacity of publics to act as citizens, as they are very much positioned as consumers. Despite the valid point that media consumption is not necessarily totally detached from (cultural) citizenship (see Hartley, 1999), this reduction is nevertheless problematic as it brings along high democratic opportunity costs.

Attempts have been made to address this imbalance structurally, by introducing the concept of communication rights. When the right to communicate was originally proposed in 1969 – by the French civil servant, Jean d'Arcy – it aimed to broaden the right to be informed, which is embedded in article 19 of the Universal Declaration of Human Rights. The right to communicate – referred to by Jacobson (1998) as a third generation human right – was very much at the centre of the UNESCO debates relating to the New World Information and Communication Order (NWICO) and the plea for a 'free and balanced flow of information'. This repositioning expanded the traditional Western 'right to be informed' and redefined communication as 'a two way process, in which the partners – individual and collective – carry on a democratic and balanced dialogue' (MacBride, 1980: 172). In practice, this implied that:

a. *the individual becomes an active partner and not a mere object of communication;*
b. *the variety of messages exchanged increases; and*
c. *the extent and quality of social representation or participation in communication are augmented* (MacBride, 1980: 166).

As Jacobson slightly ironically remarks, the MacBride commission was correct in its assumption that '[the] right to communicate [still has to] receive its final form and its full content' (MacBride, 1980: 173). Harms' definition, explicitly mentioned in the MacBride report, nevertheless remains relevant:

Everyone has the right to communicate: the components of this comprehensive Human Right include but are not limited to the following specific communication rights: a/a right to assemble, a right to discuss, a right to participate and related association rights; b/a right to inquire, a right to be informed, a right to inform, and related information rights; c/a right to culture, a right to choose, a right to privacy, and related human development rights (Harms quoted by MacBride, 1980: 173).

The concept of the right to communicate (almost) received its 'coup de grace' when the United States, as well as the United Kingdom, pulled out of UNESCO (Jacobson, 1998: 398). During the 1990s, the right to communicate disappeared almost completely from UNESCO's agenda (as well as from the agenda of other international organizations), with the exception of forums like the 'MacBride round table' (Hamelink, 1997: 298). Only in 2003, in the slipstream of the UN World Summit on the Information Society [1] was the debate on communication rights revitalized and reinvigorated, partially thanks to initiatives like the Communication Rights in the Information Society Campaign (CRIS) [2]. Still, the exact signification, formulation and span of the concept of communication rights have not stabilized. A more contemporary version can for instance be found in Hamelink and Hoffman (2004: 3): 'those rights – codified in international and regional human rights instruments – that pertain to standards of performance with regard to the provision of information and the functioning of communication processes in society'.

More important than the exact formulation of communication rights are the democratic ideals (and ideology) that support it. Communication rights have been developed as one of the many strategies for 'democratizing democracy' (Giddens, 2002: 93) or for increasing the share of decentralized decision-making. Whatever perspective on the democratic roles of media organizations is taken, all perspectives are in agreement when it comes to the vital role media play in contemporary democracies. We would like to argue that this societal importance brings along rather significant responsibilities, towards the entire polis, but also towards civil societies, economies and individual citizens. To put it differently, media organizations have a vital role to play, not just in democracy as such, but also in the much-needed project of deepening or democratizing our democracies. This unavoidably requires a repositioning of the media organizations in their relation to their publics. Although much has been said (and rightly so) about the active audience, a lot of barriers between the media and the public persist, unnecessarily reducing the level of audience activity in terms of access and participation. Communication rights contribute to this new and more intense relation between media organizations and their publics, whereby these media can become democratic gate openers rather then gate-keepers (Manca, 1989). In other words, communication rights legitimize the (symbolical) reclaiming of the media by their publics.

This book does not wish to do away with the traditional forms and conceptualizations of democracy, media, citizenship and journalism. Despite their legitimacy as such, these traditional variations need to be scrutinized and criticized whenever and wherever necessary, showing their dysfunctions and inappropriate hegemonic claims (Carpentier, 2005). At the same time, we need other and more variations of media and journalistic identities that are, for instance, more innovative when it comes to participation. We also (and desperately) need media activisms that are willing to critique the traditions and propagate the innovations. Despite the unavoidable antagonisms between traditional and participatory forms of journalism and media production, between new and old forms of citizenship, between media activists and media professionals, we believe all these identities and practices can coexist. Here we do appreciate Mao Tse-Tung's statement, 'Let one thousand flowers bloom.'

Structure of the book

The book project was initiated at the First European Communication Conference, which took place in Amsterdam in November 2005 and was jointly organized by the Amsterdam School of Communications Research (ASCoR), the European Consortium for Communications research (ECCR) and the European Communication Association (ECA). On this occasion, ECCR and ECA merged into a new European organization called the European Communication Research and Education Association (ECREA).

One of the ECREA sections, the Communication and Democracy Section organized three panels at the Amsterdam conference, entitled Communication Rights in the EU – history and contemporary perspectives; Journalism in Democracy; and Past, Present and Future of Networked Activism. These panels and their presentations provide us with the backbone of this book, both at the level of content and structure. Moreover, as many of the conference presenters and authors of this book are ECREA members, this book also provides us with an (albeit partial) overview of the work of ECREA members.

This book addresses the role of media and communication in democracies by focussing on four subsets of issues. The general theme of communication rights will be addressed (differently) in all four subsets, but will get special attention in the first subset on citizenship and public sphere, given their close relation. The three other subsets – participation, journalism and activism – all are intimately related to the (potential) democratic role of the media. To explore these key notions further, each subset of chapters will be introduced by a short conceptual text, focussing on the signification and relevance of the key concept(s) being addressed.

The first subset of chapters, Section One, focuses on citizenship and the public sphere, with special consideration to communication rights. Citizenship is, however, much more than mere rights and obligations. It also refers to the way a society mediates between different interests and seeks a societal consensus of what constitutes the public good. In other words, citizenship and the civic is also about the process to determine which rights a society upholds and which obligations it demands in return. Crucial to this process is the public sphere, the arena where this societal consensus can be forged. However, the public sphere can also be conceived as contentious, oppositional and conflictual. First, Kari Karppinen explores this tension between consensus and conflict in the public sphere through analyzing discourses on media diversity and pluralism. Next, Claudia Padovani, Arjuna Tuzzi and Giorgia Nesti analyze e-democracy discourses in a selection of documents focussing on the role of ICTs in the changing relationship between citizens and the (representative) democratic process. Finally, Margit Böck explores the usefulness of Freire's pedagogy of the oppressed for media literacy strategies.

The second subset, Section Two, elaborates further on a notion central to communication rights, namely that of participation. This subset focuses on the interconnections between the media system and the non-media professional 'other'. In this subset, the key concept is media participation, and these articles analyze how concepts as access, interaction and co-deciding materialize (or not) within the media system. Auli Harju looks at a spontaneous process of civic action in Tampere (Finland) and local journalism's way of reacting. Egil G. Skogseth analyzes the democratic and participatory potential of the experimental research project and prototype Web radio station Demostation. Tamara Witschge's chapter, finally, deals with one of the key components of participation in discussion forums, namely inclusionary and exclusionary practices.

In the third subset of chapters, Section Three, the traditional political role of the media is emphasized, drawing on long-standing research traditions in political communication, studying the media's representational role in relation to democracy and citizenship. First, Nico Carpentier's chapter gives a broad outline of the tools media professionals can use to increase the democratic and participatory nature of their practices. Hannu Niemienen looks at participatory (media) projects as ways to bypass traditional media and attempt to establish new relations with the 'people'. Finally, Anu Kantola deconstructs the way that financial journalism (and more specifically, the *Financial Times*) defines democracy through its neo-liberal lenses.

A fourth and final subset, Section Four, moves outside of the (traditional) media system, and deals with a diversity of media and communication strategies of activists. All three chapters deal with the impact of globalizing trends and technological changes on activism and activist strategies, both from the perspective of media-activism and the use of media by activists. Natalie Fenton discusses the theoretical implications of these transformations for the nature of social and political protest. The two other chapters focus more on specific cases. Arne Hintz contextualizes the efforts of media activists within global policy forums, such as the WSIS, to advocate for the communication rights of civil society media. Bart Cammaerts closes off with a chapter analyzing, from a non-mediacentric perspective, the media and communication strategies of local activists, appropriating transnational discourses and action strategies.

Notes for Introduction

[1]   www.itu.int/wsis. This summit was held in 2003 in Geneva and in 2005 in Tunis.

[2]   http://www.crisinfo.org/.

References for Introduction

Carpentier, N. (2005), 'Identity, Contingency and Rigidity. The (counter-)Hegemonic Constructions of the Identity of the Media professional', *Journalism*, 6: 2, pp. 199–219.

Couldry, N. (2002), *Media Rituals: A Critical Approach*, London: Routledge.

Curran, J. (1997), 'Rethinking the Media as Public Sphere', in P. Dahlgren and C. Sparks (eds.), *Communication and Citizenship*, London/New York: Routledge, pp. 27–57.

—— (2000), 'Rethinking Media and Democracy', in J. Curran and M. Gurevitch (eds.), *Mass Media & Society,* (3rd ed.), London: Arnold, pp. 120–54.

Foucault, M. (1984), *The Archaeology of Knowledge*, New York: Pantheon.

Giddens, A. (2002), *Runaway World. How Globalisation is Reshaping our Lives*, (2nd ed.), London: Profile.

Hamelink, C. (1997), *The Politics of World Communication*, London, Thousand Oaks, New Delhi: Sage.

Hamelink, C. J., Hoffman, J. (2004), *Assessing the Status Quo on Communication Rights*, Preliminary Report, Amsterdam: University of Amsterdam.

Hartley, J. (1999), *Uses of Television*, London and New York: Routledge.

Held, D. (2006), *Models of Democracy*, (3rd ed.), Cambridge and Stanford: Polity Press and Stanford University Press.

Jacobson, T. L. (1998), 'Discourse ethics and the right to communicate', *Gazette,* 60: 5, pp. 395–413.

Kellner, D. (1992), *The Persian Gulf TV War*, Boulder, San Francisco, Oxford: Westview Press.

MacBride, S. (1980), 'Many Voices, One World', *Report by the International Commission for the Study of Communication Problems*, Paris and London: Unesco and Kogan Page.

Manca, L. (1989), 'Journalism, Advocacy, and a Communication Model for Democracy', in M. Raboy and P. Bruck (eds.), *Communication for and Against Democracy*, Montréal, New York: Black Rose Books, pp. 163–73.

Melucci, A. (1996), 'Challenging codes', *Collective Action in the Information Age*, Cambridge: Cambridge University Press.

Mouffe, C. (1993), *The Return of the Political*, London: Verso.

Siebert, F., Peterson, T., Schramm, W. (1956), *Four Theories of the Press*, Urbana: University of Illinois Press.

US-AID (1999), 'The Role of Media in Democracy: A Strategic Approach', *Technical Publications Series*, Center for Democracy and Governance, Washington DC: US-AID. http://www.usaid.gov/our_work/democracy_and_governance/ publications/ pdfs/pnace630.pdf. Consulted 1 March 2006.

Citizenship, the Public Sphere, and Media

Bart Cammaerts

Historically, citizenship can be traced back to ancient Greek city–states. It is traditionally understood as a system whereby rights are granted to and duties put upon citizens. Citizenship can also be viewed as a way of structuring society, of enforcing boundaries that allowed the (city-) state to include, but above all to exclude. From this perspective, citizens are the 'official' and registered inhabitants of a geographically delimited territory. They are allocated specific rights by the state, which 'others' – non-citizens, foreigners, denizens, deviants, prisoners, slaves, etc. – do not have. In return, certain duties are expected from the citizen.

However, citizenship, as it is understood today, has evolved considerably since the Greek city–states or since the formation and consolidation of the nation states after the treaty of Westphalia (Münster) in 1648. Western Enlightenment, the struggle for universal suffrage and modernism, in close connection to the class struggles, as is shown in T. H. Marshall's seminal work *Citizenship and Social Class*, has considerably extended citizenship rights. Marshall (1950: 10–11) defined citizenship as being composed out of civic, political, as well as social rights:

> *The civil element is composed of the rights necessary for personal freedom [...] By the political element I mean the right to participate in the exercise of political power, as a member of a body invested with political power or as an elector of such a body. [...] By the social element I mean the whole range from the right to a modicum of economic welfare and security to the right to share to the full in the social heritage and to live the life of a civilised being according to the standards prevailing in the society.*

Later the Marshallian conceptualization of citizenship was refined, amongst others, by introducing the social welfare state as the realm in which citizenship materialized in modern societies (Esping-Andersen, 1990: 21; Pierson and Castles, 2000). Feminist authors also criticized the dominant 'pater familias' focus (Lister, 1997). Furthermore, an ethnic minority perspective was introduced (Soysal, 1994; Ginsburg, 1994). In the 1980s and 1990s, the emphasis within citizenship studies partly shifted from 'rights' to 'obligations', such as paying taxes, voting, being part of a jury or other civic duties, but also informing oneself (Etzioni, 1993; Janoski, 1998).

The assumption of an intrinsic link between the notion of citizenship and the nation/welfare state remains pre-dominant in most of these approaches. Citizenship is developed and conceptualized within the 'boundaries' of the modernist state, which remains the most important political space in which rights are voted, upheld and enforced through the rule of law (at least within democratic societies).

However, the increasing globalization of the world economy – characterized by post-Fordism and fuelled by the introduction of innovations in communication, distribution and mobility, ecological and demographic pressures, as well as ethnic and nationalistic forces – has considerably undermined the sovereignty and legitimacy of the nation state (Held *et al.*, 1999; Haque, 1996). Due to these social, economic and political transformations, it is fair to assert that the conceptualization of the Westphalian nation state, as a sovereign state linked to a geographical territory with relative material, economical, social, physical and psychological autonomy, has become very difficult to sustain (Rosenau, 1990).

Besides the effects on citizenship of the power shift from states to the market, from states to regions or to international organization/regimes, the linkage of citizenship and the nation state is also being challenged by culturalist and post-structuralist theories, which put cultural citizenship on the agenda. Cultural citizenship is 'understood as membership of an actual or virtual community based not on nation but on, for example, ethnicity, gender, sexual orientation, region, age, etc' (Hartley, 1999: 208). This form of citizenship implies the redefinition of citizenship as 'sets (plural) of different and sometimes overlapping communities that constitute individuals as competent members of sets of different and sometimes overlapping communities [...] which should ideally constitute the national (political) culture' (Hermes, 1998: 159). From these perspectives, special attention is attributed to the relationship between global media (including the Internet) and cultural globalization, and to what this means for the notion of citizenship (Lash and Urry, 1994; Rantanen, 2004).

Both the post-Fordist global economic and the culturalist challenges to citizenship have given rise to a number of 'unbounded' citizenship notions such as ecological citizenship, net.citizen(ship), transnational citizenship, cosmopolitan citizenship or denationalized citizenship (van Steenbergen, 1994; Bauböck, 1994; Hauben, 1995; Linklater, 1999; Sassen, 2002). These citizenships transcend the personal and the individual and collective rights focus inherent to formalized legal citizenship. As Mouffe (1992: 231) argued, citizenship thus becomes a 'form of identification, a type of political identity; something to be constructed, not empirically given'. This also reflects an ethical stance that sees the moral being inscribed into the political and a strong belief in change, agency and the capacity of democracy to constantly transform and adapt itself. It points to an idealized citizenship and – to a certain extent – to the impossibility of full – complete and stable – citizenship (Enwezor *et al.*, 2002).

Citizenship is thus constantly re-negotiated and increasingly linked to sexual, cultural and/or ethnic identities and sub-cultures. It points to the distinctiveness, but also (possibly conflictuous) coexistence of, on the one hand the citizen as a legal subject, linked to communities of birth, the polis and welfare state rights, and on the other hand the citizen as a normative subject, linked to social, sexual or cultural identities and practices, to communities of interest (Giddens, 1991; Beck *et al.*, 1994; Bennett, 1998). What binds both types of citizenship is that they simultaneously exclude and include; they set boundaries as to who is in or out, thereby constructing the identities of all involved.

Communication has always played an important mediating role regarding the facilitation of the debate on, the articulation of and the struggle for new citizenship rights. As Urry (1999: 318) argued, '[c]itizenship has always necessitated symbolic resources distributed through various means of mass communication'. Citizenship thus refers to the process that leads to the articulation of certain rights, the forging of a societal consensus about the nature and extent of rights and obligations, about the balance between different often conflicting rights. The public sphere is a central – albeit contested – notion in this regard.

From a liberal perspective, the public gathering is conceived as the marketplace of ideas. While pluralism is heralded as an important democratic value, at the same time, the personal autonomy of individuals is emphasized in determining which ideas prevail over others. Thus, from a liberal perspective a consensus is reached if a majority of individuals make the same or similar choices.

Opposed to this procedural and individualized conception of democracy and the articulation of the common as a marketplace of ideas, embedded in the US first amendment tradition, is a more West European conception of the public sphere, embedded in values such as equality, reason, deliberation, and discourse. The most well-known representative of this tradition is the German philosopher Jürgen Habermas. He argues that discourse becomes democratic through communicative rationality, which

> *recalls older ideas of logos, inasmuch as it brings along with it the connotations of a noncoercively unifying, consensus-building force of a discourse in which the participants overcome their at first subjectively based views in favor of a rationally motivated agreement'* (Habermas, 1990: 315).

He thereby emphasizes that communicative action ideally requires equal positions of the participants and open access for citizens to the deliberative process. Besides this, Habermas' idealtype also presupposes citizens to be rational and knowledgeable, active and informed. Deliberative processes should also be centred on the common good and not on self-interest. In addition, citizens should be willing to modify or change their views as a result of debate and discussion, and the strength of the argument is more important than the status of those who make it. From this deliberative perspective, reaching a consensus is, thus, more a process involving different actors, than a procedure to count the number of personal preferences. It should also be informed by rational argumentations, respect for difference as well as the ability to change views.

Habermas' normative account of a public sphere striving to reach a societal consensus through rational discourse within an ideal speech situation has been extensively criticized (Calhoun, 1992; Benhabib, 1996; Mouffe, 1999). The critiques that ideal speech is a flawed concept, consensus always a temporary ceasefire in a world criss-crossed by ongoing conflicts and that fragmentation leads to multiple public spheres are most relevant here. The public sphere is neither so harmonious and rational nor so unified, as Habermas would like it to be. Instead, the public sphere is seen as an arena of (antagonistic and agonistic) contention, of opposing and conflicting discourses, ideas and interests, increasingly fragmented into what Gitlin (1998) calls 'public sphericules'. Mouffe (1999: 757) points out that a conception of the public sphere must take into account the 'multiplicity of voices that a pluralist society encompasses', as well as 'the complexity of the power structure that this network of differences implies'. From a post-structuralist position, Mouffe argues that a plurality of oppositional discourses and social organization is not to the detriment of democracy, but indeed central to current notions of political mobilization and participation. Within a democratic or civic culture, passions and fierce disagreements should, according to her, not be eliminated in favor of consensus, but to be actively mobilized and incorporated into the democratic project. Post-modernist challenges to the deliberative model also point to the danger that striving towards a consensus, through debate and argumentation, between inherently conflicting interests within each society, re-enforces the hegemony and dominance of ruling elites rather then bring about empowerment and social change (Lyotard, 1984).

However, respect of other persuasions, consensus building, mutual tolerance towards difference and what Dahlgren (2005: 153) calls 'the integrative societal function of the public sphere' remain very useful normative values for any democracy. It is equally important to not slide into indifference, intolerance and outright violence between communities, religions and ethnicities. But at the same time, politics and democracy is as much about conflict and opposing conceptions of the public interest than it is about reaching a (temporary) consensus in society.

Throughout the argument developed earlier, media were always seen to be present in the background, sometimes leaping towards the front stage, facilitating or even accelerating some of the outlined developments. They represent an underlying opportunity structure, playing a crucial and instrumental role in the different struggles for the extension of citizenship rights (Meyer and Minkoff, 2004). So much so, that communication itself has been the object of a struggle on citizenship for over 25 years, with the MacBride report as an official starting point (MacBride, 1980; Traber and Nordenstreng, 1992). More than two decades later, we live in a distinctly different world with old and new challenges. After UNESCO officially abandoned the new information and communication order in 1989, the debate regarding communication rights shifted to civil society. By the end of the 1990s, several initiatives taken by activists and academics in conjunction with large coalitions of civil society organizations had adapted and refined the pleas and arguments for communication rights, to make them face up to those new challenges, without forgetting the old ones. Examples of these are the People's Communication Charter [1], The Seattle Statement (Schuler, 2000), The Communication Rights in the Information Society Charter [2] and the World Summit on the Information Society Civil Society Declaration *Shaping Information Societies to Human Needs* [3]. However, the attempts, recently invigorated by the WSIS-process, to politicize media and communication in terms of a democratic struggle for communication rights have until now largely failed. The mantra of liberalization, free trade, media concentration and copyright protection, ruling media and communication remains as strong and unquestionable as ever. This further undermines the public interests that were deemed inherent to media and communication a few decades ago. It also can be seen as one more symptom of how the citizen is increasingly being reduced to the consumer.

The communication rights discourse represents a counter-hegemonic reaction against the commodification of information and communicational tools. It pleads for a participatory and citizen-oriented approach to information and communication, embedded in an open and transparent democratic culture, with an emphasis on:

- Access to infrastructure, capabilities, skills, services, qualitative content
- Real diversity and pluralism of channels of expression and media outlets
- Vibrant and pluralistic public spheres that go beyond the mainstream and respect difference and minority views
- Independence, ethical norms and protection of journalists
- The common good, knowledge sharing and decommodification of information
- Fair trade and sustainable development
- Support for participatory citizens media initiatives.

This struggle and subsequent attempts to politicize media and communication and to move this debate away from economic interests towards a human rights and citizen-centred perspective has had a troublesome and conflictual history (Ó Siochrú, 2004; Padovani and Nordenstreng, 2005). The current dominant neo-liberal mantras of copy-right protection, of light auto-regulation regimes or reducing regulation to a technical matter and of auctioning the spectrum to the highest bidders, as well as the huge economic and above all commercial interests ruling media and communication in the post-monopoly era, do not represent a very favorable environment to adopt and enact such participatory discourses focussing on citizen empowerment, on pluralism as in diversity of content/opinions, and on normative values that go beyond the materialistic. Needless to say that there is still a long struggle ahead to make (global) communication rights more tangible and, above all, enforceable.

Notes for Section One: Introduction

[1]   http://www.pccharter.net/charteren.html.

[2]   http://www.crisinfo.org/content/view/full/98/.

[3]   http://www.itu.int/wsis/docs/geneva/civil-society-declaration.pdf.

References for Section One: Introduction

Bauböck, B. (1994), *Transnational Citizenship*, Aldershot: Edward Elgar.

Beck, U., Giddens, A., Lash, S. (eds.) (1994), *Reflexive Modernization: Politics, Tradition and Aesthetics in the Modern Social Order*, Cambridge: Polity Press.

Benhabib, S. (ed.) (1996), *Democracy and Difference: Contesting the Boundaries of the Political*, Princeton, NJ: Princeton University Press.

Bennett, L. (1998), 'The Uncivic Culture: Communication, Identity and the Rise of Lifestyle Politics', *Political Science & Politics*, 31: 4, pp. 741–61.

Calhoun, C. (ed.) (1992), *Habermas and the Public Sphere*, Cambridge, MA: MIT Press.

Dahlgren, P. (2005), 'The Internet, Public Spheres, and Political Communication: Dispersion and Deliberation', *Political Communication*, 22, pp. 147–62.

Enwezor, O., Basualdo, C., Bauer, U. M., Ghez, S., Maharaj, S., Nash, M., Zaya, O. (eds.) (2002), *Democracy Unrealized, Documenta11_Platform1*, Kassel: Hatje Cantz.

Esping-Andersen, G. (1990), *The Three Worlds of Welfare Capitalism*, Cambridge: Polity Press.

Etzioni, A. (1993), *The Spirit of Community*, New York: Crown.

Giddens, A. (1991), *Modernity and Self-identity. Self and Society in the Late Modern Age*, Cambridge: Polity Press.

Ginsburg, N. (1994), 'Race, Racism and Social Policy in Western Europe', in J. Ferris and R. Page (eds.), *Social Policy in Transition*, Avebury: Aldershot, pp. 165–86.

Gitlin, T. (1998), 'Public Spheres or Public Sphericules', in T. Liebes and J. Curran (eds.), *Media, Ritual and Identity*, London: Routledge, pp. 168–74.

Habermas, J. (1990), *The Philosophical Discourse of Modernity; Moral Consciousness and Communicative Action* (trans. C. Lenhart and S. W. Nicholson), Cambridge, MA: MIT Press.

Haque, M. S. (1996), 'Public Service Under Challenge in the Age of Privatization', *Governance,* 9: 2, pp. 186–216.

Hartley, J. (1999), *Uses of Television*, London: Routledge.

Hauben, M. F. (1995), 'The Netizens and Community Networks', http://www.columbia.edu/~hauben/text/bbc95spch.txt. Consulted on 1 March 2006.

Held, D., McGrew, A., Goldblatt, D., *et al.* (1999), *Global Transformations*, Cambridge: Polity Press.

Hermes, J. (1998), 'Cultural Citizenship and Popular Culture', in K. Brants, J. Hermes, and L. Van Zoonen (eds.), *The Media in Question. Popular Cultures and Public Interests*, London: Sage, pp. 157–68.

Janoski, T. (1998), *Citizenship and Civil Society: A Framework of Rights and Obligations in Liberal, Traditional and Social Democratic Regimes*, Cambridge: Cambridge University Press.

Lash, S., Urry, J. (1994), *Economies of Signs and Space*, London: Sage.

Linklater, A. (1999), 'Cosmopolitan Citizenship', in K. Hutchings and R. Dannreuther (eds.), *Cosmopolitan Citizenship*, London: Macmillan Press, pp. 35–59.

Lister, R. (1997), *Citizenship: Feminist Perspectives*, London: Macmillan.

Lyotard, J. F. (1984), *The Postmodern Condition: A Report on Knowledge*, Manchester: Manchester University Press.

MacBride, S. (1980), *Many Voices, One World. Report by the International Commission for the Study of Communication Problems*, Paris and London: Unesco and Kogan Page.

Marshall, T. H. (1950), *Citizenship and Social Class*, Cambridge: Cambridge University Press. See also C. Pierson and F. G. Castles (eds.) (2000), *The Welfare State Reader*, London: Polity Press, pp. 32–41.

Meyer, D. S., Minkoff, D. C. (2004), 'Conceptualizing Political Opportunity', *Social Forces*, 82: 4, pp. 1457–92.

Mouffe, C. (1992), 'Democratic citizenship and the political community', in C. Mouffe (ed.), *Dimensions of Radical Democracy: Pluralism, Citizenship, Community*, London: Verso, pp. 225–39.

Mouffe, C. (1999), Deliberative Democracy or Agonistic Pluralism?, *Social Research,* 66: 3, pp. 746–58.

Ó Siochrú, S. (2004), 'Will the Real WSIS Please Stand Up? The Historic Encounter of the "Information Society" and the "Communication Society"', *Gazette: The International Journal for Communication Studies,* 66: 3–4, pp. 203–24.

Padovani, C., Nordenstreng, K. (2005), 'From NWICO to WSIS: Another World Information and Communication Order', *Global Media & Communication,* 1: 3, pp. 264–72.

Pierson, C., Castles, F. G. (eds.) (2000), *The Welfare State Reader,* London: Polity Press.

Rantanen, T. (2004), *The Media and Globalization,* London: Sage.

Rosenau, J. (1990), *Turbulance in World Politics, A Theory of Change and Continuity,* Princeton: Princeton University Press.

Sassen, S. (2002), 'The Repositioning of Citizenship: Emergent Subjects and Spaces for Politics', *Berkeley Journal of Sociology: A Critical Review,* 46, pp. 4–25.

Schuler, D. (2000), 'The Seattle Statement: Moving the Democratic Communication Agenda Forward', *The CPSR Newsletter,* 18:2. http://www.cpsr.org/prevsite/publications/newsletters/issues/2000/Summer2000/seattle1.html. Consulted on 1 March 2006.

Scott, A., Street, J. (2001), 'From Media Politics to E-protest? The Use of Popular Culture and new media in parties and social movements', in F. Webster (ed.), *Culture and Politics in the Information Age, A New Politics?* London: Routledge, pp. 32–51.

Soysal, Y. N. (1994), *Limits of Citizenship: Migrants and Postnational Membership in Europe,* Chicago IL: University of Chicago Press.

Traber, M., Nordenstreng, K. (1992), *Few Voices, Many Worlds. Towards a Media Reform Movement,* London: World Association for Christian Communication (WACC).

Urry, J. (1999), 'Globalization and Citizenship', *Journal of World-Systems Research,* 5: 2, pp. 311–24.

van Steenbergen, B. (1994), 'Towards a Global Ecological Citizen', in van Steenbergen, B. (ed.), *The Condition of Citizenship,* London: Sage, pp. 141–52.

Chapter One

Making a difference to media pluralism: a critique of the pluralistic consensus in European media policy

Kari Karppinen

Introduction

In theorizing the relationship between media and democracy, citizens' access to a wide range of information in the public sphere is unarguably a key condition. Furthermore, notions of pluralism and diversity today seem to invoke a particularly affective resonance; to an extent that they permeate much of the argumentation in current European media policy debates. Yet opinions on the meaning and nature of these values are manifold, and they embody some of central conflicts in contemporary media policy. Based on the undisputed merits of social, political and cultural pluralism, diversity and variety in the media can even be seen as desirable ends in themselves. But as McLennan (1995: 7) noted, the constitutive vagueness of pluralism as a social value gives it enough ideological flexibility so that it is capable of signifying reactionary tendencies in one phase of the debate and progressive values in the next. From the perspective of democratic theory, it has, thus, been noted that 'pluralism is currently one of those values to which everybody refers but whose meaning is unclear and far from adequately theorized' (Mouffe, 1993a: 69). In media policy, the resonance of pluralistic discourses has been exploited accordingly in arguments for various and often incompatible objectives; for free market competition, as well as further public interventions and public service obligations.

The aim of this chapter is to deconstruct some of the paradoxes involved in the use of diversity and pluralism as media policy objectives. The argument is mainly conceptual and rooted in theoretical debates on media and democracy, but the context of contemporary European media policy debates, within political decision-making processes, as well as in expert discourses of policy analysts, serves as an illustration of the conceptual frameworks being adopted by different actors.

In both political and analytical discourses, the concepts of media pluralism and media diversity are used more or less synonymously, raising some confusion regarding the difference, or a possible hierarchy, between the two concepts. Although the purpose here is not to offer any new systematic definitions, the notion of media diversity is generally used in a more empirical or tangible meaning, whereas pluralism refers to a more diffuse societal value or an underlying orientation. In the broadest sense, the concept of media diversity refers to the heterogeneity on the level of contents, outlets, ownership or any other aspect of the media deemed relevant. Respectively, different frameworks have been suggested to analyze its different subcomponents such as source, content and exposure diversity, as well as their mutual hierarchies and relations (see McQuail, 1992; Napoli, 1999; Hellman, 2001; Doyle, 2002). In any case, both function as umbrella terms or conceptual categories whose fundamental ambiguousness and indeterminacy is the very focus of this chapter.

In this chapter, the focus lies on the definitional power involved in political uses of pluralism and diversity. Of course, the contestation over politically and ethically charged concepts is not limited to these, but is rather characteristic of the recent debates around media governance, on the national, European and global level. Similar observations could thus be made of struggles around a number of concepts such as freedom, access or any other concept that is central to the debates on communication rights and citizenship. As such, the contestation of normative concepts and the fact that they can easily be remoulded for various political purposes is not foreign, or undesirable, to any sector of politics. According to Rose and Miller (1992: 178), political discourse is by definition 'a domain for the formulation and justification of idealized schemata for representing reality, analyzing it and rectifying it'. From this perspective, analyzing policy is not so much about what concepts or words, such as freedom, diversity or democracy, mean but rather of analyzing what they do, the way they function in connection with other elements, what they make possible, the sentiments they mobilize and regimes of truth they constitute (Rose, 1999: 29–30). In accordance, the intention here is not to seek the foundations of concepts or to offer new definitions, but to find contradictions, ambiguities and instances of definitional power in their current use in politics. The purpose of this chapter is, thus, to argue for a more reflexive, open-ended understanding of pluralism as a media policy value. Equally, the contribution can be conceived as an attempt at scholarly self-reflection since academic research clearly is one of the main institutions of intellectual machinery that produce the conceptual schemata of political discourse.

Pluralism as an ambiguous social value

Of course, the emphasis on pluralism and diversity as political values is nothing new. Premised on the epistemological impossibility of unambiguously establishing truth, right or good, especially in social and political affairs, pluralism is one of the constitutive tenets of liberal democracy. According to Mouffe (2000: 18), the acceptance of pluralism, understood as 'the end of a substantive idea of the good life', is the most important single defining feature of modern liberal democracy that differentiates it from ancient models of democracy. In this sense, pluralism is understood not merely as a fact, something that must be dealt with, but rather as an axiological principle that is 'constitutive at the conceptual level of the very nature of modern democracy and considered as something that we should celebrate and enhance' (Mouffe, 2000: 19). From a Liberal perspective and in contrast with more community-centred or unitary views of society, pluralism and conflict are seen as fruitful and as being a necessary condition of human progress. Antagonism is seen as mediating progress, and the clash of divergent opinions and interests, in the realm of argument, in economic competition, and struggles in political domain, can be seen as inherently positive (Bobbio, 1990: 21–24).

In other words, pluralism, in whatever field of enquiry, refers to a theorized preference for multiplicity over unicity and diversity over uniformity. In this sense, almost all particular discourses could be conceived as reflecting some aspect of the pluralism/monism interface. Similarly, pluralism is conceived here more as a general intellectual orientation than a specific school of thought or ideology, and the specific manifestations of this orientation would, thus, be expected to change depending on the context.

At the moment though, pluralism would seem to have as good a claim as any other principle for the status of a general ordering moral principle in cultural matters. According to a number of authors, accounting for a radical socio-political pluralism and accepting multiplicity and pluralism in all social experiences, identities, aesthetics and moral standards have become the main thrusts of social and political theory (see McLennan, 1995). In part, this emphasis runs parallel to the general postmodern suspicion of universalism and unifying discourses in general. Hence, the attraction of pluralism in media policy would seem to be closely linked to the attacks on universal quality criteria or other unambiguous scales for assessing media performance. Respectively, it can be argued that the normative theories and concepts on which media policy lean have generally taken a marked pluralistic or anti-essentialist turn in recent decades. Instead of a singular notion of the public sphere, national culture or the common good, theorists today prefer stressing the plurality of public spheres, politics of difference, and the complexity of ways in which the media can contribute to democracy (see Keane, 1992, 2000; Fraser, 1992; Mouffe, 2000; Jacka 2003). In the vein of anti-essentialism, Keane (1992), for instance, has argued that political values of democracy and freedom of speech themselves should be conceived as means and necessary preconditions of protecting philosophical and political pluralism, rather than as inherent principles themselves.

This trend, within which the notions of quality, cultural value or public interest are increasingly conceived in a relativist manner, directly affects media and cultural policy by dodging the paternalism of the 'old paradigm of media policy'. With the idea that all forms of culture contain their own criteria of quality and no definition of quality can legitimately repudiate another, Nielsen (2003: 238) argues that the universal basis for defining cultural quality has unavoidably been broken. This applies particularly well to the sphere of media where the paternalism and elitism often associated with traditional public service values have come under increasing criticism, consequently spurring the need for new legitimating principles. In television policy, the use of the term media pluralism is thus linked to the debates about deregulation of electronic media that began around Europe in the 1980s, and it was in policy-making responses to the expansion of commercial broadcasting that media pluralism began to gain more and more prominence in policy debates (Collins, 1998: 62; Gibbons, 2000).

In any case, pluralism – understood here as a positive affirmation of multiplicity and heterogeneity – is something that has a distinctively affective resonance and within this 'pluralistic consensus', it might seem that all things plural, diverse and open ended are to be regarded as inherently good. But as McLennan (1995) has pointed out, in deconstructing pluralism, we are faced with questions such as Is there not a point at which healthy diversity turns into unhealthy dissonance? Does pluralism mean that anything goes? And what exactly are the criteria for stopping the potentially endless multiplication of valid ideas? Particularly in terms of the media, the unsolved problem remains, how to conceptualize the need for pluralism and diversity, inherent in all normative accounts of the public sphere, without falling in the trap of relativism, indifference and an unquestioning acceptance of market-driven difference and consumerism.

Without objecting to the ideas of diversity and pluralism themselves, it is rather easy to notice that cultural and political pluralism and diversity have a tendency to turn sacrosanct and somehow flat; politics of difference are in danger of blurring into politics of indifference. As McLennan (1995: 83) notes, although pluralism and multiplicity have been revived to counteract the greyness of modernist politics, the same principles can themselves turn into just another ontological or methodological absolute, into new privileged all-purpose abstractions.

In this chapter, a position is defended that goes against the tendency to take for granted that even in their contestedness and diffuse uses of variety and diversity, there lie some common pluralistic values or an unproblematic democratic ideal of a 'pluralistic public sphere'. Pluralism – as a concept – clearly alludes to objectivity and neutrality that seem to transcend the dilemmas inherent in terms such as quality or social responsibility in assessing media performance. While this makes it more compatible with both the needs of technocratic expert assessment and the broader ideology of anti-paternalism and multiculturalism, it can also be argued that this inclusiveness and indeterminacy serves to mask political conflicts and antagonisms in media policy and is thereby often obscuring the properly political or normative aspects of evaluating media performance and setting policy objectives.

However, this chapter is not an attempt to define but rather to re-politicize or radicalize the notions of media pluralism and diversity. This will be illustrated by analyzing briefly the contestation of these concepts in general European media policy debates, as well as in expert discourses, in which diversity is increasingly conceptualized as a measurable assessment criterion for media policy. In contrast to this tendency, it will be argued that instead of seeing diversity as a neutral performance indicator, there is a need to retain the oppositional or radical character of pluralistic orientation, to pay attention to the wider issues of media power and promote not only a plurality of media outlets, but also a plurality of perspectives in assessing those structures.

In particular, it will be argued that the failure to see the contested nature of these values contributes to the general de-politicization and technocratization of public policy. Following Nielsen's critique (2003) of evaluation practices in cultural policy, it can be argued that a formal and technocratic control discourse, with no reference to the general normative debate on the functions of the public sphere and the media, can have comprehensive consequences. These would potentially include weak public debates on the normative issues related to the organization and tasks of the media, as well as arbitrariness and unintentional consequences in setting policy objectives. Instead, there is a need for reflection of evaluation criteria, such as diversity, in relation to overall socio-political goals for the public regulation of the media. Above all, there is a need to discuss the underlying overall rationales of media policies, such as supporting a pluralistic public sphere, and their relation to other objectives such as economic growth or political integration. The obsession with objective or unambiguous criteria in policy analysis and decision-making easily obscures often contradictory goals whose relative priorities need to be politically settled.

Diversity and the structure of differences

Is more diversity always better? Based on any discussion of pluralism as a social or philosophical value, the belief that it can be unambiguously turned into a linear variable is easy enough to repudiate. While the notion of media diversity clearly denotes heterogeneity on some level, it can be defined in any number of ways and it can refer to any aspect of the media: sources, outlets, opinions as well as genres and representations. In debates on media policy, diversity can refer to the extent in which media contents reflect and serve various interests and opinions of the public, or it can refer to the general diffusion of media power in society on the level of ownership, economic structures, and political influence. Considering the variety of possible definitions, empirical evidence on the relations of different aspects of diversity tends to be very ambiguous as well. The relationship between the number of media outlets, the diversity (however defined) of available content, and the actual content that is being provided is all but straight-forward, as is shown by a number of contradictory and ambiguous studies on the effects of competition and ownership structures on content (see Meier and Trappel, 1998; Doyle, 2002; van der Wurff, 2004; Aslama *et al.*, 2004). For instance, it is entirely possible that market competition would enhance the number and variety of program types and genres available to the public, while at the same time reducing the diversity of political views or cultural representation or even excluding some contentious issues altogether. Thus, it needs to be recognized that any act of constructing the differences against which diversity is analyzed or measured is itself an act of power.

Theoretically, this has especially been stressed by Mouffe (2000) who explicitly denies the type of extreme pluralism that valorizes all forms of difference and espouses heterogeneity without any limits, because for her, such pluralism crucially misses the dimension of the *political*. Differences need to be constructed before they can be measured, and because of its refusal to acknowledge the relations of power involved in all 'constructions of differences', such naive pluralism is actually compatible with the liberal evasion of politics, converging with the typical liberal illusion of pluralism without antagonisms (Mouffe, 2000: 20).

It is clear that there are no absolute means to define or measure media diversity or pluralism, but rather they are only intelligible in relation to some criteria and definitions that are deemed more important than others. As Van Cuilenburg (1998) puts it, media diversity always has to be 'gauged' in some way to the variations in social reality. The question then arises, how to conceptualize this relationship. How are the differences – against which diversity is examined – constructed, institutionalized, and operationalized?

Although often presented as an end in itself, speaking of pluralism and diversity in any political context always requires a frame of reference in which it makes (political) sense. Most empirical studies usually follow or modify McQuail's (1992: 144–145) conceptualization in which the media is seen to contribute to pluralism in three ways: (1) by reflecting proportionately existing differences in society, (2) by giving equal access to any different points of view, or (3) by offering a wide range of choice for individuals. Each of these frames implies a different interpretation of the meaning of media diversity and the standard by which it should be assessed. Most empirical approaches, however, are based solely on the third, liberal freedom of choice perspective, while political arguments would seem to rely equally on the broader conceptions of pluralism and reflection of social and cultural differences. Respectively, choice is usually discussed in terms of the market – as expressed through the metaphor 'the free marketplace of ideas', where the limits and criteria are set by free competition and consumer choice. Social scientists, critical of these market-oriented models, have instead privileged the neo-Habermasian perspective of the public sphere as a favorite frame of reference in which the need for plurality of political views and social perspectives is conceptualized as part of rational democratic public deliberation (see Calhoun, 1992; Dahlgren, 1995, 2004; Venturelli, 1998).

The marketplace model and public sphere approach, thus, rely on very different political rationalities in interpreting diversity and pluralism as media policy goals. While the former is based on competition and freedom of choice, the latter emphasizes broader defence of 'principled pluralism', an attempt to serve the whole society with various political views and cultural values.

Further challenges to the notion of media diversity are of course posed by technological developments and the complexity of the contemporary media landscape. In particular, the suggested shift from the mass broadcasting model to a more differentiated and individualized narrow-cast model of communication only adds to the blurring of the 'old' dichotomy between public and private communication. Although the technological development would seemingly diversify the uses of media, it has also brought about concerns over fragmentation, extreme individualism, loss of common public platforms, and their consequences for the public sphere (see Gitlin, 1998). Van Cuilenburg (1998: 41) has presented some of these problems in 'diversity paradoxes', contradictions between the aspects of diversity that cannot be reconciled. For instance, the aim of increasing proportionate representation of social interests might not be compatible with ideal openness to new ideas, and increased consumer choice does not necessarily increase the visibility of minorities. The explosion of information increases choice, but also leads to high degrees of information waste and to an overload of information. Even though the expansion of channels might lead to increased choice, there is no corresponding effect on the citizens' access to relevant information. On the contrary, increase in the diversity of supply may even reduce the actual consumption of diversity (Gibbons, 2000: 308–311; Van der Wurff, 2004: 216).

Besides this, another tension can be identified, namely between two basic functions of the media in a democratic society; pluralism, and integration. The media are often seen as a central tool for creating a common culture, constructing a national identity, or a shared arena for public debate, values that would seem to be in contradiction with the strong pluralist agenda. This relates to the idea in political theory that at some point, the emphasis on diversity and pluralism runs against the imaginary presuppositions of democracy itself and that there is an inherent tension between pluralism and 'publicness' (McLennan, 1995: 92). This in turn reflects what Mouffe (2000: 64) calls 'the democratic paradox'; how to envisage a form of commonality strong enough to institute a 'demos', but nevertheless compatible with true religious, moral, cultural, and political pluralism?

In particular, with the media market increasingly being structured into smaller segments and citizens getting less and less exposed to competing views and unnoticed problems, there is a genuine fear that polarization of media consumption may lead to unwanted social fragmentation or 'balkanization' of the public, which contrasts with the traditional republican ideal of a large and heterogeneous public sphere. Based on these paradoxes, Sunstein (2003: 95) claims that the public sphere requires 'appropriate heterogeneity', thereby acknowledging that while all arguments can never be heard, the public sphere is above all a domain in which multiple perspectives should openly engage. For Sunstein (2002: 285), such a system of engagement between differing views should rely on something other than unrestricted individual choices. Citizens should, therefore, not only fall back on a range of common experiences, but should also be exposed to materials and information that they would not have chosen in advance. Similarly, Nielsen (2003: 243) declares the purpose of cultural policy rather high mindedly:

> By virtue of its empowering and enlightening objective, public cultural policy cannot be content with works or activities that only aim to please and confirm superficial preferences and opinions. On the contrary, an important element in the practice of public cultural policy is to create activities that challenge these immediate private preferences, and a central criterion for success and for quality, will be precisely whether these activities are capable of facilitating experimental processes that open the mind and senses of the public to something they didn't know they wanted.

What all these concerns express is that the varied functions of the media cannot merely be reduced to choice and satisfaction of individual preferences. So pluralism cannot be reduced merely to diversity of options as such, it is as much about a system of representation within a given society that allows for different political viewpoints and different forms of expression to be visible within the public sphere (Doyle, 2002: 14). Increases in the information available to citizens highlight the view that an increase in outlets or channels as such is not really relevant in view of a pluralistic public sphere, but that the processes of political and social representation are still central to the justification of media policies and still bear relevance to the discussion of media pluralism.

Naivety of free choice

As the political diversity discourse already indicates, the central metaphors through which almost all public policy is conceived today are the marketplace and 'choice'. As Bauman (1997: 93) puts it, freedom of choice has become the main stratifying variable in our multi-dimensionally stratified societies to an extent that making choices is everybody's fate. Only the ranges of realistic choices differ and so do the resources needed to make them.

In the tradition of the critical Political Economy of the media, models based on free competition and choice have long been criticized for ignoring that choice is always pre-structured by the conditions of competition. The belief that consumer choice directs the media in accordance with the general will of the people misses that the influence of the consumer is passive, reactive rather than pro-active, and the extent of alternatives for choice is always limited by the structural effects, such as the concentration of ownership, high costs for market entry, advertizing, unequal representations, and political influences (Curran, 2002: 227–230). Bauman (1999: 73–78) argues that choice is always pre-structured by processes of pre-selection. Throughout modernity, the principal tool for 'setting the agenda for choice' has been legislation and the rule of law. Today political institutions are increasingly abandoning this tool. However, this 'liberalization' does not necessarily mean that freedom of choice is expanding, merely that the power of pre-selection is being ceded to other than political institutions, above all the markets themselves. Consequently, the code or criteria of pre-selection is changing too, as are the values towards which choosers are trained to orient their choices. In this regard, short-term pleasure, hedonism, entertainment, and other market-generated needs come to occupy a superior place. Thus, Bauman argues that the late-modern emphasis on freedom of choice and individual autonomy has not really increased individual freedom. On the contrary, it has instead lead to 'unfreedom', to the transformation of the political citizen into a consumer of market goods.

The simplistic equation of media diversity to market competition and free choice thus obviously fails to take into account the wider relations of power in which the media are situated. Furthermore, contrary to the discourse of 'the free marketplace of ideas' – in which the market is seen as self-regulating and spontaneous mediator – the market itself is a politically designed institution, not a homogenous, unstructured, and unregulated natural entity. The actual shape of the markets is most often crafted by political and legal regulation, and it hardly emerges spontaneously as a neutral mediator of civil society. The market also imposes its own criteria of pre-selection that necessarily limits the range of public choices. Yet it seems that despite the divergent political rationalities, the discourse of consumer choice has become prevalent enough to force even the defenders of public service media to adapt to it too. Symptomatic to the commodification of politics and media, economic modes of argumentation and economic vocabularies have come to dominate European media politics in general and 'freedom of choice for consumers', in particular, has become an important signifier on which arguments are based when deciding on channel licenses, norms of regulation, or performance assessment (see Pauwels, 1998; Venturelli, 1998; Hellman, 1999; Van Cuilenburg and McQuail, 2003).

The implication of this in terms of media policy is that given its own illusion of neutrality, the neo-liberal praise of individual choice does not support any collective definition of 'quality' over any others. Still, arguing for negative freedom by invoking the value pluralism may consequently result in the contrary: individual choices, perfectly reasonable in themselves, might produce a large set of social difficulties. The reactions against the dominant neo-liberal discourse, as outlined earlier, remind us that it is only through rich and secure cultural structure that people can become aware of the options available to them in the first place. Consequently, there are important differences between consumer sovereignty and the democratic roots of media freedom and pluralism (see Sunstein, 2002: 294–295). On the one hand, the very idea of consumer sovereignty, underpinning the free markets logic, implies that consumers should increasingly 'get what they want' through freedom of choice in the marketplace, constrained only by prices and their own requirements and holdings. The concept of political sovereignty, on the other hand, builds on a very different foundation, since it does not take individual tastes or requirements as fixed or given, and it prioritizes social requirements such as democratic self-government and public deliberation.

However, conceiving social differences as categorical or static, something that can be unambiguously captured by institutional arrangements, as in the Public Service Broadcasters' (PSB) claims to serve all of the people all the time, is at least as problematic. Instead, as Keane (1992: 117) has acknowledged, it is self-evident that the repertoire of public service programmes, or any other media, can never exhaust the multitude of publics in a complex pluralist society. Instead, the claim to 'balance' is always a specific defence of virtual representation of a fictive whole. As such, this commitment to balance itself will, in some cases, close off contentious, unbalanced views, favor representatives of established social groups, and in effect 'stabilize difference'.

Thus, there is a familiar twin trap of relativism and indifference on the one hand, and foundationalism and statism on the other. Of course, as a partial answer to this, theories of media and democracy, such as the one developed by Keane, typically promote the autonomy of civil society, which is regarded as a realm of spontaneous action and a marker for a more differentiated and pluralistic system of power. While not a panacea, this would at least seem to offer some basis for making political practices more inclusive and empowering less privileged participants. The main point here, however, is to stress that the meaning of pluralism is always context dependent, and not intelligible as an absolute or linear variable.

Political appeal of diversity discourse

The more positive the images associated with a certain concept are, the more meaningful it becomes to discern the definitional power that underlies its political uses. It, thus, remains relevant to assess which articulations of media pluralism and diversity become hegemonic, and on which kind of political rationalities they rely, for these are rarely without political consequences. Taking notice of this, Gibbons (2000: 307) suggested that media diversity itself could serve as a kind of transitional concept that conveniently assists a shift from the public service dominance to the market-driven approach in European media policy. This is because the dominant articulations of the concept frame the discussion on the democratic role of the media as a reasonable difference of opinion between two different ways of achieving the same goal (diversity of media supply). Implicit in such discourses, he argues, is the idea that through development of the new media and increased competition, the problems of market failure might be corrected and the special need for public regulation would become obsolete.

This concurs, in many ways, with the concept of 'vehicular ideas', which Osbourne (2004: 441) defines as practical, usable propellants that move things along and discursively get us from one place to another. As such, vehicular ideas are contrasted to 'big ideas' or 'grand narratives' and associated with the move from the ideological to the informational politics (Osbourne, 2004: 443; see also Lash, 2002). To modify Marx's phrase that theory becomes a material force when it grips the masses, one could claim today that theoretical ideas become material forces when they are adopted into the evaluation jargon of the bureaucracy in dire need of explanatory frameworks. Furthermore, by drawing from the recent research into the role of ideas and concepts in public policy, it can be argued that the 'success' of political ideas and paradigms often rely, not on grand ideological clashes, but on their capability to become institutionalized and embedded within the norms, standard practices and calculations of policy-making and policy-makers (see Hay, 2004).

This would seem to be in accordance with Van Cuilenburg and McQuail's (2003) suggestion that explicit references to moral and normative components in European media policy debates have largely been supplanted by more market-oriented and supposedly more pragmatic concerns. The socio-political media policy paradigm, which was shaped by social and democratic struggles induced by normative concerns relating to the democratic and social responsibilities of the media, has been replaced by a new paradigm that emphasizes mainly technical and economic considerations. Such considerations are usually presented as pragmatic, problem-oriented, and unlike the political practice illegitimately justified by ideologies, rational politics is characterized by the treatment of social problems as a matter of instrumental deduction, requiring ever-increasing expert knowledge and objective analysis. Similarly, Hay (2004) associates the institutionalization of the new neo-liberal policy paradigm with a shift from normative to more normalized and necessitarian political rationalities. Political rhetoric is increasingly couched in terms of the non-negotiable character of external, either economic or empirical-objective, imperatives, painstakingly difficult to reconcile with the various normative views on what constitutes the public interest or the common good.

Given the ambiguousness of the pluralistic values, it is thus no surprise that the construction of such necessitarian political rationalities becomes pivotal to the debates on media diversity and pluralism on the political level. Accordingly, in European media policy, the effective resonance of media pluralism has been mobilized for various and often incompatible political objectives. While well suited to the contemporary emphasis on de-centralization and multiculturalism in social theory, the 'pluralistic consensus', Nielsen (2003: 238) argues, has not immediately offered new opportunities for the orientation of public policy, but instead created an open situation in which the articulations and hegemonic definitions of pluralism and diversity were and still are contested. One powerful articulation has obviously been the equation of 'diversity' with 'freedom of choice', and the general framework of the 'free marketplace of ideas'. Within the various discourses that emphasize socio-political pluralism, the belief in social centralism, rational progress, a homogenous public, and social engineering have all come to seem politically questionable. Thus, diversity, variety, and choice are generally seen as the opposite of paternalism; constructing an image of media history as a continuum from public regulation and planning towards ever-increasing freedom of choice for the consumer and freedom of operation for the industry (see Curran, 2002).

However, as influential as it has been, the neo-liberal articulation of diversity and the market is not unquestioned. Proponents of public service broadcasting in particular have adopted diversity and pluralism as the core of their remit and consequently promoted a more interventionist articulation of diversity (Collins, 1998: 62). The protocol of the Treaty of Amsterdam of the European Union, for instance, states that 'the system of public broadcasting in the Member States is directly related to the democratic, social and cultural needs of each society and to the need to preserve media pluralism' (Harrison and Woods, 2001). Similarly, the Council of Europe and the European Parliament have repeatedly promoted pluralism and diversity as key public interest values that necessitate intervention in the media market in general and give support to public service broadcasting in particular (Kaitatzi-Whitlock, 1996; Collins, 1998; Harrison and Woods, 2001; Sarikakis, 2004).

Similarly, national legislations around Europe refer to diversity and pluralism as both general principles of media policy and specific justifications or demands for public service broadcasting. Thus, the idea that democracy and public deliberation require a variety of opinions and views from diverse media sources certainly seems beyond dispute in contemporary European debate on media policy. What they mean in any given context, however, is not nearly as clear. The battling rationales of the free marketplace and the public service approach, thus, clearly attest to an inevitable tension between freedom in the negative sense and any positive social goals associated with media diversity. The free market and public service discourses rely on very different political paradigms when interpreting diversity and pluralism as media policy goals. The former is based on competition and freedom of choice and the latter on a much broader defence of 'principled pluralism', an attempt to serve the whole society with various political views and cultural values (Van Loon, 2000; Harrison and Woods, 2001; Hellman, 2001).

The definitional and discursive power that frames the boundaries of political discussion also clearly shows in the vicissitudes of media policy in the European Union. While the European Parliament consistently raised the issue of media pluralism to the Commission since the early 1990s, the attempts to build on a political and cultural definition of pluralism and diversity have repeatedly failed due to the opposition of industry groups and the Commission, as well as their inability to redefine the terms of the debate (Kaitatzi-Whitlock, 1996; Sarikakis, 2004). First, the issues of pluralism and independence of the media have been relegated under competition policy, marginalizing any problems specific to the media sector (Doyle, 1997, 2002). Second, when dealing explicitly with media contents, diversity has been defined as a choice between programme types or genres, raising an immediate concern regarding the reduction of the public service remit to produce content that is not profitable or taken care of by the commercial content providers (Feintuck, 1999: 59–61; Harrison and Woods, 2001). Internationally, similar definitional struggles have recently become prominent in the debates of the UNESCO Convention on the Protection and Promotion of the Diversity of Cultural Expressions and in its wording regarding media freedom and the possible need for positive intervention in the market to promote cultural diversity.

Appeal of empirical closure

Parallel to the struggles over the meaning and connotations of pluralistic values, there is also an opposite tendency to search unambiguous and objective definitions. According to Napoli (1999), media diversity is increasingly treated as a measurable concept, a tangible and empirically assessable construct, rather than a justification for policy initiatives or another abstract dimension of media freedom. This has taken place to an extent that there is now an established field of academic empirical diversity research in addition to the governmental and regulatory commissioned studies on the diversity of television programming (see Napoli, 1999; Hellman, 2001; Aslama et al., 2004; van der Wurff, 2004). In addition to the revival of pluralism in social thought, the popularity of the diversity discourse can also be related to the attraction of neutrality and objectivity in the criteria for evaluating public policy. Despite the paradoxes outlined earlier, pluralism and diversity seem markedly more neutral and less value dependent than the notions of quality or social responsibility, for instance, making them resistant to any remnants of paternalism in media and cultural policy.

Consequently, media diversity is more and more treated in the administrative discourse as an empirical construct, an indicator amenable to objective measurement. Indicators used in such administrative media performance assessment around Europe vary from very elaborate frameworks of qualitative and quantitative assessment to rough calculations of programme type diversity (see Hellman, 2001; Bardoel, *et al.*, 2005; Coppens, 2005). In any case, it seems that the idea of performance assessment based on 'reliable and objective evidence' is now firmly embedded in European media policy too, as it has been in the United States for some time now (see Howley, 2005). However, in the United States the demand for objective and reliable empirical evidence in assessing diversity as a policy goal has also met with resistance from various public interest groups who claim that the reduction of diversity to a single quantitative measure fails to account for the complexities of the media landscape and substitutes mechanical devices for serious analysis of media power (Howley, 2005: 103–104).

Moreover, it needs to be noted that empirical definitions and assessments of diversity are hardly ever neutral any more than its variety of political uses are. The trend of developing more and more specific objectives and performance criteria has profound effects on public service broadcasting in Europe. In part, this new accountability can be attributed to the increased criticism and scrutiny of PSB in the European Union and by the private broadcasting lobby. Especially, the concerns related to competition policy and common market have raised the need to develop tangible criteria to distinguish the domain of public regulation as an exemption from the market principles (Harrison and Woods, 2001: 499; Syvertsen, 2003: 167–168; Coppens, 2005). Moreover, the technocratic trends in media and cultural policy have been associated with a more general set of ideas about the reorganization of the public sector, known as 'the new public management', the roots of which can be traced back to the diminishing possibilities of political decisions to shape policy and the increasing needs to control social complexity (Nielsen, 2003; McGuigan, 2004). According to Nielsen (2003: 240), this has created a need for new administrative instruments of control, 'disciplining mechanisms that formally, but potentially also in practice, ensure central government's continued control over the tasks it has delegated to decentralized levels'.

It is clear that these developments are not without consequences for the classic distinction between a market-driven approach of diversity, which emphasizes choice and deregulation, and the public regulation approach, which relies on cultural–political norms of cultural diversity, civic equality, and universalism. While the market definition of diversity is rather easily quantifiable and measurable, the more qualitative and multi-faceted public service ideals clearly are not. On the contrary, the remit of public service broadcasting is especially intangible and normative, embedded in the ideas of public sphere, citizenship, pluralism, creativity, national/regional culture, all values that are notoriously difficult to define in an unambiguous way, let alone measure empirically (see Jakubowicz, 2003; Coppens, 2005). Consequently, it is not difficult to point out several problems in the administrative discourse of diversity evaluation. To critical theorists concerned with depolitization, the emphasis on instrumental reason and expert knowledge has always been problematic. As Habermas (1996: 45) put it, rationality in the choice of means often accompanies irrationality in orientation to values, goals, and needs, essentially depriving democratic decision-making of its object. With this in mind, all attempts at defining or measuring media diversity will necessarily involve political and normative choices and contestation over the meaningful norms and criteria of setting policy goals that cannot be reduced to mere facts and figures. Thus, attempts to impose common criteria or a certain conceptual framework for analyzing media (-diversity) can be deconstructed as attempts to reach political closure, or as attempts to stabilize the political contestation and hegemonize certain specific criteria and concepts.

Towards a radical-pluralist approach

As argued earlier, values and meanings associated with pluralism and diversity are open-ended, inseparable from the broader questions of political power and social representation, and subject to continuous processes of social negotiation. It is, thus, not feasible to invoke an absolute final value or an authority (scientific, moral, or political) and to establish the relevant norms and criteria for their assessment. Instead of understanding them as linear or fixed variables, there is a need for more dynamic and contextual conceptualizations of diversity and pluralism. Furthermore, representing media diversity as a measurable variable, instead of a contested political value, turns media policy away from values and public deliberation towards instrumental rationality and technocratic decision-making. In doing so, the philosophical and political ideals that media policy declarations strive for are in danger of being reduced to mere rhetoric.

But then what? Should we give up the concept and just talk about communication freedom – which is hardly less ambiguous. After deconstructing the diversity principle in media policy from a more practical perspective, Van Cuilenburg (1998: 45) subsequently claims that diversity in information and opinion is a completely fictitious, even mythical, concept with no practical meaning in today's media environment characterized by abundance. Van Cuilenburg argues that the real issue for media policy is not lack of information, but information accessibility and openness, particularly to new and innovative ideas and opinions of minority groups.

Thus, it can be argued that in the context of continuing structural power, the emphasis should be put above all on the inclusiveness of the public sphere, access to alternative voices, and contestability of all hegemonic structures; general openness instead of any tangible criteria of measurable diversity.

Similarly, Curran (2002: 236–237) argues that media pluralism should be conceived from the viewpoint of contestation that is open to different social groups to enter, rather than its traditional justification, that truth will somehow automatically arise from either free competition of ideas or open rational– critical debate. The implication of this is that a structural reform that involves levelling the field and widening social access to public debate is a key requirement of media pluralism. The task of media policy from this perspective would be to support and enlarge the principled opportunities of structurally underprivileged actors of the public sphere, create room for critical voices outside the systemic structures of the market or state bureaucracy, aiming to increase the inclusiveness, and openness of the public sphere to various forms of contestation. The debate should thus not focus on trying to measure the balance of the existing media contents, for 'balance' only makes sense from the vantage point of a certain social objectivity. Instead, the media policy debate should shift towards the structural level of media power.

However, many of the problems regarding the use of pluralism and diversity in media policy discourses, raised in this chapter, have to do with a more general problem of reflecting on values in both administrative and theoretical debates. As McQuail (1997) notes, the academic variant of media policy analysis has typically emphasized 'realism', eager to appear economically and technologically literate, and has been rather short on idealism and fundamental criticism. The reputedly more critical approaches of Cultural Studies, on the contrary, have largely shunned formal legal–economic discourses, which has often left them detached from the concrete political and regulatory concerns. Although I have emphatically criticized the way diversity is conceptualized in the administrative policy research, it is not my intention to defend any unquestioning celebration of all multiplicity and heterogeneity either, as some particular strands of Cultural Studies have done in the past. The repeated appeals to complexity, pluralism, and contingency of media culture may at their worst steer researchers away from the politically sensitive issues of media performance and the norms of evaluation.

With this, it is becoming increasingly clear that the treacherous questions of values and quality can never be totally averted in cultural evaluation and policy-making. As McQuail (1997: 49) grudgingly concedes, 'The only alternative to considered and coherent media policy seems to be the patently messy and intellectually incoherent attempt to uphold somewhat arbitrarily chosen values (with sometimes dubious undercurrents and allies)'. Although this does not sound very dignified, it captures the very basic idea of radical democratic politics. According to Keane (1992: 129), democracy is ruled by publics who make – and remake – judgements in public. That is why any system of public communication is not a 'recipe for creating a heaven of communication on earth', and it would not stifle controversies and contestations about the meaning of democracy, freedom of speech, rights, nor the criticism about paternalism or elitism. Freedom of communication or media pluralism is, thus, not something that can be realized in a definitive or perfect sense. It is an ongoing project without an ultimate solution and a project, which constantly creates new contradictions and dilemmas.

Conclusions

If the role of ideas in politics is indeed changing from ideological to informational, or 'vehicular', it also implies new aims for the criticism of political ideas. While the point here is not to argue against the importance of media pluralism, it is important to recover the contradictions and disparities in the political uses of normatively laden concepts; to criticize the tendency of certain concepts to turn sacrosanct. In this sense, as Jacoby (1999: 33) argues, pluralism and diversity have come to form a mythology of our time:

> *[They are] blank checks payable to anyone in any amount, lacking meaning or content.... Pluralism becomes the catch-all, the alpha and omega of political thinking. Dressed up as multiculturalism, it has become the opium of disillusioned intellectuals, the ideology of an era without an ideology.*

Garnham (2000: 165–166) also stressed that moral absolutes, such as freedom of speech, are especially susceptible to being mobilized for political interests because of their unquestioned and mythological status that prevents the critical examination of their premises. Thus, the core argument of this chapter is that the questions of media structure and performance are essentially political and ideological questions that imply a dialogue or conflict between different values. Democratization of communication is not seen as a one-way street but a process of contestation and negotiation.

In this sense, the concept of media pluralism itself does not conceptually offer much unambiguous basis for the demands of democratic politics on the media but is rather in itself an object of political contestation. Indeed, McLennan (1995: 85) has appositely argued that the force of any brand of pluralistic discourses depends on its ability to problematize some prevailing 'monistic' orthodoxy. In that sense, pluralism in general is a 'generic concept' or 'an intellectual syndrome', rather than a fixed paradigm or tradition. Therefore, it is inevitable that its precise connotations and implications vary according to the context. Ironically enough though, the 'pluralistic consensus' itself seems to have become the monistic orthodoxy of today's media policy.

Following a more radical pluralist orientation, Keane (1991, 1992) and Curran (2002), for instance, have suggested that all democratic media–political tools and forms of public intervention in the media can be conceived as correctives against the wishful belief in the decentralized anonymity of the market or any other superior or natural self-correcting mechanisms. Thus, it needs to be recognized that any system depends on a certain social objectivity and differentiation, to construct a system of social representation within which diversity and pluralism make sense. From this perspective, it can be argued that freedom of communication and media pluralism in a critical sense are jeopardized more than anything by cost-benefit analyzes and the search for general and substantive criteria for defining or measuring them. Instead, it has been argued that in pluralistic democratic systems, the scope and meaning of these values, as well as the process of representation, will inevitably be the object of continuous contentious, political struggles.

Respectively, the choices made to assess the state of various demands posed to the structure of communication will depend on different visions of society and the public sphere. To this end, there have been numerous calls, on which the arguments in this chapter also rely, in political theory to return to a more normative (and democratic) form of politics (Mouffe, 1993b; Hay, 2004). What these perspectives lament is the incapacity of facing and dealing with societal problems in political terms, that is requiring not simply technical, but proper political decisions, which are made between real alternatives and which imply the availability of conflicting, but legitimate projects on how to organize common affairs. In line with this, it can be argued that one of the main ways of coping with the complexities of the current media system has been to hide behind 'pluralism' and 'diversity' as supposedly neutral values that somehow transcend the problems of responsibility, quality, truth, or rationality. This chapter sets out to demystify and deconstruct some of the rationalist premises on which public legitimation of media policy is based and highlight the inherent contestability of normative concepts such as media freedom, pluralism, or diversity. For, after a closer look, it becomes evident that claims to procedural and substantial neutrality that often underlie the debate on pluralism and media diversity are more difficult to separate from the political judgements they rely on.

References for Chapter One

Aslama, M., Hellman, H., Sauri, T. (2004), 'Does Market-Entry Regulation Matter?' *Gazette: The International Journal for Communication Studies*, 66: 2, pp. 113–32.

Bardoel, J., D'Haenens, L., Peeters, A. (2005), 'Defining Distinctiveness. In Search of Public Broadcasting Performance and Quality Criteria', in G. F. Lowe and P. Jauert (eds.), *Cultural Dilemmas in Public Service Broadcasting*, Göteborg: Nordicom, pp. 57–78.

Bauman, Z. (1997), *Postmodernity and its Discontents*, Cambridge: Polity Press.

—— (1999), *In Search of Politics*, Cambridge: Polity Press.

Bobbio, N. (1990), *Liberalism and Democracy*, London: Verso.

Calhoun, C. (ed.) (1992), *Habermas and the Public Sphere*, Cambridge: MIT Press.

Collins, R. (1998), *From Satellite to Single Market: New Communication Technology and European Public Service Television*, London: Routledge.

Coppens, T. (2005), 'Fine-tuned or Out-of-key? Critical Reflections on Frameworks for Assessing PSB Performance', in G. F. Lowe and P. Jauert (eds.) *Cultural Dilemmas in Public Service Broadcasting*, Göteborg: Nordicom, pp. 79–100.

Curran, J. (2002), *Media and Power*, London: Routledge.

Dahlgren, P. (1995), *Television and the Public Sphere*, London: Sage.

—— (2004), 'Theory, Boundaries and Political Communication. The Uses of Disparity', *European Journal of Communication,* 19: 1, pp. 7–18.

Doyle, G. (1997), 'From "Pluralism" to "Ownership": Europe's Emergent Policy on Media Concentrations Navigates the Doldrums', *Journal of Information, Law and Technology*, 3, http://elj.warwick.ac.uk/jilt/commsreg/97_3doyl/ (Consulted 01/03/06).

—— (2002), *Media Ownership*, London: Sage.

Feintuck, M. (1999), *Media Regulation, Public Interest and the Law*, Edinburgh: Edinburgh University Press.

Fraser, N. (1992), 'Rethinking the Public Sphere: A Contribution to the Critique of Actually Existing Democracy', in C. Calhoun (ed.), *Habermas and the Public Sphere*, Cambridge: MIT Press, pp. 108–42.

Garnham, N. (2000), *Emancipation, the Media and Modernity*, Oxford: Oxford University Press.

Gibbons, T. (2000), 'Pluralism, Guidance and the New Media', in C. Marsden (ed.), *Regulating the Global Information Society*, London: Routledge, pp. 304–15.

Gitlin, T. (1998), 'Public Spheres or Public Sphericules?' in T. Liebes and J. Curran (eds.), *Media, Ritual and Identity*, New York: Routledge, pp. 168–75.

Habermas, J. (1996), 'The Scientization of Politics and Public Opinion', in W. Outhwaite (ed.), *Habermas Reader*, Cambridge. Polity Press, pp. 44–52. Originally in Habermas (1971), *Towards a Rational Society*.

Harrison, J., Woods, L. (2001), 'Defining European Public Service Broadcasting', *European Journal of Communication*, 16: 4, pp. 477–504.

Hay, C. (2004), 'The Normalising Role of Rationalist Assumption in the Institutional Embedding of Neoliberalism', *Economy and Society*, 33: 4, pp. 500–27.

Hellman, H. (1999), 'Legitimations of Television Programme Policies. Patterns of Argumentation and Discursive Convergencies in a Multichannel Age', in P. Alasuutari (ed.), *Rethinking the Media Audience*, London: Sage, pp. 105–29.

—— (2001), 'Diversity – An End in Itself? Developing a Multi-measure Methodology of Television Programme Variety Studies', *European Journal of Communication*, 16: 2, pp. 181–208.

Howley, K. (2005), 'Diversity, Localism and the Public Interest: The Politics of Assessing Media Performance', *International Journal of Media and Cultural Politics*, 1: 1, pp. 103–6.

Jacka, E. (2003), 'Democracy as Defeat', *Television & New Media*, 4: 2, pp. 177–91.

Jacoby, R. (1999), *The End of Utopia. Politics and Culture in the Age of Apathy*, New York: Basic Books.

Jakubowicz, K. (2003), 'Bringing Public Broadcasting to Account', in G. F. Lowe and T. Hujanen (eds.), *Broadcasting & Convergence. New Articulation of the Public Service Remit*, Göteborg: Nordicom, pp. 147–66.

Kaitatzi-Whitlock, S. (1996), 'Pluralism and Media Concentration in Europe. Media Policy as Industrial Policy', *European Journal of Communication*, 11: 4, pp. 453–83.

Keane, J. (1991), *The Media and Democracy*, Cambridge: Polity Press.

—— (1992), 'Democracy and the Media – Without Foundations', *Political Studies*, XL: Special Issue, pp. 116–27.

—— (2000), 'Structural Transformations of the Public Sphere', in K. L. Hacker and J. van Dijk (eds.), *Digital Democracy*, London: Sage, pp. 71–89.

Lash, S. (2002), *Critique of Information*, London: Sage.

McLennan, G. (1995), *Pluralism*, Buckingham: Open University Press.

McQuail, D. (1992), *Media Performance. Mass Communication and the Public Interest*, London: Sage.

—— (1997), 'Policy Help Wanted. Willing and Able Media Culturalists Please Apply', in M. Ferguson and P. Golding (eds.), *Cultural Studies in Question*, London: Sage, pp. 39–55.

McGuigan, J. (2004), *Rethinking Cultural Policy*, Maidenhead: Open University Press.

Meier, W. E., Trappel, J. (1998), 'Media Concentration and the Public Interest', in D. McQuail and K. Siune (eds.), *Media Policy. Convergence, Concentration and Commerce,* London: Sage, pp. 38–59.

Mouffe, C. (1993a), 'Liberal Socialism and Pluralism. Which Citizenship?' in J. Squires (ed.), *Principled Positions. Postmodernism and the Rediscovery of Value,* London: Lawrence & Wishhart, pp. 69–84.

—— (1993b), *The Return of the Political,* London: Verso.

—— (2000), *The Democratic Paradox,* London: Verso.

Nielsen, H. K. (2003), 'Cultural Policy and Evaluation of Quality', *International Journal of Cultural Policy,* 9: 3, pp. 237–45.

Napoli, P. (1999), 'Deconstructing the Diversity Principle', *Journal of Communication,* 49: 4, pp. 7–34.

Osborne, T. (2004), 'On Mediators: Intellectuals and the Ideas Trade in the Knowledge Society', *Economy and Society,* 33: 4, pp. 430–47.

Pauwels, C. (1998), 'From Citizenship to Consumer Sovereignty: The Paradigm Shift in the European Audiovisual Policy', in A. Calabrese and J-C. Burgelman (eds.), *Communication, Citizenship, and Social Policy,* Lanham: Rowman & Littlefield, pp. 65–76.

Rose, N., Miller, P. (1992), 'Political Power Beyond the State: Problematics of Government', *British Journal of Sociology,* 43: 2, pp. 173–205.

Rose, N. (1999), 'Powers of Freedom,' *Reframing Political Thought,* Cambridge: Cambridge University Press.

Sarikakis, K. (2004), 'Powers in Media Policy,' *The Challenge of the European Parliament,* Oxford: Peter Lang, pp. 284–310.

Sunstein, C. (2002), 'The Future of Free Speech', in L. C. Bollinger and G. R. Stone (eds.), *Eternally Vigilant. Free Speech in the Modern Era,* Chicago: The University of Chicago Press, pp. 284–310.

—— (2003), 'The Law of Group Polarization', in J. Fishkin and P. Laslett (eds.), *Debating Deliberative Democracy,* Oxford: Blackwell, pp. 80–101.

Syvertsen, T. (2003), 'Challenges to Public Television in the Era of Convergence and Commercialization', *Television & New Media,* 4: 2, pp. 155–75.

Van Cuilenburg , J. (1998), 'Diversity Revisited: Towards a Critical Rational Model of Media Diversity', in K. Brants, J. Hermes, and L. van Zoonen (eds.), *The Media in Question,* London: Sage, pp. 38–49.

Van Cuilenburg, J., McQuail, D. (2003), 'Media Policy Paradigm Shifts. Towards a New Communications Policy Paradigm', *European Journal of Communication,* 18: 2, pp. 181–207.

Van der Wurff, R. (2004), 'Supplying and Viewing Diversity. The Role of Competition and Viewer Choice in Dutch Broadcasting', *European Journal of Communication*, 19: 2, pp. 215–37.

Van Loon, A. (2000), 'Freedom Versus Access Rights in a European Context', in C. Marsden (ed.), *Regulating the Global Information Society*, London: Routledge, pp. 285–303.

Venturelli, S. (1998), *Liberalizing the European Media: Politics, Regulation, and the Public Sphere*, Oxford: Clarendon Press.

Chapter Two

Communication and (e)democracy: assessing European e-democracy discourses

Arjuna Tuzzi, Claudia Padovani, and Giorgia Nesti

Introduction

This chapter aims to articulate the conceptual nexus between communication and democracy, through a reflection on 'e-democracy' discourses. We address the connection between the 'e-' dimension and democracy as:

> *[a] political concept, concerning the collectively binding decisions about the rules and policies of a group, association or society. Such decision-making can be said to be democratic to the extent that it is subject to the controlling influence of all members of the collectivity considered as equals* (IDEA, 2002: 13).

Recent initiatives for the analysis and assessment of democratic systems, alongside efforts to clarify the articulation between e-government, e-governance, and e-democracy, offer theoretical and empirical insights towards the development of frameworks for the assessment of electronic democracy as well. From a theoretical perspective, those initiatives build on developments in democratic theory that stress a substantial vision of democratic processes; while at the empirical level they contribute in identifying criteria and indicators for the evaluation of practices, which can be relevant for both offline and online modes.

We, therefore, start by positioning societal transformations in relation to democratic practices and reviewing some of these reflections in order to identify the basic elements for a (re)conceptualization of democracy in the information age. We then proceed by investigating if and how these core elements play a meaningful role in contemporary discourses on e-democracy, through a lexical-content analysis of documents, which represent different perspectives from which the e-democracy discourse is being developed. Finally, since e-democracy is generally understood as a way to strengthen and revive democracy through the application and use of tools that enhance information flows and communication processes in society, and given the close relation between democracy and the exercise of human rights, particularly communication rights, this analysis of e-democracy discourses will identify some open issues that pertain to the potentialities and challenges of information and communication technologies'

(ICTs) applications in the promotion, protection, and realization of communi-cation rights in Europe.

E-Democracy: introductory remarks

It may be useful to outline some of the reasons why the e-democracy concept has become widely discussed and related practices introduced in recent times. We here underline three aspects [1].

First, the evolution and diffusion of ICTs in the last decade in European countries and the centrality they have acquired in many aspects of life have made ICTs' applications increasingly relevant for political systems. They challenge modes of relations which have for decades been grounded on a prevailing representative conception of democracy and open up spaces of horizontal exchange and more direct participation. At the same time, policies for ICT applications and diffusion imply innovations in policy-making processes.

Second, this potential to revive democratic practice and strengthen the opportunities for active citizenship emerges at a time when democratic countries are facing a double challenge. On one hand we observe a disengagement from the formal political life. This apparent disconnection between political elites and large parts of the population has many reasons: a growing complexity of contemporary societies (plurality of demands, different priorities, globalizing processes etc.); the loss of political socialization mechanisms through imme-diate channels such as the family and education systems to the advantage of mass mediated forms; and changes in the very essence of political commu-nication, which is highly conditioned by a media logic that is more responsive to market and commercial interests than to public interests. On the other hand there are growing visible expressions of national and transnational contentious politics denouncing the limits of public institutions' capacity to respond to demands and priorities expressed by groups and communities and the lack of legitimacy in institutional processes at all levels. These expressions are often interpreted as a generalized demand for more direct civil engagement in political processes.

Third, as Blumler and Coleman (2001: 7) remind us, the 1990s have 'witnessed a significant turn in democratic theory away from aggregative notions of preference building ... towards a more deliberative view of active citizenship'. A shift that was prompted, the authors suggest, by the need for democracies, after the end of the Cold War, to assert their values no longer 'in negative contradistinction to totalitarianism but in more positive normative terms' (Blumler and Coleman, 2001: 7).

The relationship between citizens and governments has changed in recent years, largely due to the increasing role of ICTs. Different concepts have been adopted to describe this transformation such as e-government, e-governance, and e-democracy. In many cases, such terms are used as buzzwords referring in a rather vague way to the beneficial effects of ICTs on government–citizens relations. Though meaning different things, they all refer to the use of electronic means to improve government's performance and citizen engagement (JANUS, 2001).

E-government is generally understood as the provision of government services by means of ICTs, allowing public administrations to provide traditional services in new and more efficient ways, as well as offering new services. E-governance refers to a broader set of steering processes in society embracing both e-government and e-democracy. As far as e-democracy, our starting point is an understanding of this concept as one aspect of democratic processes, which relates to the online activities of governments, elected representatives, political parties, and citizen groups (Kane and Patapan, 2004). As such e-democracy should necessarily be linked to the broader context of democratic practices and grounded in democratic theory.

There is no all-encompassing definition of the term 'e-democracy', and we find in literature several ways of describing these online activities. For some, there are different models of e-democracy (Kakabadse *et al.*, 2003): a bureaucratic one (service delivery); an information management conception focussed essentially on the potential of ICTs to foster the management of information of public relevance; a populist mode in which citizens can make their preferences known on a range of issues; and a civil society model which assumes the possibility of openness in the conduct of governmental and political practice. For others, e-democracy can be conceived as 'the use of ICTs and CMC to enhance active participation of citizens and support the collaboration between actors for policy making purposes, without the limits of time and space and other physical conditions in democratic communications' (JANUS, 2001: 39): a usage of technology that enhances citizens' empowerment and ability to control their governments, as well as communities' power to deliberate and act. E-democracy is also thought as the 'delivery of electronic democracy' which range from the simple access of citizens to governmental information, to greater interaction between citizens and governments, to online participation in governmental actions and decisions through consultations and forums (Norris, 2003: 3). According to this approach, we may distinguish between a minimalist definition of e-democracy – in which citizens would enjoy electronic access to governmental information and be offered the opportunity to interact with governmental officials and conduct on-line transaction with governments – and a more substantial conception of democracy, which implies 'a more active citizen involvement [... and] the ability to act both directly and through their chosen representatives to govern themselves and their communities' (Norris, 2003: 3).

Interestingly, all perspectives seem to be aware of the different 'degrees' of engagement that can be found in e-democracy practices, making the participatory dimension one of the elements that needs to be theoretically clarified and empirically assessed. Referring to relevant literature (OECD, 2001; The Access Initiative, 2003), we can in fact identify at least three levels of citizens' engagement that can be supported by ICTs: at the *information level* citizens may have access to relevant information – through websites, search engines, and electronic newsletters – that allows meaningful personal and organizational choices and decisions. At the *consultation level*, governments interact with citizens, adopting mechanisms, such as online forums, web-based platforms, and e-mail newsgroups, through which public debates and deliberation can inform decision-making processes. A third level is defined as *active participation*, stressing the potentialities (and challenges) for active engagement in partnerships and policy-making processes.

Thus the very idea of a more participatory style of democracy emerges as a feasible and desirable (if not needed) way to respond to something that has been neglected in representative models of democracies, namely robust deliberative processes and active citizens' participation (Barber, 1984). 'New forms of governance are increasingly consultative' (Blumler and Coleman, 2001: 6), and ICTs have a crucial role to play in this transformation, since they have the potential to enhance and facilitate citizens' involvement in discussing and deciding on issues of collective interest. In this perspective, e-democracy could be part of the recipe for strengthening democracy, since 'participation serves three important democratic values: legitimacy, justice and the effectiveness of public action' (Fung, 2005: 46).

Yet the very notion of participation becomes highly problematic when it needs to be translated into concrete modes: participation makes sense not as an end in itself but when it 'addresses pressing deficits in more conventional, less participatory arrangements' (Fung, 2005: 3). As different degrees of participation can be envisaged, very often actors that have stakes in policy processes have differentiated visions of participatory processes (Padovani and Tuzzi, 2004) and the difference between access and participation should be clearly articulated (Cammaerts and Carpentier, 2005). Furthermore, the design and management of participatory practices require addressing a number of highly relevant queries concerning the 'who', 'how', and 'what for' of participation. As far as the subjects entitled to participate, we can have different levels of 'inclusion', from the broad macro-public or public sphere, to state actors, passing through mini-publics, including lay and professional stakeholders' selection. As far as the 'how' we can have different levels of 'intensity' in participation, from a general 'sit as observers' to actively deliberate, passing through education and development of preferences. Finally, possibly the most problematic aspect remains the 'influence' that public participation in deliberation and consultation can have on decision-making processes (Fung, 2005).

Given this complexity, when it comes to the adoption of ICTs to address democratic challenges we are faced with a number of open issues: what vision of democracy informs e-democracy developments? What is the awareness, both at the institutional level and among citizens, of the challenges and opportunities brought about by the adoption of ICT to foster democratic processes? To what extent is the potential to enhance citizens' involvement actualized in practice?

A substantial understanding of democratic practice

In order to set the stage for a better understanding of e-democracy, we refer to recent attempts to conceptualize democracy beyond simple procedures. Earlier attempts to evaluate the 'quality of democracy' in contemporary societies (O'Donnel, 1994; Morlino, 2003a, b) were mostly developed within a state-centered approach to representative democracy, but the assumptions elaborated in order to develop indicators to evaluate national democratic quality may be generally applied to both offline and online practices as well as to different levels of authority, from the local to the global.

Following Morlino's conception of democratic quality, a first distinction can be made between formal and substantial democracy, that is, between the procedural aspects [2] and the content [3] dimension. A third element should also be taken into consideration, which is the result [4] (degree of satisfaction, or 'performance') of democratic systems. No full conceptualization of democracy can be developed unless all these three dimensions are considered and a multi-dimensional approach is adopted.

According to Morlino, five aspects should be taken into account, two of which relate to procedural aspects (the rule of law and accountability), one to performance (responsiveness), and two to substantial elements (respect for rights and freedoms and the implementation of a certain degree of equality). Each of these aspects can be differentiated in sub-elements and presupposes a set of democratic pre-conditions. As far as the relation between formal and substantial democracy, Morlino (2003b: 15) points to 'levels of intensity', stating that when speaking of 'procedural democracy' we refer to the 'who' and 'how' of decision-making, while substantial democracy concerns 'what' is being decided upon. Following the line of reasoning adopted earlier, who participates and how these participants interact are central elements of the procedural context of democratic practice; while the capacity of these subjects to affect the substantial output and outcome of such processes, depends on the level of influence they may exert (Pateman, 1970). Substantial democracy presupposes the procedural dimension of which it is a precious enrichment. Furthermore, if we are to evaluate democracy in substantial terms we would find several 'degrees' of democratic quality, due to the correspondence of concrete situations to an ideal of democratic practice. Morlino's proposal can be synthesized in the Table 1.

In order to further clarify the dimensions and develop an analytical framework for the assessment of e-democracy discourses, we refer to the methodology developed by the Institute for Democracy and Electoral Assistance (IDEA, 2002: 12). Starting from a review of former attempts to assess democracy (human rights surveys, governance assessments, democracy indices, democratic audits) and trying to overcome their limits, IDEA produced a multi-dimensional assessment framework, the aim of which is to raise public consciousness, contribute to public debate, and provide an instrument to effectively evaluate how democratic reforms are implemented.

Table 1:

Dimensions, elements, and basic conditions of democracy (elaboration from Morlino, 2003b)

Dimensions of democracy	Five aspects to evaluate democracy	Elements composing the different aspects	Basic pre-conditions
Procedural	Rule of law (decisional output and implementation according to the supremacy of law)	• Equal enforcement of law • Supremacy of the legal state • Independence of the judiciary and fair resolution of lawsuits • Supremacy of the constitution	• Diffusion of liberal and democratic values among both the people and, especially, elite • Existence of bureaucratic traditions • Legislative and economic means
	Accountability (obligation of elected political leaders to answer for their political decision when asked by citizen electors and other constitutional bodies) Vertical and horizontal accountability	• Information • Justification • Punishment/ compensation	• Existence of a public dimension characterized by pluralism and the participation of a range of individuals and collective actors • Political competition/ distribution of power • Well established intermediary structures (parties, media, associations that share democratic values) • Interested, educated and informed citizens who remain involved in political processes

Table 1: (*Continued*)

Dimensions of democracy	Five aspects to evaluate democracy	Elements composing the different aspects	Basic pre-conditions
Substantial	Respect for rights and achievement of freedoms Progressive implementation of greater political, social and economic equality	• Civic, political and social rights • Formal and substantial equality	• Political will • Affluence • Organized interests • Political will • Affluence • Organized interests
Result	Responsiveness (the capacity to satisfy the governed by executing the policies that correspond to their demands)	• Policies • Services • Distribution of material goods • Extension of symbolic goods	• Well established, independent, informed and engaged civil society • Concurrent presence of active intermediary structures

The starting point is that '*the key democratic principles are those of popular control and political equality*' (IDEA, 2002: 13), two very general principles which need to be sustained and realized through a set of mediating values: participation, authorization, representation, accountability, transparency, responsiveness and solidarity. Again a number of requirements (or pre-conditions) are identified, such as constitutionally recognized rights, capacities and resources, ad hoc agencies and a vibrant cultural life. It is precisely by looking at the implementation of these principles and requirements that a multi-dimensional assessment of democratic practice should be carried out.

What emerges from this quick review of democratic quality assessment exercises is a 'strong' version of democracy (Barber, 1984): a vision in which the exercise of *citizenship, rights* and *responsibilities*, and values of *participation, transparency, responsiveness, accountability* and *effectiveness* emerge as central nodes in the network of interactions that makes up a strong democratic project. These elements— citizenship, rights, responsibilities, participation, transparency, responsiveness, accountability, effectiveness— make up the initial list of concepts considered in our analysis. Besides this, since the focus here is on e-democracy, a few additional aspects have been included. The very nature of ICTs and online practices often relate to notions such as *debate, dialogue* and *consultation*, stressing the potential of information technologies to foster citizens' active participation and the expression of ideas and preferences. We have therefore inserted these concepts in our analytical framework. Finally *information* and *communication*, the first indicating unidirectional transmission flows and the second underlying the horizontal dimension of exchange and interaction, seemed to be central to our attempt to connect electronic citizenship and communication as a fundamental right, and have thus been considered in our analysis.

Framing e-democracy discourses

Research questions and selection of documents

Our main research question, in looking at the e-democracy narrative, concerned the possibility to discern a coherent approach to e-democracy or to recognize that, on the contrary, diverse and possibly competing visions are emerging. To address this question, a lexical-content analysis has been conducted on a selection of documents, chosen as somehow 'representative' of the different voices producing contemporary e-democracy discourses. The language of academic reflections and the narratives emerging from practices in the field of e-democracy, but also the discourse that characterizes European institutions on the use of ICTs to foster and facilitate the relation between citizens and institutions, are compared. Due to requirements and constrains in the use of lexical-content analysis, we have chosen written texts that are short enough to be processed by the software used (Taltac), yet contribute substantially to the definition of e-democracy. These documents are well known and widely cited in the literature, and are recent enough to offer an account of contemporary reflections. Table 2 lists the selected texts as well as the rationale for our choice.

Our main research question has been articulated further in a set of sub-questions which guided the analysis of the selected documents:

- Looking at the language used by the different authors, is it possible to identify some 'core concepts' that could be considered as conceptual references of a shared vision of e-democracy?
- Through which concepts is the narrative elaborated? Are the dimensions/ elements of democracy identified above relevant to e-democracy? What is the authors' understanding of information and communication? And what is their perspective as far as citizens' participation through on-line debates is concerned?
- Finally, which elements are specific to each document (or relatively more relevant in a document)? Is it possible to identify differences between a more academic-oriented discourse and the one that emerges from more institutional actors?

In order to answer these questions, and building on the earlier mentioned reflections on democratic quality, a set of key concepts/semantic areas have been identified in order to develop an analytical framework. We have thus looked at

Table 2:

List of the documents and rationale for their selection

J. G. Blumler and S. Coleman (2001), *Realising Democracy Online: A Civic Commons in Cyberspace*, IPPR/Citizen Online Research Publication.	A text written by two respected academics who have for many years devoted attention to changes in the sphere of political communication and more recently to the relation between democracy and technologies. Though written in an academic style, both in language and structure, it is not just an academic reflection as it develops clear-cut proposals for active intervention of institutional actors.
S. Clift (2003), *E-Government and Democracy. Representation and Citizen Engagement in the Information Age.*	The article is based on a research provided by the author to the United Nations UNPAN for the 2003 World Public Sector Report. It is grounded on the direct experience and engagement of Steven Clift in promoting and improving citizens participation through the use of the Internet since the mid 1990s, including the Minnesota E-Democracy project, one of the first consultative and participatory experiences using ICTs.
EU eGovernment Unit, (2004), *Report on 'eDemocracy Seminar'*, IS Directorate General, Brussels: European Commission.	The document is the official Report of the 'e-Democracy seminar' organized in Brussels (12 and 13 of February 2004) by the eGovernment Unit of the Information Society Directorate General of the European Commission. On that occasion over 250 experts and practitioners in e-democracy from across the European Union and beyond gathered *'to assess the current state of eDemocracy, how it is being practiced and what are the implications for the future'*. The report is an overview of the interventions and discussions and is structured around two main streams: e-Voting and e-Participation.
R. W'O Okot-Uma (2004), *Electronic Governance and Electronic Democracy: Living and Working in the Connected World*, Commonwealth Centre for e-Governance.	This document, written by Rogers W'O Okot-Uma of the Commonwealth Secretariat in London, is a chapter of a publication titled *'Electronic Governance and electronic democracy: living and working in the connected world'*. It has been selected in order to investigate the conceptual and linguistic relation and/or difference between discourses focused on e-democracy and those focused on e-governance.

---

clusters of concepts [5], identified as central to a strong reading of democracy. Concepts related to: democracy, citizenship, participation, transparency, responsiveness, accountability and effectiveness, rights and responsibilities, debate, dialogue and consultation, information and communication.

From the analysis of the entire vocabulary of our corpus [6], a number of immediate observations emerge. The term 'democracy', as was foreseeable, is often used in all documents, yet the articulation in language – as expressed in formulations such as 'participatory democracy', 'deliberative democracy', etc. – is rich and diversified in only a few documents.

The 'potentiality' dimension, meaning a focus on opportunities and potential of ICTs, seems to prevail over the recognition of the challenges or constraints brought about by ICT applications. There is also a strong normative perspective indicating directions of what 'should_be' and 'must_be' done in order to develop e-democracy.

The 'deliberative' dimension made possible by ICTs seems to prevail on the 'participative' dimension, especially in the case of institutional speakers. All documents, except the EU one, refer to a connection between a transformation in democracy and innovative governance practices. Finally, a diffused reference to the global context indicates an awareness of global challenges which could be addressed also through e-democracy.

Lexical-content analysis and focus on specific semantic areas

For each key concept in our list, we have elaborated a table that shows how the specific semantic area is articulated in the corpus. In each table, we have positioned a selection of complex textual units (CTU), thus showing how many times each textual unit (rows in table) appears in each document (columns in table). This allows to identify which formula are relevant to each speakers, while comparing similarities and differences, both from a quantitative point of view and in terms of the richness and depth of each speaker's language.

Every document is also positioned in the semantic space created by each concept, producing a graphic visualizations, which is helpful in identifying documents' specificities, allowing an immediate comparison in terms of which document is similar to which according to the language used. Each table (and figure) is followed by a short comment, while a more comprehensive inter-pretation is presented in our concluding remarks.

Lexical-content analysis of the selected documents

On democracy

As anticipated, the corpus shows a very high use of terms relating to democracy, yet it is interesting to note how the texts by Clift and Blumler and Coleman are

Table 3:
Selection of CTUs relating to democracy as a semantic area

Graphic form	Total occurrence	1 Blumler/ Coleman	2 Steven Clift	3 EU e-government unit	4 Common- wealth
E-democracy	60	5	27	28	0
Democracy	55	22	15	13	5
Democratic	40	19	20	1	0
Participatory_ democracy	13	0	13	0	0
Edemocracy	11	0	0	2	9
Democracies	10	4	6	0	0
Democratic_ process	9	0	3	6	0
Democratic_ outcomes	8	0	8	0	0
E-democracy_ policy	8	0	8	0	0
Representative_ democracy	8	5	1	2	0
E-government_ and_democracy	5	0	5	0	0
Electronic_ democracy	5	3	0	0	2
Direct_ democracy	4	2	2	0	0
E-democracy_will	4	0	1	3	0
Teledemocracy	4	0	3	1	0
Democratic_ institutions	4	1	3	0	0
Democratic_ goals	4	0	4	0	0
Democratic_ processes	4	0	4	0	0
Information-age_ democracy	3	0	3	0	0
Democratic_ participation	3	1	2	0	0
Inherently_ democratic	3	0	3	0	0
Enhance_ participatory_ democracy	3	0	3	0	0

(*Continued*)

Table 3: (*Continued*)

Graphic form	Total occurrence	1 Blumler/ Coleman	2 Steven Clift	3 EU e-government unit	4 Common-wealth
Deepen_democracy	3	0	3	0	0
Growth_of_ e-democracy	3	0	0	3	0
Nature_of_ democracy	3	0	1	2	0
System_of_ representative_ democracy	3	1	1	1	0
Citizenship_and_ democracy	2	2	0	0	0
Ict-enhanced_ participatory_ democracy	2	0	2	0	0
Service_of_ democracy	2	0	2	0	0
Commitment_to_ democratic	2	0	0	0	2
Implementing_ e-democracy	2	0	0	2	0
E-democracy_ movement	2	0	0	2	0
E-democracy_ sphere	2	0	0	2	0
E-democracy_ seminar	2	0	0	2	0
E-democracy_ process	2	0	0	2	0
E-government_and_ e-democracy	2	0	1	1	0
E-democracy_ technology	2	0	2	0	0
Challenge_for_ democracy	2	0	2	0	0
E-government_ and_democracy_ activity	2	0	2	0	0
Deliberative_ democracy_online	2	0	2	0	0

Table 3: (*Continued*)

Graphic form	Total occurrence	1 Blumler/ Coleman	2 Steven Clift	3 EU e-government unit	4 Common-wealth
Deliberative_ democracy_as	2	0	2	0	0
Deliberative_ democracy	2	0	1	1	0
Democracy_and_ e-government	2	0	2	0	0
Strengthen_ democracy	2	0	0	2	0
Democratizing_ potential	2	0	2	0	0
Democratic_ potential	2	1	1	0	0
Democratic_ citizenship	2	2	0	0	0
Democratic_ process_and_ institutions	2	0	0	0	2
Traditional_ institutions_ of_democracy	2	0	2	0	0
Government_ e-democracy	2	0	2	0	0
Nature_of_ democracy_itself	2	0	0	2	0

more similar than the other two in their articulation of democracy (cf. Figure 1). Their position towards the centre of the graph indicates the fact that these texts contain most of the terms that appear in other texts. But Clift, in particular, utilizes a very articulated terminology, referring to 'deliberative', 'participatory', and 'direct' democracy in a way that no other speaker does. On the other side of the spectrum, the EU e-government unit offers a quite static vision of e-democracy, always using the prefix and stressing the 'applicative' dimension of ICTs. Also interesting is the fact that all documents, but one – namely the Commonwealth Centre document – refer to representative democracy, and a qualitative reading of the texts indicate clearly the underlying idea that e-democracy should not be considered as an alternative to traditional representative democratic practices, but a complementary element in order to strengthen them.

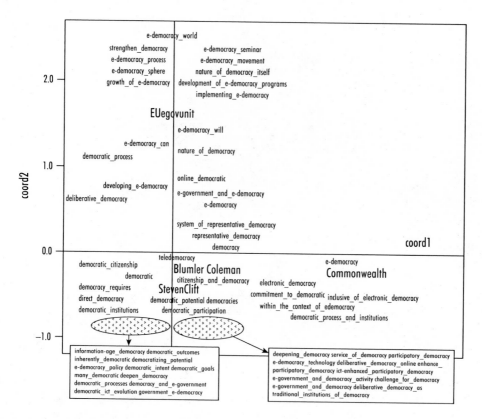

Figure 1: Visualization of documents position in the semantic space relating to democracy.

On citizenship

The theme of citizenship is much more developed and articulated in the document written by Clift than in other documents, and from his text a more elaborated conception of citizen participation emerges. The connection between citizenship and democracy is strongly expressed by Blumler and Coleman, who also stress the active role of citizens, while the EU e-government unit focuses on the idea of citizens' engagement ('engaging', 'engage', 'engagement'). The EU document also talks about citizenry and not citizenship, suggesting a vision of citizens as receivers/consumers of services. The Commonwealth Centre text is again quite different in its language, though it is interesting to note that it refers to ICTs potential to 'foster a sense of citizenship' and also to active citizen participation, alongside access to information for all citizens.

Table 4:
Selection of CTUs relating to citizenship as a semantic area

Graphic form	Total occurrence	1 Blumler/ Coleman	2 Steven Clift	3 EU e-government unit	4 Common-wealth
Citizens	107	28	54	19	6
Citizen	55	1	23	28	3
Citizens'	9	8	1	0	0
Citizenship	9	9	0	0	0
Citizenry	6	0	0	4	2
Many_citizens	5	0	3	2	0
Citizen_ participation	5	0	5	0	0
Citizen_ satisfaction_ and_service	4	0	4	0	0
Online_citizen_ engagement	4	0	4	0	0
Citizen_input	4	0	4	0	0
Citizen'	4	2	2	0	0
Citizen_ engagement	4	0	4	0	0
E-citizens	3	0	3	0	0
Informing_the_ citizen	3	0	0	0	3
Global_citizen	3	0	0	3	0
Citizens_online	3	1	2	0	0
Consulting_the_ citizen	3	0	0	0	3
Individual_citizens	2	1	0	1	0
Citizen_access	2	0	0	1	1
Citizen-centric	2	0	0	2	0
Citizens_they_represent	2	0	2	0	0
Citizenship_and_ democracy	2	2	0	0	0
E-citizen	2	0	2	0	0
Making_information_ widely_available_ to_citizens	2	0	0	0	2
Representing_the_ citizen	2	0	0	0	2
Representation_and_ citizen_engagement	2	0	2	0	0

(Continued)

Table 4: (*Continued*)

Graphic form	Total occurrence	1 Blumler/ Coleman	2 Steven Clift	3 EU e-government unit	4 Common- wealth
Involving_the_ citizen_function	2	0	0	0	2
Its_citizens	2	0	2	0	0
Role_of_citizens	2	0	2	0	0
Deliberation_ among_citizens	2	0	2	0	0
Encouraging_the_ citizen_to_vote	2	0	0	0	2
Empower_citizens	2	1	0	0	1
Engagement_of_ the_citizen	2	0	0	2	0
Engaging_citizens	2	0	1	1	0
Engaging_the_citizen	2	0	0	2	0
Democratic_citizenship	2	2	0	0	0
Consult_with_citizens	2	1	1	0	0
Global_citizens	2	0	0	2	0
Government_and_ citizens	2	0	2	0	0
Connect_with_citizens	2	0	2	0	0
Fostering_a_sense_ of_citizenship	2	0	0	0	2
Give_citizens	2	0	1	1	0
All_citizens	2	0	0	0	2
Among_citizens	2	0	2	0	0
Active_citizen_ participation	2	0	0	0	2
Active_citizen	2	2	0	0	0
Allowing_citizens	2	0	1	1	0
Citizen-based	1	0	1	0	0
Citizen_satisfaction	1	0	1	0	0
Between_ governments_ and_citizens	1	0	1	0	0
Available_to_citizens	1	0	1	0	0
Involving_the_citizen	1	0	0	0	1
Informed_citizenry	1	1	0	0	0
Governments_ and_citizens	1	0	0	0	1

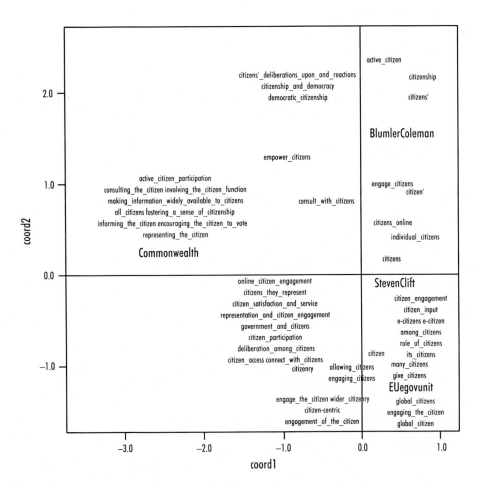

Figure 2: Visualization of documents position in the semantic space relating to citizenship.

On participation (and openness)

The nexus between participation and democracy is clear in Blumler and Coleman as well as in Clift, while the more institutional texts are rather vague in this regard. References to public and political participation are also specific to these authors. In the EU e-goverment unit text, we find recurrent reference to the 'e-dimension' (again a quite static and limited reading of participation without articulating the nature of such participation, nor the goals) and to channels for participation, thus stressing the functional role of ICTs. The graph shows once again the different language of the Commonwealth document, where reference to participation does not occur often, but it is referred to as 'active' through the enabling potential of ICTs.

Table 5:
CTUs relating to participation as a semantic area (occurrence above 2)

Graphic form	Total occurrence	1 Blumler/ Coleman	2 Steven Clift	3 EU e-government unit	4 Common-wealth
Participation	22	6	10	3	3
Participate	15	2	6	7	0
Participatory_ democracy	13	0	13	0	0
E-participation	12	0	5	7	0
Public_participation	5	2	3	0	0
Participatory	5	0	3	0	2
Citizen_ participation	5	0	5	0	0
Participating	4	0	1	3	0
Political_ participation	4	1	3	0	0
E-voting_and_ e-participation	4	0	0	4	0
Online_ participation	3	0	2	1	0
Participatory_ governance	3	0	3	0	0
Democratic_ participation	3	1	2	0	0
Enhance_ participatory_ democracy	3	0	3	0	0
More_participatory	3	2	1	0	0
Ict-enhanced_ participatory_ democracy	2	0	2	0	0
Channels_for_ participation	2	0	0	2	0
Successful_ e-participation	2	0	1	1	0
Enabling_participation_ in_the_information_ society	2	0	0	0	2
Forms_of_ participation	2	0	2	0	0
Either_e-voting_ or_e-participation	2	0	0	2	0
Participatory_audience	2	0	2	0	0

Table 5: (*Continued*)

Graphic form	Total occurrence	1 Blumler/ Coleman	2 Steven Clift	3 EU e-government unit	4 Common-wealth
Participation_ through_input_ and_consultation	2	0	2	0	0
Active_citizen_ participation	2	0	0	0	2

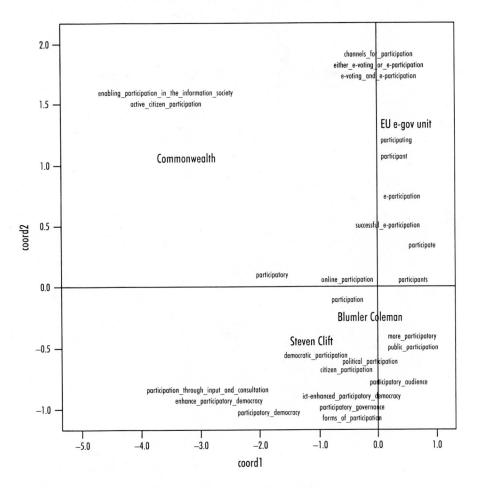

Figure 3: Visualization of documents position in the semantic space relating to participation.

On representation and representativity

As mentioned earlier, representativity and representatives remain relevant in a context that is being transformed by less-mediated communication channels: all documents but the Commonwealth one explicitly mention 'representatives' and 'representative democracy', while 'representative institutions' and the 'system of representative democracy' are relevant to both Clift and Blumler and Coleman. This last document appears, nevertheless, as the most concerned with the relation between representative democracy and democratic practice through the use of ICTs.

Table 6:

CTUs relating to representation and representativity as a semantic area

Graphic form	Total occurrence	Length	1 Blumler/ Coleman	2 Steven Clift	3 EU e-government unit	4 Common-wealth
Representatives	14	15	4	9	1	0
Representative	8	14	5	3	0	0
Representative_ democracy	8	24	5	1	2	0
Representative_ institutions	5	27	1	4	0	0
Elected_ representatives	5	23	3	1	0	1
Representation	3	14	3	0	0	0
System_of_ representative_ democracy	3	34	1	1	1	0
Representative_ processes	2	24	0	2	0	0
Representative_ bodies	2	21	0	2	0	0
Representation_ and_citizen_ engagement	2	37	0	2	0	0
Representative_ role	2	19	0	0	0	2
Effective_ representation_ and_decision-making	2	44	0	2	0	0
Effective_ representation	1	24	1	0	0	0

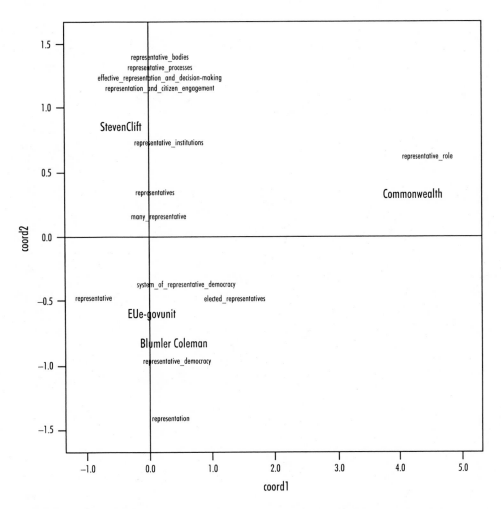

Figure 4: Visualization of documents position in the semantic space relating to representation.

On transparency, responsiveness and accountability

The analysis also shows that there is limited attention for qualitative elements of the democratic process, such as transparency, responsiveness, or account-ability, which could all be affected and strengthened by the use of ICT [7]. Few mentions are made of transparency, with a slightly higher relevance in the EU e-government unit document. On the contrary, responsiveness, as the capacity to relate to demands from individuals and communities, which could be strongly enhanced through ICT, is not mentioned in the more institutionally oriented texts, whereas accountability is mentioned in very vague terms. These aspects are, however, highly relevant to Clift and, to a lesser extent, also to Blumler and Coleman.

Overall the picture, according to our theoretical framework, is quite problematic: in spite of the recognition of the potential of new technologies, little effort is made, especially from the side of more institutional speakers, to articulate such potential with explicit reference to (strong) democratic principles.

On rights and responsibilities

Also highly problematic is the semantic area concerning rights and responsibilities, which are central aspects in a substantial vision of democracy conceived here as the realization of equality and respect for fundamental rights and freedoms. Overall these themes are not relevant to any document, though responsibilities are referred to by Clift and the Commonwealth document, while being completely absent from the EU e-government unit text. As far as human rights, a single mention of this concept in each document can be observed, without any further articulation, in spite of the fact that precisely the diffusion of ICTs and their usage to strengthen (or repair) the relation between public authorities and citizens may raise new and serious concerns with respect to the protection of fundamental communication rights such as the right to privacy and protection from surveillance of private communications.

Table 7:

CTUs relating to rights and responsibilities as semantic areas

Graphic form	Total occurrence	1 Blumler/ Coleman	2 Steven Clift	3 EU e-government unit	4 Common-wealth
Responsibilities	7	0	4	0	3
Responsibility	6	1	3	0	2
Responsible	4	2	0	2	0
Human_rights	4	1	1	1	1
Right	3	0	2	1	0
Rights_and_ opportunities	2	1	0	0	1
Rights	2	1	0	0	1
Fundamental_ human_rights	2	0	0	0	2

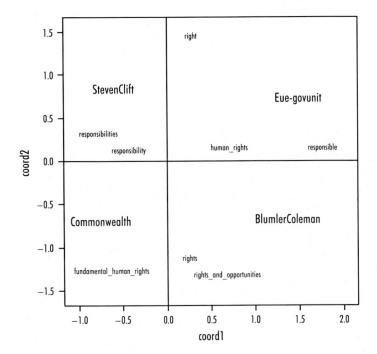

Figure 5: Visualization of documents position in the semantic space relating to rights and responsibilities.

On deliberation and consultation

Maybe less problematic than the almost inexistent reference to rights and responsibilities, but indicative of quite different understandings of the potential of ICT to enhance participatory processes, is the use of terms such as consultation and deliberation. Clift as well as Blumler and Coleman express a much more articulated vision of the interaction between consultation and deliberation in which online consultation go together with the idea of ICT to promote a deliberative arena. The EU e-government unit remains within the boundaries of applications (e-consultation) without engaging with the crucial questions of consultation for what and of what kind. The Commonwealth Centre document stands, once again, on its own, with a different language, which refers to 'consultating_the_citizen'.

On information and communication

As far as the awareness of the distinction/interplay between information and communication is concerned, it is important to stress that in all documents reference to information prevails on communication. An awareness of the

Table 8:
CTUs relating to deliberation and consultation as semantic areas

Graphic form	Total occurrence	1 Blumler/ Coleman	2 Steven Clift	3 EU e-government unit	4 Common-wealth
Consultation	20	6	12	2	0
Online_consultations	16	3	7	6	0
Consultations	16	8	2	5	1
Deliberation	15	7	8	0	0
Online_consultation	10	2	7	1	0
E-consultations	6	0	0	6	0
Public_deliberation	6	6	0	0	0
Deliberative	5	2	2	1	0
Consultative	4	2	1	0	1
Deliberate	4	3	1	0	0
Engagement_and_ deliberation	4	0	4	0	0
Deliberations	3	1	0	2	0
More_deliberative	3	2	1	0	0
Consulting_the_ citizen	3	0	0	0	3
Consulting	3	1	1	1	0
Consult	3	1	0	2	0
Citizens'_ deliberations_upon_ and_reactions	2	2	0	0	0
E-consultation	2	0	0	2	0
Deliberative_ opportunities	2	2	0	0	0
Deliberative_ democracy_online	2	0	2	0	0
Deliberative_ democracy_as	2	0	2	0	0
Deliberative_ democracy	2	0	1	1	0
Deliberation_among_ citizens	2	0	2	0	0
Deliberative_arena	2	2	0	0	0
Deliberative_polls	2	2	0	0	0
Consult_with_citizens	2	1	1	0	0
Consultation_activities	2	0	2	0	0
Participation_ through_input_ and_consultation	2	0	2	0	0

Table 8: (*Continued*)

Graphic form	Total occurrence	1 Blumler/ Coleman	2 Steven Clift	3 EU e-government unit	4 Common-wealth
Online_deliberative_ poll	2	1	1	0	0
Online_consultations_ and_events	2	0	2	0	0
Online_deliberation	2	1	1	0	0
Online_consultations_are	2	0	2	0	0

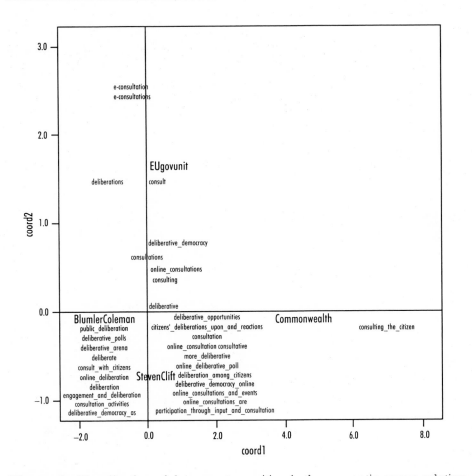

Figure 6: Visualization of documents position in the semantic space relating to deliberation and consultation.

changes in political and public communication processes, and of the challenges posed by ICTs to citizen–institutions relations, is explicit only in Blumler and Coleman, whereas in the more institutional texts 'access to information' and 'information sharing' emerge as favorite practices which can be facilitated by ICTs. The EU e-government unit is the least original text in this regard, while the Commonwealth Centre document offers a greater articulation of the two concepts, in relation to governance processes.

Different e-democracies

What emerges from the analyzes of these e-democracy narratives is not yet a common vision. The discourse is expanding, but it is being developed in

Table 9:

Selection of CTUs relating to information and communication as semantic areas

Graphic form	Total occurrence	1 Blumler/ Coleman	2 Steven Clift	3 EU e-government unit	4 Common-wealth
Information	54	13	20	10	11
Communication	20	15	2	1	2
Communications	14	10	0	3	1
Political_ communication	9	9	0	0	
Informed	8	4	3	1	0
Information_and_ communication_ technologies	8	0	3	0	5
Information-age	7	0	7	0	0
Information_access	6	0	4	0	2
Public_information	5	2	2	0	1
Inform	5	3	1	1	0
Access_to_ information	5	0	2	0	3
Channels_of_ communication	4	1	3	0	0
Freedom_of_ information	4	2	1	1	0
Information_sharing	4	0	0	2	2
Information_and_ knowledge	4	0	0	0	4
Information-age_ democracy	3	0	3	0	0
Information_age	3	0	3	0	0

Table 9: (*Continued*)

Graphic form	Total occurrence	1 Blumler/ Coleman	2 Steven Clift	3 EU e-government unit	4 Common-wealth
Informing_the_citizen	3	0	0	0	3
Information_ management	3	0	0	1	2
National_information_ infrastructure	3	0	0	0	3
New_information_and_ communication_ technologies	3	0	0	0	3
Relevant_information	3	2	1	0	0
Information_online	2	0	1	1	0
Information_and_ communication	2	1	1	0	0
Information_society_ initiative	2	0	0	0	2
Information_systems	2	0	1	0	1
Information_society	2	0	0	0	2
Communicate	2	0	1	1	0
Communication_ technologies	2	0	0	0	2
Making_information_ widely_available_ to_citizens	2	0	0	0	2
Enabling_ participation_in_the_ information_society	2	0	0	0	2
Greater_public_ access_to_information	2	0	2	0	0
Creating_the_ infrastructure_for_ the_information	2	0	0	0	2
Public_communication	2	2	0	0	0
New_information_and_ communication_ technologies_are	2	0	0	2	0
New_and_emerging_ information_and_ communication	2	0	0	0	2
Providing_ information_about	2	0	0	0	2

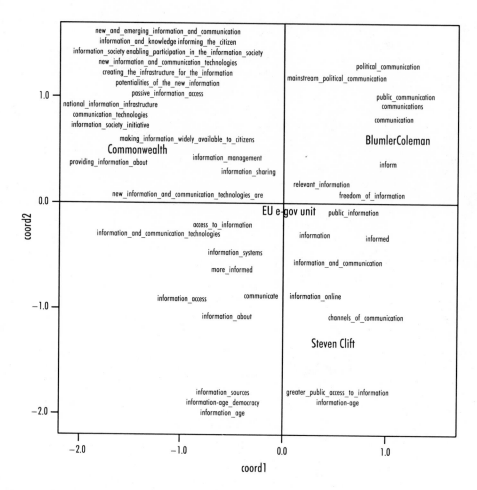

Figure 7: Visualization of documents position in the semantic space relating information and communication.

different directions; there are common linguistic elements – mostly generic references to democracy, the citizen, access to information, ICTs, but when looking at the depth of language meaningful differences can be observed.

A first line can be drawn between texts that express a more institutional approach and texts that are the outcome of reflections both from an academic point of view (cf. Blumler and Coleman) or from practice in the field (cf. Clift). From an institutional perspective, there seems to be very little reference to a theoretical understanding of democracy in spite of the fact that the seminar, of which the EU document was an outcome, was attended by more than 200 'experts' in e-democracy from different sectors. With regard to academic and practitioner discourses, a sound relation to democratic thinking and theory emerges, outlining in a more explicit way the transformative potential (and the challenges) of ICT use to foster, enhance, and strengthen political participation.

The focus of the EU e-government unit document seems to remain within the context of ICT applications (e-voting and e-participation) without a broader perspective of the challenges facing political systems which could be addressed through appropriate usage of technologies; neither is there an emphasis on the implications and potential consequences these application may have on the exercise of democracy.

Steven Clift appears as the author with the strongest interest in the actual relation between the 'e-dimension' and democracy as such. In doing so, Clift offers a very articulated vision of electronic democracy, through the use of more diversified linguistic formulations.

Blumler and Coleman, adopting changes in public and political communication as a starting point, express a similar position but are more concerned with the societal transformations e-democracy is trying to address than with the democratic potential of ICTs applications.

Finally, the language of the Commonwealth Centre document is quite different altogether and ends up being always positioned separately in the visualized semantic spaces. The document was selected precisely because of its specific focus on e-governance and not on e-democracy. Our findings, nevertheless, result quite problematic: they seem to indicate that basic principles of democratic practice are not a major concern in the context of the e-governance language, in spite of the fact that the very governance concept is one of the novel, though controversial, terms through which a re-structuring of political processes is described. As such, e-governance also refers to attempts to make decision-making and decision-finding processes more inclusive and participatory to different subjects operating at different levels of authority (Rosenau, 1999; Cammaerts, 2006; Padovani and Cammaerts, 2006).

Concluding remarks

To conclude, it is appropriate to state that democracy emerges from our analysis once again as an 'unfinished journey' (see Enwezor, *et al.*, 2002), now opening to new opportunities of deliberation and participation – a challenge to citizens and institutions alike.

However, the very idea and nature of citizenship is not being revised. Nothing is being said, for instance, about the challenges and potentials of new technologies regarding a re-articulation of citizenship in a transnational and multi-level space; an aspect that is crucial to the European experience in which the democratic deficit is widely recognized as a major challenge for democratic institutions.

Another issue that requires further reflection is that of participation. This is one of the crucial aspects that ICT application in democratic processes touches upon. In this regard, not much attention seems to be devoted to how new modes of participation will relate to and impact on representative systems, how they will redefine issues of legitimacy and how they will affect the concept of institutional accountability. Furthermore, a clearer definition of participatory mechanisms and their outcomes should also relate to the distinction between consultation and engaging in deliberation on the one hand and, possibly, decision-making or what Hemmati (2002: 2) calls 'decision-finding' on the other. The former referring to opening up channels for expressing views without any guarantee in terms of feedback and impact; the latter relating to different stakeholders' engagement in public deliberative discussions, where views may be transformed through dialogue and decisions taken in a more participatory way.

Problematic in this regard is that e-democracy discourses say very little about central features of democratic processes such as transparency, responsiveness, and accountability. ICTs can potentially influence these aspects in a positive way, yet this is not pre-given; it requires political will and precise choices from the side of all actors involved. These aspects should, therefore, play a more central role in the e-democracy narrative in order to inform practices and actions. But for this to materialize in a meaningful way, a 'culture of (e-)democracy' should be promoted among institutions and officials, as well as among citizens.

Also problematic is that information (flows, systems, technologies) is deemed much more relevant in e-democracy discourses than communication (processes, exchange, interaction). This is especially the case if we take into consideration the wide recognition that what characterizes ICTs is precisely their capacity to create horizontal (interactive) flows of exchange among individuals, groups, and peoples. It is this active orientation made possible by the use of communication technologies that would allow citizens to have a voice and express their preferences, priorities, and demands.

And finally, what really seems problematic is the almost total absence of any reference to the dimension of individual, neither collective, rights and freedoms, the protection and promotion of which should be one of the main outcomes (both in 'substance' and 'result') of strong democratic processes. These considerations lead us to conclude our discussion by referring to the nexus between developments in democratic practices and the exercise of communication rights.

By communication rights, we generally refer to 'those rights – codified in international and regional human rights instruments – that pertain to standards of performance with regard to the provision of information and the functioning of communication processes in society' (Hamelink and Hoffman, 2004: 3). Communication is increasingly seen as a right[8], closely related but not equal to the right to freedom of expression as expressed in the Universal Declaration of Human Rights and the International Covenant of Civil and Political Rights. The debate around communication rights has recently been revived in the context of the UN World Summit on the Information Society [9], where discussions have engaged different actors, both governmental and non-governmental, on the very idea of conceiving communication as fundamental to every social organization [10].

A lexical-content analysis on communication rights looking at documents and positions recently elaborated by a number of civil society actors (Padovani and Pavan, 2006), suggests that in spite of the different vocabularies and specific focuses, a somehow shared consensus on core principles of communication rights is emerging amongst civil society organizations worldwide [11]. These principles are freedom (of expression, thought, assembly, etc.), inclusion/access (to old and new media, to public information, etc.), diversity/pluralism (cultural and linguistic as well as relating to the media), participation (in cultural life and in the promotion of a democratic environment through communication), and the idea of knowledge as a common goods.

The connection between these 'communication rights principles' and the mediating values which were identified as central to a substantial conception of democracy, need to be made explicit. Some of these principles are in effect pre-conditions for the practice of democracy, for instance freedom of expression; other simply coincide with democratic values, as in the case of participation.

We can, therefore, consider democracy and communication rights as interdependent. The respect and promotion of communication rights, such as freedom of expression and respect for privacy, would enhance the democratic nature and functioning of our societies, fostering communication processes that would be grounded in the principles of pluralism and openness while at the same time strengthening democracy. Consistently, a democratic society is one in which the full enjoyment of communication rights would accompany and support transparency, effectiveness, and accountability of political institutions and inclusion of citizens in full respect of their diversity.

The application of ICTs to democratic processes, if grounded in a strong conception of democracy, could further enhance not only those processes but also the enjoyment of communication rights. At the same time, if obstacles and constraints that impede the full enjoyment of such rights are not removed – in terms of censorship as well as digital divides and non-respect for cultural diversity – the democratic potential of ICT applications will not materialize. The very limited reference to communication processes that we find in contemporary e-democracy discourses therefore is in itself a constraint. Not only e-democracy policies, practices, and strategies should be informed by mediating values of democracy in a more explicit manner, but also a stronger awareness of communication processes and related rights should constitute a theoretical and normative basis on which to design and develop ICT-supported democratic processes, if these are to foster not just increased efficiency in citizens–government relations but also legitimacy and social justice.

Notes for Chapter Two

[1]   Many other aspects should be discussed. Particularly problems related to existing divides in terms of access to infrastructure, knowledge, and skills as well as of the unbalances in information flows between and within countries should be mentioned. The scope of this chapter does not allow to fully consider those aspects; therefore we keep them in the background of our reasoning.

[2]   'In a good democracy the citizens themselves have the power to check and evaluate whether the government pursue the objectives of liberty and equality according to the rule of law' (Morlino, 2003b: 3).

[3]   'A good democracy is one in which the citizens, association and communities of which it is composed enjoy liberty and equality' (Morlino, 2003b: 3).

[4]   'A good democracy is first and foremost a broadly legitimate regime that completely satisfies citizens' (Morlino, 2003b: 3).

[5]   By clusters of concepts we mean semantic areas that relate to a specific concept. For instance, in the case of participation, we would look at all textual units, both single words and sequences of words, sharing the root 'participat' such as participation, participant, participatory, participatory_democracy, e-participation etc.

[6]   The first and second text are almost the same length (respectively 9409 and 9828 words) while the e-government unit text is about two thirds (6076) and the Commonwealth Centre text is one third (3126). This difference must be taken into consideration when referring to occurrences in the corpus and relative richness in language.

[7]   Respective tables are not re-produced due to space constrains.

[8]   Reference to a 'right to communicate' dates back to 1969 when it was first mentioned by Jean D'Arcy, then in charge of the Information Services of the United Nations, and then included as one of the controversial issues in the debates that developed around the proposal for a New World Information and Communication Order (NWICO) in the 1970s. For a historical account and a comprehensive analysis, see Padovani and Pavan (2006). On communication rights, see also 'Manuel d'évaluation des droits de la communication', *CRIS Campaign*, (2005) and Lee (2004).

[9]   www.itu.int/wsis.

[10] 'Communication is a fundamental social process, a basic human needs and the foundation of all social organizations' WSIS Declaration of Principles, Geneva, December 2003.

[11] The analysis was conducted on the following documents: the Statement on Communication Rights (World Forum on Communication Rights, WFCR 2003), the Statement by Article 19 (London 2003), the Charter of Civil Rights for a Sustainable Knowledge Society (Heinrich Böll Foundation, 2002), the International Researchers' Charter for Knowledge Societies (IAMCR, 2005), the Council of Europe Declaration (CoE, 2004), and the Charter on Rights of Citizens' in the Knowledge Society (Telecities, 2003).

References for Chapter Two

Barber, B. (1984), *Strong Democracy: 'Participatory Politics for a New Age'*, Berkeley & Los Angeles, CA: California University Press.

Blumler, J. G., Coleman, S. (2001), 'Realising Democracy Online: A Civic Commons in Cyberspace', *IPPR/Citizen Online Research Publication*, http://www.oii.org.uk. Consulted on 1 March 2006.

Cammaerts, B. (2006), 'Civil Society Participation in Multi-Stakeholder Processes: in Between Realism and Utopia', in L. Stein, C. Rodriquez and D. Kidd, (eds.), *Making Our Media: Global Initiatives Toward a Democratic Public Sphere*, Cresshill, NJ: Hampton Press. Forthcoming.

Cammaerts, B., Carpentier, N. (2005), 'The Unbearable Lightness of Full Participation in a Global Context: WSIS and Civil Society participation', J. Servaes and N. Carpentier (eds.), *Towards a Sustainable Information Society. Deconstructing WSIS*, Bristol, UK and Portland, OR, USA: Intellect, pp. 17–50.

Clift, S. (2003), *E-Government and Democracy. Representation and Citizen Engagement in the Information Age*, http://www.publicus.net/e-government/. Consulted on 1 March 2006.

Enwezor, O., Basualdo, C., Bauer, U. M., Ghez, S., Maharaj, S., Nash, M., Zaya, O. (eds.), (2002), *Democracy Unrealized – Documenta11_Platform1*, Kassel: Hatje Cantz.

European Commission eGovernment Unit (2004), *Report on 'eDemocracy Seminar'*, Brussels: IS Directorate General.

Fung, A. (2005), 'Varieties of Participation in Complex Governance', paper prepared for *Theorizing Democratic Renewal*, workshop University of British Columbia, Vancouver, 10–11 June, http://www.archonfung.net/papers/FungVarietiesOf Part.pdf. Consulted on 1 March 2006.

Hamelink, C. J., Hoffman, J. (2004), *'Assessing the Status Quo on Communication Rights'*, Preliminary report, Amsterdam: University of Amsterdam.

Hemmati, M. (2002), *Multi-Stakeholder Processes for Governance and Sustainablility: Beyond Deadlock and Conflict*, London: Earthscan.

IDEA (2002), *Handbook on Democracy Assessment*, The Hague: Kluwer Law International.

JANUS (2001), Joint Analytical Network for Using Socio-economic research - IST-2001-33300, deliverable 1.5 Final Glossary of terms and definitions, S. Hoorens, L. Cremonini, S. Bearne, *et al.*, *'eGovernment, eGovernance and eDemocracy'*, pp. 39–44.

Kakabadse, A., Kakabadse, N. K., Kouzmin, A. (2003), 'Reinventing the democratic governance project through information technology? A growing agenda for debate', *Public Administration Review*, 63: 1, pp. 44–60.

Kane, J, Patapan H. (2004), 'Challenge and Promise of E-Democracy', *Griffith Review*, 3 (Autumn): pp. 201–207.

Lee, P. (2004), *Many Voices, One Vision. The Right to Communicate in Practice*, London: Southbond and WACC.

Morlino, L. (2003a), *Democrazie e Democratizzazioni*, Bologna: il Mulino.

Morlino, L. (2003b), 'La qualità democratica. Note introduttive', paper presented at the SISP Congress, Trento (Italy), 14–17 September.

Norris, P. (2003), *Democratic Phoenix. Reinventing Political Activism*, Cambridge: Cambridge University Press.

O'Donnel, G. (1994), 'Delegative Democracy', *Journal of Democracy*, 5: 1, pp. 55–69.

OECD (2001), *Citizens as Partners. OECD Handbook on Information, Consultation and Public Participation in Policy Making*, Paris: OECD.

Padovani, C., Cammaerts, B. (2006), 'Il World Summit on the Information Society: esercizi di e-governance fra 'Spazi di Luogo' e 'Spazi di Flusso', *ComPol*: Forthcoming.

Padovani, C., Pavan, E. (2006), The emerging global movement on communication rights: a new stakeholder in global communication governance? Converging at WSIS but looking beyond, in D. Kidd, C. Rodriguez and L. Stein (eds.), *Making Ourmedia: Mapping Global Initiatives toward a Democratic Public Sphere*, Cresshill, NJ: Hampton Press, Forthcoming.

Padovani, C., Tuzzi, A. (2004), 'WSIS as a World of Words. Building a common vision of the information society?', *Continuum. Journal of Media and Society*, 18: 3, pp. 3603–79.

Pateman, C. (1970), *Participation and Democratic Theory*, Cambridge: Cambridge University Press.

Rosenau, J. (1999), 'Towards an Ontology for Global Governance', in M. Hewson and T. J. Sinclair (eds.), *Approaches to Global Governance Theory*, Albany, NY: State University of New York Press, pp. 287–301.

The Access Initiative (2003), *Assessing Access to Information, Participation and Justice for the Environment. A Guide*, World Resource Institute, http://www.accessinitiative.org/. Consulted on 1 March 2006.

W'O Okot-Uma, R. (2004), *Electronic Governance and Electronic Democracy: Living and Working in the Connected World*, Commonwealth Centre for e-Governance, http://www.electronicgov.net/pubs/research_papers/eged/contents.shtml. Consulted on 1 March 2006.

Chapter Three

Reducing communicative inequalities towards a pedagogy for inclusion

Margit Böck

Framing

This chapter has two broad aims. One is the larger social and political aim referred to in the first part of the title. The reference to the work of Paolo Freire (1972) is entirely deliberate. The other, derived from the first, is to reflect on the social and political purposes of the academic field of Communication Studies [1] to increase its relevance for analyzing and developing solutions for pressing issues such as 'the digital divide', 'the knowledge gap/information gap', and others.

Theoretically, this entails connecting the macro-level of the purposes and aims of communication policy – particularly in relation to communication rights – with the micro-level of habits, practices, and structures of information use in the everyday life of social actors. This necessitates an extension of Communication Studies theory, as it has been conceptualized within mainstream academic thinking in the German speaking areas. In this tradition, phenomena are often studied under the heading of 'media-effects'. In this chapter, communication is framed differently by introducing the notion of 'learning'. 'Socialization' processes are central to any theorizing and development of policies and proposals for action in relation to communicational inequalities, and these processes are best described by the notion of 'learning as knowledge production'. 'Learning' describes the process of change in the learner through the changes in the learner's resources, gained in the process of knowledge production. In this way, both the concept and the processes become an essential component of a theory, which can then achieve the link between macro- and micro-levels of analysis.

The stance being developed in this chapter is grounded in an ethnographic study, which was carried out between 2001 and 2004 in a remote rural area in Austria (Böck, 2003, 2004a, 2004b). The groups that were studied are sometimes characterized as 'information poor', 'communication poor', 'informational have-nots', 'avoiders of information', and so on. The main research question was where and how do people get the information they need in their everyday life. One of the aims in that study was to think about how one might connect or include such groups into the contemporary knowledge society, i.e. a society in which information, knowledge, and therefore learning are central resources and processes. The study attended to patterns of interaction and took note of what types of information were important, in what form, etc. Moreover, representations of the everyday made by members of these groups – specifically photographs – were also analyzed (see Böck, 2003). Enquiries into their life trajectories served to get a sense of their social, communicational, and personal 'mobility'. In other words, the research question included and transcended the issues being discussed in debates on the notion of the 'digital divide'.

From this research the concept of the 'information habitus' emerged. 'Habitus' (Bourdieu, 1982, 1993) is a sociological notion that is a useful tool in Communication Studies as it accounts for the manifold links between social structures and individual dispositions/practices. Bourdieu (1993: 97–114) makes that connection through the notion of 'socialization experiences'. He describes the genesis of habitus as growing into one's life-world, by 'incorporating' existing structures, values, meanings, and forms of acting. The essential ingredient in the process is the 'agency' of the individual, whose recognition of, and action on, the always-existing potentials for choice between alternatives produces individual practices and dispositions (Bourdieu, 1993: 110 ff.), even though the choices on offer might be of a banal nature. As explained above, these processes are better understood and more fully explained by the concept of learning, borrowed from pedagogy. In particular, 'learning' opens up the opaque area of 'incorporating' existing structures for a more detailed account, while at the same time connecting it with an understanding of individual 'knowledge' (more or less held consciously) as the effect of learning processes. Gains in knowledge are gains in potentials for action, and as such constitute the central element in any project of bringing about (social) mobility, itself central in the reduction of inequality.

Digital media and their environment

The label 'digital divide' has many meanings (e.g. Carpentier, 2002), each of which brings with them particular kinds of problems. A focus on digital media alone is too reductionist. It tends to narrow the perspective onto debates centred around technology and digital media, thereby only focussing on issues of 'access' and of technical, computer-oriented competences. It avoids taking account of humans as sense-making beings for whom the integration of media has to be meaningful in the environment of their wider 'media menus', that is, the environment of all the media they have available for their use and which are significant in their everyday lives. The real issue is what effects are produced by the whole web of connections between socio-structural aspects such as education, class, gender, ethnicity, age, and their interplay with habits of use of specific media.

Two further consequences of the narrow focus on the 'digital' are that the traditional (mass) media are often forgotten and interpersonal communication tends to be downplayed or excluded altogether. As mentioned earlier, in the

German speaking academic tradition Communication Studies have traditionally concentrated its efforts on forms of public communication (e.g. for critical comments Löffelholz and Quandt, 2003), and it also tended to analyze mass communication independently of forms of interpersonal communication. If one regards communication as an essential resource for dealing with all the aspects of the personal and social life, then all of its forms will need to be integrated into one theoretical framework.

The study analyzed in this chapter was holistic in its outset, detailed, qualitative, micro-level ethnographically oriented, and bound to forms of the everyday in its assessment of patterns of communication. It shows that a full understanding of the concerns related to the 'digital divide' can only be achieved if it is integrated into an understanding of the whole 'bandwidth' of communication. That bandwidth needs to be established on different levels – of the individual, groups, and larger social organizations. This study shows that media use and communicative habits are an integral part of people's life-worlds. The issue then becomes one of analyzing and describing relevant features of life-worlds and establishing their interconnections with all features of media and communication.

Life-worlds are socially, materially, geographically, and culturally defined spaces. With their characteristics and the manner in which their features are interpreted by its members, they create frames of potentials for action. They shape possibilities, structures, and practices of communication, which shape and transform the life-worlds in their turn. The structures of communication involve media and their usage – where 'media' needs to be interpreted in the widest possible fashion. The example developed further below is based on one of several interviews (as well as many other less- or unstructured encounters) with a young woman – whom, for purposes of privacy, shall be called Karin. She was a central figure, both in her group and in the study as such. She talks about the media she used in order to get information during her first pregnancy, largely about giving birth. Besides specific media, she mentions a wide range of sources. The close and entire interrelation of the structures (and characteristics) of her life-world and the 'bandwidth of communication' are clear to see, not only as in the media she used, but also in their significance for her and for this specific issue.

Information into knowledge: the basic resource for social action and participation

Society is changing. These transformations have many causes, and not all of these have to do with 'the digital'. Historic expectations of a relatively equitable, democratic society embedded in the modernist ideals of the Enlightenment, are being superseded, at different rates in different localities, by the neo-liberal capitalist paradigm and new patterns of consumption; the notion of the 'citizen' is being displaced by that of the 'consumer' (Gandy, 2002). Expectations suggesting that 'citizens' should have the possibilities and the resources to adequately cope with the changing conditions in their society are increasingly difficult to fulfil. The wish to understand this shift and perhaps to consider intervening may be one important motivation for having a special interest in communication and the media. It seems clear that the need for 'understanding' will not diminish when one substitutes the rights and obligations of the state and the citizen with the rights, needs, and demands of the market and consumers. At one level, it concerns an understanding of the roles that communication and the media play in the everyday, what functions they have, as well as how they might support social actors in shaping and managing their lives. At another level, the contents of media have the potential to assist social actors in solving problems in their everyday life (Saxer, 1997). Such problems might be anything from 'how do I spend an evening at home by myself', 'what to do to cheer myself up', choosing a different hair color, to finding a new job, getting myself informed about the political situation in a place I am about to visit, etc.

In Communication Studies, as in Cultural Studies, a distinction has been made between an objective perspective (maybe more characteristic of [mass] Media Studies) and a more subject-oriented perspective (maybe more characteristic of Cultural Studies) (e.g. Bonfadelli, 2001: 175). In this chapter, a subject-oriented approach will be adopted, focussing on the perspectives of social actors in their life-world (Selwyn *et al.*, 2005: 23 f).

In the next example, Karin explains how she obtained information about the many issues concerned with pregnancy. Some brief segments from the transcript of one conversation are follows [2]:

The first thing is, people, no matter who it is, a girlfriend, my sister-in-law, anyone you might meet in the street, first thing is 'how are you doing?' That is simply the first question. Then, if you're feeling ok, you say, 'yeah, ok, I'm feeling ok'. Then they say, you know, well, with me it was like this sort of. And then blahblahblah. I tell you, the stories you hear! All the way, from vomiting to....
Well, you know, I did go and buy those little parenting magazines [literally: the Parents' Magazine]. Some I got from the doctor for free. And I did look for them a bit by myself too.
Well, you know, I did go and kind of look in the Encyclopaedia too.
The times when I did need a bit of paper was to be able to write all that down, that was each time I had my examinations with the gynaecologist. You know, I have a female gynaecologist, she's already got a child too.
Brochures, sort of, yeah, and little magazines, that kind of thing. (Interview Karin, 4 September, 2002, translations by the author)

Karin refers to quite a few sources of information as follows:

- First, members of her (closer) social environment ('people') who already know about her condition, social actors whom she mentions specifically, and who actively engage with her (relatives, girlfriends, acquaintances). The site of contact is the street, a public space. The others initiate the interaction ('how are you doing?'); they have a notion of what is relevant in this situation ('Then they say, you know, well, with me it was like this sort of'). Karin categorizes this information with a genre-label – 'little stories' – and provides an evaluation – 'All the way, from vomiting to…'.
- Second, this time, more actively initiated by herself, the parenting magazine, a special interest magazine that she got from her General Practitioner (GP) and of which she considers herself a member of the audience. Her formulation – 'I did look for them a bit myself too' – suggests distinguishing herself from other women, who were less active in their seeking out of information than she was.
- Third, an encyclopaedia: from her perspective a highly valued medium of information, and an integral part of the media that ought to be consulted ('Well, you know, I did go and kind of look in the Encyclopaedia too'). It is not quite clear whether her attribution here refers to the book qua medium *book*, or as a compendium of approved content in the form of a 'reference book', the consultation of which implies a targeted seeking out of information.
- Fourth, there is her gynaecologist, a woman who also had experience in giving birth herself. This specification implies a special kind of information source: 'interpersonal' (e.g. with the possibility of dialogical communication in case one has not understood everything), 'professional' and 'experienced'. Her GP is very likely to take her cue on how to act from Karin's own behavior: her questions, her speech, her behavior more generally – more or less anxious or more or less secure, her professional knowledge or status, and – very important for Karin in different situations – knowledge based on experience. Karin used this source of information very precisely and carefully and had prepared a list of questions ('The times when I did need a bit of paper, was to be able to write all that down, that was each time I had my examinations with the gynaecologist').

Her formulations contain evaluative comments concerning both the sources and the information and reveal what she takes for granted in these situations.

For Karin, getting information is a process in which she has a lot of responsibility and which she can control. She turns all of that information into knowledge for herself:

Well, you know, I found out quite simply that each birth is different. You know, you simply can't say that my experience was like yours afterwards. That was simply totally, everyone told me something totally different. Quite slowly it dawned on me that no one can tell me how it really is, because, you know, quite simply you have to experience that for yourself. (Interview Karin, 4 September 2004, translation by the author)

The earlier quotation shows some of the variety of information and sources of information; they vary according to situation and topic. For Karin, in her situation of being pregnant, knowledge that comes from experience is of particular importance. She distinguishes between 'little stories' ('Gschichtln') and experiences she hears from acquaintances on the one hand and the professionally founded and supported knowledge of her female gynaecologist on the other. Regarding the latter, she stresses the personal experiences of the gynaecologist as particularly important; it guarantees the authenticity of the information for her and shows empathy with her situation and understanding of her insecurities.

The media Karin uses as sources – besides interpersonal, face-to-face communication – are print media, and these are relevant for her in different ways. Most useful is the parenting magazine. Many of its contributions are written by people who are themselves parents, who report on their experiences. As with her specialist, their knowledge has been derived from personal experience. As such, the information she gets from the print media becomes personalized.

In her professional life, Karin is a dressmaker. She uses professional, factual literature – journals and magazines, and in the part-time course she is taking to train as a childcare worker she regularly uses other media (e.g. professional textbooks) in quite specific ways. One reason for this difference – apart from the proximity of being pregnant, the private sphere, and her aspiration to be a professional child-carer – might be that the latter entails further professional development, for which textbooks are (at that time still) classic media. By contrast, being pregnant and becoming better informed on pregnancy and birth hardly count as professional development and hence do not lead her to that kind of text and medium. In her role as child-carer, the information she accumulates is directed outward – towards the care of the children – whereas the information on pregnancy and birth is directed towards herself and the baby to come. This differential practice and evaluation points towards the question of the legitimization of actions in and by a social group: what sources of information am I entitled to use to get the information I need to answer a question arising from a particular domain of my life?

A possible definition of information, which relates the 'life-world' to 'information' and 'knowledge', goes as follows: Information is that which is selected by actors in their life-worlds and transformed by them into knowledge in order to solve a problem.

This definition partially coincides with the situated approach of Brenda Dervin's (1980) looking from the perspective of those who seek information. The approach adopted here focuses on the embeddedness of social actors in their life-worlds, on their active selection of contents (and media) available to them in relation to a problem – more or less experienced and understood by them – which needs to be solved. The chosen information is 'appropriated' and 'integrated', which represents a process of learning. Through that process and in conjunction with the prior knowledge/resources of the learner, information is transformed into the knowledge, needed as a tool for solving the problem considered relevant.

Information habitus: information, knowledge, and learning

The earlier-mentioned definition of information connects information and knowledge (both terms are often very loosely used; see Stehr, 2001: 53). Knowledge is always the result of processes of transformation, evoked and shaped by the existence of a problem. In this, the learner's – and social actor's – knowledge resources are constantly changed, expanded, and legitimated. Knowledge is the object of constant processes of transformation. This concurs with Stehr's (2001: 62) approach, taking 'knowledge' as the basis of social action in order to solve problems – from choosing a hair color to acquiring political information. Stehr (2001: 62) talks about 'knowledge' as a 'potential for action'. This 'potential for action' includes the potential for acting on the environment ('external action'), as well as the means for thinking ('inner action').

Knowledge is thus a consequence of learning. In learning, the learners are active in processes of transformative engagement with an issue or an aspect of the environment, in which the environment, the learner, and the tools used in that engagement are transformed. These transformations constantly bring about changes of the learner's resources, tools, and in the learner (Kress, 2006).

It is possible to systematize Karin's practices of getting, using, and valuing of information and sources, and her use of these in relation to specific issues and circumstances. It is this systematic use, its relative stability, as well as its effects, which need to be interlinked with the notion of the 'information habitus'. Following Bourdieu (1993), the information habitus could be conceptualized as a means of describing and understanding habits and strategies of access to, as well as means of obtaining and using information. These could be seen as 'systems of enduring and transferable dispositions, structured structures, made to function as structuring structures, that is, as generative and ordering bases for practices and conceptions' (Bourdieu, 1993: 98; highlighting in the original, translation by the author). The information habitus includes schemata of recognition, of thought, principles of evaluation, and of acting (Bourdieu, 1993: 101). This refers to the relevant knowledge as to what information is available, possible (and necessary) to obtain, the means for obtaining such information – interpersonal, mediated, institutional, etc., and how these are to be used. Included in the information habitus are subjective evaluations of 'sources of information', of 'strategies of information', and of 'forms of representation'. The latter are modes of communication – writing, image, speech, gesture; media of communication – information book, newspaper, TV; and genres – news, talk shows, soaps. The information habitus also specifies an awareness of which 'information strategies', of which 'sources of information' etc., are legitimate for social actors to use in their social environment.

Given its immediate plausibility, Bourdieu's notion of habitus has been widely taken up, in a variety of academic disciplines, whether in debates around multiculturalism and multilingualism (the 'monolingual habitus', see Gogolin and Nauck, 2000), in debates relating to Media Studies/Media Policy (Couldry, 2003), or in Organizational Communication (Mutch, 2003). One common, persistent, and unresolved problem is whether to take Bourdieu's definitions and work with them, and as such dealing with the real theoretical difficulties regarding structure and agency, durability and transformation, or to attempt to adapt the concept as seems warranted within in-depth readings of Bourdieu's work (see e.g. Krais and Gebauer, 2002 [3]; as well as comments in a similar vein by, e.g. Couldry, 2003 and Mutch, 2003).

The latter is the position adopted here. Hence the information habitus is taken to be produced in the context of specific life-worlds, with their own characteristics and demands. It is socially and historically determined and is the result of the many and varied experiences of socialization. The information habitus also mediates between social actors and the conditions of their life-worlds (Bourdieu, 1993). Social actors (with their histories – embedded in their life-worlds) are at the centre of attention in this concept.

The information habitus provides explanations for the genesis of forms of practice (Bourdieu, 1993: 97ff.; here communicative practice of the everyday) for the conditions of production, as well as for their continuous change, produced as an effect of the social trajectories of the actors, their resources in the form of economic, cultural, and social capital, the changes in their life-worlds, and so on. For communication theory in German speaking domains, the concept of habitus provides a means of getting beyond the still dominant individual-based approaches to communicational action.

Whose responsibility is it to be(come) informed?

Within the information habitus, two fundamental dispositions towards the supply and/or obtaining of information can be distinguished – 'Bringschuld' and 'Holschuld' – as follows [4]:

- 'Bringschuld' (literally, an obligation, a 'debt', which the source of information owes to the recipient to provide or to 'bring' information) names a structure in which the responsibility and the obligation to supply the necessary information for whoever needs it, lie with the relevant authority. In other words, the suppliers of information are responsible.

- 'Holschuld' (literally, an obligation, a 'debt', which whoever needs information owes to her/himself to get or 'fetch' that information) names a structure in which the responsibility and the obligation lie with whoever needs the information, to seek and obtain it. In other words, those who need information are responsible.

The current changes in the social and media landscape are producing a situation in which the agency of the individual is ever more focal. 'Becoming informed' can be approached from two perspectives: either responsibility for providing information lies with the source of information or responsibility for obtaining information lies with whoever needs the information.

From the first perspective, the 'obligation to fetch', Karin – as the actor – regards herself as responsible for obtaining the information she needs. If we read her comments on a meta-theoretical level (even though expressed in her dialect), she describes where and how she obtained the information regarding her pregnancy as follows (more detail in Böck, 2004a):

> It's like this, you've really got that many examinations, where it's really talked about, well, where it can be talked about, if you play your part in it. Well, I'd say, for me that goes without saying, 'cause, if I sit there and say 'yeah, ok, that's right' then she [the specialist] won't know what questions I have, what I am interested in knowing, really it's up to me to let her know that. (Interview Karin, 4 September 2002, translation by the author.)

The pause and the reformulation 'where it's really talked about, well, where it can be talked about' emphasizes Karin's sense that visiting her specialist would not have automatically resulted in getting the information she needed or would have liked to receive. This requires that she takes the initiative, she acts, and she sees very much as her own responsibility.

The second perspective of the 'obligation to bring' implies that the medical practitioner would as a matter of professional ethos tell patients all they need to know or that it is relevant for them to know. Gerlinde, another participant in my study, tells a different story of her two pregnancies; she didn't have to ask much, her specialist and her GP told her all she needed to know. She hardly talked with other women about her pregnancy, nor did she read about it in books, though she did look at the brochures her doctor gave her.

With the 'obligation to bring' the responsibility to provide or supply information lies with those who have it and to a much lesser extent with those who need the information. If that information is not coming, then these (potential) sources of information are responsible, not those who needed (but did not seek) the information. It is essential to focus on these profoundly distinct dispositions in any attempt to develop strategies for overcoming inequalities. This will be taken up again later.

Media, as well as other technologies of communication, are implicitly structured along these lines (e.g. television leans more towards 'Bringschuld' while the Internet is more oriented towards 'Holschuld'), so the concept can be quite readily transferred to media use (Böck, 2003). For instance, it is quite possible to be satisfied with the information supplied in the main news programmes on television or radio. Equally, it is quite possible – easy even – to look out for more extensive discussion programmes, or to read at greater length in newspapers or newsmagazines, to go to the Internet, and of course it is possible to talk about issues with others. Depending on the individual's information habitus – and on the specific topic and domain of interest, etc. – strategies will vary.

There is one further issue. This concerns the extent to which information is 'prepared' for those who seek or need it, or the extent to which they themselves can and need to transform information, which is not necessarily 'tailored' to their habitus (Böck, 2003). In interpersonal communication, the interlocutor does this work, by and large. The adjustment is an integral part of the interaction, as we are unlikely to select that person again as a source of information if this adjustment is not made. By contrast, in classical mass communication, there is a one-way relation from communicator to recipient, and the issue there is very much the aptness of the content and the expectations and capacities of the audience to 'decode' and use information appropriately. Karin's reluctance to refer to the encyclopaedia may be a case in point.

The dispositions of 'Holschuld' and 'Bringschuld' are profoundly different forms of the information habitus, and it is precisely here that the major challenges for policy reside.

A pedagogy for inclusion

A pedagogy for inclusion is both a 'pedagogic' and a 'political' project. As a pedagogic project, it is concerned with individuals and their needs; as a political project it has to do with social issues such as changed (social) affiliations, different distributions of power both for individuals and groups, different potentials for individual and social action. It aims at changes 'in' the individual in order to achieve social change and at social change in order to produce changes in any individual's potential for action. The political aims of this pedagogy are to assure democratic, equitable outcomes for social, cultural, economic, and political participation at the widest level (see Freire, 1972; Cope and Kalantzis, 1993, 2000; Bernstein, 1996; Gee, 2000; Giroux, 2001).

Learning as producing knowledge is fundamental for all aspects of social life; a pedagogy for inclusion focuses on an individual's dispositions towards learning or producing knowledge and aims at inducing specific changes.

What is meant by 'a pedagogy' and 'pedagogy for inclusion'? As it is used here, 'pedagogy' describes the social relations of the participants (as learners and as social actors) in the situation in which learning takes place

(Bernstein, 2001: 3–24; Kress, 2006b); the social place and social relations of the participants involved in the pedagogic process – how do those who are 'teachers' see learners? What power is attributed to learners or to teachers? What status does the curriculum have? Whose authority stands behind the curriculum? And what relations exist between all these? The 'curriculum' on the other hand specifies 'what is to be learned'.

At this level of analysis, we need to consider both formal and so-called informal learning. While in Communication Studies informal learning has received much attention, the increasing emphasis on life-long learning must lead to an expansion of focus for both Communication Studies and pedagogy. This will result in a closer relationship between the interests of Communication Studies and pedagogy. What Communication Studies might be able to offer schools – and the educational system as such – would be a relevant question in this regard.

The term 'pedagogy for inclusion' implies at the same time the content of the curriculum and the political project of the pedagogy. It implies an existing structure of inclusion and exclusion of groups of learners and others, and it suggests means for overcoming those exclusions, namely the curriculum. What structures of social relations are needed in order to foster people's mobility? While this concerns, in principle, all people and all groups, it has a specific significance in relation to groups which have had negative experiences regarding (formal) learning, as well as developing social relations.

As with pedagogy, there is also a need to specify what is included in the curriculum. The main content and task of the curriculum is to provide the resources needed as a means of 'making mobile' independently of content and strategies. 'Moving' a learner or a group of learners from one state (not having certain kinds of knowledge, skills, values) to another (having those skills, knowledge, values) is a quite traditional pedagogic task. 'Movement' is implied in all pedagogy, as in all learning (and teaching).

For a social–political project, such as a 'pedagogy for inclusion', questions of social relations and power are central, and they have effects on every aspect of the strategies to be adopted in programmes of action (e.g. Foucault, 1980; Bernstein, 1996: 3–24).

The essential features or components of a pedagogy for inclusion are the following:

- An essential precondition is an apt theory of communication, learning, and 'making knowledge'. This necessitates reframing existing theories.
- A basic aim of any pedagogy is always promoting mobility, whether of individuals or of groups. Both learning and knowledge production expand the resources and horizons for individuals and for groups (of learners as social actors), whereby the expansion of horizons is understood as promoting mobility.

- The political aim of a pedagogy for inclusion is to change horizons, potentials, and affiliations of individuals and groups with the aim to connect 'excluded' individuals and groups with groups who can be situated in the mainstream.
- A sine-qua-non of a pedagogy for inclusion is engaging learners, as social actors in their own right, as always significant and as experts of their own life-worlds. This relates to seeing and treating those who belong to 'excluded groups' as knowledge makers and learners already.
- Those who are the objects of a pedagogy for inclusion have to be accorded full recognition of their position and the achievements in their lives, in their life-worlds. They have to be made aware of their practices as achievements and of their position as learners and makers of knowledge.

An apt theory of communication, learning, and of making meaning
As listed earlier, one essential pre-requisite is an apt theory of learning and meaning production, leading to the reframing of existing theories – both in terms of communication and pedagogy. This will enable recognizing the intrinsic connection of learning and knowledge production and focus on the actions of individuals as knowledge makers in all areas of their everyday lives. This gives proper recognition to the significance and potential of everyday actions and acknowledges both that individuals are constantly involved in processes of learning and 'knowledge production' and 'learning' are two sides of the same coin.

Mobility or 'making mobile'
If a basic aim of 'pedagogy' is to promote mobility, whether of individuals or groups, then the difference in the aims of a 'pedagogy for inclusion' lies in the specific direction and the goal of that movement. In this regard, it is essential not to confuse 'transport' with 'making mobile'; the latter implies a particular disposition on the part of the learner – 'being mobile', which the former does not presuppose. Similarly, 'inclusion' implies a reciprocal relationship between 'feeling a part of' and 'being included'. Such movements have social effects and are political in the everyday sense of bringing about changes in social affiliations and distributions of power, etc.

The movement envisaged in the pedagogy for inclusion can be seen in different ways: as the expansion of the horizons of those located in one life-world to include forms of actions, knowledges, practices, habits from other life-worlds; as a movement across life-worlds from one to another, or as connecting one life-world to another. It ideally results in the linking-up of an individual to other possibilities of life and to the expansion of the potentials for action. Seen at the micro-level of the individual, the main issue here is 'difference' – in the everyday, in practices, etc. At the social macro-level, in the presence of power, phenomena, such as discrimination and exclusion, come to the forefront. Important in this regard is the political question that deals with the interrelation of life-worlds and the effects of expanding horizons. Any political project of intervention – of which the pedagogy of inclusion is one – will invoke profound ethical and power issues, and of the legitimacy of such a project.

Seeing practices and lives in a wide social context is to recognize that seemingly 'mere' individual differences have a social dimension. It always implies excluding individuals and their group from the social, cultural, and economic benefits/goods of their wider society. Hence the subjective perspective always needs to be seen from a wider social perspective.

Directions of movement: the political aim of changing potentials and affiliations of individuals and groups

The aim of a pedagogy for inclusion is that of connecting individuals and groups who are 'excluded' with groups who can be situated in the mainstream of cultural, social, economic, and technological processes. Here again arises the political question of the relation of life-worlds towards each other, and the expansion of horizons of potentials, perceptions and expectations for individuals and groups (Selwyn *et al.*, 2005: 19ff.). On the political level, it is essential to link a focus on the individual within their own specific life-worlds with the macro-level of the social, characterized by its inequalities and differences. This would make it possible to develop proposals for actions in which an understanding of individual lives and their horizons is central – through the notion of the information habitus. In this way individuals can be connected to the horizons of mainstream social groups, situated on the other side of the digital divide, so to speak.

Ideally, this implies the possibility of offering all members of a society the same potentials for action – independently of their membership of specific life-worlds. A banal example would be that Karin could have researched forms of surgical intervention that might be used in the processes of the baby's delivery in hospital through consulting the Internet. This would have given her the basis for a much more focussed discussion with her GP. The example is both banal and profound: given her information habitus, and the limitations of the horizons of knowing which the habitus imposed, much information that is now available and regarded as essential for informed decision-making was not available to her. This relates to the question of Karin's independence of action, her autonomy in seeking information in order to construct the knowledge she needs in relation to her problem. However, she needed to approach someone whom she regarded as competent, without actually knowing what she might need to get from this person; or could she act on her own account in shaping her search for information and knowledge production? The effects of the information habitus can be seen here – the different possibilities for action in combination with various sources of information, issues, and their evaluation. Karin and others can find themselves in a form of exclusion not necessarily wanted by anyone or determined by any structure but nevertheless detrimental to her in this crucial part of her life.

Politics of a pedagogy for inclusion as a politics of intervention: putting agentive learners central

A pedagogy for inclusion is at all times a political project, and as such it raises ethical, social, and political issues. This presupposes that those who are potential subjects of a pedagogy for inclusion are already active and possess agency in their life-worlds. A cornerstone of a pedagogy of inclusion is seeing agency both as the starting point and as the centre of pedagogic action. In other words, learners and their actions are paramount to this pedagogic strategy. But, being a political project, these subjects also have to be seen as social beings, as full, significant, valuable participants in their life-worlds. As such, any engagement has to take place 'on their own terms', from within their life-world, in which they are (usually/often/always) already experts.

Learning and knowledge production expand the resources and horizons of the involved learners. The expansion of horizons brings about the potential for doing things differently and can thus promote mobility. The aim of this mobility is the expansion of the potentials for action in specific areas and to open up forms of action, which had hitherto not been taken into consideration or had not been recognized as a possibility. Such an expansion of horizons is the democratic goal of maximal participation by all citizens.

A curriculum for inclusion: what is it that is to be learned?

A *pedagogy* describes the social relations of those who are engaged in the processes of (teaching and) learning and knowledge production. A curriculum then is or describes 'what is to be learned'. We can view a curriculum in different ways though always as altering the resources, which are available to the learner: it 'fixes a lack'; it supplies what is missing, what might be needed. From this follows the question what the lack is which needs to be fixed by this curriculum. The changed resources transform the individual's potentials for action, which can potentially change the notion of the self as a social actor. At the most general level, the curriculum aims at dispositional changes; at other levels more specific aims appear.

The aims of a curriculum for inclusion have to be in harmony with the pedagogy for inclusion. If the aims of the latter are to promote mobility, the aims of the former are to provide the means for achieving these aims. The different elements of a curriculum can be summarized as follows:

- Means for producing changes in the information habitus in general, in all forms, at all levels. In particular, moving away from a disposition of 'Bringschuld' towards a disposition of 'Holschuld'. For Karin, this might mean that there are other sources of information than acquaintances or (professional/ non-professional) experts in the wider social environment, for instance factual literature, or the Internet.

- Means for producing specific dispositional changes: finding means of showing the fragility of 'the already achieved'. This can be expressed as 'I am happy with what I have, where I am, I would not get any further anyway, I have got a steady/secure job, it makes no sense for me to do a course, etc' [5]. It is crucial to continue to provide recognition of the subjects' present position while also showing the intrinsic (e.g. seeing Adult Education as simply instrumental, job-oriented) and extrinsic (e.g. there are no secure jobs any more) difficulties and limitations of the position. This perspective provides a full picture of education as a personal (leisure time, health, living) and as a professional (development in a job and for other occupations) project. Any challenge to existing achievements must not lead to a denigration of present achievements as real achievements. However, it is important to see the insistence on 'I am happy where I am' as an implicit acknowledgement of fear. While the present might be unsatisfactory, anxiety about the unknown prevails.
- To initiate a changed sense of self, and changes in the self-image, and the individual's valuation of her or himself. 'Who am I, where do I stand? What does change mean for my potentials to do things differently in my everyday life? If I change my knowledge, my competences, will I then also give up my own sense of expertise?' If I change it might/will change my position in my life-world, for instance power-relations might become questioned (McGivney, 1990), and different roles become recognized.
- To expand potentials for action and to insist on the legitimacy of changing common practices so that the individual can see, think, and act differently. A first step is that actors have to become aware of these possibilities. The essential second step is that of recognition – to recognize possibilities as relevant and legitimate for themselves.
- To expand knowledge around sources of information, making learners as social actors aware that there are other sources of information than those that have been used within their everyday practices. This entails specific elements in the curriculum such as providing research skills. This entirely connects with the agenda of information and communication rights and freedoms.
- To provide (the means of gaining) access to the knowledge resources available to all. This entails engendering a disposition of seeing learning as a socially centred means of access. A central problem for the knowledge society is that those who are excluded might remain excluded, causing the gap to widen even more, due to the movement of society as a whole. This requires that they are provided with strategies and specific means for catching up, thereby creating an environment of equal chances [6].

A curriculum for inclusion, thus, starts from the recognition that social actors already possess a specific information habitus with specific strategies for obtaining information, a particular stance towards learning, and so on. While that information habitus might be limiting or even counter-productive from the perspective of a pedagogy for inclusion, the argument being made here is that citizens need to be respected for the capabilities they already have and learners need to be approached as knowledge producers, taking them seriously as experts, and as such according them recognition in a real sense. The point is to find means and strategies to align this with the demands of the knowledge society. Central to that – both for those who are developing these strategies and for those who become the subjects of the pedagogy – is seeing learning as the central means, process, and resource in the pedagogy for inclusion, a resource for all aspects of managing life.

Re-theorization

This brings us back to the task of re-theorizing Communication Studies. This chapter started by outlining two broad aims: the larger social and political aim referring to Freire, and the other, inseparable from the first, to reflect on the potential social and political uses of Communication Studies in relation to the ever more pressing problems around issues such as 'the digital divide', 'the knowledge gap/information gap', and so on. My theoretical proposal for both, but in particular for connecting the macro-level purposes and aims of communication policy with micro-level of habitus, practices, and structures of information use in the everyday life of social actors, was to introduce the notion of 'learning' into the set of terms used in communication theory.

As a conclusion of this chapter, the arguments regarding 'learning' developed in this chapter will be summarized in three main points: (1) the response of communication theory to social and economic change; (2) the difficulties which exist in relevant areas within theories of communication; and (3) the political purposes of Communication Studies for many of its practitioners, that is, the attempt to affect potentials for equitable social outcomes through theorization and analysis. These are as follows:

(1) The inexorable move in 'developed economies' towards a situation in which information and/or knowledge define both the dominant forms of economic activity and salient features of society – the so-called information or knowledge societies – has profound consequences for members of those societies, whether (still) as citizens, as consumers, or as part of the labor force. With the rise of the post-industrial economy, its required flexibility and the abundance of information; an individualized and stable sets of skills may no longer suffice to meet the demands of the labor market and of society. Phrases such as 'life-long', 'life-wide learning' respond to this situation (e.g. Gee *et al.*, 1996). The economy and its spokespersons, as much as politicians, demand that schools should produce a flexible, dynamic, innovative, creative population of young people for that market. But as demands for change affect everyone, irrespective of age and increasingly also of social position, the question arises whether communication theory needs to expand its role into this field, where socialization, pedagogy, and

communication intersect and interact. In any case, issues, such as the 'digital divide', are an integral part of the concerns of communication theory, as are many (maybe all?) of the issues of information and knowledge. They too are, without question, central to this area. But so are the processes, the environments, and the effects of learning. In the manner being described and defined in this chapter, learning and the production of knowledge are interconnected.

(2) Learning describes the processes of change within the learner through the changes produced by the learner in the learner's resources, gained in the process of knowledge production. At this point, learning becomes once again a central concept in relation to the theoretical issues raised on habitus/disposition and the need for communication policy to find ways and means of reconnecting (with) those who are in danger of being excluded in the course of social and economic developments. What is needed for members of these groups are precisely these changes in their dispositions/habitus in order for them to become re-mobilized socially, culturally, economically, and psychologically. Such changes of disposition pose a problem for present conceptualizations of habitus (see my earlier brief reference to that). The issue is one of stability, persistence, and durability versus dynamism, change, and flux. In (contemporary socio-cultural) theories of learning (see e.g. Gee *et al.*, 1996; Daniels, 2001), the processes of learning are described more in terms of processes of constant transformative engagement and change by a learner with her or his environment. The effect of that process is a change in the resources of the learner, in terms of a changed capacity for action, for instance. But this is very similar to a change in/of disposition by the learner – a change in habitus. Theories of learning of this kind relate to durability as much as to change – a relative durability, an apparent inertia even combined with incessant transformation of usually the smallest kind. In this way, both the concept of learning and the processes invoked by that term become an essential component of a theory of communication, which can then achieve the link between macro- and micro-levels of analysis.

'Socialization' processes are central to any theorizing and development of policies and proposals for action in relation to communicational inequalities, and in my view these processes are best described by the notion of 'learning as knowledge production'. In this approach, the relative durability of structure is given; there is no suggestion of 'things being thrown over'. Yet agency, similarly, is given and brings along the constant transformative engagement of socially formed and located actors with their visions on the shape of their worlds, and their dispositions.

(3) That brings us to the third issue, an older political purpose of Communication Studies for many of its practitioners, namely to have an effect on potentials for equitable social outcomes through theorization and analysis. The effects of economic, social, political, cultural, and technological change – implied in terms

such as 'the digital divide', as much as in other communication-related 'divides' and inequalities – demand a response on the part of Communication Studies. This chapter hopes to contribute to that attempt.

Notes for Chapter Three

[1] References to Communication Studies in this section relate to the mainstream German tradition, which focuses still, to a large extent, on public communication in the traditional mass-media (the Press, TV, Radio, though also now the Internet). Its main concerns are processes of production, mediation, and reception (Deutsche Gesellschaft für Publizistik und Kommunikationswissenschaft, 1999; for critical comments see Löffelholz and Quandt, 2003), with the transmission of information as often also quite central (see here the critical comments by Klaus, 2003).

[2] The conversation was conducted in the local dialect, of which we are both speakers. Many of the nuanced meanings of dialectal forms – of all kinds – are inevitably lost or smoothed out in the translation, even if it would be 'translated' into standard German.

[3] 'Der Habitus ist kreativ, er variiert, geht mit neuen Situationen anders um als mit alten' – 'the habitus is creative, varies, and deals with new situations differently to old' (Krais and Gebauer, 2002: 79).

[4] I have not as yet produced a good translation into English, so I will gloss each concept and then use two terms 'obligation to bring', and 'obligation to fetch'.

[5] As one of my 'informants' said to me in the context of a different project, concerned with establishing paths to courses in 'Basic Education'.

[6] This is a quite different situation for those who have the intellectual, educational, social, and economic means for remaining connected but make a deliberate decision to adopt a different position.

References for Chapter Three

Bernstein, B. (1996), *Pedagogy, Symbolic Control and Identity: Theory, Research, Critique*, London: Taylor & Francis.

Böck, M. (2003), 'Information, Wissen und Medialer Wandel', *Medien Journal*, 27: 1, pp. 51–65.

—— (2004a), 'Informationshabitus und Lernen in der Informationsgesellschaft', in M. Krainz-Dürr, H. Enzinger, and M. Schmoczer (eds.), *Grenzen überschreiten in Bildung und Schule*, Klagenfurt: Drava, pp. 163–74.

—— (2004b), 'Life Worlds and Information Habitus', *Visual Communication*, 3: 3, pp. 281–93.

Bonfadelli, H. (2001), *Medienwirkungsforschung I. Grundlagen und Theoretische Perspektiven*, (2nd ed.), Konstanz: UVK.

Bourdieu, P. (1982), *Die Feinen Unterschiede. Kritik Der Gesellschaftlichen Urteilskraft*, Frankfurt/Main: Suhrkamp.

—— (1993), *Sozialer Sinn. Kritik Der Theoretischen Vernunft*, Frankfurt/Main: Suhrkamp.

Carpentier, N. (2002), *Bridging Cultural and Digital Divides. Signifying Everyday Life, Cultural Diversity and Participation in the on-line Community Video Nation*, http://www.re-creatiefvlaanderen.be/srv/pdf/srcvwp_200205.pdf. Consulted on 1 March 2006.

Cope, B., Kalantzis M. (eds.) (2000), *Multiliteracies: Literacy Learning and the Design of Social Futures*, London: Routledge.

—— (1993), 'Histories of pedagogy, Cultures of Schooling', in B. Cope and M. Kalantzis (eds.), *The Powers of Literacy: A Genre Approach to Teaching Writing*, Pittsburgh: University of Pittsburgh Press, pp. 38–62.

Couldry, N. (2003), 'Media, Symbolic Power and the Limits of Bourdieu's Field Theory', *Media@LSE Electronic Working Paper*, Nr. 2. http://www.lse.ac.uk/collections/media@lse/mediaWorkingPapers/ewpNumber2.htm. Consulted on 1 March 2006.

Daniels, H. (2001), *Vygotsky and Pedagogy*, London: Routledge.

Dervin, B. (1980), *Communication Gaps and Inequities: Moving Toward a Reconceptualization*, in B. Dervin and M. Voigt (eds.), *Progress in Communication Sciences*, vol. 2. Norwood NJ: Ablex, pp. 73–112.

Deutsche Gesellschaft für Kommunikationswissenschaft (1999), *Die Mediengesellschaft und ihre Wissenschaft*, Deutsche Gesellschaft für Kommunikationswissenschaft.

Foucault, M. (1980), *Power/Knowledge: Selected Interviews and Other Writings, 1972–1977*, New York: Pantheon.

Freire, P. (1972), *Pedagogy of the Oppressed*, Harmondsworth: Pengiun.

Gandy, O. (2002), 'The Real Digital Divide: Citizens Versus Consumers', in L. Lievrouw and S. Livingstone (eds.), *The Handbook of the New Media. The Social Shaping and Consequences of ICTs*, London: Sage, pp. 448–60.

Gee J. P. (2000), 'New People in New Worlds: Networks, The New Capitalism and Schools', in B. Cope and Kalantzis M. (eds.), *Multiliteracies: Literacy Learning and the Design of Social Futures*, London: Routledge, pp. 69–91.

Gee, J. P., Hull, G., Lankshear, C. (1996), *The New Work Order: Behind the Language of the New Capitalism*, Sydney: Allen & Unwin.

Giroux, H. A. (2001), *Theory and Resistance in Education: Towards a Pedagogy for the Opposition*, Revised and expanded edition, Westport, CT: Bergin & Garvey.

Gogolin, I., Nauck, B. (2000), *Migration, Gesellschaftliche Differenzierung und Bildung*, Opladen: Leske + Budrich.

Klaus, E. (2003), 'Produzieren für die Spaßgesellschaft. Unterhaltung als Beruf', in M. Löffelholz and T. Quandt (eds.), *Die neue Kommunikationswissenschaft. Theorien, Themen und Berufsfelder im Internetzeitalter. Eine Einführung*, Opladen: Westdeutscher Verlag, pp. 303–320.

Krais, B., Gebauer, G. (2002), *Habitus*, Bielefeld: Transcript.

Kress, G. R. (2006a), 'Thinking about Meaning and Learning in a World of Instability and Multiplicity', *Pedagogy*, 2: 1, Forthcoming.

—— (2006b), 'Towards a Semiotic Theory of Learning', in M. Göhlich, C. Wulf, and J. Zirfas J. (eds.), *Pädagogische Theorien des Lernens*, Paderborn: UTB, Forthcoming.

Löffelholz, M., Quandt, T. (2003), 'Kommunikationswissenschaft im Wandel. Orientierung in Einer Dynamischen, Integrativen und Unüberschaubaren Disziplin', in M. Löffelholz and T. Quandt (eds.), *Die neue Kommunikationswissenschaft. Theorien, Themen und Berufsfelder im Internetzeitalter. Eine Einführung*, Opladen: Westdeutscher Verlag, pp. 13–42.

McGivney, V. (1990), *Education's for Other People. Access to Education for Non-Participant Adults*, Leicester: National Institute of Adult Continuing Education.

Mutch, A. (2003), 'Communities of Practice and Habitus: A Critique', *Organisation Studies*, 24: 3, pp. 383–401. http://www.findarticles.com/p/ articles/mi_m4339/ is_3_24/ai_99699577. Consulted on 1 March 2006.

Saxer, U. (1997), 'Medien als problemschaffende und problemlösende Systeme: Zur Notwendigkeit der Annäherung der Medienforschung an ihren Gegenstand', *Publizistik*, 42: 1, pp. 73–82.

Selwyn, N., Gorard, S., Furlong, J. (2005), 'Whose Internet is it Anyway? Exploring Adults' (Non)Use of the Internet in Everyday Life', *European Journal of Communication*, 20: 1, pp. 5–26.

Stehr, N. (2001), *Wissen und Wirtschaften. Die gesellschaftlichen Grundlagen der modernen Ökonomie*, Frankfurt/M.: Suhrkamp.

Section Two: Introduction

Participation and Media

Nico Carpentier

Participation is a highly fluid and contested notion, or a concept that can be called – following Laclau and Mouffe (1985) – an empty signifier. In practice, this means that – as Pateman (1970: 1) puts it – 'the widespread use of the term [...] has tended to mean that any precise, meaningful content has almost disappeared; "participation" is used to refer to a wide variety of different situations by different people'. It is tempting to see this process of the emptying of the signifier participation as a neutral event or as an accident of history. A more critical analysis shows that this is actually an ideological process, which aims (or threatens) to remove the more radical meanings from the concept of participation.

Attempts to counter this softening-down of (the signifier) participation have been based on the construction of dichotomized systems of meaning. In these dichotomies, specific forms of participation are described as 'real' and 'authentic', while other forms are described as 'fake' and 'pseudo'. In the field of so-called political participation, for example, Verba (1961: 220–221) points to the existence of 'pseudo-participation', in which the emphasis is not on creating a situation in which participation is possible, but on creating the feeling that participation is possible. An alternative name, which is among others used by Strauss (1998: 18), is 'manipulative participation' [1]. An example of an author working within the tradition of participatory communication who uses terms as 'genuine' and 'authentic participation' is Servaes. In his *Communication for development* (1999), he writes that this 'real' form of participation has to be seen as participation '[that] directly addresses <u>power</u> and its distribution in society. It touches the very core of power relationships' (Servaes, 1999: 198; my emphasis). Moreover, this shows how crucial power is to the definition of participation, as is also emphasized by White (1994: 17):

> *It appears that <u>power</u> and <u>control</u> are pivotal subconcepts which contribute to both understanding the diversity of expectations and anticipated out-comes of people's participation.* (My emphasis).

Other strategies consisted out of the construction of hierarchically ordered and multi-layered systems. A seminal example is Pateman's (1970) book *Democratic Theory and Participation*. The two definitions of participation that she introduces are 'partial' and 'full participation'.

Partial participation is defined as:

A process in which two or more parties influence each other in the making of decisions but the final power to decide rests with one party only (Pateman, 1970: 70; my emphasis),

while full participation is seen as:

A process where each individual member of a decision-making body has equal power to determine the outcome of decisions (Pateman, 1970: 71; my emphasis).

Through the UNESCO-debates on the New World Information and Communication Order (NWICO), the distinction between access and participation was defined. While their definition of access stressed the availability of opportunities to choose relevant programs and to have a means of feedback, participation implied 'a higher level of public involvement […] in the production process and also in the management and planning of communication systems' (Servaes, 1999: 85, see MacBride, 1980). Within Communication Studies, attempts have been made to introduce the notion of interaction as an intermediary layer between access and participation (Grevisse and Carpentier, 2004). From a Policy Studies perspective, complex typologies have been developed to tackle all variations in meaning – see, for instance, Arnstein's ladder of citizen participation (1969). Also illustrative in this context is the OECD's (2001) three-stage model, which distinguishes information dissemination and consultation from active participation.

When focussing more explicitly on the media's role, and the importance of media participation, we need to distinguish between participation 'in' the media and 'through' the media, in a similar way that Wasko and Mosco (1992: 7) distinguished between democratization 'in' and 'through' the media. Participation 'in' the media deals with the participation of non-professionals in the production of media output (content-related participation) and in media decision-making (structural participation). These forms of media participation allow citizens to be active in one of the many (micro-)spheres relevant to daily life and to put their right to communicate into practice. Second, these forms of micro-participation are to be considered important, because they allow people to learn and adopt a democratic and/or civic attitude, thus strengthening (the possible forms) of macro-participation. Verba and Nie (1987: 3) briefly summarize this as follows: 'a participatory polity may rest on a participatory society'. Although mainstream media have attempted to organize forms of audience participation (Livingstone and Lunt, 1994; Carpentier, 2003; McNair *et al.*, 2003), especially alternative media have proven to be more successful in organizing more deepened forms of participation in the media (Girard, 1992; Downing *et al.*, 2000; Rodriguez, 2001).

Participation 'through' the media deals with the opportunities for extensive participation in public debate and for self-representation in the public spheres, thus, entering the realm of enabling and facilitating macro-participation (Couldry, 2003). Starting from a broadly defined notion of the political, consensus-oriented models of democracy (and participation) emphasize the importance of dialogue and deliberation and focus on collective decision-making based on rational arguments à la Habermas. Other authors (Fraser, 1990; Mouffe, 1994) stress more conflict-oriented approaches. They point to the unavoidability of political differences and struggles and see the media as crucial sites for struggles for hegemony (Kellner, 1992: 57). Both consensus- and conflict-oriented models enable to stress the need for citizens to participate in these processes of dialogue, debate, and deliberation.

Both participation 'in' the media and 'through' the media see the (mass) communicative process not as a series of practices that are restrictively controlled by media professionals, but as a human right that cuts across entire societies. When the right to communicate was originally proposed in 1969 by the French civil servant Jean d'Arcy, it aimed to broaden the right to be informed, which is embedded in article 19 of the Universal Declaration of Human Rights. Although the definition of the right to communicate was highly debated, Jim Richstad and Michael Anderson wrote in their 1981 book on *Crisis in international news*, that the right to communicate included (amongst other rights) the right for active participation in the communication process. A necessary condition to remain an effective and inextricable part of the right to communicate is the protection of participation from significatory reductionisms. These reductionisms try to remove the politicized notion of power balances from its meaning and attempt to conflate participation with interaction. As an endangered species, this key notion needs – more than ever – our attention, care, and protection.

Notes for Section Two: Introduction

[1] The well-known rhyme, which according to myth appeared some time around the beginning of the 1970s on a Paris wall, also refers to this dichotomy between 'real' and 'fake' participation. 'Je participe, tu participes, il participe, nous participons, vous participez, ils profitent'. (Verba and Nie, 1987: 0)

References for Section Two: Introduction

Arnstein, S. R. (1969), 'A Ladder of Citizen Participation', *Journal of the American Institute of Planners,* 35, pp. 216–24.

Carpentier, N. (2003), 'BBC's Video Nation as a Participatory Media Practice. Signifying Everyday Life, Cultural Diversity and Participation in an on-line Community', *International Journal of Cultural Studies,* 6: 4, pp. 425–47.

Couldry, N. (2003), *Media Rituals: A Critical Approach*, London: Routledge.

Downing, J., with T. V. Ford G. Gil (2000), *Radical Media. Rebellious Communication and Social Movements*, London: Sage.

Girard, B. (ed.) (1992), *A Passion for Radio*, Montreal: Black Rose Books.

Grevisse, B., Carpentier, N. (2004), *Des Médias Qui Font Bouger. 22 Expériences Journalistiques Favorisant la Participation Citoyenne*, Brussel: Koning Boudewijn Stichting.

Fraser, N. (1990), 'Rethinking the Public Sphere', *Social Text,* 25/26, pp. 56–80.

Kellner, D. (1992), *The Persian Gulf TV War*, Boulder, San Francisco, Oxford: Westview press.

Laclau, E., Mouffe, C. (1985), *Hegemony and Socialist Strategy: Towards a Radical Democratic Politics*, London: Verso.

Livingstone, S., Lunt, P. (1994), *Talk on Television, Audience Participation and Public Debate*, London: Routledge.

MacBride, S. (1980), *Many Voices, One World. Report by the International Commission for the Study of Communication Problems,* Paris and London: Unesco & Kogan Page.

McNair, B., Hibberd, M., Schlesinger, P. (2003), *Mediated Access Broadcasting and Democratic Participation in the Age of Mediated Communication*, Luton: University of Luton Press.

Mouffe, C. (1994), 'For a Politics of Nomadic Identity', in G. Robertson, M. Mash, L. Tickner, J. Bird, B. Curtis and T. Putnam. (eds.), *Travellers' Tales: Narratives of Home and Displacement*, Routledge: London, pp. 105–13.

OECD (2001), *Citizens as Partners: Information, Consultation and Public Participation in Policy-Making*, PUMA: OECD.

Pateman, C. (1970), *Participation and Democratic Theory*, Cambridge: Cambridge University Press.

Richstad, J., Anderson, M. H. (eds.) (1981), *Crisis in International News: Policies and Prospects,* New York: Columbia University Press.

Rodriguez, C. (2001), *Fissures in the Mediascape. An International Study of Citizens' Media*, Cresskill, NJ: Hampton Press.

Servaes, J. (1999), *Communication for Development. One World, Multiple Cultures*, Cresskill, New Jersey: Hampton press.

Strauss, G. (1998), 'An Overview', in F. Heller, E. Pusic, G. Strauss, *et al.* (eds.), *Organizational Participation: Myth and Reality*, New York: Oxford University Press, pp. 8–39.

Verba, S. (1961), *Small Groups and Political Behaviour*, Princeton: Princeton University Press.

Verba, S., Nie, N. (1987), *Participation in America: Political Democracy & Social Equality*, Chicago: University of Chicago Press.

Wasko, J., Mosco, V. (eds.) (1992), *Democratic Communications in the Information Age,* Toronto and Norwood, NJ: Garamond Press & Ablex.

White, S. (1994), *Participatory Communication: Working for Change and Development*, Beverly Hills: Sage.

Chapter Four

Citizen participation and local public spheres: an agency and identity focussed approach to the Tampere postal services conflict

Auli Harju

Introduction

> *Today, citizenship still generally evokes the notion of a subjectivity positioned publicly – even if a 'public' context can be very small-scale. Yet, with the public and private having become intertwined, citizenship as an identity becomes interlaced with our dimensions of the self. However, if citizenship is a dimension of the self, this does not mean that people necessarily give the word 'citizen' a meaning that resonates with them; they may have other vocabularies* (Dahlgren, 2000: 318).

Is citizenship an identity and if so, what kind of identity is it? Do people experience themselves as being citizens when they engage in public performances? Peter Dahlgren states that seeing citizenship as part of one's identity allows us to avoid viewing citizenship in a mono-dimensional way, as something that shapes us into one single form when it comes to acting as citizens (Dahlgren, 2000: 318). Hence, identity is an important concept in regard to citizenship since it creates a connection between people's everyday lives and their public activity as citizens.

This position is very different from the more traditional definitions of citizenship. Traditionally, when citizens get involved in politics, as voters or as participants in public discussions, they are expected to detach their private matters, interests, and commitments from their public performances. They are expected to adopt a particular form of social agency and act as a citizen.

This dichotomized ways of thinking about citizenship is problematic. The boundaries between the public and the private are actually debated in the public sphere, and they cannot be considered settled before the actors enter the public sphere. This implies that there is a need for all actors that operate within the public sphere to recognize and include the diversity of identities that connect to people's activities and forms of involvement. The public sphere should not only be a place for rational discussion à la Habermas but also a place for achieving social solidarity. According to Craig Calhoun (2002), bracketing identity-related issues carries a heavy price, as it causes the exclusion of some of the most important citizens' concerns. In order to avoid this exclusion, individual life histories need to be related to the public sphere and public policies.

In this chapter, I first want to explore the concept of the 'citizen' and the connections between citizenship and the public sphere. Second, I want to ask whether the identity dimension of social agency and participation has been taken into account thoroughly enough when theorizing the notion of citizenship. I then want to look at other forms of social agency, such as consumerhood, and discuss their potential relationship with citizenship. Finally, the relation of citizenship and journalism will be linked to this discussion. The case study of a conflict of the Finnish postal service and local residents will be used as a case study. This case study is based on the analysis of newspaper articles and letters to the editor of a local newspaper *Aamulehti* and interviews with the active members of local neighborhood organizations.

The conflict over mail deliveries took place in the city of Tampere in a few old neighborhoods in the spring 2003 and was initiated by the postal service's ambition to rationalize its mail delivery system. Because of this business strategy, the residents were ordered to group their mailboxes in their home street instead of keeping the mailboxes in close proximity of each house. The residents, with the help of local neighborhood organizations [1] opposed the order. The issue was not a big social problem, it did not affect all the citizens of the town, but it still caused a considerable local public debate that was frequently covered by the local newspaper and other local media. Further discussions between the representatives of the postal service and the heads of the neighborhood organizations were carried out behind closed doors. The public debate faded away during the summer 2003, and the negotiations resulted in 91 per cent of the households moving their mailboxes according to the orders of the postal service in October 2003.

However, the debate changed the traditional ways of action of the neighborhood organizations when they took the lead of the residents' opposition against the postal service. Also the residents' way of getting local media's attention in the beginning of the conflict showed that these 'ordinary people' were aware of the importance of publicity. Furthermore, the conflict made the residents momentarily cross the borders between audiences and publics.

My basic claim is that studying local civic action and citizens' views on participation is important for understanding contemporary forms of citizenship – for understanding how people take part in the public sphere as agents whose private selves, emotions, experiences and interests inform, stimulate and contribute to their political/civil activities.

Citizenship and identity

The notion of citizenship is a key concept when exploring local civic action. Sociologically, 'citizenship' can be defined as a set of practices that make people competent members of a community (Turner, 1994: 159). Citizenship can also be defined as the status of an individual within a polity, where a citizen has both rights and obligations. The more sociological definition has the advantage that it allows incorporating civic action, citizens' attitudes and their commitment to their communities (Turner, 1994: 159; Dahlgren, 2000: 317; Heikkilä, 2001: 23–28; Rättilä, 2001: 195).

The word citizen is a modern concept. It was introduced during the fourteenth century, referring only to the inhabitant of a city. Later, the concept was first linked to the rights that originated from state membership. After that, it also came to include the obligations and duties attributed to the individual [2]. In the eighteenth century, the term became connected with modern notions of individualism. But altogether, 'citizen' still referred to 'an individual with the ability to act – an agent – in a political community' (McAfee, 2000: 13; see also Habermas, 1996: 496–497).

Traditionally, the individual's political role in a democracy was limited to the functioning of governments, whether by voting, demonstrating, or writing letters to their (elected) representatives. The government claimed the public realm and the leftovers – the private sphere – belonged to its citizens (McAfee, 2000: 83). The notion of citizenship thus involved the idea of a shared national political structure and culture.

The understanding of politics has changed in the twentieth century, and the earlier described modernist version of citizenship now finds itself in contradiction with the postmodern aspects of our contemporary cultures (Turner, 1994: 165–166). Giddens' notion of life politics describes this change: the questions that move people now relate to their everyday life, self-conception, and their worldviews. People's engagement in politics is becoming less institutionalized. Instead of engaging in long-term and stable relationships with traditional political organizations, they form temporary alliances around diverse issues (Giddens, 1991: 214–217; Melucci, 1996: 8; Dahlgren, 2000: 312). When 'the private' enters into the public sphere, this move also changes the way that people define political actors. When the gates of politics are opened for the politicization of everyday life, this actually (at least potentially) increases the presence of politics in people's lives. They become potential political actors. From this perspective, identities can be seen as a resource for civic action.

> *Against the grain of democratic theory, I argue that the democratic citizen is not a species apart from the subject, from the welfare recipient, the bureaucratic client, the exploited worker, or the therapeutic patient. Being 'just another number,' 'dependent,' or ' in need of help' is not the antithesis of being an active citizen. Rather it is to be in a tangled field of power and knowledge that both enables and constraints the possibilities of citizenship* (Cruicshank, 1999: 20).

Barbara Cruicshank continues to argue that separating subjectivity, agency, and citizenship from subjection, domination, and powerlessness is misleading.

She suggests that a person can be both an active citizen and the subject of government. Even as a subject of bureaucratic control, one still has the opportunity to resist definitions and regulations (Cruicshank, 1999: 23).

How do you become a citizen in contemporary societies then? For example, do active residents recognize that their actions are based on notions of citizenship? Do they consider themselves as citizens when acting on behalf or against some issue? It is more likely that they would call themselves parents, or consumers, or members of a local community – depending on the issue in question.

The concept of identity illuminates the existence of aspects in citizenship that relate to 'private' emotions and experiences. Citizenship as an identity includes the idea of belonging to a community, which can be a locality as a neighborhood or a city, or a larger collectivity, a society and so forth (Calabrese, 1999: 268–269; Dahlgren, 2000: 317–318). However, a collective identity not necessarily depends on geographical proximity. It is merely a system of relations and representations. A communal, cultural identity can be born for instance in a process where people engage in urban movements or other community organizations, through which common interests are discovered and defended (Castells, 1997: 60–62; Carpentier *et al.*, 2003: 53–54).

In the case of the mail delivery conflict, the residents involved in the debate identified themselves strongly with the neighborhood community and its neighborhood organization. However, the conflict made the traditional neighborhood organizations to change at least momentarily their ways of action from traditional cooperation to opposition, showing that in conflicts the identity of a collective actor is challenged (Melucci, 1996: 75). This brought along the need of public attention for their case, although seeking media publicity was not a common part of the 'toolkit' of these organizations. Through this process, the organizations not only politicized their mailbox issue but also themselves as collective actors.

A key question then becomes is there a place for different and contingent forms of citizenship? Is there a place for a voter, and for an active member of a neighborhood community, and for an activist belonging to a social movement? And are there participatory means and practices available for those who actually find these new civic identities more appealing than the traditional forms of citizenship?

Different forms of agency in civic action

There are, of course, many other subject positions available in society apart from citizenship. One interesting other subject position is consumerhood. Citizens and consumers are often positioned in opposition, linking it to an active/passive dimension. Consumption has been considered a merely reactive action. In contrast to this perspective, consumers can also be seen as active users, who modify and change products to meet their own needs and purposes (Turner, 1994: 164). For example, fan culture can be easily associated with consumerism because of the vast media production (tv series, movies, artists, etc.) that is marketed for them. However, opposing elements can be found in fan cultures, when fans are seen 'poaching' (Jenkins, 1992), modifying, and recycling media products (Nikunen, 2005).

Moreover, Liesbet van Zoonen has shown similarities in the activities of fans and citizens participating in political practices and ceremonies. She pointed to the fan behavior of citizens who supported a political candidate or celebrated her/his victory. She argued that these practices do not differ vastly from the emotions and admirations that a group of fans exhibit for a movie star or a sports athlete (van Zoonen, 2004).

Acts of consumption can also become highly political as they have direct relevance concerning, for example, the quality of the lived environment. Citizens' joint efforts, boycotts, and demonstrations – often led by non-governmental organizations – to make companies change their ways can be considered as private experiences, worries, and feelings of responsibility becoming politicized through action.

The mail delivery conflict offers an illustrative example of different subject positions actualized in civic activity. The resistance of the residents could be seen merely as an expression of the Not in My Back Yard (NIMBY) [3] phenomenon, but actually the worries of the residents extended from their houses to aspects related to the development of the welfare society and to the citizens' abilities to have a say in the demands posed to them. The residents not only felt they were treated unfairly as citizens and clients by the postal service but also expressed their frustration over structural societal changes such as the ongoing process of commodification, the decrease of public service provisions, and the lack of control on their own daily lives. The debate was also remarkably well covered in the local media (see later). This example shows how politicized everyday-life issues may have social connections that move beyond the implications of Giddens' notion of life-style politics.

The residents were occupying many different positions during the debate. They saw themselves simultaneously as neighbors, members of the local community, citizens, clients, elderly people, activists defending 'the rights of ordinary people', etc. A multiplicity of identities and interests informed and structured their activities. In the conflict with the postal service the residents' private interests became politicized. At the same time, the political became personal for the residents (see also McAfee, 2000: 159–160).

Identities that work as resources actually strengthen people's ability to act in public. In case of local civic action, these identities collide with the views of local power holders, revealing an important paradox. Politicians and other governmental actors often publicly express the need for citizen participation in localities, but the so-desired 'active citizen' actually remains framed in the traditional restrictive interpretation of citizenship, in which private experiences and interests are still bracketed (or chained).

This is combined with the tendency in Finnish municipalities to increasingly address local citizens as clients. People are first and foremost seen by the local administration as individual users of the services that the municipality is offering. One of the consequences of this is that the channels that residents can use to have a say about the services are constructed as feedback channels and not as participatory channels (Harju, 2002: 160; see also Eliasoph, 1998: 213).

Since the 1990s, Finnish municipalities have also introduced new participatory tools for local planning and decision-making in order to get citizens more involved. It still remains to be seen how these different forms of involvement are linked together and how they are used. Moreover, despite the labelling of these new tools as participatory, they still in many cases construct a client-oriented relation between the city and its residents. When local residents become aware of these new participatory opportunities, they often react by claiming more participation also in areas that are considered by the administration as their prerogative. Slightly increasing participation thus only exposes the structural lack of participation.

In everyday life, different subject positions become intertwined and citizens are shifting fluently from one position to other. In contrast, the practices of municipalities structurally constraint participation, as they tend to define citizens still in more traditional ways, or as they revert to other (less threatening) models such as consumer-oriented identities. The civic positions they are willing to offer show a structural scarcity, only strengthening the conflicts with citizens' expectations that want to move beyond this narrow and rigid path.

However, in the case of the conflict with the postal service, even the adopted practices of local cooperation did not work, since the opposite side was not the city but a company. Finnish Postal Service has been traditionally a public service, state-owned, non-profit company, but it has moved increasingly (during recent years) into the field of private markets, for instance, by addressing people more as customers or clients in selling their services. Even though the practices of the postal service may seem to belong to private profit-oriented business sector, there still remains one difference in its relation to the customers in comparison to private companies: people do not have the option to choose from different companies in the field of postal services, as Finland Post Group still holds the monopoly as a public service to deliver 'ordinary' mail to Finnish people.

A similar kind of shift between the public and private can be seen in the residents' ways of opposing the changes demanded by the postal service. The first reaction against the postal service's orders originated from residents' earlier experiences in cooperating with city officials and the notion of how they should – and should not – be treated as local citizens. The most crucial mistake the postal service made was that they did not follow the protocol for organizing a 'planning meeting' to both 'inform' people and invite them to 'discuss' the matter. In city governance, this has become a routine practice in local planning.

Instead the postal service 'ordered' the residents to change the places of their mailboxes and announced a 'briefing' that was planned to take place within short notice. The letter announcing the informational meeting came only a couple of days before the actual meeting was scheduled in the middle of the summer holiday season.

Even the residents resisting the change admitted that they could have accepted it but:

> Nobody asked us anything beforehand. There was only this letter from the Post Office that ordered us to implement the new rules of mail delivery. And this wasn't even the first time that the postal services worsened during last ten years. (Interview with local resident 1).

Thus, in the beginning, the postal service acted as an old-fashioned state enterprise and subjected residents to the authority of the enterprise. But the residents, having lived the changes in the attitudes of city administrations in the 1990s that took on more open attitudes towards civic participation and cooperation with local citizens, did not approve of the way that the postal service approached them.

Another notable difference between the postal service's first contact and the way the residents expected to be addressed was that the residents were used to act in matters related to their neighborhood using the neighborhood organization as a representative tool, but the postal service approached 'individuals' by sending the new orders of mail delivery to each house of the area instead of immediately involving the neighborhood organization.

Journalism and active citizens

Media are unavoidably bound to the development of citizenship. Hence, the relation between media and the different forms of agencies people occupy needs be further explored (see also Ridell, 1999a) as the earlier mentioned political sciences and sociological approaches to civic action do not spend enough attention to the public sphere and the media.

Apart from the categories of the informed citizen or the passive audience, there are other agencies and subject positions through which people are addressed in different media contents and genres. Media not only raise issues that have considerable importance in people's everyday life, but they also take part in forming our understanding of the potential sites and means of civic participation. Moreover, new technologies, such as the Internet, instant messaging services, mobile phones, etc., are broadening citizen's media practices and are diversifying their entries and activities in the public sphere.

Through the blurring of the boundaries between different genres, issues that are traditionally considered private are brought out together with topics related to conventional politics. Media features that are usually labelled as 'popularization' can make links to people's everyday life and maybe even serve as mobilizing force in society (Dahlgren, 2000: 314).

Media pretend to know their audiences through marketing technologies generating institutional knowledge (Ang, 1991). But what is the ability of media to address us as citizens? Politics has been – and still is – the key focal point for journalism. One of the traditional and modernist tasks of journalism is to inform the citizenry, facilitating their informed choice at election times. Traditional journalism does also (exceptionally) side with citizens when it takes on its watchdog role, but more often this becomes part of the power struggle between media and politics, waged over the heads of audiences and citizens.

Although local journalism usually focuses on local issues that are important to local audiences, its ability to help citizens making connections between their everyday life and politics, as well as its capacity to encourage local people to participate in political debates, or even provide them with the skills needed in local politics, are rarely used to its maximum (Eliasoph, 1998: 210).

Both administrative actors and journalists have difficulties in facing and engaging with active citizens. Active citizens are 'useful' for journalists when these citizens are defending or opposing positions in local matters. These conflicts produce highly dramatic material, which is considered very suitable for news stories, guaranteeing wide attention among dispersed audiences. At the same time these journalists tend to be careful not to associate themselves too closely with the active citizens they present in their stories, as professional journalistic principles do not allow them to breach the imaginary line between reporting and advocacy.

A central part of journalism's self-understanding as a profession is based on the ideas of autonomy and independence (Carpentier, 2005; Kunelius, 2006 (forthcoming)). Following the principles of their professional code, journalists tend to see active citizens from the perspective of the uninvolved, detached, and distant spectator in order to protect their impartiality. This prevents them from providing a structural space for citizens' arguments in the public discussion. It especially prevents them from presenting citizens as actors that are to be taken seriously (Harju, 2005). Citizens are not treated as experts of everyday-life issues, in the same sense as economic experts are considered knowledgeable on economic matters, or as parliamentary representatives are allowed to make their arguments known in relations to the state of affairs of the nation.

In Seija Ridell's (1999b: 24–25) research on readers' relations to their local newspaper, one of the key findings was that the questions people wanted to put to decision-makers or other authorities remain absent from the newspaper pages. The readers that were interviewed by Ridell even suspected that journalists do not ask questions 'difficult enough' for those in power. The absence of these questions deemed relevant by citizens has partly to do with the journalistic style of writing: the news story is written in a way that it forms a consistent whole, offering thought-through information, which is easy to read.

Journalistically produced and represented information is never neutral. It always includes specific viewpoints of actors. Journalism tends to universalize the information it presents, and at the same time it reproduces the legitimacy of elite actors, while excluding access to others. If the interests behind the facts presented by journalism were acknowledged and made visible, the constructedness of information would be better understood and opened up for criticism. In that way, instead of focusing on 'facts' and 'truths' and on the journalism's ability to pass them on to their audiences, attention could be paid to the epistemological questions: whose knowledges, and ways of knowing, is journalism supporting. That would also reveal the active role journalism is playing in the production of social subjectivities as well as the potential role it might play facilitating citizens' participation (Ridell, 2000: 147–148; Kunelius, 2006 (forthcoming)).

One of the reasons for the extensive public attention the mailbox conflict gained was the residents' activeness in contacting the local media. They directly called journalists of the local newspapers, radio stations, and even the small local television company. PR work has for long been included in the daily work of social movements who need media publicity to get public attention for their issues (Rentschler, 2003: 538–539). In the case of the mailbox debate, the determined, instant, and systematic aim of the residents to get their issue in the local media also shows how 'ordinary citizens' are becoming media-savvy, knowing the importance of gaining public attention to their issue.

In conflict situations, media can however hinder the potential emergence of a productive public dialogue between the participants by maintaining the distinction between citizens and administration or other power holders. In my case study, exploring the newspaper articles clearly showed the difference between the residents and the postal service as news sources. The representatives of the postal service had their views presented in the main news pages of *Aamulehti*, as facts presented by an authoritative source, whereas the residents mainly got to present their arguments in the local news part of the newspaper, with big pictures showing them standing next to their mailboxes, in stories written in a popular, colorful style. It seemed that a dialogue between the participants was more often prevented than encouraged by the newspaper, since it kept the participants separated in the different corners of its pages. Furthermore, journalism's emphasis on the conflictuous aspects of the problem was potentially bringing the different parties even further apart (see also Ridell 2003, 14):

The atmosphere was intense, angry, almost aggressive. When it started to be somewhat difficult to get one's voice heard, everybody shouted. Those who had the loudest voices got to represent all the others, and the crowd was apparently unanimous. You could notice that when the public started to laugh at the questions posed or the answers given. (News article in Aamulehti, May 23, 2003).

Is the 'ideal citizen' of journalism, thus, a loud and angry person, who rises up against the ones in power supported by fellow citizens, and so provides material for colorful stories and dynamic pictures to spice up the more serious assortment of daily news? The way journalism presented the voices of the participants in the debate can be seen a formative for citizens' ideas of what are their possibilities to act. By dividing the voices of the residents and the representatives of the postal service, and by placing them in different articles and even in different news pages *Aamulehti* may have reinforced the residents' impression that their attempts to have any effect were hopeless. The decisions were firmly in the hands of the postal service, whose representatives got to present their 'facts' in the official news segment, separated from the residents' 'opinions'.

In the arguments of the residents, the debate over their mailboxes was intrinsically linked with large social questions. However, the connections to these larger questions were mainly made by the residents in the letters to the editor segment. The journalists did not use these questions to develop the debate any further, although it could have resulted in a more in-depth discussion, fulfilling the newspaper's function of stimulating public discussions about socially relevant matters (See also Eliasoph, 1998: 226–228).

The residents themselves were quite happy with the publicity the debate received in *Aamulehti*. They needed the publicity to improve their position to resist the postal service's orders and *Aamulehti* fulfilled this need. However, the residents did not see the local newspaper as a participant or a resource that could have offered more than only access to a larger audience. The residents even felt that the journalists were alternatingly working for both parties of the conflict:

Q: *How did the news articles in Aamulehti present your opinions and the opinions of the postal service?*

A: *Well, it somewhat depended on who had ordered the story, did it originate from us or from the postal service, there was a clear difference in that. The postal service defended their opinions and we defended ours. And you really could tell, who had ordered the story.* (Interview with local resident 2).

Despite the way journalism often presents citizens' arguments, there are also positive effects resulting from the media's publicity for local civic actions. For instance, in the Tampere region *Aamulehti* has been paying a lot of attention to issues that citizens have been trying to bring into the public discussion, such as land-use questions, controversies over construction plans and projects, the destruction of old buildings and so forth. Although citizens have mainly been positioned as described earlier in this chapter, disconnected from the decisions, they are still presented in an active role, trying to make a difference, acting together, arguing on behalf of their issues. And even though the mail delivery debate turned out to be not so successful for the residents, there have been at least some other processes where the opposition of local citizens has resulted in changes in the plans of the city administration, which can be seen as encouraging people to act out in public as citizens.

Whatever the result has been in different cases of local civic action, *Aamulehti* has presented its readers with a model of the active citizen, who is not satisfied with merely voting or using other tools of a representative democracy, but who enters the public sphere with his or her demands and arguments. In the case of mail delivery debate, the residents' unwillingness to accept the subjection to the orders of the postal service can be seen as an echo of this active citizen's identity.

Conclusions

In order to study civic action and its relation to local media, one should explore the local cases in which people take the initiative to act. The postal service debate analyzed in this chapter gave a possibility to take a look at a spontaneous process of civic action and local journalism's way of reacting to that action. Studying local cases also reveals how people shift between different subject positions and on which agencies they base their activities and arguments. For instance, in the case of the residents' disagreement with the postal service, the residents felt they were wrongfully treated, not just as postal service clients, but also as citizens. As clients, they felt the continuous reduction of the postal services' provisions unfair. As citizens, they were worried about the dominant profit-making mentality and about the inability to have a say in issues that affected their lives.

It also became clear that when citizens take action, they consider local media extremely important, and so media are actively drawn into the process. The residents' use of local media was active, but it was limited to seeking public attention. The other resources journalism could have offered – creating and maintaining a dialogue between participants and so forth – were not perceived or demanded by the residents. More than showing the lack in political imagination of the residents, this shows how intensely the media's detachment has been normalized.

Despite the fact that the debate was well covered in the news pages of *Aamulehti* and the residents got quite extensive publicity, local journalism still failed to take the active citizens seriously. In the news stories the residents were presented as 'an angry and irrationally acting crowd'. The local journalism recognized and supported the activism of the residents but did not manage to overcome their categorization through the standardized formula of 'little people [that] have had enough' (Eliasoph, 1998: 214).

The journalists did not grasp the existing potential of the mail delivery debate to be widened as a discussion about citizens' possibilities to have some effect on the issues close to their everyday lives or about the ongoing problematic tendencies in the society. The residents, trying actively and publicly to arouse discussion about the postal service's action, though not believing their true possibilities to change the course of events, did not get much support from the local newspaper for their attempts to act as active citizens, since the paper presented their opposition mainly as a brave but hopeless struggle.

In relation to the cases of local civic action, media's and especially journalism's role needs to be brought into the picture. In today's mediated society, media can represent citizens actively and show their opinions and interests. This matter needs further and concrete exploration, not only at the level of textual analysis but also in studying existing professional journalistic practices. The blurring boundaries between citizenship and consumerhood should be attributed equal importance – avoiding a binary relation between them (see also Couldry, 2004). It is more fruitful to look at situations where they intertwine, at the point where consumption becomes politicized. To give another example, the Finnish branch of Amnesty International asked a Finnish designer to design a collection for their campaign – clothes and accessories printed with images related to human rights. They also asked Finnish actors and musicians to act as a campaign model and wear the clothes. This example again shows the politicization of consumer culture (more specifically of design) or to put it differently, the use of consumer culture to make civic statements.

Popular culture and political culture have also become intertwined. For instance, the campaigns of the Finnish presidential candidates have utilized popular culture imaginaries. A supporter of the President Tarja Halonen can be seen wearing a red t-shirt with the presidential face printed in black, which resembles the pictures of Che Guevara or Lenin that in turn have been commercially exploited to a very high degree. Although the shifting between the imaginaries of the political and the cultural is not a new phenomenon, these examples and my postal service analysis show that the frontiers between politics and consumption have continued to blur. Understanding that the political transcends a representative system of institutionalized political practices, parties and voters, and seeing the presence of the political in people's everyday life activities becomes a crucial step in understanding contemporary politics, cultures, and civic identities.

Notes for Chapter Four

[1] In Finland, neighborhood organizations (or so-called home owners' associations) are a traditional way to form a (kind of) representative organization for people living in the same small neighborhoods. These organizations have also been recognized by local administrations as legitimized partners in planning and decision-making that concern these neighborhoods. Neighborhood organizations have, thus, become a link between city administrations and neighborhood residents.

[2] It should be noted that the full membership in the community as a definition for citizenship has throughout history implied the exclusion of certain groups,

for instance women and other marginalized members of a state who have not gained full member status (Tupper, 2002).

[3] The often made connection of NIMBY phenomenon with selfishness suggests that local protest is less important if it is not based on wider social or environmental concerns. However, there has also been argued that actions based on individuals' self-interest should actually be considered rational within a capitalist system. Furthermore, several studies have shown how the opposition of local people is not only aimed at defending their own interest but is based on concerns of the impact of new developments. (Burningham, 2000: 57; Peltonen, 2004; Ridell, 2005: 37–38).

References for Chapter Four

Ang, I. (1991), *Desperately Seeking the Audience*, London and New York: Routledge.

Burningham, K. (2000), 'Using the Language of NIMBY: A Topic for Research, not an Activity for Researchers', *Local Environment*, 5: 1, pp. 55–67.

Calabrese, A. (1999), 'The Welfare State, the Information Society, and the Ambivalence of Social Movements', in A. Calabrese and J-C. Burgelman (eds.), *Communication, Citizenship, and Social Policy*, Lanham: Rowman & Littlefield, pp. 259–77.

Calhoun, C. (2002), 'Imagining Solidarity: Cosmopolitanism, Constitutional Patriotism, and the Public Sphere', *Public Culture*, 14: 1, pp. 147–71.

Carpentier, N. (2005), 'Identity, Contingency and Rigidity. The (Counter-) Hegemonic Constructions of the Identity of the Media Professional', *Journalism*, 6: 2, pp. 199–219.

Carpentier, N., Lie, R., Servaes, J. (2003), 'Community Media: Muting the Democratic Media Discourse?' *Continuum: Journal of Media & Cultural Studies*, 17: 1, pp. 51–68.

Castells, M. (1997), *The Power of Identity*, Oxford: Blackwell.

Cruicshank, B. (1999), *The Will to Empower. Democratic Citizens and Others*, Ithaca: Cornell University Press.

Couldry, N. (2004), 'The Productive 'Consumer' and the Dispersed 'Citizen'', *International Journal of Cultural Studies*, 7: 1, pp. 21–32.

Dahlgren, P. (2000), 'Media, Citizenship and Civic Culture', in J. Curran and M. Gurevitch (eds.), *Mass Media and Society*, London: Oxford University Press, pp. 310–28.

Eliasoph, N. (1998), *Avoiding Politics. How Americans Produce Apathy in Everyday Life*, Cambridge: Cambridge University Press.

Giddens, A. (1991), *Modernity and Self-Identity. Self and Society in the Late Modern Age,* Cambridge: Polity Press.

Habermas, J. (1996), *Between Facts and Norms: Contributions to a Discourse Theory of Law and Democracy*, Cambridge: MIT Press.

Harju, A. (2002), 'Kunnat Keskustelua Oppimassa [Municipalities Learning to Discuss]', *Kunnallistieteellinen Aikakauskirja,* 30: 2, pp. 156–67.

Harju, A. (2005), 'Asukkaat Ja Mediajulkisuus Tamperelaisessa Postilaatikkokiistassa [The Residents and the Media Publicity in the mail Delivery Controversy in Tampere]', *Yhdyskuntasuunnittelu,* 43: 1, pp. 50–60.

Heikkilä, H. (2001), *Ohut Ja Vankka Journalismi. Kansalaisuus Suomalaisen Uutisjournalismin Käytännöissä 1990-luvulla. [Thin and Strong Journalism. Citizenship in Finnish News Practices in the 1990s.]*, Tampere: Tampere University Press.

Jenkins, H. (1992), *Textual Poachers. Television Fans and Participatory Culture,* New York: Routledge.

Kunelius, R. (2006, forthcoming), 'Good Journalism? On the Evaluation Criteria of Some Interested and Experienced Actors', *Journalism Studies*, 7(5).

McAfee, N. (2000), *Habermas, Kristeva, and Citizenship*, Ithaca: Cornell University Press.

Melucci, A. (1996), *Challenging Codes. Collective Action in the Information Age,* Cambridge: Cambridge University Press.

Nikunen, K. (2005), *Faniuden Aika. Kolme Tapausta Tv-ohjelmien Faniudesta Vuosituhannen Taitteen Suomessa. [Fan Time - Television, Fan Cultures and Popular Publicity.]*, Tampere: Tampere University Press.

Peltonen, L. (2004), 'NIMBY-Kiistojen Asukaskeskeiset Ja Kontekstuaaliset Selitykset. [Resident-Centered and Contextual Explanations of NIMBY Disputes]', *Alue Ja Ympäristö,* 33: 2, pp. 43–54.

Rentschler, C. A. (2003), 'Expanding the Definition of Media Activism', in A. N. Valdivia (ed.), *A Companion to Media Studies*, Oxford: Blackwell, pp. 529–47.

Ridell, S. (1999a), 'Tutkimus Julkisoa Tuottamassa. Paikallisuus Verkkomediassa – Hanke Irtiottona Kulttuurisen Yleisötutkimuksen Käytännöistä [Provoking and Promoting the Public]', *Tiedotustutkimus,* 22: 3, pp. 28–41.

—— (1999b), *Lehti Lukijoidensa Puntarissa. Aamulehti Yleisöryhmän Arvioitavana.* [What Reader Groups Make out of the Local Newspaper: The Aamulehti Case], Audience Studies in the Suburban Journalism Project. Report II, February 1999, University of Tampere, Journalism Research and Development Centre.

—— (2000), 'Ei Journalismi ole Tärkeää, Julkisuus on' [Journalism Is Not Important - Publicness Is], *Journalismikritiikin vuosikirja 3, Tiedotustutkimus,* 23: 1, pp. 144–55.

—— (2003), 'Kansalaislajityypit Verkkodemokratian Rakennuspuina. [Civic Web Genres as Constituents of Digital Democracy]', *Alue Ja Ympäristö,* 32: 1, pp. 11–22.

—— (2005), 'Mediating the Web as a Public Space', *Nordicom Review,* 24: 1, pp. 31–48.

Rättilä, T. (2001), 'Kansalaistuva Politiikka? Huomioita Kuntalaisaktiivisuudesta Poliittisena Toimijuutena [Towards Citizen Politics? Notes on Local Resident Activism as Political Subjectivity]', *Politiikka,* 43: 3, pp. 190–207.

Tupper, J. (2002), 'The Gendering of Citizenship in Social Studies Curriculum', *Canadian Social Studies,* 36: 3. Downloaded on 20 July 2005 from http://www. quasar.ualberta.ca/css/Css_36_3/index36_3.htm.

Turner, B. S. (1994), 'Postmodern Culture/Modern Citizens', in B. van Steenbergen (ed.), *The Condition of Citizenship,* London: Sage, pp. 153–68.

van Zoonen, L. (2004), 'Imagining the Fan Democracy', *European Journal of Communication,* 19: 1, pp. 39–52.

Chapter Five

Towards fair participation: recruitment strategies in Demostation

Egil G. Skogseth

Introduction

The experimental research project and prototype Web radio station Demostation (www.demostasjon.net) is based on the optimistic notion that technologies like Internet and telephony, with their cheap production, communication, and distribution possibilities, incorporate a potential for participatory–democratic deliberation. Furthermore, the Norwegian editorial/research group [1] behind the experiment cherishes the assumption that if the opportunity is seized, this potentiality may be used to stimulate the further spread and cross-fertilization of emancipating journalistic genres and formats.

Demostation 1 and 2 (that were respectively operational in April and in September 2005) were, therefore, experiments in how these (both new and old) technologies could be used to create new Web radio formats, based on participatory–democratic principles. The goal was to develop a format that also incorporated a fair and representative participant selection procedure, which contributed to the maximization of the participants' expressive freedoms. In this chapter, I will discuss to what extent Demostation 2's strategy for recruitment facilitated this fair participation.

Ideally, when the principle of equality would be applied radically, the inclusion of all citizens in the area – served by the media organization – would need to be ensured, at least if they wished to be included. Since Demostation 2's five programmes were aimed at serving the entire Norwegian population, this was not a viable possibility. Fair participation and selection was, therefore, operationalized by involving equally sized proportions of the different socio-economic groups in society (i.e. a stratified representative selection was generated).

In order to provide a theoretical framework for the concept of fair participation and to deduce the tools to analyze fairness in the participatory process of Demostation 2, I will first briefly discuss four main democratic traditions and their linkages to Habermas' theoretical public sphere tradition. Five values are then deduced from these theoretical strands to be combined in a normative public sphere model called *Publicity for Empowerment*. The next section outlines my methodological approach to analyzing the recruitment strategy in Demostation 2. This section also raises one of the experiment's main questions: does the balanced selection of participants of a radio programme, in which most of the airtime is reserved for them, contribute to egalitarian programmes with extensive expressive freedoms for the participants? The third section is a description of the strategy developed for recruiting the Demostation 2 participants. In the fourth section, the selection strategy and its implementation, is evaluated in relation to one of the five core values, openness. That section also tentatively addresses the earlier mentioned research question. The last section features the project's evaluation and discusses both criticisms and possible solutions and improvements. In sum, this chapter aims to use Demostation to illustrate why a fair strategy for recruiting citizens as participants (and not only as consumers) should be developed and implemented by all media organizations that cherish (the deepening of) our democratic values.

Theoretical approach

The theoretical framework in this chapter is based on a discussion about the interconnections between the public sphere, participation, and modern democracy. This debate was revitalized in the 1960s by Jürgen Habermas, who in his *The Structural Transformation of the Public Sphere* describes or/and outlines a normative ideal, built on the democratic importance attributed to the British bourgeois public sphere as could be found in clubs and coffee houses [2]. According to Habermas, this was a sphere where land owning men engaged in unrestricted deliberation where the best argument did not only win the discussion, but also eventually affected policy decisions [3] (Habermas, 1989 [1962]). He also emphasized the importance of varied, high quality, and lasting discourse.

Although these values still bear merit, there are also problems in Habermas' account/theory. After being severely criticized for several years, he recognized that his original model's lack of openness formed a major flaw. Although the bourgeois public sphere was based on the principles of universal access, women were excluded and only educated land owning men had the financial means to participate:

> [...] unlike the institutionalization of class conflict, the transformation of the relationship between the sexes affects not only the economic system but has an impact on the private core area of the conjugal family. [...] Unlike the exclusion of underprivileged men, the exclusion of women had structuring significance (Habermas, 1992: 428).

Habermas thus emphasized that universal access is a prerequisite for fair participation. But even though this adjustment positively broadens Habermas' scope, it is not difficult to agree with Colin Sparks when he argues that 'the classical bourgeois sphere that Habermas identified in eighteenth-century England was only tenuously connected even to the most minimal forms of democratic politics' (Sparks, 2001: 76). Despite the contemporary acceptance and even dominance of the view that universal access to the public sphere's deliberations is necessary and citizens should be able to influence democratic institutions [4], the necessary degree of access and participation in democracies is still highly debated and dependant on one's perspective on democracy.

Skogerbø distinguishes four major theoretical democratic models: elite/market, communitarian/discursive, participatory, and deliberative democracy [5] (Skogerbø, 1996: 11–14). The earlier presented normative public sphere theory is closely related to particularly the participatory and deliberative models. These models allow a strong involvement of people in ruling the political unit; they also appear to be good analytical tools for assessing Demostation (Deetz, 1999), and they are close to Demostation's sources of inspiration and aims (Nyre, 2006).

Participatory democracy has its roots in the ancient Greek direct democracy which emphasized the citizens' ability to present their views and to be directly involved in the functions of the state (such as the legislative and judicial functions) (Held, 2000: 17). Although more modern versions of this tradition do not necessarily go as far as they did in the Greek city states, the citizen is not only perceived as a voter, but also as a co-producer of the democratic processes:

A common normative thread is the desirability of maximising the participation of citizens in the public decision that affects their lives. To do this, they should, to the extent feasible, be active participants in the public sphere as part of an ongoing process (Gamson, 2001: 57).

Discursive democracy promotes the idea of creating meeting places for dialogue. In discussions, citizens should be treated equally and decisions should be based on the best argument. The model is derived from the ideas of liberal ideologists such as John Stuart Mill. Mill argues that the truth will prevail as long as everything is openly discussed, without any restriction or forms of censorship (Mill, 2001 [1859]). Another source of inspiration is John Dewey, who argues in *The Public and its Problems* that a broad and democratic dialogue is at least as important as achievements in politics (Dewey, 1927). The most important mission for the press is, therefore, to facilitate a public discourse between citizens and politicians – the political community. This emphasis on community has connected Dewey to the communitarian tradition.

Deliberative democracy also focuses on rational debates among free and equal citizens as the best approach to reach democratic decisions (Elster, 1998: 1). Whereas the discursive model (at least the way Habermas described it) is influenced by the ancient Greek spatialized agora conception, the deliberative democratic model allows more variation in the deliberative sites. John B. Thompson stresses that the deliberative conception of democracy is still dialogical, but unlike the discursive model it promotes the idea that '[...] mediated quasi-interaction can stimulate deliberation just as much as, if not more than face-to-face interaction in a shared locale' (Thompson, 1995: 256).

Both the deliberative and the discursive models have (to some extent rightly) been criticized for being utopian. Critics have questioned whether it is possible to reach consensus through dialogue, raising the question whether the interests of those involved in debates of our times are not too different to be reconciled. Chantal Mouffe argues that the display of the different stances in a discussion, or agonistic pluralism as she labels it, is more constructive than covering up opposing views through what appears to be a consensus (Mouffe, 1999) [6].

One can of course also argue that the modern polis – the democratic nation state – is too densely populated to allow all citizens to participate at an equal level (Dahl, 1998: 105–108). Balanced representation – reflecting societal plurality – is, therefore, perhaps in modern societies a more realistic demand than universal participation (Touraine, 1997 [1994]: 34). Nevertheless, since media 'space' is – after the introduction and spread of the Internet – no longer a scarce resource, it is (at least in theory) possible to grant all citizens the opportunity to express themselves. But even then, a strategy is required to make sure that their participation is fair and to avoid that the elite strata in society and those who can produce and distribute their own media content dominate the process.

Based on the earlier discussion, five values can be selected to form the core of the *Publicity for Empowerment* model that is developed more in-depth elsewhere (Skogseth, 2005). These five components are as follows:

1. Open for as many as possible (both users and producers)
2. Thematically varied
3. Constructive and of high quality (with a cooperative dialogue)
4. Independent of market and state and
5. Instructive for larger public spheres and policy decisions.

Since this chapter discusses and evaluates strategies for ensuring fair parti-cipation in mediated public spheres, the first value – (1) to be open for as many as possible – is highlighted in this analysis. Furthermore, given the problems of 'total' participation in large societies, openness is translated here as representative participation. The other four principles constitute the chapter's normative and theoretical background.

Methodological approach

While preparing the launch of Demostation 2, the editorial/research group realized that a strategy to recruit participants was needed, not only to ensure that the experiment would work, but also to ensure that it would live up to its participatory–democratic claims. This necessitated the development of a recruitment strategy, based on the notion of representativeness, to be defined before the Demostation 2 programmes started. One of the first problems that the editorial/research group faced was the difficulty, if not impossibility, to precisely define the level of representativeness required for the Demostation participants to be representative of the population served by the station. To solve this problem, a matrix was constructed, containing a series of preset categories of participants we wanted to see included in each programme.

After the five Demostation 2 programmes ended, the theoretical principles described in the model *Publicity for Empowerment*, were used to analyze the participatory aspects of the experiment, by looking at how fair participation was operationalized, and at how well the participants matched with the matrices used for their selection. This part of the experiment would be considered successful if (given that the technical and editorial aspects of Demostation worked) the actual participant selection was a representative selection of the population and if this representative selection contributed to the production of an egalitarian programme format, guaranteeing maximum expressive freedoms for the participants.

The analysis in this chapter is based on qualitative data from the log of the editorial/research group's evaluations of the programs and on quantitative statistical data about the participants in Demostation 2. Data and self-reflexive triangulation were used to increase the quality of the analysis. I have also critically questioned my role as editorial secretary in Demostation and my analytical approach while writing this chapter.

Demostation 2's recruitment strategy

I worked as editorial secretary for Demostation 2 and recruited 38 citizens [7] and 15 representatives of political parties who participated in the five 1-hour programmes in September 2005. I also helped to organize – and participated in – Demostation 1 in April 2005. In this first version, much effort was put into testing the technical aspects of Web radio and citizen's participation through the IP-telephony system Skype. The strategy developed for recruiting participants for Demostation 2 is, therefore, partly based on the Demostation 1 experience of having no overall selection strategy. Still, thanks to a hectic last minute effort, the editorial/research group managed to recruit 43 participants [8] for the six Demostation 1 programmes. However, all participants in Demostation 1 were friends or colleagues of the members of the editorial/research group. Consequently, the vast majority of the participants were either students or researchers within the fields of journalism and media studies, and the participants could not be considered as a representative selection of the population served by Demostation. Because of this strong bias in the selection, the Demostation 1 experiment could not be considered as case of fair participation at the level of participant composition.

In contrast to the first version, Demostation 2 actively sought public attention for its (Web-streamed) programmes. These programmes addressed national political issues before, during, and after the parliamentary elections in Norway in September 2005. With Demostation 2's focus on the social and editorial aspects of the experiment, we wanted to show that Web radio – based on participatory–democratic principles – can also work outside academia and can facilitate fair participation by the adult Norwegian population. Given this point of departure, selecting participants that covered the entire adult Norwegian population was deemed essential.

To recruit (and to persuade) participants to join a radio programme might sound somewhat authoritarian in a country where the citizens have the democratic right to chose 'not' to get involved in politics (and even not to vote) (Eriksen and Wigård, 1999: 153). However, the reason why it might be considered authoritarian is influenced by the neo-liberal ideology that has had a severe impact on Norway (and on many other Western democracies), resulting in the domination of the definition of people as consumers. Contrary to this, the recruitment strategy in Demostation 2 is inspired by the twentieth century's social democratic approach to social engineering as a way to achieve equality. It is furthermore inspired by the ancient Greek direct democratic tradition where all citizens (free men) were expected to participate in all areas of the polis. But the Demostation strategy does not take its ambitions as far as Pericles did, when he wrote 'we do not say that a man who takes no interest in politics is a man who minds his own business; we say that he has no business here at all' (cited in Held, 2000 [1997]: 17). Those approached to participate in Demostation were invited and not enlisted. But, even though a refusal to participate was accepted, the persuasive attempt to include them in the programme was somewhat insistent.

The initial goal was to recruit 80 participants who would participate in the programme via telephone, Skype or other forms of IP-telephony, and in the radio studio [9]. Five programmes were produced on weekdays from 2 PM to 3 PM, from 7 to 13 September (see Appendix). Each participant was to be given 3 minutes to talk about the selected programme topic [10]. This would allow including 16 participants in a 1-hour programme [11].

When the editorial/research groups had their first planning meetings, a discussion emerged between those who favored a form of minimal journalism (or microphone stand journalism) (Nyre, 2006) and those who preferred forms of more traditional journalism. In Demostation 1, a preset speaking time had been allotted to each participant. Initially, this concept was planned to be used in Demostation 2 as well. However, the majority of the editorial/research group found this approach too rigid, and the editorial/research group decided to apply a more traditional journalistic approach, enabling the hosts to decide when each participant's airtime ended. In an editorial meeting towards the end of Demostation 2, this strategy was explicitly articulated: the quality of the argumentation should be the parameter for the duration of each participant's airtime.

Before Demostation 2 started, the editorial/research group was aware of the importance of promotion. Unless the Demostation team managed to spread the word about the programmes, it could not be expected that many people would take the initiative to participate in the programmes. In this scenario, the vast majority of the participants had to be recruited. Two main participant categories were defined: those who defended a (party-political) position and those who could use their own life situation as a point of departure for political deliberation. Those who represented a party would be put on air towards the end of the programmes. This strategy was preferred in order to reduce the effects of differences in public speaking capacities between party activists/representatives and citizens. Introducing them at the end of the programmes also avoided that those representing a political party dominated the first and most defining part of the programme.

Based on the earlier mentioned points, the following strategy for recruiting participants was developed:

- Publish an announcement that members of the public are welcomed to participate in the programmes on www.demostasjon.net.
- Get coverage in the mainstream media through press releases and personal contacts. Mention that Demostation wants to get in touch with people who want to participate in interviews.
- Post information in news groups/blogs.
- Get in touch with potential participants through email and telephone, based on searches in web search engines and the phone book. In addition to (1) randomly selected people, these following groups are to be explicitly invited: (2) participants from Demostation 1 (mainly friends and colleagues of the editorial/research group); (3) other people in the network of the members of the editorial/research group (2 and 3 are not representative groups); (4) interview respondents of the Cultural Techniques-project, of which Demostation is a part of (all these participants live in Bergen in West Norway); (5) party activists/ representatives who are recruited through county [12] party offices.
- In case people called during the live streaming of the programmes, it would be the responsibility of the editor to decide whether or not they should be put on air.

Naturally, this strategy affected the choice of the method used for selecting the participants. Non-probability sampling methods were considered the most suitable (see Ringdal: 2001: 149–151), which resulted in the choice for the quota method. This meant that people had to fit into specific (demographic) categories of the matrix, but within these categories, they were to be selected at random. Especially members of the public that contacted Demostation but also people contacted through searches on the Web were selected through this method. Also the snowball method was used, as some of the participants were (indirectly) selected through the editorial/research group's network.

Variables	50 Percent		50 Percent	
Gender	Male		Female	
Age	<40 years		>40 years	
Occupation/Social class	Blue collar		White collar	
Variables	**1/3**	**1/3**		**1/3**
Political sympathies [13]	The left	The centre, do not know and shall not vote		The right

Figure 1: Matrix used to recruit the citizen-participants.

The selection matrix was constructed on the basis of the following variables: gender, age, occupation/class, area of residence, political preference (left, centre, right, none/do not know), and predicted voting behavior (shall vote/shall not vote). The choice of these variables (especially gender, occupation/class and political preferences) relates to the earlier discussion about the limitations in Habermas' bourgeois public sphere. In addition to these variables, attention should be spent on potential participants who expressed special interest in one of the topics of the programmes.

The 12 citizen-participants in each programme were to be distributed in the way as discussed in Figure 1.

The variables occupation and class were not used when recruiting activists/representatives. Only four activists/representatives were granted access per programme, to make sure that the citizen-participants got enough speaking time to express their views. At least one of the political activists/representatives was to be affiliated with the centre/right government, one with the centre/left coalition, and one with the Progressive Party/small parties [14]. The political parties were requested to ask one of their activists (or representatives) to participate in one of the programmes. Political parties could also propose election candidates and MPs to participate, but activists were preferred as they usually are less experienced in speaking in public than representatives are. For the first four programmes, the following parties were asked to provide Demostation with either one or two (2) participants: the Progressive Party (FrP – a right-wing populist party), the Conservatives (H) (2), the Liberals (V), the Christian-Democrats (KrF) (2), the Coast Party (KystP.), the Centre Party (Sp – a former agrarian party), Labor (Ap) (2), the Socialist Left Party (SV) (2) [15], and the smaller parties the Green Party (De Grønne) and the Communists (RV). In the last programme, which was streamed on the day after the elections, representatives of the winning coalition and of the FrP should be invited to participate.

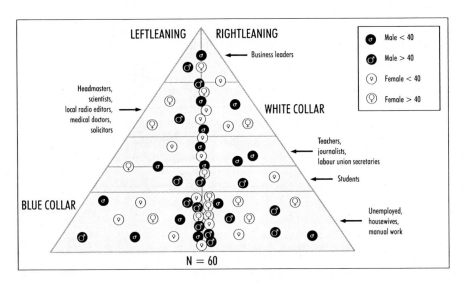

Figure 2: The planned demographical distribution of the citizens participating in Demostasjon 2.

Eighty participants were scheduled to take part in the five programmes. Some programmes were oriented at participants and users belonging to specific regions (see Appendix). Programmes with only participants from Hordaland and Bergen, and Møre og Romsdal/Volda were produced because these were the

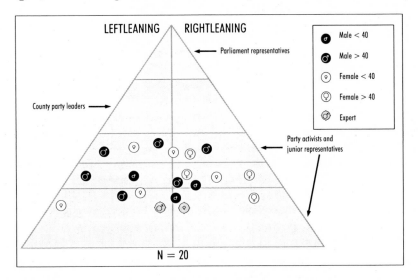

Figure 3: The planned distribution of representatives from political parties in Demostasjon 2.

areas where the members of the editorial/research group (and most of their social networks) lived. Furthermore, the regions Trøndelag and Sørlandet were chosen at random. This implies that there was no systematic plan to include proportions of people from each part of the country, which in practice led to the underrepresentation of the Northern and Eastern part of Norway.

In sum, the selection strategy could not – for practical reasons – be too time-consuming and elaborate, but was still considered crucial in its contribution to the realization of Demostation's core objectives: to make radio programmes based on participatory–democratic principles and to give a broad selection of both citizens and representatives of political parties the opportunity to participate.

Evaluation of the recruitment strategy

This section evaluates how the distribution of participants in Demostation 2's programmes relates to the normative ideal to be as open as possible, for as many as possible (both users and producers). In other words, the question is to what extent Demostation 2 has facilitated – in its practical realization – fair participation. Efforts were made to give a demographically balanced group of participants enough time to elaborate their views. None of the participants were recruited completely by chance, but some searches for participants on the Web came close. Most of the participants were recruited using a snowball method initiated through the members of the editorial/research group.

The first programme already proved that it was too difficult to recruit 16 participants on the basis of the matrix. In the first programme, only twelve people participated [16]. The editorial/research group considered this number of participants sufficient, and for the next programmes the maximum number of participants was consequently reduced from 16 to 12. This was compensated by giving each citizen-participant 4-minute airtime ($12 \times 4 = 48$ minutes) instead of three as initially planned. The new target (of 12 participants) was not met in the remaining four programmes, which only had between 9 and 11 participants. In total, the five programmes counted 53 participants, of which 38 were citizen-participants. Although they were not positioned as activists/representatives, some of them were politically active.

Looking at the demographics of these citizen-participants (and excluding the representatives from the political parties), it becomes clear that a large majority (31 out of 38) of them were men. Although there were quite a few participants that were in their 20s and 30s (22 out of 38 were less that 40-years old), all age groups of the adult Norwegian population (up to 72 years) were represented. Thirty-three of the 38 participants were students or educated white collar workers. Almost half of the participants leaned towards the political left. Those associated with the political centre and right were thus underrepresented. Still, the quite large group of people who claimed to be

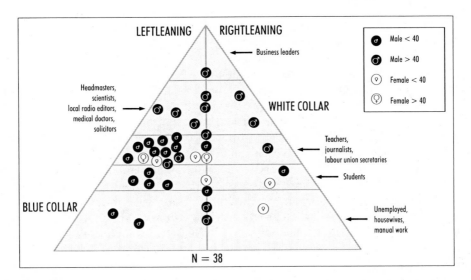

Figure 4: The actual demographical distribution of the citizens participating in Demostasjon 2.

neutral, or would not answer the question (7 out of 38) might include a high portion of people associated with the political centre and right. The variable predicting voting behavior (shall vote/shall not vote) was not used extensively (even in the programme about doubt and mistrust towards the political system) because it was hard to recruit people who were certain that they would not vote.

The citizens' unbalanced demographics are of course partially related to the practical elaboration of the recruitment strategy. Although the five days period that was set aside to recruit participants, was increased to approximately nine, it turned out to be very difficult to persuade enough people to participate. Since so few people contacted the editorial/research group asking to participate, people who did not fit into the demographical matrix soon had to be accepted in order to get enough participants for each programme. Part of the explanation is that Demostation is still a relatively anonymous mini public sphere. Furthermore, www.demostasjon.net only started their promotional activities a few days before the programmes started. Due to time constraints, too little work was invested into getting mainstream media coverage and very little information was posted in news groups and blogs.

Especially in the two first programmes, participants were selected because they featured on the interviewees' list of the Cultural Techniques-projects. Others were selected through searches on web sites of NGOs, educational and cultural institutions, companies, labor unions, the employers' federation, a trade chamber, newspapers, religious and ethnic communities, and residents associations. Participants were recruited through these organizations and institutions because this strategy made it easier to get hold of a diverse group of people, and partly because these people would be able to live up to the editorial/research group's quality-of-argument criterion. Most of the participants in the three last programmes were people that the editorial/research group knew (or were suggested to them by people they knew) and representatives from political parties. Although this biased selection of participants made the experiment problematic at the level of the participant selection, it nevertheless gave interesting results at the level of the programme content.

Since there is limited demographic information available about the people who were asked to participate, but declined, it is difficult to assess if the distribution would have been more balanced if they had indeed accepted to participate. However, it is clear that more women and more business professionals and managers declined than other groups. While more positive replies from women would have made the gender distribution more balanced, there is also reason to believe that an increase in participation of business leaders would have implied more participants that adhered to the political centre or right.

Out of a total of fifteen, nine men and six women represented a political party. Out of these people, seven were under 40 years. Thirteen were students or had white collar jobs. While five of them lived in Hordaland, three in Trøndelag, two in Rogaland, and two in Møre og Romsdal, none of the representatives lived in Oslo. As 13 of them were recruited through party offices, using organizational and election secretaries at the parties' county offices as intermediaries proved to be a fairly successful strategy. This was in most cases not too time-consuming, and the parties did manage to delegate a person for the programme. Still, in the first four programmes, for a diversity of reasons that were beyond Demostation's control, Labor, the Progressive Party, the Green Party, and the Socialist Left Party had one participant less than planned [17]. In the programme the day after the election, a representative of the Liberals was included alongside the Progressive Party and the winning side of Labor, the Centre Party, and the Socialist Left Party.

The Demostation team preferred party activists but allowed the party secretaries to choose for themselves. This strategy turned out to be beneficial as several party secretaries were not sure if an activist could be delegated (or if they had party activists at all). However, as ten of the fifteen representatives from the parties were candidates and/or board members of the party county branch, there was probably a more considerable distance between party representatives and the members of the public than planned [18]. Of the remaining five party representatives, two of them were party secretaries and only three were local activists who held no prominent position. Two of these three participants represented or had represented their party in municipal councils.

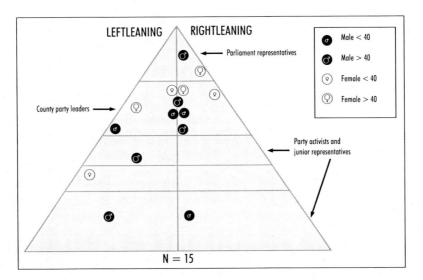

Figure 5: The actual distribution of representatives from political parties in Demostasjon 2.

Both in the case of citizens and representatives of the political parties, especially Hordaland/Bergen, but also Møre og Romsdal/Volda, Trøndelag, and Sørlandet were overrepresented. In addition, Oslo had more participants than planned (eight out of 38) while other parts of East and North Norway were underrepresented.

As the participants' demographics were not in accordance with the selection strategy, and a series of biases skewed the equal distribution of the citizens-participants, this part of the Demostation experiment can hardly be considered successful. However, at a number of other levels, the project was still a success. The exchanges between the participants in Demostation were more vibrant in comparison to existing talk radio platforms on channels such as BBC London and LBC (also based in London) (Nyre, 2006). The Demostation participants had up to 8 minutes of dialogue without intervention from the hosts. It illustrates the expressive freedoms they did have.

In total, the hosts talked more than the minimal journalistic approach in Demostation would have allowed them. But this was mainly in situations where participants clearly expected to engage in a conversation or needed questions to continue their reflections. Demostation 2's use of a parameter (the argumentative quality) to decide on the duration of the interventions was less egalitarian than in Demostation 1, where the hosts allocated a preset amount of time to each speaker. But because of the reduction of the number of participants per programme from 16 to 9–12, all participants still had extensive

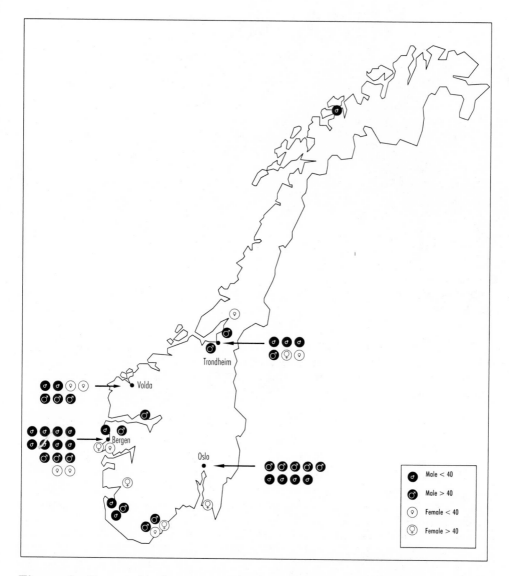

Figure 6: Geographical representation in Demostasjon 2. Citizens and representatives of political parties: N = 53.

opportunities to express themselves. It can, therefore, be argued that despite the problems in the selection procedure, the five Demostation 2 programmes still had an egalitarian profile, which supported the expressive freedoms of the participants.

Concluding Remarks

Theoretical and methodological evaluation

To what extent can media research be normative? Is it plausible, through experiments and prototypes, to attempt to influence the journalistic practices in the media sector and government media policies? The editorial/research group behind the experimental prototype Demostation definitively (as the reader probably has understood) give a positive answer to this question. However, as these interventionist approaches to research also can be problematic, more efforts should be invested into developing a more thorough theoretical and methodological foundation for experiments and prototypes in 'normative empirical media research'. One of the disadvantages is that the Demostation team had to develop the theoretical and methodological foundation for themselves, which generated an important learning experience, but also unavoidably caused a number of problems. Still, as an experimental prototype for participatory democratic media production, Demostation can form a unique [19] basis for new practices in the media production and policy sectors.

Demostation is based on a technologically optimistic approach, as it assumes that new digital production, communication, and distribution technologies embody a potential for democratic deliberation, and that:

1. This potential may be transformed into newly mediated public spheres based on fair participation
2. It offers a model that can be used to persuade governments, media organizations that control (most of) the existing mediated public spheres, and their editors and journalists to facilitate fair participation and use their media as tools for societal deliberation
3. It can be used to influence the attitudes among journalist students and
4. It ultimately can empower citizens to become active agents who can influence political representatives and other more powerful groups.

As these values and objectives can (at least partially, especially 2 and 4) be found in traditions, such as Public and Civic Journalism (Rosen, 1993), some of these ideas can hardly be considered new. Similar to these traditions, the values that feed into Demostation may be considered utopian. But Demostation has realized its important objective, by showing that it is socially, journalistically, and technically feasible to produce a talk-only radio station based on participatory–democratic ideals.

It is nevertheless important stressing that the experiment has had numerous problems. The earlier discussed problems with the selection of participants are only one set of problems. Moreover, even a highly competent editorial group cannot guarantee that the conversation does not turn into a cacophony. Demostation's deliberations will have to find ways of dealing with participants whose behavior is destructive towards the process of deliberation itself. These interventions would harm the core value of openness and the principle of representativeness, but they would – ironically – contribute at the same time to Demostation's ideal of becoming a policy sphere and facilitate the training of the participants in public speaking. It is also relevant to mention that no more than twenty people listened to the actual content – the highly appraised deliberation – at any point in time. As each programme only featured between 9 and 12 participants, this might be in accordance with C. W Mills' understanding of the word public as 'virtually as many people express opinions as [they] receive them' (cited in Habermas, 1989 [1962]: 249). This does, of course, raise the question how socially relevant a permanent version of Demostation, and similar mini public spheres, would be if they remained confined to this small scale.

It can furthermore be argued that if Demostation's long-term participatory objectives should be upheld in talk radio, the selected area needs to be smaller than the Norwegian nation-state. However, if this strategy is preferred, it decreases the possibility of this public sphere to affect policies. This problem can be captured by reformulating Robert A. Dahl's fundamental democratic dilemma (Dahl, 1998: 109–110). The smaller the area that a mediated participatory public sphere tries to reach, the greater is its potential for equal participation (by including everybody who wants to) and the lesser is the need for representatives. The larger the mediated public sphere (both in terms of geography and users), the greater is its capacity to influence policy decisions on issues that are important to the citizens, and the greater is the practical necessity for these citizens to have representatives who can speak on their behalf.

Demostation's technologically optimistic approach, which relies on the publics' access to modern digital communication technologies, is also problematic. Most participants were asked if they had access to the IP-telephony programme Skype. Since only two participants had IP-telephone/Skype (a third participant did not get on air because of technical problems), most participants used a fixed line, and in some cases they used a cell phone. This reduced the technological threshold in Demostation 2 (in comparison to Demostation 1). Because the editorial/research group wanted to treat everybody equally, none of the participants were invited to the studio. Telephone/cell phone possession is very widespread in Norway, and the likelihood that the choice for this technology to access Demostation excluded many people is very small. More surprisingly, also none of those who were asked to participate declined because of the lack of access to a computer with a Windows Media Player and an Internet connection [20]. But some did agree to participate although they (because of practical reasons) did not have the opportunity to listen to the programme.

Nevertheless, even though a high proportion of the Norwegian population has Internet access, a fair share of the population cannot listen to Web radio. This digital divide remains a problem, which should not be forgotten while enthusiastically promoting the brave new World Wide Web.

Achievements, criticism, and proposals for improvement

Did the recruitment strategy and its implementation facilitate fair and representative participation? At the theoretical level, it can be argued that the matrix should have included a geographical/regional variable and variables, such as occupation/social class, should have been better operationalized (instead of using only the two categories 'blue collar' and 'white collar'). More variables could also have been added. Still, although the developed strategy was by no means perfect, its successful application could nevertheless have resulted in a fairly representative group of the Norwegian adult population. The main problems were situated at the practical level as time constraints, limited resources, the airing of the programs during the daytime (excluding quite a few people who worked at this time of the day [2–3 PM]), and lack of experience in effectuating such a recruitment strategy, prevented its successful implementation.

Strategies for recruitment, similar to the one used in Demostation 2, can still be implemented in future research and more general in media practices, but it has become clear that sufficient resources must be allocated to the recruiting phase. This recruiting phase also needs to be seen in connection with all other participatory components that characterize Demostation 2. Simply copying this one component would be meaningless, as the participatory nature of the entire project is built on an interrelated set of components that are based on a normative framework, supported by the 'participatory attitude' (Carpentier, 2003: 442) of its initiators.

Demostation 2 has shown that it is possible to facilitate deliberation by using the phone-in concept for Web radio. Well-educated, predominantly leftist, middle class people and representatives of political parties with all sorts of ideologies did effectively participate. Although other groups were represented as well, the selection of participants was not balanced enough, and some of the constraints were too present to allow Demostation 2 becoming an open public sphere where the airtime is fairly distributed among the different societal groups. One may argue that this remains possible, but even though much effort was put into establishing a fair recruiting procedure, Demostation 2 was not a success in this regard.

There are good reasons to believe that this procedure would be easier to achieve by large and well-established radio stations, if they desired to do so. Still, Demostation 2 participants are generally more representative than is the case of most current affairs programmes in Norway. This experiment suggests that radio programmes where most of the airtime is reserved for the participants and where their selection is based on the principles of representativeness can lead to more egalitarian programmes that provide participants with extensive expressive freedoms. Demostation 2 shows the importance of having a well-thought-through recruitment strategy that is based on participatory–democratic ideals and needs to be taken into account by all mainstream media programming that claims to play a democratic role.

Notes for Chapter Five

[1]   The Demostation experiments were part of the research project Cultural Techniques, funded by the Norwegian Council of Research for the period 2003–2007. The thirteen members in the editorial/research group were students, engineers, and media researchers of the University of Bergen and Volda University College.

[2]   Even though Habermas has only recently started to adress public spheres on the Internet, his theories are used here because they are useful for describing the notion of the public sphere. Although *Structural Transformation* has been criticized, Jacobson and Kolluri have argued that it can be used to theorize participatory media (such as Demostation): 'His analysis of the public sphere could provide the basis for an analysis of media institutions in so far as they facilitate democratic participation through public discourse' (Jacobson and Kolluri, 1999: 266).

[3]   This relates to Bennett and Entman's division between public and policy spheres. The 'public' sphere includes all physical and virtual spaces where ideas and feelings related to politics (broadly defined) can be communicated freely and openly. The 'policy' sphere is a subset of the public sphere where ideas connected to policy change are communicated to government officials, parties, and politicians holding office, who may decide on the outcome of the issue (Bennett and Entman, 2001: 4).

[4]   As one cannot guarantee that state media are in favor of universal access, media should ideally be independent from the state and the market.

[5]   While the former is connected to the 'realist' position, the three latter have been termed 'idealist'. Elite and market democracy and communitarian and discursive democracy, respectively, have of course differences but share some common values.

[6]   The negotiations in the World Trade Organization seem to be a modern example of a problematic approach to consensus democracy.

[7]   One citizen participated twice and is counted as two participants (i.e. 37 individual citizens).

[8]   Six participated twice (i.e. 37 individual citizens).

[9]   The idea to invite participants to the studio was abandoned later.

[10] The topics were chosen by the editorial/research group. Topic selection criteria were that the topics had to relate to the different stages of the election campaign (and look beyond the election), be somewhat original (compared to the mainstream media coverage), and not presuppose too much knowledge about political processes amongst the participants (see Appendix).

[11] $3 \times 16 = 48$ minutes and five programmes $\times 16 = 80$ participants. The four representatives of the political parties/experts that participated in each programme were all given 4 minutes of airtime, bringing the total up to 52 minutes. The remaining 8 minutes were to be used by the producer and hosts for jingles, introductions, questions, and small talk.

[12] 'Fylke' in Norwegian.

[13] This distribution was not to be used for the programme about doubts and mistrust towards the political system on 9 September. Ideally, none of the participating citizens in this programme were active voters. The symbol for each of the participants in the Demostation 2 programmes who do not vote are unsure, or neutral politically, are put in the centre of figures 2–5. Figures 2–6 are designed by Jørgen Furuholt.

[14] In the programme on 9 September, this distribution model was not used as only two activists/representatives were invited.

[15] These eight parties were represented in Parliament during the period 2001–2005. This high number is explained by the traditionally relatively strong periphery in Norway (Rokkan, 1987) (manifested by four parties: SP, V, KrF, and KystP.), and by the election system with proportional representation from multi-member majority constituencies. Since 1961, no political party has had a majority in Parliament and coalitions had to be formed in order to enable the formation of majority governments. In the 2005 elections, the centre–left coalition (AP, SP, SV) competed against the centre–right coalition (H, V, KrF). The opposition centre–left coalition won.

[16] This number included the four representatives of political parties and one caller who was asked to call in 'spontaneously'.

[17] This was due to (1) a robbery, (2) no reply after contacting the party office several times, (3) no answer when the producer called the person before the programme, and (4) a last minute cancellation.

[18] This distance was reduced by the hosts who did not distinguish between citizens and representatives from political parties.

[19] Web radio is – technologically speaking – by no means new, but Demostation's conscious participatory–democratic and research-driven approach to the new (and old) communication and distribution technologies

offers a new contribution to the genre. We do of course acknowledge that participatory media projects exist, (or have existed) both in the mainstream (Livingstone and Lunt, 1994; Carpentier, 2003, McNair *et al.*, 2003) and in the alternative media sphere (Engelman, 1996; Atton, 2002; Meikle, 2002; Curran and Couldry, 2003; Gilmor, 2004; Skogseth, 2005). Furthermore, similar research projects have been conducted earlier. The Australian Youth Internet Radio Network (YIRN – http://cirac.qut.edu.au/yirn/) is for instance similar to Demostation 2 in the sense that both explore the way Internet technologies can be used to create public spheres (Web radio stations), which can enhance participation. Still, while Demostaton 2 focused on adult citizen's involvement in political issues, YIRN's focus is on how Web radio can be used as a channel for artistic expression for youngsters, leaving 'explorations of citizenship and participation' as a 'bi-product' (Tacchi *et al.*, 2004). Other differences include YIRN's ethnographic action research method. This implies including competent users as producers – and not mere 'ordinary' participants – and analyzing them when they take part in the process. Furthermore, unlike the research group behind Demostation, YIRN takes a more positive stance on the commercial potential of new media.

[20] The editorial/research group were contacted by colleagues from Department of Information Science and Media Studies (University of Bergen) who argued that demanding that users should have a computer with commercial software installed on it was not democratic. This is a fair point, but the editorial/ research group could, due to time constraints, only partly solve it by offering a direct hyperlink to the streaming audio on www.Demostasjon.net.

References for Chapter Five

Atton, C. (2002), *Alternative media,* London: Sage.

Bennett, W. L., Entman, R. M. (2001), 'An Introduction', in W. L. Bennett and R. M. Entman (eds.), *Mediated Politics: Communication in the Future of Democracy,* Cambridge: Cambridge University Press, pp. 1–29.

Carpentier, N. (2003), 'BBC's Video Nation as a Participatory Media Practice. Signifying Everyday Life, Cultural Diversity and Participation in an On-line Community', *International Journal of Cultural Studies,* 6: 4, pp. 425–47.

Curran, J., Couldry, N. (2003), *Contesting Media Power: Alternative Media in a Networked World,* Lanham, M: Rowman & Littlefield.

Dahl, R. A. (1998), *On Democracy,* New Haven and London: Yale University Press.

Deetz, S. (1999), 'Participatory Democracy as a Normative Foundation for Communication Studies', in T. L. Jacobson and J. Servaes (eds.), *Theoretical Approaches to Participatory Communication,* Cresskill, New Jersey: Hampton Press, pp. 131–67.

Dewey, J. (1927), *The Public and its Problems,* Athens, Ohio: Swallow Press/Ohio University Press.

Elster, J. (1998), 'Introduction', in J. Elster (ed.), *Deliberative Democracy,* Cambridge: Cambridge University Press, pp. 1–18.

Engelman, R. (1996), *Public Radio and Television in America: a political history,* London: Sage.

Eriksen, E. O., Weigård, J. (1999), *Kommunikativ Handling og Deliberativt Demokrati,* Bergen: Fagbokforlaget.

Gamson, W. A. (2001), 'Promoting Political Engagement', in W. L. Bennett and R. M. Entman (eds.), *Mediated Politics: Communication in the Future of Democracy,* Cambridge: Cambridge University Press, pp. 56–74.

Gillmor, D. (2004), *We the Media,* Sebastopol, CA: O'Reilly.

Habermas, J. (1989 [1962]), *The Structural Transformation of the Public Sphere: an Inquiry Into a Category of Bourgeois Society,* Cambridge: Polity Press.

—— (1992), 'Further Reflections on the Public Sphere', in Calhoun, C. (ed.), *Habermas and the Public Sphere,* Cambridge, Mass.: MIT Press, pp. 421–61.

Held, D. (2000 [1997]), *Models of Democracy,* Cambridge: Polity Press.

Jacobson, T. L., Kolluri, S. (1999), 'Participatory Communication as Communicative Action', in T. L. Jacobson and J. Servaes (eds.), *Theoretical Approaches to Participatory Communication,* Cresskill, New Jersey: Hampton Press, pp. 265–80.

Livingstone, S., Lunt, P. (1994), *Talk on Television: Audience Participation and Public Debate,* London: Routledge.

McNair, B., Hibberd, M., Schlesinger, P. (2003), *Mediated Access Broadcasting and Democratic Participation in the Age of Mediated Communication,* Luton: University of Luton Press.

Meikle, G. (2002), *Future Active: Media Activism and the Internet,* London: Routledge.

Mill, J. S. (2001 [1859]), *On Liberty,* London: Electric Book Co.

Mouffe, C. (1999), 'Deliberative Democracy or Agonistic Pluralism?', *Social Research,* 66: 3, pp. 745–58.

Nyre, L. (2006), *Minimum Journalism: Experimental Procedures for Democratic Participation in Sound Media.* Unpublished Manuscript.

Ringdal, K. (2001), *Enhet og Mangfold,* Bergen: Fagbokforlaget.

Rokkan, S. (1987), *Stat, Nasjon, Klasse: Essays i Politisk Sosiologi,* Oslo: Universitetsforlaget.

Rosen, J. (1993), *Community Connectedness Passwords for Public Journalism: how to Create Journalism that Listens to Citizens and Reinvigorates Public Life,* St. Petersburg, Florida: The Poynter Institute for Media Studies.

Skogerbø, E. (1996), *Privatising the Public Interest: Conflicts and Compromises in Norwegian Media Politics 1980-1993,* Oslo: Department of Media and Communication, University of Oslo.

Skogseth, E. G. (2005), *Indymedia – Journalistic Anarchy on the WWW.* Bergen: Institute of Information Science and Media Studies, University of Bergen. http://www.ub.uib.no/elpub/2005/h/704004/. Consulted on 1 March 2006.

Sparks, C. (2001), 'The Internet and the Global Public Sphere', in W. L. Bennett and R. M. Entman (eds.), *Mediated Politics: Communication in the Future of Democracy,* Cambridge: Cambridge University Press, pp. 75–95.

Tacchi, J., Lewis, D., Hartley, J. (2004), *The Youth Internet Radio Network: Can We Innovate Democracy?* Melbourne: Paper Presented at the Australian Electronic Governance Conference, Melbourne, VIC. http://www.public-policy.unimelb.edu.au/egovernance/papers/36_Tacchi.pdf. Consulted on 1 March 2006.

Thompson, J. B. (1995), *The Media and Modernity: a Social Theory of the Media,* Cambridge: Polity Press.

Touraine, A. (1997 [1994]), *What is Democracy?* Boulder, Colorado: Westview Press.

Youth Internet Radio Network (2006), *Connecting Queensland Youth Through Music and Creativity.* http://cirac.qut.edu.au/yirn/. Consulted on 1 March 2006.

Appendix: the five programmes

Wednesday, 7 September: What does it take to make you satisfied? Participants: citizens less than 40 years and representatives from political parties from Hordaland and Bergen (West Norway).

Thursday, 8 September: Which needs do you have where you live? Political visions and ambitions for the next four years. Participants: citizens who are more than 40 years and representatives from political parties from Trøndelag and Sørlandet (Central and South Norway).

Friday, 9 September: Doubt and mistrust towards the political system – on why people do not vote or are unsure about which party they should support. Nationwide participation. The plan included two non-partisan experts in addition to two representatives from political parties as participants in the programme, but the non-partisan experts could not be found in time.

Monday, 12 September: Media's role in the run up to the election. What role can media actors such as Demostation play? Participants: citizens and representatives from political parties from Møre og Romsdal/Volda (Northern part of West Norway).

Tuesday, 13 September: Will the elected government coalition fulfil its promises? Nationwide participation.

Chapter Six

Representation and inclusion in the online debate: the issue of honor killings*

Tamara Witschge

Introduction

The Internet is often praised for its ability to provide spaces for every person to present her or his view. In doing so, the Internet potentially allows for more inclusion and participation in the public debate, as everyone who has economic and social access to the Internet has at least the opportunity to take on the speaker's role. Each individual that wants to participate in the debate – either through reading or writing – is free to do so in the online environment. The social advantages of taking on this speaker's role are expected to be the largest for those groups that have been excluded from this role, either in the media or in other areas of the public sphere. Because of the low costs of publishing, participation in the public sphere is considered attainable for people 'beyond elites in wealthy societies' (Bohman, 2004: 137), and for those outside the centre of politics:

> It is clear that the Internet permits radical groups from both Left and Right (...) to construct inexpensive virtual counter-public opinions (...). The opinions of these groups have traditionally been excluded or marginalized in the mass-media public sphere. The Internet offers them a way not only of communicating with supporters, but also the potential to reach out beyond the 'radical ghetto' both directly (disintermediation) and indirectly, through influencing the mass media (Downey and Fenton, 2003: 198).

The Internet is, thus, seen as a new discursive space that allows groups normally silenced in traditional media to 'voice themselves and thus become visible and make their presence felt' (Mitra, 2004: 493). It is seen as being able to challenge traditional media because societal groups, institutions, or states do not have to compete for access; it 'can be used by anyone, at any time, from any place on the planet' (Karatzogianni, 2004: 46).

Considering these arguments concerning the potential democratic and participatory benefits of the Internet, the central research question of this chapter

---

* This research is funded by the Dutch Science Foundation (NWO), grant number 425.42.008.

is 'to what extent do Internet discussions indeed provide in practice a platform for inclusion and discussion of both dominant and marginalized voices'? In an ideal democracy, citizens have access to the entire range of opinions and arguments that exist on a specific issue. According to deliberative democracy theories (see for instance Bohman, 1996; Bohman and Rehg, 1997; Elster, 1998; Dryzek, 2000), such access should be provided through participation in public debates. Currently, the prevailing idea is that newspapers and other traditional media do not take on this role sufficiently; many scholars (for instance Papacharissi, 2002; Albrecht, 2003; Liina Jensen, 2003; Janssen and Kies, 2004; Dahlgren, 2005; Wiklund, 2005) have, thus, turned to the Internet as a possible key for participation in public discourse.

This chapter will zoom in on a specific issue – honor killings – to see which actors and positions are represented. How broad is the range of viewpoints and how inclusive is the online debate? Inclusion, one of the central features of the democratic debate (for an overview of different criteria for democratic debate, see Ferree *et al.*, 2002), ideally results in the actual representation of difference, in terms of actors, positions, and arguments. Not only the voicing of all relevant issues, arguments, and representations is a requirement, also the opportunity to access all of these different positions and arguments becomes important.

Honor killings

The inclusiveness of the online representations is examined through the analysis of a case study, which offers discourses on a particular issue situated within the broader public debate on immigration and integration in the Netherlands. The specific issue that is chosen for this purpose is 'eerwraak', which can be translated as 'honor revenge'. This broad term not only includes so-called 'honor killings' but also refers to other forms of (physical) violence in order to 'restore' the honor of a family [1]. This issue has received increased media attention after a number of honor killings. Amongst many others, the public statements of a member of parliament, Ayaan Hirsi Ali, have drawn public attention to this issue. As these statements have created an upsurge in the debate, they provide the timeframe and material for the analysis in this chapter.

This case study allows for a comparative analysis of newspaper articles and online postings in web forums. The selected newspaper articles consist of the articles that are intended to allow public participation and opinion formation, namely editorials, opinionating articles, and letters to the editor. Both types of media products will be analyzed in relation to the actors that are given voice and to the content level. Although these newspaper articles and online postings have a number of similarities (see for instance Liina Jensen, 2003: 370), they can hardly be equated, as for instance the selection procedure differs strongly. Morrison and Love (1996: 45–46) summarize this as follows:

Typically, editors select well-written and cogently argued contributions (...) rather than openly offensive pieces (...) and these are generally in keeping with the established ideological direction of the publication. (Morrison and Love, 1996: 45–46.)

Selection of the issue and timeframe

Ayaan Hirsi Ali, a then member of the Dutch parliament for the VVD (a liberal right-wing party), gave an interview in *De Volkskrant* on 4 February 2005. Some of her statements in this interview were specifically related to honor killings [2]:

The perpetrators of honour killings know the Dutch legal system. They put a [male] minor on the girl, because he will get a less severe punishment. The boy does the job, reports himself with the police, says he acted on an impulse and the case is closed. The justice department has a murder, a murder weapon and a perpetrator. Case closed. Finished. The whole family keeps silent and the justice department leaves it as it is. That's why I propose to do things completely different. We recently got a new terrorism law. That law says that information from the intelligence services can be used in court as evidence. Why don't we put those services onto the families of the hundreds of women who are currently in hiding? They are talking about it in those families! Why don't we keep them under permanent surveillance, why don't we tap their phones? [3].

This interview was published a week before a parliamentary debate that was scheduled to take place on 10 February 2005. Both in the newspaper articles and online forums, the number of contributions to the debate on honor killings increased after Hirsi Ali's statements. This analysis will include the public statements made until 1 month after Hirsi Ali's comments were published (4 February 2005–4 March 2005). The rationale for choosing this period is twofold: both the newspaper and the online debates have died out after 1 month, and such a timeframe provides a feasible number of articles for analysis.

Selection of the newspaper articles and web forums

The newspaper articles in the chosen timeframe come from seven newspapers. Six national newspapers were selected for analysis [4]. In addition, one free newspaper – *Metro*, which is mainly distributed at train and bus stations throughout the Netherlands – is included. In utilizing *Lexis Nexis*, all editorial articles and letters to the editor that mention 'eerwraak' (honor killings) were selected [5]. This resulted in a total of 21 editorial articles and nine opinion pieces and letters to the editors. The distribution was as shown in Table 1.

The selected online discussions come from the sample of forums used in my Ph.D. research, which exists of seven popular sites (in terms of the number of readers and postings). The sample includes rightwing-oriented (both extreme

Table 1:
Distribution of articles in newspapers

Newspaper	Frequency
Volkskrant	6
AD	4
NRC	3
Trouw	4
Parool	4
Metro	5
Telegraaf	4
Total	30

and moderate) and leftwing-oriented websites, as well as ethnic minority websites. On these forums, a search to find discussions on honor killings was performed. Only the web forums fok.nl, weerwoord.nl, and maroc.nl contained relevant material within the timeframe [6]. The three forums represent different types of websites as follows:

- 'Fok' is a general Dutch discussion website with thousands of members [7] that have posted almost 30 million postings in 700,000 threads [8]. Here, a discussion was started in the political section of the website on 4 February 2005 at 15 : 25 by Umm-Qsar. The thread was titled *Honour killings not Terrorism*. The thread stopped within 48 hours, with the 36th posting on 6 February at 13 : 51.
- 'Weerwoord' is a discussion forum that focuses on political topics. It has almost 8,000 threads in which 1,800 registered users posted over 200,000 messages. Here, Koos posted a message in the section 'Immigration and Integration' on 4 February 2005 at 4 : 08. The thread was called *Hirsi Ali wants to deploy the AIVD [Dutch Intelligence Service] against honour killings*. There were 64 reactions to this initial posting. The last posting dates from 6 February at 18 : 40.
- *Maroc* is a website that is specifically aimed at people of Moroccan descent living in the Netherlands, but increasingly sees 'native' Dutch people populating the forum. It has almost 2 million postings in 125,000 threads and 46,000 members. Here, a thread called *The debate on honour killings* was started by Te quiero, who initiated the discussion by quoting a newspaper column on honor killings (by Anil Ramdas) that appeared in *De Volkskrant* on 14 February 2005. Te quiero made this posting on 20 February 2005 at 00 : 44. There were 37 reactions within 2 days; the last message was posted on 21 February at 20 : 47.

Debate on honor killings
The selected newspaper articles and web postings were then coded, using the actor [9] as a basic level of analysis. Both in the newspaper articles and web postings, this

first quantitative content analysis focuses on who is given voice, and on their characteristics. In a second analysis, the emphasis is placed on the positions that are taken and the practices of inclusion and exclusion. Here a quantitative content analysis is combined with a critical discourse analysis (Chouliaraki and Fairclough, 1999, see also Philips and Jørgensen, 2002 for a good overview).

Who is represented?

Table 2 shows a fairly varied distribution in terms of sex and origins among the 22 people that were given voice in the newspaper debate on honor killings. Ten out of 22 actors are female, and ten are male (two people's sex was unknown).

Table 2:

Voices in newspapers

Sources quoted/authors	Freq.	Position	Sex	Descent
VVD-MP Hirsi Ali	12	Politician (g.p.)	Female	Immigrant
CDA-minister Donner	10	Politician (g.p.)	Male	Native
Chairman of the VVD party, Van Aartsen	4	Politician (g.p.)	Male	Native
PvdA-MP Albayrak	4	Politician (opp.)	Female	Immigrant
LPF-MP Kraneveldt	3	Politician (opp.)	Female	Native
CDA-MP Sterk	3	Politician (g.p.)	Female	Native
W. Timmer, police coordinator	3	Administration	Male	Native
Researcher C. van Eck, VU	2	Academic	Female	Native
VVD-minister Verdonk	2	Politician (g.p.)	Female	Native
Civil servant of the department of Justice	1	Administration	—	—
GroenLinks-MP Azough	1	Politician (opp.)	Female	Immigrant
F. Bouali	1	Columnist	Female	Immigrant
K. van der Donck	1	Citizen	—	Native
J.A.A. van Doorn	1	Columnist	Male	Native
G. Dorsman (50), lawyer	1	Citizen	Male	Native
CDA-MP Van Haersma Buma	1	Politician (g.p.)	Male	Native
Pamela Hemelrijk	1	Columnist	Female	Native
T. Hesseling (43), housewife	1	Citizen	Female	Native
K. Hooreman (Haarlem)	1	Citizen	Male	Native
R. van Kaam (23), student	1	Citizen	Male	Native
Frank van Pamelen	1	Columnist	Male	Native
A. Ramdas	1	Columnist	Male	Immigrant
Total	56			

NB: (g.p.) stands for a politician from a government party (at the national level), including ministers; (opp.) stands for a politician whose party is in the opposition.

In terms of origin, the table shows that five actors are of immigrant descent, whereas sixteen actors are native Dutch. If this number is compared to the number of immigrants in Dutch society, actors of immigrant descent are thus reasonably represented. However, if one holds the view that the issue of honor killings affects immigrants more and that they should therefore take part more in the debate, they are rather poorly represented.

Looking at the types of actors that are quoted in terms of the number that belongs to the political elite (and both the 'governmental' politicians and the 'oppositional' politicians), the picture is very different. Six out of 22 actors are politicians from governmental parties (including two ministers). Another two are linked to the administration. Only three members of the opposition are included; together, the political elite grasps more than two third (44 out of 56 quotations) of times that people are given voice in the newspapers. Furthermore, even though five of the quoted actors are (presented as) citizens, they only have five quotations out of the total number of 56 quotations.

Furthermore, Table 3 shows that these citizens only get a voice in the free newspaper, the *Metro*. Readers of the *Volkskrant* only have access to the voices of the government on this matter. In contrast, *Algemeen Dagblad* quotes opposition politicians five times. As a whole, newspaper readers are only confronted with oppositional political voices in six out of 30 newspaper articles. In seventeen articles, the readers can read the statements of governmental politicians.

Online, we can see a different distribution (see Table 4). First, and very prominently, there is an unequal distribution of sex, most specifically on Fok. Women are almost totally absent (one women posted one message out of a total of 36 postings). On Weerwoord, no information is provided about the sex of the

Table 3:
Actors quoted per newspaper

Newspaper/ source	Volks- krant	AD	NRC	Trouw	Parool	Metro	Tele- graaf	Total	Number of actors
Politician (governmental party)	8	6	5	3	3	1	5	31	6
Administration	2	1			1			4	2
Politician (opposition party)		5	1	1	1		1	9	3
Citizen		1				4		5	5
Columnist			1	3		1		5	5
Academic		1			1			2	1
Total	10	14	7	7	6	6	6	56	22

Table 4:
Online participants

Participant	Frequency	Sex	Total No. of posts	Average	Member since	Origin
Participants on Fok.nl						
opa	9	Male	1683	23	Oct-99	
pool	6	Male	7730	390	Dec-03	
sjun	4	Male	12438	420	Apr-03	
Musketeer	3	Male	138	17	Jan-05	
desiredbard	2	Male	1711	180	Nov-04	
Jereon	2	Male	2627	120	Jul-03	
SCH	2	Male	66794	1980	Nov-02	
Umm-Qsar	2	Male	1057	60	Apr-03	
Chewy	1	Male	4341	150	Jan-03	
GewoneMan	1	Male	7270	360	Jan-04	
Gia	1	Female	13877	240	Apr-00	
IntroV	1	Male	1391	25	Jan-01	
pberends	1	Male	38534	1440	Jul-03	
tommytheman	1	Male	1133	60	Jan-04	
Total	36		11480	390		
Participants on Weerwoord.nl						
Koos	20	Male	391	65	Nov-04	
Alfatrion	7	—	2420	73	Aug-02	
Theo	7	Male	3677	141	Mar-03	
Xeno	7	—	1547	50	Oct-02	
Anne	4	Female	1486	57	Mar-03	
Torero	4	—	2449	66	Apr-02	
Moppersmurf	3	—	609	55	Jun-04	
waarbenik	3	—	702	47	Feb-04	
Circe	2	—	1102	38	Dec-02	
Gert	2	Male	73	2	Dec-01	
John Wervenbos	2	Male	3795	74	Feb-01	
curacaoteam	1	—	3971	95	Nov-01	
Eduard Genen	1	Male	1440	206	Oct-04	
Olga	1	Female	206	11	Oct-03	
P040	1	—	616	41	Feb-04	
Total	65		1632	68		

(Continued)

Table 4: *(Continued)*

Participant	Frequency	Sex	Total No. of posts	Average	Member since	Origin
Participants on Maroc.nl						
Ron Haleber	10	Male	4109	137	Nov-02	NL
sjaen	6	Female	1109	101	Jun-04	NL
mark61	4	Male	17071	1004	Dec-03	—
Goodnight	3	Female	6992	388	Nov-03	Morocco
tr_imparator	3	Male	1279	426	Feb-05	Turkey
Mill	2	None	2308	68	Jul-02	—
S@deeQ	2	Male	722	52	Mar-04	Morocco
Simon	2	None	8712	235	Apr-02	Liechtenstein
Te quiero	2	None	618	103	Nov-04	NL
~Panthera~	1	Female	13226	357	Apr-02	NL
Couscousje	1	Female	19740	439	Aug-01	NL
Japio	1	None	76	8	Aug-04	Spain
Rabi'ah	1	Female	4417	147	Nov-02	Suriname
Total	38		6183	266		

users, but when the names of the participants are used as indicators [10], only two 'obvious' female names can be found, in contrast to five male names. On Maroc.nl, a more equal situation can be found, as five women are represented, in contrast to four males and four 'onzijdig' (male nor female)' [11].

With regard to the origins of the participants, very little information was found on both Fok and Weerwoord, and very little variety is suggested when taking names as indicators. On these two forums, thirteen out of 29 have 'Dutch' names and in only two cases there is a reference to other nationalities (*desiredbard*, who refers to Ireland as his home country, and *curacaoteam*, who refers to Curacao as his/her country of origin). On Maroc, information on the 'national affiliation' is available, as participants are asked to choose a flag when registering. Even on this site, which focuses on people of immigrant descent (in specific Dutch Moroccans), the majority of the flags are Dutch. This, of course, does not necessarily imply that the participants cannot be of immigrant descent, but they are at least not representing themselves as such through their flag selection. In addition to the Dutch flag, only the following 'national affiliations' are represented in the honor killings discussion through their flags: Moroccan, Spanish, Surinamese, Turkish, and Liechtenstein [12].

In terms of the type of online users, specifically Maroc and Fok show heavy users. However, on all of the websites there are also less frequent posters participating. Moreover, heavy users do not dominate this specific discussion in terms of the number of contributions per participant. Likewise, 'young' and 'old' (in terms of their registration date) are equally present on all of these forums; neither group dominates the discussion. When looking at the dynamics of the discussion, particular participants do dominate the discussion. On all three forums, the top three posters are responsible for more than half of the contributions. On Weerwoord, one of the contributors is responsible for one third of the messages. This concurs with other studies into the dynamics of online discussions, as is discussed in Witschge (2004). The question is, however, to what extent this influences the content of the debates. In the next section, I will turn to the diversity with regard to positions and arguments in the debate.

Which positions are represented?

Looking at both the online and the newspaper debate, the most prominent disparity is the difference in the amount of information. The newspaper articles focuses on the *process* of the debate instead of the 'content' of the debate. Only in 9 out of 30 articles, the content of the proposal of how to deal with honor killings made by Hirsi Ali is considered. (In five of the articles, a negative position was taken, in one a positive, and in three articles the issues was considered without taking on a negative or positive position.) Hirsi Ali's suggestions were not taken well by government actors and some opposition actors. Most of the newspaper's attention was devoted to these critiques. Statements that did relate to honor killings showed surprisingly little variety. Most of these statements dealt with the question whether or not honor killings should be seen as terrorism or whether the new terrorism law should indeed be utilized to deal with honor killings. Only two statements favored linking honor killings and terrorism, the other ten were negative.

What remained remarkably absent in the newspaper debate was an argumentation developed on honor killings in general and on its relation to terrorism in particular. No information was given about honor killings – barring one article that reported on an interview with the national police coordinator in charge of dealing with honor killings [13]. Almost no information was provided about the nature of honor killings, its possible causes, or alternative solutions.

In contrast, this kind of information *was* found in the online debates. The participants discussed the issue, provided arguments, reacted to each other, and shared information (see Table 5).

Online participants used different types of sources to inform each other, to provide additional information or to dispel fallacies. In addition, the range of viewpoints and ways of looking at honor killings is much broader. The online debate was clearly focused on the legal aspects of honor killings and on its nature, making these elements much more apparent than was done in the newspapers.

In analyzing the online discourses, two main themes were identified: (1) how should honor killings be interpreted? and (ii) how should honor killings be dealt with? Within each of these two themes, two additional topics emerged.

Table 5:

Types of utterances on web forums

	Frequency			
Type of utterance	Fok	Weerwoord	Maroc	Total
Providing information	6	13	2	21
Personal attack	0	0	6	6
Meta-talk about the discussion	0	2	1	3
Statement about honor killings	14	20	3	37
Argument for statement on honor killings	7	18	1	26
Reaction to others	12	36	1	49
Asking for information	2	4	1	7
Alternative solution	7	17	0	24
Total number of messages	36	65	38	139

Note: Not every message contained one of these types of utterances, and some contained more than one type of utterance.

Within the first theme – how honor killings should be interpreted – two perspectives on honor killings can be distinguished. Honor killings are articulated (a) as a terrorist act and (b) as a cultural or religious phenomenon. In terms of how honor killings should be dealt with – the second main theme – again two perspectives can be identified: who should deal with honor killings, from a legal point of view (i.e. is the intelligence service indeed the right organization, as Hirsi Ali suggests); and whether honor killings should evoke a signal of disapproval (from the media, public opinion, or politicians). Before discussing these themes, it is important to point out that all four perspectives are very much interdependent and intertwined.

First, the question of 'who' should deal with honor killings is closely related to the question of 'how' honor killings are seen. Should honor killings be seen as 'normal' murders, as the Dutch minister Donner suggests in *De Volkskrant*? Or are they inherently different, and should they consequently be dealt with differently? And if so, what makes the difference with other murders? These questions, while hardly touched upon in the newspapers, formed the focal point of the online debate.

Honor killings were not seen as a normal crime, as is illustrated by the following example. These statements seem to not only suggest that honor killings are different from other murders but they are worse.

> *Young sons that slaughter their sisters, being ordered by the family, with a cultural/religious motive, I do not see that as a 'normal' crime.* (Koos, WW, 4 February 2005, 14:26.)

There seems to be an intensity scale underlying the different crimes: 'normal' murder, honor killings, and terrorism. One of the participants used this scale in his reasoning as to why honor killings should not be treated as terrorism:

> *By calling cases that are clearly not terrorism-related, such as honour killing terrorism, she [Hirsi Ali] doesn't take real terrorism serious enough. A real terrorist has the intention to overthrow the state, disrupt society, create fear, etc.* (Pool, Fok, 4 February 2005, 15:39.)

This links up with the notion that the AIVD, the Dutch Intelligence Service, should not deal with honor killings, as they should be dealing with more 'serious' crimes such as terrorism.

In opposition, there are also participants that did see parallels between terror and honor killings. First, a number of discussants looked at it from the victim's perspective; for them, the victims are clearly being terrorized.

> *I find honour killing terror. Often against the woman, and certainly against the individual.* (John Wervenbos [moderator], WW, 4 February 2005, 19:07.)

In reaction to this view, there were also counter-positions.

> *Of course, honour killing is a normal crime and not terrorism. Family terror is no terrorism.* (Gert, WW, 6 February 2005, 18:15.)

It became clear that participants hold very specific and varying notions of what terrorism is. For some, the individual being terrorized signifies that the crime itself should be seen as terrorism, while others disagree. Other debaters take on a different perspective and argue that honor killings can be viewed as a form of resistance against Dutch society, as they prioritize cultural values over Dutch law.

> *Whether you can call it terror, I don't know, but you can see it, I think, as a ritual murder by people that find their culture/religion more important than our laws. And that requires a different approach than normal crimes.* (Koos, WW, 4 February 2005, 19:17.)

For some it can, thus, be defined as 'full' terrorism.

> *Honour killing has characteristics that are similar to terrorism: 1) Honour killing is preferably acted out in public [...] 2) The community often pressures the father or the brother to revenge the honour. The murder is thus planned by a* **network** *of people.* (Koos, WW, 5 February 2005, 01:16, emphasis in original.)

The earlier quotes refer to the cultural character of honor killings and what sets them apart from other crimes, a second theme in the discourse on the interpretation of honor killings. Here the cultural or religious character of honor killings is emphasized. This will be discussed separately in the next section, as this theme shows the mechanisms of exclusion that are at work in the honor killings discourse.

With regard to how participants feel that honur killings should be dealt with, there are two perspectives: the legal issue and the societal response issue. In terms of the legal approach to honor killings, online discussants explore a broader range of possible ways of dealing with honor killings (in comparison to the newspaper content). They view the issue from multiple angles and try to determine whether or not the new terrorism law should really be utilized in dealing with honor killings. In this respect, many of the discussants feel that the present-day police powers concerning the tracing of criminals should be sufficient for dealing with this crime and that the Dutch Intelligence Services (AIVD) should not be involved.

> *What do these people have to do with state security? Police business ... they can also tap phones.* (waarbenik, WW, 4 February 2005, 11:39.)

The argument here is that the AIVD already has too much to do. Additionally, they are not considered the right institute to deal with this type of crime. In contrast, others do agree with Hirsi Ali that the AIVD should deal with honor killings. These proponents mostly provide us with pragmatic reasons such as the following quote demonstrates:

> *But the AIVD does have the means to track and map these sorts of crimes. That it's not terrorism is no reason. And that it's not possible by law [to use the AIVD] isn't a reason either. Then they should just change the law.* (Moppersmurf, WW, 4 February, 22:24.)

Some participants were very ingenious in thinking of alternative ways of dealing with the issue of honor killings. One example is the proposal to establish a CARE police force.

> *There used to be a 'zedenpolitie' [vice squad] that dealt with 'zedendelicten' [sex offences]. (Does it still exist?) Why don't we expand this or have a new squad that deals with infringements against the general norms and values (which used to be called 'zeden' [14]) of ethnical, cultural and religious background. CARE-police ('Culturele Achtergronden Religies en Etniciteit' [Cultural Backgrounds Religions and Ethnicity]).* (Eduard Geenen, WW, 5 February, 13:43, emphasis by author.)

The discourse in the online debates shows that honor killings are considered to be a very severe crime (some called it terrorism, others still considered it an 'ordinary' crime). It is also apparent that respondents do not feel that this crime is being given the attention it deserves. Both in a penal as in a political sense, the seriousness of the issue is being underestimated according to the online discussants. Part of the problem for them is that the legal, political, and public signals of disapproval are too weak. Therefore, a call is made to amplify this societal signals to demonstrate the 'Dutch' aversion to this crime.

In any case [there should be] more severe punishments and attention in the media. I also think that the ministers Verdonk and Donner should speak out on this matter. (Koos, WW, 5 February 2005, 00:27.)

In this respect, even the term 'eerwraak' is challenged. As explained earlier, the Dutch term is used both for honor killings as for other violence with regard 'to protecting or restoring the honor'. One of the participants linked this term to the way this issue is viewed.

Such a premeditated murder shouldn't have such a euphemistic name as 'eerwraak'. In my opinion, it is better to mercilessly expose the immaturity and unscrupulousness of those people that are involved in this murder. (sjun, Fok, 6 February 2005, 08:35.)

In addition, others linked the Dutch societal condemnation of the crime with a possible condemnation by the community in which honor killings are practiced.

That's why it's so important that honour killing is going to be condemned within the [Islamic] community. *For that to happen, politicians will first have to communicate the view that honour killing is not tolerated.* (Koos, WW, 5 February 2005, 17:21, emphasis by author.)

In general, the call for condemnation in Dutch public discourse is concurrent with the notion of honor killings originating from cultural values of ethnic and religious minorities within the Netherlands. Many discussants linked the practice of honor killings explicitly to culture and religion. This particular perspective is explored more in-depth in the following section.

Discursive exclusions

Within the discussion on honor killings, three exclusionary (linguistic) mechanisms can be traced. First, people and positions were explicitly treated as inferior, although this did not happen very often. For example, one of the participants referred to another participant's educational level ('VMBO', the lowest level of Dutch secondary school), suggesting an inferior quality of argumentation. The same participant called people that hold a different opinion than he, 'Dumbos'. As such, these participants are treated unequally and their positions are not taken seriously. Another example of this exclusionary mechanism is the exclusion of one of the participants of Maroc.nl, who said he resisted integration. He is told to 'veil himself in exotic clothes and build some wooden huts and dig his own well' (sjaen on Maroc.nl). Here, failure to integrate into Dutch society is clearly equated with being 'backward' or 'primitive'. Resistance against integration is ridiculed.

The second exclusionary mechanism – othering – is much more widespread. Martin Rojo (1995: 50–51, emphasis in original) describes this process as follows:

> *The exclusion is articulated on two axes: DIVIDING, that is, establishing the categories which will be opposed in the conflict–us, with several different referents, vs them, or, nearly always, him; and REJECTING, that is, segregating, marginalizing, creating a negative image. The creation of an enemy, them or him, makes it possible to establish, as the opponent, an inclusive subject, we, which is defined simply by opposition. In the same way, the construction of a negative image of the enemy, using the fact that he flouts a series of established values and is given negative features like irrationality or madness, provides the inclusive we, by opposition, with a positive image. The result is a we which is indefinite but which evokes a set of shared values that remain implicit. Both the subject and the values are thus underdefined, but despite this the reader absorbs them and becomes part of them.*

Participants in the online discussions feel strongly about what is Dutch and what is not. Throughout the online discussions (and at times also the newspapers), it is apparent that honor killings are seen as something 'outside' of Dutch society. Basically, the idea is that this phenomenon has no place in the Netherlands. This, of course, conforms to the conception of crime, which has to be placed outside social normality. Unlike the ways in which other crimes may be discussed, honor killings are seen as 'foreign' to Dutch society, and its values and practices. Some examples that illustrate this are as follows:

> *In any case, it [honour killing] is not normal, at least not in* our *culture YET.* (xeno, WW, 4 February 2005, 17:52, emphasis by author.)

> *It should be made clear that honour killing is not tolerated anymore* over here *(...). So, no more keeping silent, as the Netherlands still do, but making it clear that we find this outrageous.* (Koos, WW, 4 February 2005, 19:17, emphasis by author.)

The discourse that aims to eradicate honor killings from the Netherlands is focused on its perpetrators. The participants of online forums discussed whether or not these perpetrators can or should still be viewed as Dutch citizens, showing that honor killings are not just any crime, but impinge on the nation state itself. Some view it as terrorism, as something that challenges the very basis of the Dutch legal system. Some examples are as follows:

> *[Honour killing is] murder with the aim to* resist the ruling system. *In that sense you could compare honour killing to terrorism (...). The slogan: 'Your nation state is not mine' has taken root in Holland.* (opa, Fok, 4 February 2005, 23:10, emphasis by author.)

> *It [The Netherlands] is* their *nation state.* They *will deny it, particularly the duties that come with it, but yet these duties still apply. We are entitled to enforce these duties, which brings along the enjoyment of these rights.* (Pool, Fok, 4 February 2005, 23:30, emphasis by author.)

The online discussion later turned to the subject that not all Dutch citizens are considered equal. As one of the participants stated, 'I would like to see all citizens of Holland as fellow citizens.' (opa, Fok, 5 February 2005, 00:11, emphasis by author). He 'would like to' see them as fellow citizens, but his formulation suggests that he does not.

Analysis of the discussion also reveals that the nature of the crime is very much interwoven with its perpetrators. The following examples illustrate how some notions, such as honor killings and terrorism, have strong ethnical or religious connotations.

> *There's bound to be natives that have killed a family member, something that can resemble an honour killing. That's why I don't think it is terrorism.* (pberends, Fok, 4 February 2005, 20:34.)

> *As honour killing takes place in different cultures, like the Christian, you can impossibly call it terrorism, in my opinion.* (anne, WW, 6 February 2005, 15:42.)

Feelings of superiority further strengthen the view that honor killings are incompatible with Dutch cultural values and are not practiced by 'Dutch' people. Honor killings are not only seen as 'foreign' but also as 'backward' and 'barbaric'. The position that enables the participants to condemn honor killings is one of 'enlightenment' that has not yet touched the 'foreign and backward'.

> *We view honour killing as an offence, and in the Netherlands (where we fortunately still live) it is considered a crime (...). To me it seems particularly useful to monitor all types of acts that are inspired by backward foreign 'values'.* (Torero, WW, 6 February 2005, 00:02, emphasis by author.)

We're fed up with all this Islam shit. Taking a firm position on this is the only remedy for such barbaric matters! (GewoneMan, Fok, 4 February 2005, 23:36, emphasis by author.)

If it is not a Dutch phenomenon, but 'foreign' to the Dutch, the question in the debate becomes whose problem is it, anyway? Does the Dutch society have to deal with this, and is the Dutch society really affected? In this respect, the following quote claims that 'our' wives are not affected by honor killings.

Bad idea, the AIVD already has her hands full with the followers of the 'Lachende doder' [Laughing slayer] [15] *that has it in for our society (...). That they also make their own wives' lives miserable is annoying, but that has to be dealt with in a different way.* (xeno, WW, 4 February 2005, 8:57, emphasis by author).

The notion that it is not an issue for the Dutch to deal with becomes clearer through the solution people present for this issue. Participants cared more about 'where' honor killings take place (not in Holland) than to 'whom' it happens. The discourse seems to suggest that participants do not inherently condemn it, as long as it does not take place on Dutch soil.

Honour killing is completely unacceptable in the Netherlands (...). People who want such a society, should build it elsewhere, for where I'm concerned, but not here in the Netherlands. (John Wervenbos (moderator), WW, 5 February 2005, 0:01.)

This position is questioned by one of the participants by raising the following question: who should be deported? What if they are Dutch or Surinamese? However, the solution proposed by this specific discussant is still exclusionary, even though it deals with a slightly narrower group of people.

You also have madmen amongst the Dutch-white-townspeople-and-country folk ethnicity [sic]. What do you want to do with them? Deport them as well? Or Surinamese or Antilleans? I do think, however, that those with double nationalities should be mercilessly deported and have their Dutch citizenship withdrawn, when there is conclusive evidence of serious criminality. Children or no children, rich or poor. I couldn't care less ... deport these corrupting forces. (Eduard Geenen, WW, 5 February 2005, 13:14, emphasis by author.)

An alternative solution that is less popular, but still advocated by some, is an attempt to bring about cultural changes within the group that practices honor killings. This change is mostly envisaged to occur through a 'simple' transferral of Dutch values. In the 'inburgeringscursus' (a course that aims to teach immigrants the Dutch language as well as Dutch cultural values) the 'other' can be taught how 'the Dutch' deal with family life. The following quotes illustrate how the discussants view this cultural transformation.

> *The honour killing phenomenon has a clear cultural (specifically Turkish) background (...). Only a change in culture will really solve the problem with this group (...). Demanding that the honour killing issue becomes an explicit part of the 'inburgeringspakket' [a set of (educational) instruments that should enable immigrants to become a citizen of the Netherlands] (how we DO deal with this in Holland) would be much more realistic.* (Theo, WW, 4 February 2005, 17:11, emphasis in original.)

This example shows the perceived simplicity of cultural value changes. The 'other' is shown the 'Dutch' way, which will lead to the necessary shift in practices and values. There are a few discussants, however, that propose a slightly less one-directional solution and put more agency with the community in which honor killings are considered to be a tolerated and practiced phenomenon. These discussants called for emancipation from within the community in order to bring about societal change.

> *The resistance against primitive matters such as 'honour killing' will eventually have to come* through the emancipation of Muslims themselves. (curacaoteam, WW, 5 February 2005, 20:17, emphasis by author.)

Even though different in outlook, this discourse is also filled with stereotypes of the Islamic community. The issue nevertheless seems to be at least a shared issue, proposing to involve 'the other'.

Conclusions

The Dutch national newspaper analysis showed that the issue of honor killings was only described through the procedure of the (parliamentary) debate. Rather than representing different viewpoints, the issue was described formally, without defining the issue and without having different perspectives explored and questioned. Even though some variety of actors (in terms of gender and ethnicity) was given voice, almost no citizens or other non-governmental actors were represented in the newspaper debate.

The online debate, in contrast, explored the issue differently. Even though more perspectives on the issue were represented and more facets of the issue were explored, the analysis also allowed pinpointing a number of problems that nuance the optimistic-democratic approach towards the Internet. No genuine counterargument was found in the online debate. No one maintained that honor killings could be a good way of societal organization, and no one provided an alternative or complementary mechanism to the Dutch legal system. All discourses focussed on ridding the Dutch society of honor killings. If the Internet allows for these counter-positions to be made public, it was not done on the platforms examined here [16].

Second, while citizens remained absent from the newspaper debate, no members of the political elite could be found on the web forums. Rather, references to the 'common man' or to 'ordinary people' – both in the way users named themselves and in the online postings – seems to suggest that those discussing online distinguish themselves from the political elite.

Third, in the online debate very little suggested that those of immigrant descent were represented. No discussion between the different groups could be found. Many references were made in terms of what religious or ethnic minorities should do in relation to honor killings, but no dialogue could be found in the forums that were analyzed. Even on the Moroccan-Dutch web forum, the debate was dominated by 'native' Dutch.

Moreover, although the online debate explored honor killings more broadly than the newspapers, it contained a number of exclusionary mechanisms: exclusion of certain practices and members of Dutch society, and exclusion through the process of othering. No open debate was found in the web forums. One could argue here that this is to be expected, because of the nature of the topic: honor killings are illegal in Dutch society and the debate is naturally focused on how to eliminate crime. However, the discourse focused on the 'foreignness' of the crime and on how these honor killings could be banned from *Dutch* society. The general (or global) elimination of this deadly practice was not discussed as such. Some participants remained indifferent towards honor killings as long as it is committed elsewhere, in their 'own' country and not in the Netherlands. Here the discourse transcends the condemnation of just a crime, and here the exclusion and the processes of othering cruelly take shape.

Notes for Chapter Six

[1]   In the online debates, the commonly attributed meaning is honor 'killings', and other acts of violence are rarely implied or mentioned. The focus of this chapter will be on honor killings, even though the Dutch word encompasses more than 'killings'.

[2]   Hirsi Ali resigned in May 2006. The rest of the newspaper article demonstrated her view on Dutch 'multicultural' society in general.

[3]   All quotes were originally in Dutch and have been translated by the author.

[4]   The selected newspapers are *De Volkskrant, Trouw, De Telegraaf, NRC Handelsblad (NRC), Het Parool,* and *Het Algemeen Dagblad (AD)*. Also only

web forums with a national focus (which are not specifically aiming at, or originating from, a specific region) are included in the analysis.

[5]   *Metro* was manually searched by checking the archived PDF-files of the entire newspaper, which can be found on www.clubmetro.nl; the selected articles contained the word 'eerwraak'.

[6]   On the other forums, there was no discussion on honor killings within the timeframe of the study. The archives of nieuwrechts.nl and politiekdebat.nl, two other websites in the sample, were not available at the time of the data collection.

[7]   The exact number of users is not made public.

[8]   The statistics of the three forums stem from February 2006.

[9]   To be selected, actors have to have made statements regarding honor killings. They also need to be quoted or paraphrased in 'the newspaper article. Interpretations or evaluations of the actor's expressions are excluded (for a similar method of coding, see Ferree *et al.*, 2002).

[10]   Whether this is less reliable method than the method of taking the self-presentation of their gender remains a question. However, it is the representation I am after, that which is perceivable by others. This representation can come as much from a name as from a gender sign.

[11]   Here, participants can indicate their sex by choosing for female, male and 'onzijdig'.

[12]   I do not wish to imply that these are then necessarily the countries from which the participants originate. It is, however, these countries that are now represented for the other participants in the discussion. They do seem to suggest some affiliation. That these are not static attachments is illustrated by the fact that half a year after the data collection, the participant holding the flag of Liechtenstein now holds the flag of Luxembourg (the participant does seem to have a preference for small states). However, none of the other participants have changed their flags.

[13]   W. Timmer, a highly ranked member of the police force and a national expert on honor killings.

[14]   The Dutch word 'zeden' can refer to (in)decent behavior, but also to customs and values.

[15]   Mohammed B., who murdered Theo van Gogh, called the prophet Mohammed 'de lachende doder' or the 'laughing slayer'.

[16]   Having said this, I need to come back to the nature and limitations of the study. Only a small selection of web forums has been studied, as all postings

came from three (albeit sizable) web forums. However, this selection of web forums does represent a rightwing, an immigrant, and a general forum. Also, as another part of my Ph.D. research shows, these web forums are often chosen by participants for their variety in terms of participants and perspectives. However, this variety does not seem to be present in the case of honor killings. This might be because of the specific nature of the issue – the issue of honor killings being a contested and emotionally charged political issue. On the other hand, one could argue that the benefits of the Internet to bring together people with different perspectives should be the greatest with regard to such issues, as written language and physical distance may open up the possibilities to discuss contested issues. Perhaps we need to seek instances of dialogue on forums on a smaller scale.

References for Chapter Six

Albrecht, S. (2003), *Whose Voice is Heard in the Virtual Public Sphere? A Study of Participation and Representation in Online Deliberation, Research Symposium 'Information, Communication, Society'*, Oxford: University of Oxford.

Bohman, J. (1996), *Public Deliberation: Pluralism, Complexity, and Democracy*, Cambridge: MIT Press.

—— (2004), 'Expanding Dialogue: The Internet, the Public Sphere and Prospects for Transnational Democracy', in N. Crossley and M. Roberts (eds.), *After Habermas: New Perspectives on the Public Sphere*, Oxford: Blackwell Publishing, pp. 131–55.

Bohman, J., Rehg, W. (1997), *Deliberative Democracy: Essays on Reason and Politics*, Cambridge, Mass.: MIT Press.

Chouliaraki, L., Fairclough, N. (1999), *Discourse in Late Modernity: Rethinking Critical Discourse Analysis*, Edinburgh: Edinburgh University Press.

Dahlgren, P. (2005), 'The Internet, Public Spheres, and Political Communication: Dispersion and Deliberation', *Political Communication*, 22, pp. 147–62.

Downey, J., Fenton, N. (2003), 'New Media, Counter Publicity and the Public Sphere', *New Media & Society*, 5: 2, pp. 185–202.

Dryzek, J. S. (2000), *Deliberative Democracy and Beyond*, Oxford: Oxford University Press.

Elster, J. (1998), *Deliberative Democracy*, Cambridge: Cambridge University Press.

Ferree, M. M., Gamson, W. A., Gerhards, J., *et al.* (2002), *Shaping Abortion Discourse: Democracy and the Public Sphere in Germany and the United States*, Cambridge: Cambridge University Press.

Janssen, D., Kies, R. (2004), *Online Forums and Deliberative Democracy: Hypotheses, Variables and Methodologies, Empirical Approaches to Deliberative Politics,* Florence: European University Institute.

Karatzogianni, A. (2004), 'The Politics of "Cyberconflict"', *Politics*, 24: 1, pp. 46–55.

Liina Jensen, J. (2003), 'Public Spheres on the Internet: Anarchic or Government-Sponsored – A Comparison', *Scandinavian Political Studies*, 26: 4, pp. 349–74.

Martin Rojo, L. (1995), 'Division and Rejection: From the Personification of the Gulf Conflict to the Demonization of Saddam Hussein', *Discourse and Society*, 6: 1, pp. 49–80.

Mitra, A. (2004), 'Voices from the Marginalized on the Internet: Examples from a Website for Women of South Asia', *Journal of Communication*, 54: 3, pp. 492–510.

Morrison, A., Love, A. (1996), 'A discourse of Disillusionment: Letters to the Editor in two Zimbabwean Magazines 10 years After Independence', *Discourse and Society*, 7: 1, pp. 39–75.

Papacharissi, Z. (2002), 'The Virtual Sphere: The Internet as a Public Sphere', *New Media & Society*, 4, pp. 9–27.

Philips, L., Jørgensen, M. W. (2002), *Discourse Analysis as Theory and Method*, London: Sage Publications.

Wiklund, H. (2005), 'A Habermasian Analysis of the Deliberative Democratic Potential of ICT-Enabled Services in Swedish Municipalities', *New Media & Society*, 7, pp. 247–70.

Witschge, T. (2004), 'Online Deliberation: Possibilities of the Internet for Deliberative Democracy', in P. Shane (ed.), *Democracy Online: The Prospects for Political Renewal through the Internet*, New York, NY: Routledge, pp. 109–22.

Journalism, Media, and Democracy

Nico Carpentier

Nordenstreng's (1995) description of the journalist as 'a walking paradox' already shows the difficulty that any attempt towards defining journalism has to face. A nevertheless comfortable starting point is McNair's (1998: 4) definition in *The Sociology of Journalism*.

> *Any authored text, in written, audio or visual form, which claims to be (i.e. is presented to its audience as) a truthful statement about, or record of, some hitherto unknown (new) feature of the actual, social world.*

Journalistic practices are embedded in a wide range of discourses. Journalistic ethics and ritualistic procedures (Tuchman, 1972) that try to convert these discourses into materialized practices are necessary guarantees for the integrity, reliability, and status of journalists as 'truth speakers' (by analogy with Foucault, 1978) or 'truth-reporters'. McNair (1998: 13) refers to a system of professional ethics, aesthetic codes, and routine practices that orient the journalist's work. Oledzki (1998: 286–288) calls this entanglement the 'triad of professionalism', in which next to technical skills, also relevant knowledge and ethics/deontology figure.

Furthermore, journalists are also embedded in organizational structures that are often commercial entities. Despite the seperatist tendencies, they can rarely be detached from the organization in which they operate and in which they are often (under different statutes) employed. These media organizations also form important frames of reference for journalists. Not only do they receive (as beginning staff members) an 'on the job training' (or socialization) (McQuail, 1994: 200) in this organization, which makes them accustomed to the current practices and teaches them the necessary skills and capabilities; at the same time these environments form micro-biotopes of peers ('a private world' as Burns already remarked in 1969). Or as Schlesinger (1987: 107) puts it, 'to over-simplify a little, the argument goes that journalists write for other journalists, their bosses, their sources, or highly interested audiences.'

A number of core concepts structure the identity of journalists. At the level of identity formation, these identity components can be attributed hegemonic ambitions, as they are considered to be so crucial to the journalist's identity that it is difficult to see beyond their taken-for-grantedness. Lichtenberg (1996: 225) has called objectivity 'a cornerstone of the professional ideology of journalists in liberal democracies'. Westerståhl's model of objectivity (1983) links a wide set of concepts – factuality, relevance, truth(fullness), impartiality, balance, and neutrality – to this key notion of objectivity. Especially factual accuracy is considered vital to the journalist's professional activity, as it is with 'no doubt the most sacred belief held among journalists worldwide' (Norderstreng, 1995: 115). Another set of elements is linked to the notions of autonomy and independence, or the need to resist different forms of (internal and external) pressures. Being part of the traditional paradoxes, which characterize capitalist (media) economies, this is combined with the need for professional employment, which necessitates different protective strategies to negotiate the employer – employee relationship and to prevent infringements on journalistic autonomies. A third group of concepts that structure the journalistic identity are responsibility, property, and management (Carpentier, 2005). Journalists are responsible within their organization for the professional production of specific media products. From this position, they can exert forms of psychological property (Wilpert, 1991) and act as managers of a diversity of resources – from technology via content to people – to realize these professional goals. Consequently, the relationships with the non-professional 'other' needs to be regulated, and notions as respect, confidentiality, privacy, consent, taste, and decency (see Campbell, 2004: 132–141) thus become integrated within these identity discourses.

The more traditional models attempting to explain the media–democracy relationship stress the crucial importance of the journalist's role in distributing information that enables citizens to exercise formal (through elections) and informal (through 'public opinion') control over the state. In this line of thought, journalists also fulfil a controlling function by taking on the role of watchdog or the fourth estate, bringing the dysfunctions of state and market to the attention of the citizenry. More critical approaches have emphasized the role of ideology in these representational practices that sometimes renders the watchdog into a lapdog or even a guard dog (protecting vested interests) (Watson, 2003: 105).

The main argument here is that journalists and media organizations are not situated outside ideology and will influence and be influenced by the ideologies, which circulate in society at a given time and space. Hall (1973) here distinguishes between the formal and the ideological level of news value, the latter belonging to the moral-political discourse in society. He refers to a 'double articulation' that 'binds the inner discourse of the newspaper to the ideological universe of the society [...] Events enter the domain of ideology as soon as they become visible to the news-making process.' Similar support for this line of thought can be found in Westerståhl and Johansson's (1994) model of news factors in foreign news, where ideology is placed at the very core of the model.

These critiques launched at the traditional approach towards journalism and at its minimalist attitude towards the journalist's democratic 'functions' have also generated a number of journalistic reform projects. These reform projects emphasize that journalism has more than one democratically valuable role to play and use a more maximalist perspective on the media–democracy relationship. This also implies that they aim to rearticulate (some of) the earlier mentioned key concepts that structure the hegemonic journalistic identity.

Both development [1] and emancipatory journalism and public journalism have reacted against a too absolutist interpretation of neutrality. In development and emancipatory journalism, it is explicitly stated that neutrality does not apply when universal values – such as peace, democracy, human rights, (gender and racial) equality, (social) progress, and national liberation – are at stake. The US-based public journalism-tradition takes a similar position in their plea for reviving the public debate, for centralizing democracy as a universalized value and for a tighter link between community and journalism – the so-called 'community connectedness'. The critique aimed at the traditional articulation of impartiality and the resulting 'detachment from the community', does not mean that any other form of objectivity should be rejected. In his book *Doing Public Journalism* Charity (1995: 144) summarizes this pithily, 'journalism should advocate democracy without advocating particular solutions'. The area of tension between involvement and neutrality, and the new interpretation that the concept of neutrality consequently receives, is captured by Manca's (1989: 170–171) concept of 'pluralist objectivity'.

Traditions like new journalism and human-interest journalism have pleaded for the centralizing of subjectivity (instead of objectivity). Especially in new journalism – developed in the United States during the 1960s – the undermining of the principle of objectivity is an explicit goal. On the one hand this applies to the subjectivity of the journalist, who now participates in the events, '[the new journalists] developed the habit of staying with the people they were writing about for days at a time, weeks in same cases' (Wolfe, 1973: 38). The literary techniques used in new journalism are in many cases functional towards the outlining of the personality (or otherwise put, the exposing of the identity) of the 'characters' that appear in the pieces. Human-interest journalism will – together with what Campbell (2004) calls entertainment journalism and lifestyle journalism – build on this tradition by putting the accent on soft news and authenticity and by resisting the neutrality, impersonality, and factuality of 'traditional' journalism. Narrative aspects of the news also become more important in the human-interest (news) tradition; Schudson (1978) refers in this regard to 'story journalism'. The emphasis on narration turns the media professional more into a storyteller than into an 'authorized truthteller' or a 'licensed relayer of facts' (McNair, 1998: 65), as he/she is called in 'traditional' journalism. Though widely used, human-interest journalism, thus, still remains distinct from (and contested by) 'traditional' journalism, as for instance Meijer (2001: 193) puts it, 'the conventional view [still highlights] rationality, conflict, and content rather than emotionality, dialogue and impact'.

Finally, also in the alternative media models that explicitly foreground participation, heavy critique on the hegemonic articulation of the professional identity can be found. In contrast, two-way communication and the right to communicate figure prominently in these models. Seen by Jacobson (1998: 135) as a human right of the third generation, connected to the New World Information and Communication Order (NWICO) movement, the right to communicate transcends the traditional Western right to be informed; 'communication is [...] seen as a two way process, in which the partners - individual and collective- carry on a democratic and balanced dialogue' (MacBride, 1980: 172). These alternative models support in other words the democratization of communication, in which the receiver is seen as point of departure and in which is pleaded for increasing participation and for making media more accessible to non-professionals from different positions and backgrounds. This of course also pressurizes the privileged position of the 'traditional' male/white journalist, who is seen as part of the (media) elite. One of the basic starting points of, for example, the community media movement is precisely the idea that journalistic tasks must not (and should not) be taken on exclusively by media professionals, but that members of the community – within which such media are active – can also take this role on them. The resistance against the professionalized media is seen as one of the reasons for the origin and existence of the community media in which an anti-elitist discourse is to be considered crucial (Girard, 1992; McQuail, 1994: 131).

In offering both alternative identities and practices, these journalistic reform projects show that it is possible to resist the hegemonic articulation of the journalist's identity. Their existence illustrates that journalism is a house with many rooms or, to put it less metaphorically, there is not just one journalism but a diversity of journalisms. This diversity of journalistic identities and practices also leads to a diversity of positions towards our western democracies, some of which will be more maximalist, whilst others will remain to be more minimalist. Especially these maximalist approaches will allow journalists to be more than gatekeepers and to act as 'gate-openers' (Manca, 1989).

Notes for Section Three: Introduction

[1] Development journalism is the older and more common name for this tradition. Emancipatory journalism has been developed as a model by Shah (1996) later on, and puts more stress on the role of journalists within new social movements.

References for Section Three: Introduction

Campbell, V. (2004), *Information Age Journalism. Journalism in an International Context*, New York: Arnold.

Carpentier, N. (2005), 'Identity, Contingency and Rigidity. The (Counter-) Hegemonic Constructions of the Identity of the Media Professional', *Journalism*, 6: 2, pp. 199–219.

Charity, A. (1995), *Doing Public Journalism*, New York: Guildford.

Foucault, M. (1978), *History of Sexuality, Part 1: An Introduction*, New York: Pantheon.

Girard, B. (1992), *A Passion for Radio*, Montréal: Black Rose Books.

Hall, S. (1973), 'The Determination of News Photographs', in S. Cohen and J. Young (eds.), *The Manufacture of News: Social Problems, Deviance and the Mass Media*, London: Constable, pp. 226–43.

Jacobson, T. L. (1998), 'Discourse Ethics and the Right to Communicate', *Gazette*, 60: 5, pp. 395–413.

Lichtenberg, J. (1996), 'In Defence of Objectivity Revisited', in J. Curran and Michael Gurevitch (eds.), *Mass Media and Society*, London, New York, Sydney, Auckland: Arnold, pp. 225–42.

MacBride, S. (1980), *Many Voices, One World. Report by the International Commission for the Study of Communication Problems*, Paris and London: Unesco & Kogan Page.

Manca, L. (1989), 'Journalism, Advocacy, and a Communication Model for Democracy', in M. Raboy and P. Bruck (eds.), *Communication for and Against Democracy*, Montréal – New York: Black Rose Books, pp. 163–73.

McNair, B. (1998), *The Sociology of Journalism*, London, New York, Sydney, Auckland: Arnold.

McQuail, D. (1994), *Mass Communication Theory. An Introduction*, London: Sage.

Meijer, I. C. (2001), 'The Public Quality of Popular Journalism: Developing a Normative Framework', *Journalism Studies*, 2: 2, pp. 189–205.

Nordenstreng, K. (1995), 'The Journalist: a Walking Paradox', in P. Lee (ed.), *The Democratization of Communication*, Cardiff: University of Wales Press, pp. 114–29.

Oledzki, J. (1998), 'Polish Journalists: Professionals or Not?', in D. H. Weaver (ed.), *The Global Journalist. News People Around the World*, Cresskill, New Jersey: Hampton press, pp. 277–97.

Schlesinger, P. (1987), *Putting 'Reality' Together*, London and New York: Methuen.

Schudson, M. (1978), *Discovering the News*, New York: Basic Books.

Shah, H. (1996), 'Modernization, Marginalization, and Emancipation, Toward a Normative Model of Journalism and National Development', *Communication Theory*, 6: 2, pp. 143–66.

Tuchman, G. (1972), 'Objectivity as a Strategic Ritual: an Examination of Newsmen's Notions of Objectivity', *American Journal of Sociology*, 77, pp. 660–79.

Watson, J. (2003), *Media Communication: An Introduction to Theory and Process*, New York: Palgrave Macmillan.

Westerståhl, J. (1983), 'Objective News Reporting', *Communication Research*, 10, pp. 403–24.

Westerståhl, J., Johansson, F. (1994), 'Foreign News: News Values and Ideologies', *European Journal of Communication*, 9: 1, pp. 71–89.

Wilpert, B. (1991), 'Property, Ownership, and Participation: on the Growing Contradictions Between Legal and Psychological Concepts', in R. Russell and V. Rus (eds.), *International Handbook of Participation in Organisations (ii.), Ownership and Participation*, Oxford: Oxford University Press, pp. 149–64.

Wolfe, T. (1973), *The New Journalism*, New York, Evanston, San Francisco, London: Harper & Row.

Chapter Seven

Coping with the agoraphobic media professional: a typology of journalistic practices reinforcing democracy and participation

Nico Carpentier

Introduction

This chapter offers a prescriptive typology of journalistic practices reinforcing democracy and participation [1] that wants to provide the broadest answer possible to the following question: how can mainstream media, active within non-fiction, stimulate active citizenship and work in a democracy-supporting way? The starting point for this question, (and thus for this chapter), validates active citizenship and a well-developed democracy, from a formal-democratic point of view as well as from a perspective that focuses on democratic practices and cultures; from a (narrow) approach of the political system, as well as from a (broad) perspective of the political as a dimension that entails the social. Moreover, this starting point brackets (at least initially) the specific democratic developments of specific states, as it is contented that in all European states (albeit in sometimes very different ways) the media system's democratic role still need to grow and to be expanded.

After a quick and superficial reading, it appears to be quite easy to generate a number of singular answers to this question. However, its basic concepts, citizenship, and democracy cannot be easily defined in a singular way, since they encapsulate very different – sometimes even contradictory – meanings. The media's role in this myriad of meanings and significations, thus, also becomes problematic to be univocally described, and we now need to find a way to deal with the lack of a homogenous theory regarding the role of the media, the media professional [2] and the citizen within democracy.

The main explanation for this significatory complexity and dispersed answers to this simple question can be found in the theoretical and ideological positions that structure the models that claim to answer the question. They are all based on specific worldviews that have different ways of dealing with Western basic values such as freedom, equality, and justice. However, this does not imply that all models carry an equal weight and their impact on the social is evenly balanced. Some of these models have indeed managed to conquer a dominant position in the theories and practices related to the media and democracy. At the same time, Sayyid and Zac's (1998: 262) words need to be kept in mind: 'Hegemony is always possible but can never be total'. Their words remind us that there are attempts – alternative media models and journalistic reform projects – that try to break with these hegemonic articulations of the media/democracy relationship.

Given the diversity and richness of these models, the traditional approach to simply list and compare them can quickly be abandoned. In stead, both the dominant and the alternative models are re-analyzed and scrutinized in relation to the democratic and participatory tools they have to offer. This also implies that the general truth claims, ethical values, or practical relevance of the separate theoretical frameworks is not under discussion; their ideological load is (temporarily) bracketed. The premise of this article is that the democratic and participatory practices that are promoted by these different models are complementary (and sometimes overlapping) and can be grouped into one overarching typology. The models that theorize – all in their own way – the media/democracy relationship will be used as building block for this typology.

Normative theory, journalistic reform, and democracy

It is no coincidence that in the Western media studies literature the theories on the (democratic) role of the media within society can be found under the denominator of 'normative theories'. The often quoted American starting point here is the book *Four Theories of the Press* written by Siebert, Peterson, and Schramm (1956), based on the work of the Hutchins commission (1947) that even today contains quite a few positions that remain surprisingly contemporary. In this book, the authors describe four theories regarding the (written) press, of which two models [3] are especially relevant in this context: the liberal (or libertarian) model and the model of social responsibility.

The liberal model focuses strongly on information, but this media function is complemented by their role as a watchdog in order to control the authorities and by the need to create an independent forum for debate, a so-called market place of ideas. In the social responsibility model, these functions are further completed by stressing the importance of correct representations of social groups [4] and of providing a 'truthful, comprehensive and intelligent account' of 'the day's events in a context which gives them meaning' (Hutchins, 1947 quoted by Siebert *et al.*, 1956: 87). As the *Four Theories of the Press* was considered to be too reductive [5], McQuail (1994) added two more models: the development model and the participatory–democratic model [6]. Both models focus on the participatory role of the mass media. They support the right to communicate, defining communication as a two-way process, based on dialogue and interaction. This is combined with an emphasis on the democratization of communication, facilitating non-professionals' access and participation in the content as well as in the content-producing media organizations.

Five basic components that provide the foundations for the media/democracy relationship can be deduced from these normative theories [7]. These five basic functions are:

- The informative function
- The control function
- The representative function
- The forum function
- The participatory function.

Inspired by the research of Drijvers and his colleagues (2002) and driven by the need to avoid a too functionalist approach, this list of five media functions is reworked in four clusters that will structure the typology. First, the strictly informative cluster groups the informative and control function, as both functions focus on the production of information, be it critical or not. Second, as the difference between the representation of communities and subgroups on the one hand and the representation of the political on the other is vital in this context, the representative function is divided into two clusters, one regarding the representation of the social, focussing on a community and its subgroups. A second cluster deals with the representation of the political. Both clusters contain elements of the forum function. These forums create spaces for self-representation (as individuals, but inevitably also as members of societal subgroups) and contain a diversity of discourses (cluster 2). As the forum function also relates (indirectly) to creating 'market places of ideas' and/or 'public spheres', this function is also related to the representation of the political as such (cluster 3). But the strongest link is between the forum function and the participatory function, as these forums are (at least) aimed at enhancing audience participation. Given the importance of media access, interaction, and participation, these aspects are grouped in the fourth participatory cluster (cluster 4).

Despite the importance of these normative theories, media functions, and the resulting clusters, more input for this typology is required as the normative models (for obvious reasons) remain rather generalist in their approach. This additional input can be found in a number of journalistic reform projects [8] that all offer specific toolkits for media reform. These models will play a supportive role in this text, although they will be – whenever necessary – slightly adapted for usage in a European context.

A first group of reform projects is development and emancipatory journalism, peace journalism, and public or civil/c journalism. Crucial to these projects is their resistance against a too absolute interpretation of the principle of neutrality. In the tradition of development and emancipatory journalism – which should mainly be situated in developing countries – it is explicitly stated that neutrality does not apply when universalized [9] values such as peace, democracy, human rights, equality (gender and racial), progress (social), and national liberation, are at stake. Peace journalism puts the emphasis on avoiding conflict-oriented journalism and on the importance of structural and solution-oriented approaches, building on the universalized value of peace. And quite similarly vice versa the two previous reform projects, the US-based public journalism tradition pleads for reviving the public debate and for centralizing democracy as a universalized value. At the same time, advocates of public journalism plead for a tighter link between community and journalism – the so-called 'community connectedness' (Rosen, 1994: 371). This connectedness runs counter to the detachment that is said to be contained in the concept of impartiality. Their critique on impartiality and the 'detachment from the community' that lies behind it does not imply that any other form of objectivity should be rejected. In the words of Merritt (1995: 116), journalists still have to keep their 'neutrality on specifics'. Media have to respect the social pluralism and promote it in order to establish and preserve the democratic achievements. The area of tension between involvement and neutrality, and the new interpretation that the concept of neutrality consequently receives, is captured by Manca (1989: 170–171) and his concept of 'pluralist objectivity'.

A second group of journalistic reform projects combines new journalism and human-interest journalism. These traditions plead for the centralizing of subjectivity (instead of objectivity). Especially in new journalism – developed in the United States during the 1960s – the undermining of the principle of objectivity is an explicit goal. This also applies to the subjectivity of the journalist, who now participates in the events: '[the new journalists] developed the habit of staying with the people they were writing about for days at a time, weeks in same cases' (Wolfe, 1973: 38). The literary techniques used in new journalism are in many cases functional towards the outlining of the personality (or put otherwise: the exposing of the identity) of the 'characters' that appear in the pieces. Human-interest journalism will, in part, build on new journalism by putting the accent on soft news and on authenticity, and by resisting the neutrality, impersonality, and factuality of 'traditional' journalism. The additional emphasis on the 'personal lives, joys, tragedies, and varied activities of other people, particularly those in high places or in familiar settings' (Graber, 1994: 212) will also lead to a shift towards the private sphere, a process that Van Zoonen (1997) describes as intimization [10]. Third, the narrative aspects of the news are also stressed in the tradition of human interest (news): Schudson (1978) refers in this regard to 'story journalism'. The emphasis on narration turns the media professional more into a storyteller than an 'authorized truthteller' (McNair, 1998: 65). Though widely used, human-interest journalism still remains distinct from (and contested by) 'traditional' journalism, as for instance Meijer (2001: 193) puts it: 'the conventional view [highlights] rationality, conflict, and content rather than emotionality, dialogue and impact'.

Four clusters of the typology

As mentioned before, the structure of this typology of democratic and participatory journalistic practices is based on the discussion on normative theory, which resulted in four clusters: a strictly informative cluster, a cluster on the representation of the social as a community with her constitutive subgroups, a cluster regarding the representation of the political, and a participatory cluster. Within each cluster, different dimensions are defined. When elaborating these specific dimensions, inspiration was mainly found in the practices promoted by the different journalistic reform projects. Although the structure of this typology, with its four clusters and twelve dimensions, is partially inspired by the analysis of a journalists' survey (Drijvers et al., 2002), it of course remains only one of many possible forms of systematizing this complex reality.

Cluster 1: Information and control

The democratic importance of information is emphasized in most theoretical models. The liberal model touches the heart of this argumentation, affirming that independent media – by putting information at people's disposition – enable citizens to formally and informally control the state (or in other words, the political system). The media's watchdog function follows naturally from this line of argument: any dysfunction of the state (and by extension: of the market) should be tracked down and brought to public attention by the media. Offering critical information is, therefore, considered an important democratic media task.

One should however keep in mind that information is not a neutral concept. On a first level the, problems of the selection and distribution of information and the related processes of societal surveillance has been part of academic scrutiny for decades. Only the question of whose information will be offered illustrates the difficulties hidden behind the notion of information. Furthermore, it is epistemologically impossible to map out the exact boundaries between 'factual' information and the representations information contains. Factuality builds on representational regimes that are unavoidable in their presence, varied in their nature, and at the same time targeted by hegemonic projects. A specific problem here is that these informational flows sometimes provide us with representations that we can only describe as stereotypical. A classic example is that of the information given on the African continent, which is strongly associated with conflict and underdevelopment (and with 'hunger' in particular; see Boschman et al., 1996).

Despite the importance of these nuances, the distinction between information and representation remains crucial for analytical purposes, as some of the potentially democracy enhancing practices are well embedded within this strictly informative cluster. In this first cluster, five dimensions are included, which all (potentially) enable citizens (individually or collectively) to participate (more and better) in a democratic society. Within all five dimensions, the truthfulness of the information is considered a necessary condition. These aspects are:

Dimension 1: comprehensible and accessible information
Dimension 2: information oriented on social (inter)action
Dimension 3: positive information
Dimension 4: structural information
Dimension 5: critical information (the control and watchdog function)

The first dimension formulates the necessary condition for all democratic communication, namely its comprehensibility and accessibility, in order to prevent mechanisms of exclusion. The three following dimensions are (each in their own way) related to the empowerment of the audience. Information oriented on social (inter)action (dimension 2) makes it possible to – as affirmed by Alex Puissant (2000: 28) in his comments on the instruments of Public journalism – 'systematically inform people about all the occasions they are given to participate in discussions and civil activities [considered relevant]'. This kind of information also pays attention to initiatives from within civil society, aimed at complementing the information on the political system.

Positive information (dimension 3) also contains such an action-oriented component by for instance giving 'large and small examples of people who had made some difference' (Merritt, 1995: 89). The underlying reason is that an overload of negative information risks creating paralyzing effects. Consequently, such an overload would not motivate or stimulate citizens' active engagement. Structural information (dimension 4) allows audiences to contextualize news events and to see them as part of long-term evolutions and social phenomena. Although structural information is often seen in contrast to personalized information, an underestimation of the socio-political value of private and/or individual experiences should be avoided. This structural information dimension is related to the fifth dimension, which focuses on critical information, which – as has been said before – reveals dysfunctions within the functioning of the state and the market.

These five dimensions of the strictly informative cluster find themselves in a complex field of tension towards each other. The dimensions (and the entire typology) should, therefore, be seen as a scale. The plea for more comprehensible information, for instance, is not a retreat into simplicities and is not aimed at (completely) undermining the expert's status. In the same way, the plea for more communication that stimulates social (inter)action should not be interpreted as a legitimization for narrowing down (or dumbing-down) the information on the political system. Finally, the plea for an increase in positive news should not be used as an excuse to (further) cut down on more critical journalism. This typology of journalistic practices aimed at reinforcing democracy and participation structurally incorporates the permanent need for balancing the more traditional practices with some of the alternatives introduced here.

Cluster 2: The representation of the social: community/ies and constituting social subgroups

The concept of representation has also obtained a prominent place in different normative models, emphasizing the need to avoid misrepresentations and stereotyping. Building on this need for fair – sometimes also called 'correct' – representations of more traditional social groups like immigrants and women [11], a broader approach is introduced here. This broadened approach considers the audience as a conglomerate of all kinds of subgroups, small- and large-scale communities, criss-crossed by differences related to class, ethnicity and gender. This diversity also includes (representations of) 'ordinary people' [12], seen here as active citizens capable of participating in the public debate. 'Ordinary people' are often shown and given the floor in order to access their authentic experiences. In this fashion, these experiences gain public relevance, thus granting them (possible) political relevance (Livingstone and Lunt, 1996: 102). The importance of respectfully representing the citizenry within the public sphere should however not remain limited to accessing individual affects. Representing citizenship includes the creation of imaginaries of citizens organizing themselves in order to rationally and emotionally defend their (collective) interests and developing a series of public activities from within civil society. It is this complex combination of individuals and collectivities, organizations, and societal categories that shapes the nation as an 'imagined community' (Anderson, 1983) or as a political community. Finally, the importance of self-representation cannot go unmentioned in the discussion of the second cluster. Emphasizing the importance of access and participation (see later in cluster 4) of for instance marginalized and misrepresented groups, often via so-called community media, enables these groups to control their own representations, and be present in (one of) the public sphere(s).

This cluster includes two specific dimensions, on the one hand, an orientation towards the audience and the community (dimension 6), and on the other hand, the importance of pluriform representations (dimension 7). Media products aiming to reinforce democracy and participation need to focus on their audiences and communities, instead of using a medium-oriented – one could also say self-centred – approach. At the same time, one needs to take the complex, situated, and multi-layered meaning of the term 'audience' into account. The 'audience' is always part of all sorts of intertwined groups, communities, and organizations and cannot be reduced to merely quantitative behavioral data.

Putting these complex and active audiences at the centre of the media attention allows articulating them as directly concerned stakeholders and enables the media to increase their community connectedness.

The seventh dimension starts from the (representation of) specific (misrepresented) groups. Based on the argument of equality, it can be argued that all social groups have to be able to gain access to the media landscape. Likewise, these social groups have the right to feel correctly represented. The mere presence of members of different social subgroups, avoiding what Tuchman (1978) has called their symbolic annihilation, is a first necessary condition. One step further is to focus on their active presence, avoiding that they disappear into the background. Third, it is important to guard against the presence of stereotypes [13]. Smelik and her colleagues (1999: 45) summarize these points by contrasting forms of stereotypical representation (that are to be avoided) with the notion of what they call 'pluriform representation'. Here, members of misrepresented groups are actively present. Moreover, the duality of the oppositions that characterizes stereotypes is deconstructed, thus, enabling a greater diversity of societal representations. Hall (1997: 274) adds to the list of possible strategies the importance of working from within the complexities and ambiguities of representation. He pleads in other words for 'contest[ing stereotypes] from within'.

Cluster 3: Representation of the political

The representation of political and democratic practices *an sich* also plays an important role in this typology. In this context, it is essential to first assess which interpretation is given to the floating signifier [14] 'democracy', as it is often wrongly assumed that 'democracy' is a stable concept with a fixed signification. This way, three essential elements are ignored: the variety of democratic manifestations and variants, the distinction between formal democracy and democratic cultures and practices, and the distinction between the narrow-political system ('politics') and the broad-political dimension of the social (the 'political').

Especially this last distinction is of importance in this context: the political can be defined, following for instance Schumpeter (1976), as the privilege of specific competing elites, while it can also be broadly defined as a dimension of the social. To put this differently, this interpretation deals with the distinction between centralized and decentralized societal decision-making. In the construction of this typology, the emphasis is placed on the more decentralized societal decision-making [15], since this is a necessary condition for active citizenship. Another essential difference is the distinction between consensus and conflict-oriented approaches of the political. Here, it does remain of crucial importance to take both the consensus and the conflict-oriented approaches into account. The rationale for this choice can be found in the radical contingency of the social that leads to an oscillation between stability and conflict. A mere focus on stability and consensus would foreclose the openness of the social and would imply an almost Hegelian belief in the end of history.

Consensus-oriented models of democracy largely built upon the notion of societal dialogue and deliberation, where collective decision-making takes place based on rational arguments, 'with the participation of all who will be affected by the decision or by their representatives. [...] it includes decision making by means of arguments offered by and to participants who are committed to the values of rationality and impartiality' (Elster, 1998: 8). As Glasser and Craft (1998: 213) rightfully remark, this does not necessarily mean that everybody is given the floor, but it does mean that 'everything worth saying gets said'. In contrast, conflict-oriented models focus on political differences and struggles. Although even these approaches still need to be based on a total ('hegemonic') consensus regarding basic democratic values, within the boundaries of this core consensus, a complete lack of consensus on any other theme is perfectly possible and acceptable. In such a pluralist democracy, decision-making takes place on the basis of political struggle and debate. As Mouffe (1994: 109) writes, 'The prime task of democratic politics is not to eliminate passions, nor to relegate them to the private sphere in order to render rational consensus possible, but to mobilize these passions, and give them a democratic outlet'. This position shows some similarities with Edward Said's (1995: 12) broader plea for a 'universal' criterion 'regarding the suffering and the oppression of mankind [...] in spite of political party bonds, national background or ingrained loyalty', however without falling back into an essentialist interpretation of the social and the political. It is suggested in this chapter, for this discussion on media and democracy, that this 'universal' criterion holds five universalisable values: democracy, peace, freedom, equality, and justice. Following Mouffe, it remains important to emphasize that the concrete interpretation and articulation of these basic values are embedded in political struggles.

Three dimensions of the typology fall within this cluster. The more general dimension that covers the orientation towards a broad political and decentralized societal decision-making (dimension 8) is complemented by two more specific dimensions: providing an argument-based balance (dimension 9) and the defence of values considered universalized, a dimension that is termed here pluralist neutrality [16] (dimension 10).

Dimension 8 refers to the importance of societal deliberation, dialogue, and debate. Care is taken to avoid the reduction of the political to the political system and of news and information to what Gans (2003: 45) calls 'top-down news'. At the same time, this is a plea for more solution-oriented approaches. But this text cannot be seen as an over-simplified plea for the dialogue/deliberation model and the solution-oriented model, which would again contradict the ambition to avoid a dichotomization of the typology. I do however plead for a more balanced approach between dialogue/deliberation and debate, between (information regarding) social consensus and social conflict, and between (information about) solutions and problems. In a mediated context, this implies that one represents issues as a conflict only when these issues really do take place within the framework of a (serious) conflict. And even in that situation, sufficient attention should be spent to conflict resolution, effectively representing a diversity of opinions, without generating polarization (a requirement articulated in peace journalism).

The notions of dialogue/deliberation and debate can also be applied to two basic components of the media professional's identity, namely strive for balance (dimension 9) and for neutrality (dimension 10). This again allows the re-articulation of these components in a way that is supportive towards social deliberation, dialogue, and debate. The ninth dimension pleads for a more argument-based balance (in stead of a party- or person-related balance) in journalism. This dimension is strongly tributary to the theoretical reflections on deliberation, where the arguments (and not the persons) take in a central position. Their application implies that the social diversity of discourses and arguments, and the context within which they are situated, are taken into account.

The tenth dimension directs the focus towards the ideological-normative context. Especially in reform projects as public journalism and development journalism, journalistic neutrality is said to be no longer valid in situations where the values considered universalized are under threat. As mentioned before, the universalisable values that can be mentioned in this context are restricted in numbers: democracy (and resistance against dictatorship and tyranny), peace (and resistance against war and violence), freedom (and resistance against human right violations), equality (and resistance against discrimination), and justice (and resistance against oppression and social inequality).

Cluster 4: The participatory role

From a participation-oriented point of view (in the strict sense of the word participation – see Pateman, 1970: 70–71), access of non-professionals to media organizations (and to their media professionals) and participation in the production of media output and in media decision-making is seen as an – often unequally balanced – power process. Not withstanding this inequality, power relations need to be considered in a Foucauldian sense as mobile and multidirectional. In short, no one is ever rendered completely powerless and resistance against unequal power balances always remains a possibility. Power relations are two-way relations, even when the power of one actor seems limited in comparison to that of the other actor [17]. The questions formulated in the context of mass media-production regarding this power process are relatively simple: who 'can' take what decision and what degree of participation is allowed for? In order to formulate an answer to these questions, a distinction is made between content-related participation and structural participation.

On the one hand, participation can be considered in relation to the produced content (dimension 11), which puts the media product in a central position. Consequently, the following questions become relevant. To which extent can citizens participate in the production process of specific content? What are the power relations between the media professional and the members of 'the audience' within this production process? To which extent (and how) can these citizens be present in the media product itself? When this kind of civil participation becomes visible, it also supports more active representations of citizens and their presence within the public sphere. The British television and web project *Video Nation* illustrates that the obstacles can effectively be reduced when the involved media professionals adopt an open, honest, respectful, process-oriented, and (micro-)participatory attitude, based on a thorough analysis of the power processes and imbalances (Carpentier, 2003).

On the other hand, it is possible to focus more on structural media participation (dimension 12), putting the media organization and its policies at the centre of attention. In this case, the emphasis is placed on the power balances within the decision-making processes of media organizations and on the participation of members of the audience in the programming, policy, and administration [18] of media organizations as such. An example can be found in the French 'Société des lecteurs du Monde' (SDL) that held in 2005 10.43% of the stock shares of the Le Monde SA group [19]. The legitimization for this kind of participation can be found in the rationale that (when decentralizing democracy) the democratic principles also need to be implemented within the different (organized) micro spheres of the social, thus including the different media organizations. This form of participation enables citizens to be active within one of the many micro spheres of the social, where decisions are made that have a real impact on – and are relevant to – citizens' daily lives. At the same time, it needs to be accepted that because of its radicalism, this form of participation is the most difficult to realize.

Four clusters, twelve dimensions, and one typology

When the different dimensions are (finally) brought together into one model, this results in the overview rendered in Table 1. It cannot be stressed enough that this typology is based on the plea for the reorientation of the existing choices made within contemporary media systems. It does not support the ambition to privilege one side of the model over the other, just the plea for finding new balances.

From the perspective of continued and deepened democratization, the situation that is considered most desirable for the media cannot be simply found on one side of the typology, but requires complex considerations of the different building blocks of this typology, without disregarding the context in which the mainstream media operate. At the same time, it is hardly feasible to take all twelve dimensions into account for the analysis – or for the production – of one specific media product. Rather, his typology has the ambition to offer a variety of possibilities, like a menu from which to choose *à la carte* but with good taste, depending on the (national) contexts but also on the ambitions of those involved.

Table 1:
Typology of democracy and participation-enhancing journalistic practices

Cluster 1: Information and control	
Dimension 1: Comprehensible and accessible information	No attention for comprehensible and accessible information
Dimension 2: Information oriented towards social (inter)action	No information oriented towards social (inter)action
Dimension 3: Positive information when possible and negative when necessary	Negative information
Dimension 4: Structural information	Personalized information
Dimension 5: Critical information (the control and watchdog function)	No critical information

Cluster 2: Representation of the social: community/ies and constituting social subgroups	
Dimension 6: Orientation towards the audience and the community	Media-oriented
• Active audience	• Passive audience
• Multi-layered audience	• Uni-dimensional audience as aggregate or mass
• Spaces for direct forums (direct forum function)	• No spaces for direct forums
• Community connectedness	• Detachment
• Empowerment of community as stakeholders	• Elite-oriented
Dimension 7: Pluriform representation of social subgroups	Stereotypical representations of social subgroups

Table 1: *(Continued)*

Cluster 3: Representation of the political	
Dimension 8: Orientation towards the broad-political and a decentralized societal decision-making	Orientation towards politics in the strict sense and a centralized societal decision-making by elites
• Solution-oriented when possible and conflict-oriented when necessary	• Conflict-oriented
• Orientation towards dialogue and deliberation when possible and towards debate when necessary	• Orientation towards debate
Dimension 9: Argument-based balance (indirect forum function or control function in the broad sense)	Party or people-based balance or no balance
Dimension 10: Pluralist neutrality (control function in the broadest sense)	Absolute or no neutrality

Cluster 4: Participatory role	
Dimension 11: Content-related participation	No attention for content-related participation and power balances
Dimension 12: Structural participation	No attention for (forms of) structural participation

Conclusions

The twelve-dimensional typology of journalistic practices described here that reinforce democracy and participation first of all illustrates the variety and the broadness of the arsenal of methods and practices that are at the media's disposal. The choice for an approach that tries to respect and extend the different ideologically inspired interpretations and projects has enabled me to build a model that encompasses a wide variety of possibilities. In spite of the fact that the mainstream media already make important contributions to our democracies, plenty of space for additional steps remains available. This typology makes it possible to validate existing practices as well as to implement new practices. They show – each in their own way – that it is possible and feasible to overcome prejudices and constraints in order to foster our democracies even more.

At the same time, the actual typology reveals the complexity of such practices. As is always the case when analyzing the workings of democracy, an ideal pathway does not exist, but needs to be negotiated and constructed over and over again.

The paths we finally choose to follow and the decisions that are made on the road are the result of an alternation between confrontation and dialogue, and remain always susceptible to criticism, contestation, and re-articulation. Therefore, the dimensional nature of the typology (including both poles) was explicitly articulated as part of the typology. This way the necessity to obtain a balance between both poles of each dimension and between the different dimensions is structurally integrated in this typology.

Implementing the choices that originate from this model is far from easy. The context in the different European states can be very different, and in some cases political resistance is to be expected. Not all states applaud when 'their' media become further engaged in the process of democratization. Other boundaries on which the media professionals and organizations stumble are also not to be underestimated. Putting democracy and participation to practice often demands more expertise, time, and financial resources than is considered relevant or acceptable by contemporary capitalist media organizations. For these reasons, external support (which could for instance be provided by a European fund for media democracy) seems to be a necessary condition for the sustained development of similar practices. At the same time it also demands the willingness of the media to question their own position and share more power than is the case at this moment in time.

It is, however, especially this kind of attitude and willingness that makes it possible to find creative solutions for these boundaries. Through continuous experimentation, it can be shown that many of these journalistic practices that reinforce democracy and participation demand less investment (except for an investment in willingness and goodwill) than expected. This way the mainstream media organizations can each find their own way to – as Drijvers *et al.* (2002) suggested – conquer their agoraphobia, to contribute in taking on their social responsibility and to reinforce the democratic quality of the mass media as a whole.

Notes for Chapter Seven

[1] This typology was developed as part of the 'Media and citizens' campaign of the Koning Boudewijn Foundation. The resulting publications are Carpentier *et al.*, 2002a, b, Carpentier and Grevisse (2004), and Grevisse and Carpentier (2004).

[2] The concept 'media professional' covers a broadly defined journalistic identity, including popular journalism (see Meijer, 2001).

[3] The authoritarian and Marxist-Leninist model are considered less relevant in the contemporary Western context.

[4] Siebert *et al.* (1956: 91) provide here the following (out-dated) clarification of this position: '[...] this requirement would have the press accurately portray

the social groups, the Chinese and the Negroes, for example, since persons tend to make decisions in terms of favorable or unfavorable images and a false picture can subvert accurate judgement'.

[5] See Nerone, 1995.

[6] In the fifth edition, the six models were replaced by the following four models: the liberal-pluralist model, the social responsibility model, the professional model, and the alternative media model (McQuail, 2005: 185–186).

[7] A relatively similar list can be found in Biltereyst *et al.*, 2000: 22.

[8] For a description of development and (specifically) emancipatory journalism, see Shah, 1996; for new journalism, see Wolfe, 1973, and Thompson, 1980; for human-interest journalism, see Harrington, 1997, and Meijer, 2000, 2001; for peace journalism, see Galtung and Vincent, 1992; and for public journalism, see Rosen, 1994, Merritt, 1995, 1998, Glasser and Craft, 1998, and Puissant, 2000.

[9] Values of course risk receiving Western interpretations. To better capture the required process of cultural dialogue when articulating them, the words 'universalized' and 'universalisable' are preferred.

[10] Van Zoonen (1997: 217) describes intimization as 'a growing attention to human interest subjects, an intimate and personal mode of address and the treatment of political behavior and issues as though they are matters of personality'. In this text, the evoluative aspect of this description – which lies in Van Zoonen's term 'growing' – is not taken into account, so that the accent on the personal can also be seen as a factual condition.

[11] In spite of the fact that Communication Studies focus on these two subgroups, it is evident that the discussion cannot be narrowed down to them. Others, like handicapped persons, gay/lesbian/bisexual people, children and elderly people (sometimes) also find themselves in inferior power positions. More radical examples of these social subgroups are homeless and poor people, prisoners and prostitutes.

[12] The concept of 'ordinary people' is often – following the footsteps of Laclau (1977) and Hall (1981) and Fiske (1993) – defined in a negative way by comparing it to the elite, the power bloc or – in the words of Livingstone and Lunt (1996: 9) – the 'elite representatives of established power'.

[13] Keeping Dyer's (1984) differentiation between types and stereotypes in mind.

[14] Based on Laclau and Mouffe (1985: 112–113).

[15] This plea for maximizing the possibilities of decentralized societal decision-making does not imply the abolishment of representative democracy, but offers an opportunity to deepen it.

[16] As Manca's (1989) concept of pluralist objectivity is considered too broad, it has been renamed as pluralist neutrality.

[17] More specifically, this approach is based on Foucault's (1984) so-called analytics of power.

[18] Here can be referred to Prehn's (1991: 259) interpretation of participation (in relation to community media) as 'involving people directly in station programming, administration and policy activities'.

[19] For more information, see the SDL-website at http://sdl.lemonde.fr/. In addition, the 'Société des Rédacteurs du Monde' (SRM) held in 2005 another 29.58% (Deshusses, 2005: 1). For a history of the SRM, see Eveno (2004).

References for Chapter Seven

Anderson, B. (1983), *Imagined Communities: Reflections on the Origin and Spread of Nationalism*, London: Verso.

Biltereyst, D., Van Bauwel, S., Meers, P. (2000), *Realiteit en Fictie: Tweemaal Hetzelfde?* Brussel: Koning Boudewijnstichting.

Boschman, B., Buckens, L., Rijsdijk, L. (1996), 'De Derde Wereld in Beeld. Beeldvorming als Sociale Constructie van de Realiteit', in J. Servaes and R. Lie (eds.), *Communicatie in Sociale Verandering, een Culturalistisch Perspectief*, Leuven: Acco, pp. 155–67.

Carpentier N., Grevisse B., Harzimont M. (2002a), *Tussen Woord en Daad. Journalistieke Praktijken die de Betrokkenheid van de Burger Vergroten*, Brussel: Koning Boudewijnstichting.

—— (2002b), *Médias et Citoyens sur la Même Longueur d'onde. Initiatives Journalistiques Favorisant la Participation Citoyenne*, Brussel: Koning Boudewijnstichting.

Carpentier, N. (2003), 'BBC's Video Nation as a Participatory Media Practice. Signifying Everyday Life, Cultural Diversity and Participation in an On-line Community', *International Journal of Cultural Studies*, 6: 4, pp. 425–47.

Carpentier, N., Grevisse, B. (2004), *Media in Beweging. 22 Journalistieke Experimenten om Burgerparticipatie te Versterken*, Brussel: Koning Boudewijnstichting.

Charity, A. (1995), *Doing Public Journalism*, New York: Guildford.

Deshusses, A. (2005), 'Plan de Recapitalisation du Groupe «Le Monde»: Pourquoi? Comment?', *Lettre de la Société des Lecteurs* 2 June 2005, 54, 1. http://sdl.lemonde.fr/fichiers/lettres/sdl_juin2005.pdf. Downloaded on 29 December 2005.

Drijvers, J., Galant, C., Cieters, P. (2002), 'Tussen Woord en Daad. De Opinie van de Mediaprofessionals', in N. Carpentier, B. Grevisse and M. Harzimont (eds.), *Tussen Woord en Daad. Journalistieke Praktijken die de Betrokkenheid van de Burger Vergroten*, Brussel: Koning Boudewijnstichting, pp. TNS 1–23.

Dyer, R. (1984), 'Stereotyping', in R. Dyer (ed.), *Gays and Film*, New York: Zeotrope, pp. 27–39.

Elster, J. (1998), *Deliberative Democracy,* Cambridge, Cambridge University Press.

Eveno, P. (2004), *Histoire du Journal Le Monde 1944-2004,* Paris: Albin Michel.

Fiske, J. (1993), *Power Plays/Power Works*, London and New York: Verso.

Foucault, M. (1984), *De Wil tot Weten. Geschiedenis van de Seksualiteit 1*, Nijmegen: SUN.

Galtung, J., Vincent, R. (1992), *Global Glasnost: Toward a New World Information and Communication Order?*, Cresskill: Hampton Press.

Gans, H. (2003), *Democracy and the News*, New York: Oxford University Press.

Glasser, T. L., Craft, S. (1998), 'Public Journalism and the Search for Democratic Ideals', in T. Liebes and J. Curran (eds.), *Media, Ritual and Identity*, London: Routledge, pp. 203–18.

Graber, D. (1994), *Processing the News: How People Tame the Information Tide*, Lanham, New York, London: University Press of America.

Grevisse, B., Carpentier, N. (2004), *Des Médias Qui Font Bouger. 22 Expériences Journalistiques Favorisant la Participation Citoyenne*, Brussel: Koning Boudewijnstichting.

Hall, S. (1981), 'Notes on Deconstructing "The Popular"', in R. Samuel (ed.), *People's History and Socialist Theory*, London: Routledge and Kegan Paul, pp. 227–40.

—— (1997), 'The Spectacle of the Other', in S. Hall (ed.), *Representation: Cultural Representations and Signifying Practices*, London: Sage, pp. 223–90.

Harrington, W. (1997), *Intimate Journalism: the Art and Craft of Reporting Everyday Life*, London: Sage.

Hutchins, R. (1947), *'Commission on the Freedom of the Press',* a Free and Responsible, Press. Chicago: University of Chicago Press.

Laclau, E. (1977), *Politics and Ideology in Marxist Theory: Capitalism, Fascism, Populism*, London: New Left Books.

Laclau, E., Mouffe, C. (1985), *Hegemony and Socialist Strategy: Towards a Radical Democratic Politics*, London: Verso.

Livingstone, S., Lunt, P. (1996), *Talk on Television, Audience Participation and Public Debate*, London: Routledge.

Manca, L. (1989), 'Journalism, Advocacy, and a Communication Model for Democracy', in M. Raboy and P. Bruck (eds.), *Communication for and Against Democracy*, Montréal, New York: Black Rose Books, pp. 163–73.

McNair, B. (1998), *The Sociology of Journalism*, London, New York, Sydney, Auckland: Arnold.

McQuail, D. (1994), *Mass Communication Theory. An Introduction*, (3rd ed.), London: Sage.

—— (2005), *McQuail's Mass Communication Theory. An Introduction*, (5th ed.), London: Sage.

Meijer, I. C. (2000), 'Het Persoonlijke Wordt Publiek. De Maatschappelijke Betekenis van Intieme Journalistiek', *Tijdschrift voor genderstudies*, 3: 3, pp. 16–30.

Meijer, I. C. (2001), 'The Public Quality of Popular Journalism: Developing a Normative Framework', *Journalism Studies*, 2: 2, pp. 189–205.

Merritt, D. (1995), *Public Journalism and Public Life*, Hillsdale, NJ: Lawrence Erlbaum Associates.

—— (1998), 'Public Journalism-Defining a Democratic Art', in E. Dennis and R. W. Snyder (eds.), *Media & Democracy*, New Brunswick: Transaction Publications, pp. 119–25.

Mouffe, C. (1994), 'For a Politics of Nomadic Identity', in G. Robertson, M. Mash, L. Tickner, J. Bird, B. Curtis and T. Putnam. (eds.), *Travellers' Tales: Narratives of Home and Displacement*, Routledge: London, pp. 105–13.

Nerone, J. C. (1995), *Last Rights: Revisiting Four Theories of the Press*, Urbana and Chicago: University of Illinois Press.

Pateman, C. (1970), *Participation and Democratic Theory*, Cambridge: Cambridge University Press.

Prehn, O. (1991), 'From Small Scale Utopism to Large Scale Pragmatism', in N. Jankowski, O. Prehn and J. Stappers (eds.), *The People's Voice. Local Radio and Television in Europe*, London, Paris, Rome: John Libbey, pp. 247–68.

Puissant, A. (2000), *Een Stem voor de Burger? De 'Public Journalism'-Queeste in de Verenigde Staten van Amerika*, Brussel: Koning Boudewijnstichting.

Rosen, J. (1994), 'Making Things More Public: on the Political Responsibility of the Media Intellectual', *Critical Studies in Mass Communication*, 11: 4, pp. 363–88.

Said, E. (1995), *Manifestaties van de Intellectueel*, Amsterdam/Antwerpen: Atlas.

Sayyid, B., Zac, L. (1998), 'Political Analysis in a World Without Foundations', in E. Scarbrough and E. Tanenbaum (eds.), *Research Strategies in the Social Sciences*, Oxford: Oxford University Press, pp. 249–67.

Schudson, M. (1978), *Discovering the News*, New York: Basic Books.

Schumpeter, J. (1976), *Capitalism, Socialism and Democracy*, London: Allen and Unwin.

Shah, H. (1996), 'Modernization, Marginalization, and Emancipation, Toward a Normative Model of Journalism and National Development', *Communication Theory*, 6: 2, pp. 143–66.

Siebert, F., Peterson, T., Schramm, W. (1956), *Four Theories of the Press*, Urbana: University of Illinois Press.

Smelik, A., Buikema, R., Meijer, M. (1999), *Effectief Beeldvormen. Theorie, Analyse en Praktijk van Beeldvormingsprocessen*, Assen: Van Gorcum.

Thompson, H. (1980), *The Great Shark Hunt*, London: Picador.

Tuchman, G. (1978), 'Introduction: The Symbolic Annihilation of Women by the Mass Media', in G. Tuchman, A. Daniels and J. Benet (eds.), *Hearth and Home: Images of Women in the Mass Media*, New York: Oxford University Press, pp. 3–38.

van Zoonen, L. (1997), 'A Tyranny of Intimacy? Women, Femininity and Television News', in P. Dahlgren and C. Sparks (eds.), *Communication and Citizenship*, London: Routledge, pp. 217–36.

Wolfe, T. (1973), *The New Journalism*, New York, Evanston, San Francisco, London: Harper & Row.

Chapter Eight

Disobedient media – unruly citizens: governmental communication in crisis

Hannu Nieminen

Introduction

During the previous years, the demand for critical research in governmental communication in Finland has been on the increase. Several governmental agencies have commissioned academic institutions to critically examine their communication activities. An invitation to produce policy proposals to enhance citizens' participation and other democratic activities is often included. In this chapter, I want to ask why this research interest has emerged and why it is situated at the present day.

My initial answer is that this interest results from the political elite's need to find new ways of communicating directly to citizens and of circumventing the 'corrupting' influence of the media and journalists. Among authorities, the feeling is widespread that the media today do not function properly and fail in providing citizens with the information that is deemed necessary to maintain an informed and democratic citizenship.

A web of distrust

This feeling of distrust hides a second layer of distrust, which is situated between the political elites [1] and the citizens. This second layer provides us with the starting point of our analysis. A number of research projects from different European countries show us that this gap between top decision-makers and citizens is deeply rooted and cannot be easily overcome (see e.g. Borg, 2005; ESC, 2005). The referendums on the EU Constitution in early summer of 2005 in France and the Netherlands showed not only the distance between popular sentiments and the government in those countries but more generally, the weaknesses in the European Union's legitimacy.

Reactions from both the European Union and national elites were illuminating. First, the ignorant voter was blamed: people were misinformed and based their votes on illuminate causes. Second, the European Union's PR work was blamed, and the European Union was expected to further improve its image among the Europeans. Third, the media and journalists were blamed: they put too much emphasis on the negative sides of politics in general and of the European Union in particular [2].

My basic thesis is that in order to understand the origins of the distrust that reigns between the political elites and the media, we have to elaborate how the elites assess the role of the media. Based on recent research, it appears that according to political elites, a major change has taken place within the last two decades. As a result of this, political elites see journalists and the media as disobedient: they do not fulfil their proper social and political role as defined by political elites. As journalists do not provide citizens with relevant information, citizens are said to be lacking the 'correct guidelines' for their actions, which in turn leads to political and social unruliness.

From the point of view of political elites, there is a web of distrust with the media in its centre as follows:

- Citizens do not trust political elites because of the media's disinformation;
- Political elites cannot trust citizens because they are misinformed by the media; and
- The media are responsible for the gap between the political elite and citizens.

Dichotomy between 'yesterday' and 'today'

Many recently produced research projects have generated interesting and detailed material on the relations between political elites and the media (see Kantola, 2002a; Alho, 2004; Korkiakoski *et al.*, 2005; Hakala *et al.*, 2005a, 2005b). Anu Kantola found in her study that during the late 1980s and early 1990s, a major attitudinal shift took place in Finnish elite groups. She characterizes this shift as a transformation towards a managerial ethos [3]. The change coincided with the deep economic and financial crisis of the early 1990s, which was even more radical and disruptive in Finland than in most European countries. In Kantola's study, elite members spoke of a major difference between 'before', i.e. before the crisis, and 'after', i.e. after the crisis. The difference was described by using dichotomies like ineffective/productive, politics/expertise, irresponsibility/responsible, public sector/private enterprizes, national/international, consensus/competition, virtual/real, sick/healthy, greedy/disciplined, bad/good, etc. (Kantola, 2001: 62).

Kantola concludes:

In the past world the scale was national. Finland was governed by forest industry, forest owners, trade unions and agricultural producers, whose mutual contracts guided the society. In the new world the scale of society has changed: economy has grown global and national contracts do not suffice any more. In the past world much depended on politics; in the new situation the use of reason and economic expertise are employed as a way to manage things (Kantola, 2002a: 267).

The new world was not totally harmonious, though. One of the problems for the elites was publicity and the media. For the financial elite, 'the main lesson from the crisis was the notion of publicity as a swamp which could suck a careless speaker down, and sink the whole national economy with him [...]' (Kantola, 2002a: 210). Politics was discussed and decisions were taken in unofficial discussions and meetings, as a public debate would get too easily out of reins and turn uncontrollable. There has been a traditional tension between politicians and journalists, but there are signs that these relations are now worsening (Aula, 1991: ix–xiii and passim; Kantola, 2002a: 220–1, 238–39, 300; Kantola, 2002b: 266, 275, 282. See also Alho, 2004: 296–97, 311–17.).

Although the interviews in Kantola's analysis originated from 1995 and she did not focus specifically on the relationship between political elites and media, her findings are most helpful when interpreting the more recent research results [4]. The managerial ethos that Kantola describes has effectively spread in the mid-2000s, even to the local or municipal level. Interestingly enough, the distinction between 'before' and 'after' as described earlier receives a different meaning when it is applied to the relationship between the elites and the media in the light of recent research results (Alho, 2004; Hakala et al., 2005a, b; Junnila, 2005; Korkiakoski et al., 2005).

Although the major change took place in the early 1990s, the danger that publicity and the media pose to elite politics now appears to be much more articulated and pronounced. The 'good' that was achieved with the transformations of the early 1990s, now seems to be jeopardized by the irresponsibility and unpredictability of journalists. 'Yesterday' now refers to a mythical past, when the relations between decision-makers and journalists were assumedly correct and mutually fruitful, and where the media could be trusted to fulfil its democratic mission. 'Today' now refers to a situation that is characterized by the loss of trust as journalists seek out negative news and focus on scandals in their pursuit for commercial success (see Korkiakoski et al., 2005: 28–33, 43–44).

As one informant in Korkiakoski et al.'s (2005) research project on municipal democracy in Imatra [5] stated:

> Among the decision-makers we have a common understanding that in the recent years the news reporting has worsened. Before that there might have been even a bit too much consensus, stating that all is well in the realm even when something negative had happened, but now again small issues are blown out of proportions and things are heated up without reason (Korkiakoski et al., 2005: 31, my translation).

The report concludes by stating as follows:

> Several decision-makers think that the reporting of the local newspaper has worsened compared to the earlier situation, although opinions differ why. One decision-maker states that the attitude of the local paper used earlier to be even too positive. Today the press unreasonably exacerbates issues (Korkiakoski et al., 2005: 31, my translation).

In order to better understand the logic behind the distinction between 'yesterday' and 'today', as it is found in Korkiakoski *et al*'s study, I will outline the arguments in more details [6].

Yesterday

When an important decision had to be made, the normal procedure for the decision-maker (minister, top governmental official, city mayor, and so on) was to order the PR officer to write a press release which included the basic information but left the news editing to journalists. The press release was then distributed to the media through the routine channels. A journalist would respectfully edit the material and write a news story, which would normally be printed or broadcasted according to its assumed newsworthiness. Thus the message – the information on the decision – was disseminated to the public in more or less the form that the decision-maker had originally intended. As there was a tacit understanding of the importance of governmental information, shared by all major media, there were no major variations in the editing and deliverance of the message. This procedure guaranteed that the information that decision-makers deemed important 'got through' and that citizens were 'properly' and 'objectively' informed. In this model, the decision-maker decided on the newsworthiness, and the news angle was already defined in the press release.

Today

When an important decision is made 'today', the decision-maker orders the PR officer to write the press release. Compared to earlier practice, the situation however differs in two major ways. First, it is not enough to merely write the press release and wait for the journalist to do the editing. Today, the PR officer not only has to provide the journalist with information on the decision as such, but the PR officer has to process and shape the information into a news story, preferably with pictures, ready to be published and printed as such. Second, it does not suffice to provide journalists with a ready-made news story but it has to be 'sold' to them, i.e. journalists have to be convinced and persuaded of the importance of the issue. This has lead to the emergence of an expert known as a 'spin doctor' [7].

Unlike earlier, the journalist would not just edit the press release and make it suitable for publication. Today he or she has to carefully assess its newsworthiness, using criteria more and more based on commercial considerations:

Figure 1: The process of governmental communication 'yesterday'.

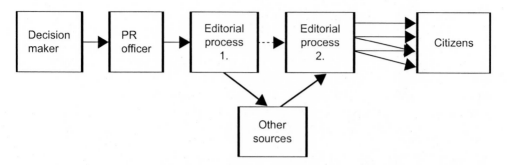

Figure 2: The process of governmental communication 'today'.

why should the issue be of interest to the reading public? Are there conflictual elements, disagreements between different governmental agencies, hidden motives? Are there other sources contradicting the 'official' information? Only if the issue fulfils these criteria, it is allowed entering the editorial process. And only then will be decided on the news angle. Because of the application of these criteria, the angle may diverge radically from what the PR officer originally intended. The final result may even fundamentally contradict the original message and seriously question the intentions of the decision-maker [8].

The interviews with the decision-makers appear to show that the shift from 'yesterday' to 'today' alters the relationship between political elites and journalists, even to this degree that despite the elite's attempts to better control the media – as the earlier mentioned examples of pre-editing the news and spin-doctoring indicate – the media have become today, from the elites' point of view, increasingly unpredictable in their behavior. This only increases the concern to find better ways to 'get the messages through' to the citizenry (see Åberg, 2005: 37, 38).

One municipal decision-maker is quoted in Junnila's (2005) research project on local public spheres, stating:

> *Before all what needs improvement is that we can better control ourselves what is communicated, when it is communicated, and also how it is communicated. So it would be an improvement, a big improvement that we would not be then at the mercy of the media as it often happens that it comes at a wrong time, when the issue under decision-making is still in preparation and it is not yet ready, or then it comes public through totally other values than what we want to stress and we know what is really the major matter* (Junnila, 2005: 57, my translation).

To put it bluntly, from the elites' viewpoint, journalists are seriously misguiding people. Today, news criteria are more and more determined by commercial goals, and citizens are missing out on much of relevant and necessary information when publishing it is not considered commercially interesting and profitable. For political elites, this results in citizens that are ignorant of the realities of decision-making and the underlying 'real' choices in matters of, for example, economic policy, security policy, or municipal economy. This is not only clearly reflected in opinion polls but also increasingly in the formation of one-issue-movements. These movements are seen by decision-makers as material evidence of how poorly informed people 'really' are, when they take stands based on emotional reactions while informed reasoning would naturally bring them to quite different positions (see Kantola, 2001: 65; Kantola, 2002b: 279–81, 284, 286; Junnila, 2005: 51–52; Korkiakoski *et al.*, 2005: 31–32).

From the elite's point of view, this unavoidably leads citizens to making 'wrong' choices. Because of the 'lack' of media responsibility, people do not understand the realities that frame decision-making. Because of their 'lack' of understanding, they cannot form 'correct' opinions and make the 'right' decisions. This lack also feeds into the continuous danger of political populism: the elite fears aspiring politicians who, in their opinion, sell simplified solutions to dire problems and try to capitalize on voters' potential anti-elitism. One way of formulating this fear is as follows:

> *Basically the question is that citizens' expectations and political realities do not meet, and the gap between them is expanding. The media could act as an intervening force and decrease citizens' expectations, making them thus more realistic and increasing citizens' understanding on the conditions of decision-making and municipal issues more generally. If these kinds of intervening forces do not exist, there is a danger that more so-called one-issue-movements will emerge* (SM, 2004, my translation).

This quotation is taken from an internal memorandum of the Ministry of Internal Affairs [9]. It points to the increasing fear for local civic movements that undermine the traditional balance of power between local parties and local authorities. Local media are expected to support and safeguard this balance and guard off 'unrealistic' criticism. What especially concerns the Ministry is that this kind of criticism is put forward more and more by professionals and by highly educated local groups such as doctors and teachers. From the point of view of the elites, their demands have gained too much weight and received too much attention in local media, leading to the mobilization of what the memorandum calls one-issue-movements [10].

Consequences: entertainmentalization of politics?
The recent studies cited earlier seem to confirm earlier analysis on how the loss of trust between decision-makers and the media on the one hand and between the elites and citizens on the other is experienced (see e.g. McNair, 1999; Meyer, 2002;

Louw, 2005) [11]. Four trends that stand out in the contemporary Finnish political life and which strengthen this spiral of anti-trust can be distinguished.

First, there is a tangible distance between members of political elites and ordinary 'back-benchers'. Members of the political elite – be they elected politicians or civil service mandarins – tend to identify themselves with the establishment and vested interests, not with the legislative or popular will as expressed in Parliament [12].

From the point of view of the elite, the danger with Parliament is its embedded bias towards populism, which the media and journalists today feed. As citizens are 'wrongly' informed by the media, they also vote in elections on 'false' premises. This means that they potentially vote for 'wrong' candidates, i.e. the candidates who promise most. After the elections, these politicians have to try to please their voters in order to get re-elected – which means that their first loyalty is towards their voters, and does not lie with the political elite. This is why, from the point of view of the elite, the Parliament and ordinary MP's are not trustworthy (Kantola, 2002b: 286; Alho, 2004: 296–97, 299) [13].

Second, as a result of the lack in trust, decision-making continues to withdraw from media publicity. Journalism's constant quest for negative issues and contradictions is considered to hinder reasonable public decision-making. In line with Habermas's well-known thesis on the re-feudalization of the public sphere, the political elite believes that the pre-decision phase – planning and preparation – can best do without publicity. It is preferred to smooth out the differences and disagreements in the confinements of a smaller circle without media attention, as this attention might bring about populist political panics. Only final decisions are brought into the public eye; the decision-making process, the argumentation, and the political debate are left non-public (Kantola, 2002a: 210–12, 220–21, 300; Alho, 2004: 299; Junnila, 2005: 53; Korkiakoski *et al.*, 2005: 22–26).

Third, there is a change in the recruitment of decision-makers. As decision-making and decision-makers try to shield themselves from the media and their interferences, politicians who know to differentiate between what they say in public and what they do behind closed doors, are advantaged. The net result is that the ethics of civil service takes over from open political contestation, which leads to the professionalization of politics, or to expert politics. This process does not favor innovative and popular and/or populist politicians but those who closely follow the 'governmental line' and restrain from bringing out new ideas or alternative solutions to political issues (Helander, 1998: 61–64; Kantola, 2001: 67; Kantola, 2002a: 280–81, 320–22; Alho, 2004: 296–97; Korkiakoski *et al.*, 2005: 22–26).

Fourth, and contradictory to the previous point, media attention is the only way forward for the political career of young politicians. Media visibility and media charisma are a necessity as there are today very little other means to contact potential voters. This leads to an almost symbiotic relationship between aspiring politicians and journalists. The problem is, however, that in order to get promoted in politics and to be able to fight for cabinet positions some day – which is often considered the ultimate aim by politicians – politics cannot be spoken about publicly, i.e. you are not allowed to bring about conflictual issues, which the media can use to create havoc. Acting otherwise might seriously harm your career (Kantola, 2002b: 287; Korkiakoski *et al.*, 2005). Polly Toynbee recently asked in *the Guardian* why the critical non-Blairite Labor MPs do not rebel, and answered by herself: 'Because for the very good reason that dissension in government is the fast-track route to opposition' (*The Guardian* 28 October 2005). Criticizing the Government means that you do not only harm yourself but also damage the party (Aula, 1991: 209–10; Alho, 2004: 298; Korkiakoski *et al.*, 2005: 42).

These four processes pave the way to political entertainment. This means that politicians fight for media attention amongst each other and with other celebrities. And they revert to trivial issues: what their favorite hobbies are, how their family life is, how they spend their summer vacations, and if they have any marital problems. 'Real' politics is kept behind closed doors and is not performed in front of journalists and citizens (Aula, 1991: 215–16; Alho, 2004: 297; Louw, 2005: 59–92).

How to surpass the media

For political elites, the media and journalism seems to be the destabilizing main factor – or at least one of the main factors – that endangers the legitimacy of the political system. When journalists 'mislead' citizens, these citizens cannot be expected to act in a reasoned and responsible way. Moreover, the normal 'democratic' ways for controlling and regulating the media have not been successful enough. What other means are still available to re-establish 'yesterday's' situation, when governmental messages still successfully 'got through' and were received as intended by citizens?

There are two inter-related approaches by which decision-makers try to circumvent the media and establish more direct links with citizens. First, authorities are seeking ways and channels to approach citizens directly, without the 'corrupting' influence of journalists. Second, authorities are promoting different forms of non-mediated interaction between them and citizens, such as for instance citizens' hearings, both on a local and on a national – mostly via the Internet – level (see SM, 2004; and Korkiakoski *et al.*, 2005 for concrete examples).

Especially when it comes to the Internet and its potential capacity to get round the media in order to inform citizens directly, authorities have great expectations (see e.g. Åberg, 2005: 37; Huhtala, 2005: 47). This is exemplified by the following statement by Matti Vanhanen, the PM of Finland:

The mass media – traditional and the new media as well – produce news with an accelerating speed. Competition between different media has hardened. Although many actions and measures of the governmental administration have long lasting effects – not only for individual citizens but for the whole society – they do not make big headlines. This is why the state administration finds itself in a situation where it has to make special investments in order to get its messages through, in an arena occupied by the media. In this task, the administration is much assisted by new media technologies and especially by the departmental web pages. We have invested much in these means in the last few years and my hope is that this development will only be consolidated (see Hakala *et al.*, 2005a, my translation) [14].

This emphasis on Internet-based governmental informational strategies and PR can also be clearly found in the guidelines for governmental communication, which the Prime Minister's Office has adopted. These are to be followed at all levels of the state administration (VNK, 2002; see also Hakala *et al.*, 2005a).

But even the Internet can pose problems. One top decision-maker – quoted in the Imatra research project – stated the following at the open Internet-based question-and-answer forum, which the city council had provided for citizens:

It functions easily as a destructive method, as people read the questions. Many of them are very negative, so all they read them and start developing them even more negatively. Thus they create a negative spiral, which is not aimed at seeking solutions but probes more problems. Those who are supposed to answer on these questions are on defensive, and there is no real interaction. This method is destructive (Korkiakoski *et al.*, 2005: 44, my translation).

The result was that the Imatra City Council's open Internet forum was closed down for an unspecified period of time. In the summer of 2006, its reopening and reorganizing was still under consideration.

Evaluation: the 'real' yesterday and its aftermath

How should we evaluate this 'yesterday–today' thesis describing the relations between political elites and media? Is it only a myth or is it based on evidence?

In general, the distinction is based on a real development, familiar to all European countries. The thesis is right in stating that between the 1970s and the 2000s deep-cutting changes have taken place in the relations between political elites and media, creating increasing tensions and even hostilities among them. It is however blatantly wrong in solely blaming the media and media's commercialization for this.

The thesis is also wrong in describing the relationship between decisions-makers, the media and citizens as once ('yesterday') being a more or less unilinear and one-directional 'chain of command', starting from the authorities, going through the media towards the citizen-audience. The situation in Finland in the 1970s was much more complex than this romanticized picture allows. In the 1970s, there was still a thick network of civil society organizations acting as

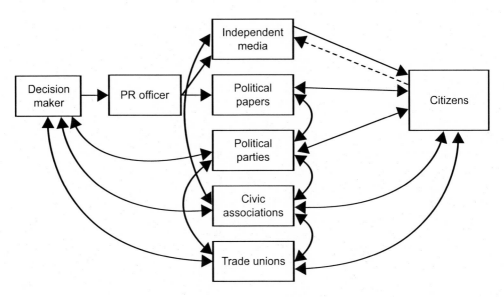

Figure 3: The process of political communication in the 1960s/1970s.

mediators between the state authority and citizenry. The media were one of the institutions that did not only mediate both 'upwards' and 'downwards' but also internally interacted constantly in many different ways. This means that the media's functioning was complemented by the workings of many other institutions, political, social, and cultural organizations, trade union movements, political parties, civic associations etc. (Aula, 1991: 207–11; Siisiäinen, 2000; Siisiäinen, 2003: 74–6, 77–9; see also Nieminen, 2004).

Problems started in the course of the 1970s with the decline in social and political mobilization. In the beginning, this was not very obvious and mediating networks seemed to function as they had always functioned. The decline in mass participation did not become immediately apparent. Even when the networks got thinner and more brittle, and most of their outer layers started to break away, eventually leaving only the political core visible, the political structures and their functioning did not change. Political elites tried to continue as if nothing has changed although its major supporting structures had all but vanished (Siisiäinen, 1998, 2000; Jokinen and Saaristo, 2002: 244–54; Nieminen, 2004).

At the same time, the space of public politics has narrowed dramatically. Compared to the situation of some 30 years ago, the public sector in Finland has been downsized considerably, especially when compared with the private sector. As the nature of politics is (to a great extent) about re-distributing public resources, there are today less and less resources to redistribute. As a result of the neo-liberal politics – extensive privatization programs and the overall reduction of the public sector – the political elite has much less power as it used to have (Kantola, 2001: 65; Kantola, 2002b: 281, 292; Kalela, 2005: 250–64).

The natural result is that due to this public authority's declining capacity in providing public services and public goods, citizens have turned more and more towards the market in order to satisfy their needs and expectations. There is not much that people can expect from politicians and politics any more, as the rapidly declining number of voters shows, not only in Finland but in most European countries (see Kalela, 2005: 260–62).

The change in the media's role has to be firmly placed in this context. If we try to apply the dichotomy 'yesterday–today' here, we can say that 'yesterday' the media and journalism were interlinked with other civil society institutions in many different ways. They had to share the stage with a diversity of institutional interests – be them political parties, trade unions, or cultural and social movements. 'Today', there is much less traditional civil society left, as civic activities have been organized in quite different ways. This means that the media do not have to accommodate the interests of civil society in the same way any more. The media have lost much (if not all) of its mediating functions in relation to the authorities and citizens. This also grants media more freedom from civil society and the state, but also less and less freedom from the market. This is clearly a problem for state authorities. Should it be a problem for citizens too?

Role of critical communication researchers

I started this chapter by referring to the increasing demand for critical research on governmental PR and communication activities. To be more exact, there have been two types of invitations. First, researchers have been approached as PR experts. They have been asked for advice on how to make governmental messages more attractive, how to deal more effectively with the media and journalists, and how to improve the public appearance of members of political elites. Second, researchers have been approached as consultants in helping to enhance citizens' participation. In this respect, they have been asked to assist in looking at strategies to increase people's political and social level of activity, to develop new forms of direct communication, e.g. through Internet, and in creating dialogical and trusting relations with civil society actors.

The question is how to answer to these invitations without losing the critical edge necessary for social scientists. It is easy to conclude that the first kind of invitation is a slippery slope: although it can be rewarding for individual academics in short term, it is not really the critical researchers' core business. The second kind of invitation is more difficult to assess critically, as it can be linked to the democratic and social activist role for academics. The question that remains is that the democratic perspective, sought-after by governments tends to be top-down or even paternalistic so that academics find themselves in the position of legitimizing pseudo-participation. On the other hand, it can be interesting to see whether academic research could have a real and lasting impact to governmental practices.

In my own experience, there are three major issues, which the researcher must make clear to him/herself before engaging in such a project. First, it should be emphasized that problems in citizens' political activities are basically structural in their nature and cannot be solely solved by increasing the level of communication. Second, there will always be a tension between the distance that critical research requires and the demand of ethical commitment, necessary for democratic academic practices. And third, the critical researcher will always have to negotiate a position between his/her own interests as a researcher, the government's urge to incorporate the academia for administrative purposes and the social and cultural movements' needs to use the researcher's expert knowledge for their particularistic goals.

Notes for Chapter Eight

[1]   When using the concept of political elite, I am referring to both top politicians, such as ministers and city councillors, and top civil servants such as heads of governmental offices etc. In Finland, it is sometimes claimed that the country's core political elite can sit comfortably at the back seat of a taxi. Here the expression is used somewhat more widely. (See also Alho 2004; Kantola 2002a, 55–56; Moring 1989; Nieminen 2000, 50.)

[2]   See e.g. leaders in Suomen Kuvalehti, 3 June 2005, and in Helsingin Sanomat, 24 July 2005. See also the Economist 2 June 2005.

[3]   Kantola analyzed 32 interviews of Finnish highest-level political decision-makers. The interviews were conducted in 1995. (Kantola, 2001: 61; Kantola, 2002b: 271.)

[4]   As a part of a larger research on governmental communication, Leif Åberg analyzed 20 interviews of highest level governmental officials, including ministers, in 2004–2005 (Hakala *et al.*, 2005b). As a part of a research project on the local public sphere in the town of Imatra, Jaana Korkiakoski *et al.* analyzed 29 interviews of the inhabitants in the town of Imatra (spring 2005), including nine municipal decision-makers and officials (Korkiakoski *et al.*, 2005). As a part of her MA thesis on the local public sphere in the town of Somero, Asta Junnila analyzed seven interviews with local decision-makers in the spring of 2005 (Junnila, 2005). The illustrative citations that are used in this chapter are based on the published reports on these studies, but the writer was also informed by all of Korkiakoski *et al.*'s interviews.

[5]   Imatra is a small Finnish declining industrial town of ca. 30,000 inhabitants in Eastern Finland, close to Russian border.

[6]   It needs to be emphasized that this description is only exploratory. It attempts to outline a series of arguments for further research and does not claim to present final conclusions. See also Aula (1991) for an interpretation of the origins of this development.

[7]   Although this phenomenon is not (yet) so ubiquitous in Finland as for instance in the United Kingdom (see e.g. Louw, 2005), 'spin doctoring' is a part of a common political landscape.

[8]   For a good illustration of the 'politics-as-strategy-cycle', see Louw, 2005: 70.

[9]   The memorandum is based on a seminar discussion between municipal decision-makers and ministerial civil servants.

[10] This interpretation was confirmed by a series of informal discussions in the spring of 2005 with the members of the local elite. See also an interview with the ex-mayor of the City of Vantaa Erkki Rantala (2005).

[11] See also Norris's (2000: 3–12, 309–10) account; however, her own contradictory conclusions cannot be addressed here.

[12] The same is the case at the local level with the municipal council, as the case of Imatra shows us.

[13] Again, this development applies also at the municipal level, as seen e.g. in Korkiakoski *et al.*, 2005: 22–26.

[14] A statement by the PM of Finland Matti Vanhanen on 7 April 2005, when he received a committee report on the monitoring and assessment system for governmental communication.

References for Chapter Eight

Åberg, L. (2005), 'Strategia I. Analyysi: Strateginen Näkökulma Viestintään ja Sen Arviointiin' ['Strategy I. Analysis: Strategic Approach to Communication and its Assessment'], in Hakala, S., Huhtala, H., Nieminen, H. *et al.* (eds.), *VISA, Osa II*, pp. 31–9.

Alho, A. (2004), *Silent Democracy, Noisy Media*, Helsinki: Helsinki University Press.

Aula, M. K. (1991), 'Poliitikkojen ja Toimittajien Suhteet Murroksessa? [The Relations Between Politicians and Journalists in Transformation?]', *Tutkimusraportti 5/1991*, Helsinki: Yleisradio.

Borg, S. (2005), 'Kansalaisena Suomessa. Kansalaisvaikuttaminen Pohjoismaissa ja European Social Survey 2002. [To be a Citizen in Finland: Citizens' Participation in Nordic Countries and the European Social Survey 2002.]' *Oikeusministeriön julkaisu 3/2005*, Helsinki: Oikeusministeriö [Ministry for Justice].

ESC (2005), *Stakeholders' Forum on 'Bridging the Gap: How to Bring Europe and its Citizens Closer Together?'*, 7–8 November 2005 by European Economic and Social Committee. A Press Release. http://www.esc.eu.int/stakeholders_forum/index_en.asp. Downloaded on 27 December 2005.

Hakala, S., Huhtala, H., Nieminen, H., *et al.* (2005a), 'VISA – Valtionhallinnon Viestinnän Seuranta- ja Arviointijärjestelmä. [VISA – the Monitoring and Assesment System for Governmental Communication.]', *Valtionhallinnon Viestintä 2007 -Hanke. VNK:n Julkaisusarja 2/2005*, Helsinki: Valtioneuvoston Kanslia [Prime Minister's Office].

――― (2005b), 'VISA – Valtionhallinnon Viestinnän Seuranta- ja Arviointijärjestelmä', *Valtionhallinnon Viestintä 2007 – Hanke, Osa II: Tutkimusraportit. VNK: julkaisusarja 4/2005*, Helsinki: Valtioneuvoston kanslia.

Helander, V. (1998), 'Julkisvalta ja Professiot' [The Public Sector and Professions], in J. Mykkänen and I. Koskinen (eds.), *Asiantuntemuksen Politiikka. Professiot ja Julkisvalta Suomessa. [Politics of Expertise. Professions and Public Sector in Finland.]*, Helsinki: Helsinki University Press, pp. 48–64.

Huhtala, H. (2005), 'Strategia II. Analyysi: Viestinnän Toimijoiden Näkökulmia Ministeriöiden Viestintään' [Strategy II. Analysis: Communicators' Approaches to Ministries' Communication], in Hakala, S., Huhtala, H., Nieminen, H. *et al.* (eds.), *VISA, Osa II*, pp. 40–7.

Jokinen, K., Saaristo, K. (2002), *Suomalainen Yhteiskunta. [The Finnish Society.]*, Helsinki: WSOY.

Junnila, A. (2005), *Paikallisjulkisuuden Vaikuttajat. Tapaustutkimus Varsinaissuomalaisessa Pikkukaupungissa. [Influential Actors in Local Public Sphere. A Case Study of a Small Town in Varsinais-Suomi.]* Viestinnän pro Gradu-tutkielma. Tammikuu 2006. [MA thesis in Communication.], Helsingin yliopisto.

Kalela, J. (2005), 'Perinteisen Politiikan loppu' [The end of Traditional Politics], in V. Pernaa and M. K. Niemi (eds.), *Suomalaisen Yhteiskunnan Poliittinen Historia. [The Political History of Finnish Society.]*, Helsinki: Edita, pp. 244–64.

Kantola, A. (2001), 'Leaving Public Places: Antipolitical and Antipublic Forces of the Transnational Economy', *Javnost*, 8: 1, pp. 59–74.

Kantola, A. (2002a), *Markkinakuri ja Managerivalta. Poliittinen Hallinta Suomen 1990-luvun Talouskriisissä. [Market Discipline and Managerial Power: Political Governance in the Financial Crisis of the 1990s in Finland.]*, Helsinki: Pallas.

――― (2002b), 'Se Keskustelu Jäi Käymättä. Poliittinen Eliitti ja Talouskriisin Julkisuus' [That Debate Never Happened. Political Elite and the Publicity of the Economic Crisis.], in U. Kivikuru (ed.), *Laman Julkisivut. Media, Kansa ja Eliitit 1990-luvun Talouskriisissä. [Facades of the Economic Crisis. Media, People and the Eelites in the Depression of the 1990s.]*, Helsinki: Palmenia, pp. 263–300.

Korkiakoski, J., Lehmusto, L., Luhtakallio, E., *et al.* (2005), *Kuuleeko Kunta Kansalaista? Paikallinen Julkisuus ja Kunnallinen Demokratia Imatralla. [Does the Local Authority Listen to Citizens? The Local Public Sphere and Municipal Democracy in the Town of Matra.]* Sisäasiainministeriön Jjulkaisuja 20/2005, Helsinki: Sisäasiainministeriö [Ministry for Internal Affairs].

Louw, P. E. (2005), *The Media and Political Process*, London: Sage.

McNair, B. (1999), *An Introduction to Political Communication,* (2nd ed.), London: Routledge.

Meyer, T., Hinchman, L. (2002), *Media Democracy: How the Media Colonise Politics*, Cambridge: Polity.

Moring, T. (1989), 'Political Elite Action: Strategy and Outcomes', *Commentationes Scientiarum Socialium 41*, Helsinki: The Finnish Society of Sciences and Letters.

Nieminen, H. (2000), Hegemony and the Public Sphere: Essays on the Democratisation of Communication, School of Art, Literature and Music, Department of Media Studies, Series A/44, Turku: University of Turku.

Nieminen, H. (2004), *Kansalaisyhteiskunta ja Media. Muistio Sitralle 25.5.2004.* Helsinki: Suomen Itsenäisyyden Juhlarahasto Sitra. http://www.sitra.fi/ Julkaisut/Muut/Nieminen.pdf. Downloaded on 27 December 2006.

Norris, P. (2000), *A Virtuous Circle: Political Communication in Postindustrial Societies*, Cambridge: Cambridge University Press.

Rantala, E. (2005), 'Erkki Rantala: Kuntapäättäjät Helisemässä Lastenvaunulähetystöjen Kanssa'. [Municipal Decision-Makers in Difficulties with Young Mothers' One-Issue-Movements], *Helsingin Sanomat*, 30 December 2005 (A6).

Siisiäinen, M. (1998), 'Uusien ja Vanhojen Liikkeiden Keinovalikoimat'. [The Means and Resources of New and Old Social Movements], in K. Ilmonen and M. Siisiäinen (eds.), *Uudet ja Vanhat Liikkeet. [The New and Old Social Movements.]*, Tampere: Vastapaino, pp. 219–43.

—— (2000), 'Järjestöllinen Pääoma Suomessa'. [Associational Capital in Finland], in K. Ilmonen (ed.), *Sosiaalinen Pääoma ja Luottamus. [Social Capital and Trust.]*, Jyväskylä: SoPhi, pp. 144–69.

—— (2003), 'Muuttuvat Yhdistykset'. [Associations in Transformation], in H. Melin and J. Nikula (eds.), *Yhteiskunnallinen Muutos. [Societal Change.]*, Tampere: Vastapaino, pp. 63–79.

SM (2004), *Imatra-Case. Muistio.* Sisäasiainministeriö, Kuntaosasto 7.9.2004. *[The Case of Imatra. A Memorandum.* Ministry of Internal Affairs, Department of Municipalities].

Toynbee, P. (2005), 'The Fight Over the Half-Inch of Turf that Perverts our Politics', *Guardian*, 20 October 2005, p. 23.

VNK (2002), *Valtioneuvoston Kanslian Suositukset Valtionhallinnon Viestinnässä Noudatettavista Periaatteista ja Toimintatavoista. [Guidelines for the Principles and Procedures of Governmental Communication by the Prime Minister's Office.]*, Helsinki: Valtioneuvoston Kanslia 23.5.2002. http://192.49.226.41/files/pdf/viestintasuositus.pdf. Downloaded on 23 December 2005.

Chapter Nine

On the dark side of democracy: the global imaginary of financial journalism

Anu Kantola

Introduction

Economic globalization and market liberalization have challenged national politics and political imaginaries during the last 20 years. With the rise of the market liberalization and market-oriented policies the faith of the nation state has become a matter of intense discussions (e.g. Hirst and Thompson, 1996; Strange, 1996; Habermas, 1999; Hardt and Negri, 2000).

In the new globalized condition, states are seen as competing on the 'hypermobile' capital (Warf, 1999) and tackling the increasing power of the multinational corporations as transnational multinationals and international finance capital have become increasingly influential in politics (Schmidt, 1995; Sklair, 2002). The state has been seen to evolve to a competition state (Cerny, 1990: 220–47) or an entrepreneurial state (Harvey, 1989: 178; Warf, 1999: 239), which tries to appear as an appealing place for investments by lowering taxes, providing cheap, flexible, or skilful labor, industrial sites or parks. The new global condition for the state and national democracies has been labelled for instance as flexible capitalism (Harvey, 1989, 2001), supermodernity (Auge, 1995) or hyperglobalization (Hay, 2004: 520).

With regard to democracy, the greatest worry has perhaps been whether a progressive separation of power from politics will take place (e.g. Bauman, 1999: 24–31, 120; Habermas, 1999). These worries have been enhanced by the problems of politics and public communication (Blumler, 1995; Franklin, 2004; Louw, 2005). These processes might mean that representative democracy and its institutions are weakening. Or to be a little more cautious, at least it seems like the scope and spaces of democratic politics and processes are currently under negotiation due to the processes of globalization (e.g. McNair, 2000; Dahlgren, 2001).

The aim here is to examine the role of journalism in these processes. As it is well known, journalism has a crucial role to play in modern mass democracies. Journalism offers information on political issues, gives an opportunity to bring up new political issues, creates opportunities for an ongoing dialogue and acts as a watchdog of the decision-makers. Moreover journalism contains a view of the world, a social cosmology or a political imaginary by which our societies and life are imagined (Anderson, 1983; González-Veléz, 2002; Taylor, 2004: 50). As Benedict Anderson (1983: 14–49) has pointed out, modern polities are to a certain extent imagined communities. Polities and political life are maintained through public arenas where the citizens of the polity do not actually meet, but rather imagine themselves belonging to a common community. Journalism can thus be understood as an imaginative exercise, which formulates social and political imaginaries. Modern polities are imagined through the endless stream of everyday journalistic texts; by the news, articles, columns, comments, and leaders which describe, analyze, interpret, debate, and contest the political.

Historically, journalism has had a particularly central role in building up national imaginaries by having tight connections with national imaginaries and democracies. As the global economy has been liberalized and the premises of the nation state have been questioned, journalism has a role to play in this process as well. As political imaginaries are changing and globalized political imaginaries are created (Cameron and Palan, 2004), it can be assumed that these global imaginaries are reflected also in journalism and, moreover, that journalism has a role in their construction.

In his sense, especially the role of financial journalism, and the role of the *Financial Times* (FT) in particular, form an interesting subject of study. Most on the media as well as on journalism is still very much nation-based and directed to national readership. There are, however, also media, which have been increasingly internationalized and can be seen as a constitutive for the new global imaginaries. International financial journalism can be seen as reflecting these new political forces and imaginaries of mobile finance capital. The aim here is to understand the role of international financial quality journalism by describing the political rationality of the FT. The analysis concentrates on the ways the FT apprehends national democracies. How does international financial journalism treat national democracies? How are the national imaginaries rewritten by internationally oriented financial journalism?

Forerunner of globalization

The FT has its roots firmly in the United Kingdom but the international scope has been a central one for the paper right from the start. The paper was founded in the late 1880s together with the *Financial News*, as London was emerging as the financial capital of the world markets and the enhancing Stock Exchange of the British Imperium provided a promising potential readership as well as advertisers for a financial newspaper (Kynaston, 1988: 1–2.). The birth of the paper thus took place in the heydays of British imperialism and colonialism, which has had a strong impact on the paper. The scope of the paper was global as the FT – already in the early twentieth century – boldly announced having 'the largest circulation of any financial newspaper in the world' and the emphasis on the global view was substantiated in for instance the 'Empire Section', published weekly from 1910 (Kynaston, 1988: 61–5).

During the twentieth century, the FT has been a forerunner of contemporary financial globalization by paying increasing attention to the internationalization of the economy. A strong developmental work regarding the paper's foreign news took place after the Second World War (Kynaston, 1988: 148–49). A foreign department was founded in 1951 (Kynaston, 1988: 213) and from the 1960s onwards internationalization became, in David Kynaston's (1988: 373) words, 'the single major direction of the newspaper'. The paper was billed in early 1970s with a slogan 'Europe's business newspaper'. The stringer network had 100 stringers around the world and the number of full-time foreign correspondents, almost 30, was larger than in any newspaper, with the exception of the *New York Times*. Moreover, there were regional specialists based in London but travelling frequently (Kynaston, 1988: 375–6). In 1979, the FT launched an international edition printed in Frankfurt and to highlight the increasing internationalization of finance a section titled the 'World Stock Markets' appeared (Kynaston, 1988: 421–4).

By the beginning of the twenty-first century, the FT represents a branch of journalism trying to convey the news to the internationally oriented investor. The paper claims to reach more senior decision-makers than any other international title across Europe. In opinion leader surveys, the FT has proved to be the most widely read international daily amongst the most important opinion formers in government, business, the media, academia, and international organizations (*Financial Times*, 2005a). The FT has also been ranked as the most widely read international business title among Europe's senior business people, and the paper has increased its circulation especially in the Asian countries. (*Financial Times*, 2005b).

Thus it is interesting to look at the political imaginary of the FT as it apprehends national democracies around the globe. How does international financial journalism treat national democracies? How are the national imaginaries rewritten?

The empirical material consists of the FT coverage on national parliamentary elections from 2000 to 2005. The material covers 32 general parliamentary elections between 2000 and 2005 and consists of the most notable national economies in the world, i.e. the OECD countries in combination with the most notable economies outside the OECD. The countries included are Mexico, Italy, United Kingdom, Norway, Poland, Denmark, Portugal, Ireland, France, the Czech Republic, Sweden, Slovakia, Germany, Turkey, the United States, Austria, the Netherlands, Finland, Iceland, Russia, Greece, Spain, India, Canada, Japan, and New Zealand. Six countries had two elections during the researched period and both elections are included.

The research material, 219 stories of which 23 are leading articles, was gathered during a period of a fortnight (1 week before and 1 week after the respective election). All the stories that have the election and the political situation as their main theme were included [1]. The election stories were retrieved from the FT.com website archive. The stories that had appeared in the printed edition, either in the United Kingdom or in the FT European edition were included and stories that have appeared only on the FT.com website were excluded. In order to concentrate on the FT's journalism, stories written by an 'outsider', i.e. a writer noted for other affiliation than the FT, were excluded.

The historical hard core of FT's journalism perceives the world through the lenses of international capital analyzing the prospectuses for investments. And as business can be done in every walk of life and is affected by politics, social, and cultural life, financial journalism has never restricted itself solely to the world of finance. In 1945, the new editor Hargreaves Parkinson described the challenge of the paper showing how the investor's point of view had become a relevant issue for men and women 'in every walk of life':

> *A great body of readers, men and women in every walk of life, find that, in this difficult mid-twentieth century world, questions which used to be the exclusive concern of the economist and the business man exert a profound influence on their daily life. Never have readers been do avid for guidance on everything bearing on full employment, inflation, taxation, the future of Government controls and similar problems.* (Cited in Kynaston, 1988, 153.)

The study of the election coverage of the FT from 2000 to 2005 shows that the paper covers national politics widely around the world. Albeit the paper was interested in the financial issues, but also issues such as welfare, taxation, healthcare, unemployment, immigrants, populism, wars, and civil unrest, voting practises and frauds as well as the individual politicians were covered. In the election stories analyzed the main themes were:

- Stories concentrating on the prospective popularity, success, and tactics of the various parties and prime minister candidates
- Stories on politics from the point of general economic policies concerning fiscal, monetary, and welfare policies
- Stories on the reactions of the financial world: the investors, business leaders, stock exchanges, and exchange market reactions and
- Stories on the non-economic election issues, such as the war on Iraq, immigration, populism, or terrorism.

Reporting democracy

When looking at the election coverage stories, it became clear that the FT often positions itself in favor of democracy and calls for enhanced democracy. The countries and elections are evaluated by standards of democracy. In the more 'consolidated' democracies of Western Europe, the FT's most important indicator of democracy is the voter turnout. For instance, in Italy the turnout of

80 per cent is greeted and framed positively in the name of democracy as 'a great day for democracy in Italy' [2]. Democracy is also in the Dutch elections presented in a positive light as the election result is endorsed 'The old arrogant style of the main parties has been forced to give way to more democracy. That is a positive benefit' [3].

The non-western countries are often assessed by their ability to conform to the western standards of democracy. India is praised in a leading article on its 2004 elections 'The sheer size of an election in India, with all its chaos and exuberance, is a magnificent and humbling spectacle, which rightly commands respect across the world' [4].

The Mexican election results in 2000 are greeted as a revolution, as 'a transition from one-party rule to pluralist democracy' which 'completes Mexico's long transition from one-party dominance to pluralist democracy, adding political maturity to a more competitive market economy'. The defeat of the leftist Institutional Revolutionary Party is greeted with satisfaction as a step towards 'political maturity', i.e. the western style of democracy of changing governments [5].

Democracy and elections are also celebrated in the case of Japan in 2005 as an enthusiastic voter is interviewed in an analysis story:

> *Although not herself a supporter of Mr Koizumi, she argues that he has performed a big service to those who aspire to a more robust and transparent democracy. 'This is a marvellous moment, something for which Japanese democracy has been waiting for half a century', Ms Hama says. 'In this election, people have to say what they mean and mean what they say. They can't get away with being wishy-washy – something unprecedented in Japanese politics'* [6].

Prime Minister Koizumi is praised in a FT leader for his efforts to transform Japan into a western-style democracy:

> *Just as post-war Japan has never wholeheartedly adopted western competitive capitalism, so it has never been a western-style competitive democracy except in its structure. By challenging the old factions in the LDP, gathering power in his own hands at the centre of the party, insisting on an ideological election platform and fighting a televisual campaign, Mr Koizumi has become a political moderniser* [7].

In Turkish elections, the defeat of the ruling party is greeted as a revolutionary act of the voters. It is described in a positive tone by using the voices of the man-on-the street:

> *'We needed a clean-out of the old system,' said Behic Ozek, 50, a businessman. Candan Ersoy, a 28-year-old child-minder, agreed. 'The best thing about this*

election is that we won't have to see the same ugly old faces any more, and that the new government, at the end of its term in office, will not be able to say 'oh we were not able to keep our promises because we lacked a parliamentary majority' [8].

In the Russian elections, the election story describes the dismal state of the Russian democracy with a worried tone:

On the whole, Russians probably did freely express their choices on Sunday. But the system they voted for remains far removed from a western-style idea of democracy centred around a strong parliament that counters the power of the executive. Low voter turnout of barely 50 per cent coupled with a sharp rise in protest votes 'against all' to 5 per cent show that a significant proportion of the Russian electorate feels disenfranchised. Voters are increasingly disengaging from the political process little over a decade after totalitarianism collapsed [9].

In a leader on the Russian, elections the worries over democracy are expressed in a clear way:

For Vladimir Putin, the Russian president, Sunday's parliamentary election was a triumph. But for the cause of political freedom in Russia it was a serious defeat. The forces of authoritarianism marshalled by the Kremlin have pushed further into territory once occupied by democracy [10].

Thus the FT clearly carries the flag of western democracy when assessing the elections. The ideals of the western democracy are used when analyzing the election results and the principles and practises of the western democracy are supported and recommended for the non-western countries.

Call for reforms

Beside democracy, another common theme in the research material is the constant and insatiable emphasis on reform, which seems to be the cornerstone of the political imaginary of the twenty-first century FT. The idea of reform is a central element in modern political imaginaries. The story of progress and the idea of revolution as a way to a progressive society are central myths of modernity (Taylor, 2004: 176). Alan Touraine sees the modern world saturated by the idea of revolution. The idea of a struggle against an 'ancient régime' is a central element in the idea of revolution, which triumphed in the West during the eighteenth and nineteenth centuries and spilled over to the Soviet and Chinese revolutions (Touraine, 1990: 122–3). Liberalism, most notably in the French revolution, alongside Marxism, forms a system of thought based on the idea of revolution. The old system has to be dismantled and a new system introduced. This seems to be the case also with the political imaginary of the FT. Twenty-first century financial journalism joins the modern political programs of reform.

The notion of reform appears in the research material over 300 times, and it is the most common theme related to politics and elections. The political communities are assessed by their ability and readiness for reform and change. The politicians are classified as pro-reform or anti-reformist, and their actions are evaluated by their readiness for reform or alternatively by their capability for reform [11]. The news stories and commentaries are posed from the point of the necessity of reform. Are the parties reformative or anti-reformative? Will the election result help the reformers? Are the reformers winning? Can the anti-reformative winners still become reformers?

As a new government faces its new term, the commentaries are often framed as summing up a list of reform or change challenges [12]. Politicians are evaluated by their capability to enforce reforms as well in Mexico as in Germany [13]. Often the reform is a given, an unquestionable key for solving large-scale societal, political, and economic problems. For instance, when Silvio Berlusconi wins the Italian elections in May 2001, his main challenge is formulated in an analysis story by pondering 'Berlusconi's commitment to reform' and by framing his first task, backed by the authority of international economists:

He comes to office with a largely untried team taking charge of an economy that has underperformed all of its main European Union partners for the last five years. Growth last year reached 2.9 per cent but international economists urge structural reforms to sustain the performance in the medium term [14].

There is a call for general reforms, such as *structural reforms* or *liberalizing reforms*, which seem to be linked to the overall economical liberalization and privatization of the national economy. Moreover, there is a host of more specified reforms such as *tax reform, labor market reform, public sector reform, regulatory reform, land reform, reform of the welfare state, the public sector, the health and social services*, and *the labor market*. Most of these reforms, thus, fit together with the tradition of market liberalism. During the last 20 years, there has been a liberal call for change and transformation of the state and welfare system, tax policies, and social policies in political talk (Clarke, 2004: 11). Judging from the research material, the FT seems to join the call of the late twentieth century for market-oriented reforms. As the reforms are addressed, the state and public sector seem to be most in the need of reformatory actions. The reforms seem to point almost without exception to the decreasing role of public funding and taxes in the economy. Having a history as a paper of the international investor and emphasizing financial discipline, the FT follows up on its tradition and consequently applies market liberalism to countries worldwide by framing its election stories, columns and leaders in terms of liberal economic reforms and emphasizing the primacy of fiscal discipline over welfare spending.

For instance, in the case of the Portuguese election in 2005, the new Prime Minister José Socrates announces that his target is a 'Nordic social democracy'. The FT clearly delineates in a news story what that means in practice for Portugal 'tough reform and austere approach to public spending'. This will mean in concrete terms cuts in the public sector:

> *Disciplining expenditure will involve cutting back an army of 700,000 public employees with a wage bill equivalent to 15 per cent of gross domestic product. Mr Socrates says he will cut 75,000 public sector jobs in four years without imposing redundancies* [15].

The massive cuttings of the public sector employment are presented as a simple and an unquestionable route to 'Nordic prosperity' for Portugal, a country with an already much smaller public sector and higher unemployment than the Nordic countries.

In the Japanese elections in 2005, the state is described in rather bleak terms in a 'Lex Column':

> *For all the talk of reform and smaller government, the state reaches into much of Japan. Government fingerprints are on everything from the lottery to universities, telecoms to railways. The government has slashed funding to special public corporations – essentially subsidised entities – but will still channel $35bn their way this year. These groups waste resources and their management is hobbled by the practice of amakudari, whereby government officials 'descend from heaven' into cushy pre-retirement postings* [16].

The discourse of reform has also a strong Anglo-Saxon element, which is reflected for instance in the way Germany is seen. From the FT's perspective, Germany is clearly the country most badly in need of a structural economic reform. In the 2002 elections after the red–green government had won, the FT points out the need of reform. In an analysis story, Germany is seen as a failing economy [17] and the election leader on Germany gives firm guidance how to interpret the election results:

> *In a country chronically averse to change, Mr Schröder campaigned on a platform of minimal economic reform, with his challenger offering little better. But it would be a tragedy for Germany and Europe if the chancellor-elect now interpreted this near dead heat as a mandate for further drift* [18].

In a similar vein in the context of the 2005 elections, the FT interprets in a news story the failure of the conservative Angela Merkel of not gaining a definitive majority with dismal tones by seeing the result as sending 'shockwaves around the European Union' and leaving 'supporters of economic reform in despair' [19].

Roll over elections! The master plan of economics

When the elections result is backing economic reformers or the parties that are counted as reformatory, the FT stories can be written rather easily. Countries, which seem to pass the test of economic reform and democracy, are treated favorably. Thus, for instance, India is labelled in a pre-election story in 2004 as 'the new star of Asia combining democracy and economic growth' [20].

In Eastern Europe, the Slovakia's centre-right government is getting a positive coverage as the result is described as a phoenixlike performance. Slovakia is noted as one of the very few post-communist countries that has won a re-election 'while pushing through tough reforms', and the results are seen as a very positive indication:

The new government should be welcomed by foreign investors and financial markets. It will be more coherent than the current fractious left-right coalition, allowing it to press ahead with painful budget cuts and reforming the public sector [21].

However, when the election result is in conflict with the economic reformers, financial journalism becomes a tricky task and the reasonable voice of journalism is used to establish the order between the discourses of economy and democracy.

The most common way of positioning the economic reform as primary over democratic discourses is to present the economic reform program as an inevitable and unquestionable 'task' or 'sole option' for politics. This task or challenge is stated as a matter of fact in similar ways in both the news stories and the more opinionated leaders and columns.

The journalistic voice of the FT seems also to have a clear sense for 'right' policies and a clear conception on what is to be done in different countries – despite the election result or the voters' will. The economic reform is the premier issue that has to be taken care of, and only after that there is space for democracy and politics. For instance, in Slovakia in a 2002 news story, the major task of politics is claimed to be 'in the fiscal area which will not be very popular'. Thus 'there will need to be a consensus on economic reform' [22].

In many cases the election result is openly questioned, and in some cases the FT even seems to invalidate the election results by maintaining that the policy programs, which have been defeated in the elections, should still be implemented. For instance in India, the problems start with the outcome of the 2004 election, which wipes out the reformers [23] and their 'genuinely liberal economic reforms' [24]. The defeat of the reformers is discussed in an extensive article, which brings out the various interpretations of the reform [25]. Finally, the FT commentary story ends with the following conclusion:

In the short run, India's economic reformers will be discouraged by yesterday's decisive verdict. But once the shock has been digested the conclusion might as easily favour more comprehensive economic reform [26].

Also Sweden needs to rethink its policies. Social Democrats have won the elections with a clear anti-reformative program, as the FT describes:

There has been no confusing Mr Persson's message. Improving schools, social services and the public health service go before any tax cuts. The main opposition party, the conservative Moderates, who proposed large tax cuts, had a disastrous result, losing around a third of its support [27].

Despite the election results and Persson's victory, Sweden is getting a clearly contradictory piece of advice. In a rather definitive and even threatening tone, the FT concludes that the new prime minister should implement policies that have just been defeated in the elections. The FT picks up the loosing agenda of tax cuts and recommends the prime minister to move on with them despite the election results:

But he [Mr. Persson] needs to do more if Sweden is to reverse its long slide from near the top to the middle of the world prosperity league. He should cut taxes - among the highest in Europe - to stop the corporate exodus and to foster small business. He could pay for this by streamlining public services and pruning welfare abuse. These moves should be on the agenda for his new term [28].

A similar negligence of the election results is visible in the 2002 Czech elections. As Vladimir Spidla, a clearly articulated leftist, has won the elections, the FT news story notices that the new prime minister 'obstinately resisted fundamental reform as minister and pledged to defend the welfare state during the (election) campaign'. The FT then formulates in an analysis story the main challenge for the new prime minister '[t]he question is can he also transform himself into a reforming leftwing premier?' The FT leader reminds the new Czech government on the primacy of economic discipline despite the election promises on welfare spending:

The new government must recognise that sound public finance comes first, followed by further economic restructuring. Otherwise the gains of the past few years will be lost, as will recent success in attracting foreign investment [29].

After the German red-green victory in 2002, it is warned that if the government should fail to make economic reforms its priority, the poll's result could have an adverse effect on growth. Ludwig Georg Braun, president of the assembly of the German Chambers of Commerce calls for a reform 'master-plan' focused on higher labor market flexibility, lower non-wage labor costs, modernization of the social security system, and a working education system [30].

This idea of economic reform as a master plan of politics is a central element in the political imaginary of the FT. The political community is described as a primarily economic community, and the complicated political issues are simplified and presented as having simple economic answers. The actual contents of these reforms are, however, often discussed vaguely. Rather they are thrown into the text as black boxes, reasonable solutions that float over the struggling polity as if the problems of society had a simple economic solution and as if there was a uniform and unquestionable understanding of the laws and functions of the economy. The question is not how to make an economy successful, but rather whether a society is willing to make the economy successful as the way to economic prosperity consists of a clearly delineated and well-known package of actions. The task of journalism is not to describe or discuss the various alternative solutions to a given country's problems but rather to assess whether the voters and politicians are bright enough to adopt the reasonable solution entitled economic, liberal, or fiscal reform.

Problem with the democratic process: the voters

The clash between the discourses of economic reform and the discourses of democracy is also clearly seen in the ways the voters are positioned. The 'will of the voters', deduced from the election results, forms one of the backbones of the democratic process. However in the researched election coverage stories, the FT does not show a great respect on their voice as voters are described rather seldom in positive light.

Somewhat exceptionally the German correspondent interprets in his column the 'will of the voters' in a favorable way 'Germans are ahead of their politicians in their willingness to accept reforms and change. All they need now is leaders with the courage to put that into practice' [31]. But especially in cases where the election result does not support economic reforms, the voters are labelled in unfavorable ways by questioning their reasonability and motives. Voters are also often characterized being lead by emotions and instincts rather than reason. They are considered emotional in opposition to the rationality of the rational economic reforms. A leader describes the situation after the Czech election in 2002:

> Reformist governments have struggled to win elections in ex-Communist central and Eastern Europe. Voters, angry with the pain of economic restructuring, have generally voted for a change of government when they have had the chance [32].

Besides being 'angry', voters are 'against change' [33], 'instinctively reform-shy' and 'alarmed' [34], 'taking revenge' [35], 'venting their anger' [36], 'spoilt' [37], their 'fears are exploited' [38], and, in the French case, they have 'superficial distrust' of global capitalism [39].

In France, the FT leader formulates a clear recipe challenging the voters' priority:

The government may be tempted to pour its energies into law and order – the voters' priority – and do little else. That would be a mistake. Consequently the leader lists a variety of 'unavoidable' reforms such as tax cuts, the reform of the 'bloated' bureaucracy and privatization [40].

The problems of the political system are often seen to lie within the irrationality of the electorate and framed in terms of irrational populism and nationalism. Alongside with the problems of populism [41] and 'hard-nosed' nationalism [42], the notion of xenophobia is mentioned as a problem, at least in Italian, Danish, Swedish, Russian, Austrian, Turkish, and Indian political life [43]. Sometimes, especially in the rare stories where voters are interviewed – thus including the 'real voice' of 'the man on the street' – they are described as passive bystanders, not interested in politics [44] and dissatisfied with politics in general.

In many cases, the inevitable reforms and the voters are seen as oppositional. In Russia 'the biggest problem for Putin is that modernization has to enter a stage where reforms really hurt' [45]. In an US election story, it is stated that the true problems of the economy cannot be discussed in elections, as the solutions would see Americans worse off and 'this is the problem with the democratic process' [46]. In Germany, the problem of the unreasonable and also morally suspect voters is clearly delineated in an analysis story on the 2005 election. The article takes off by saying 'no one doubts that Germany needs radical tax reform', but:

There lies the great dilemma. It seems that you cannot win a German election if you promise too much reform, even if all the party leaders know that pensions, the health service, the labour market and tax system need radical action [47].

The voters are criticized for being troubled by self-interest and for not warming up to the idea of a flat tax:

Yet Prof Kirchhof's flat tax solution is too radical for German voters to swallow. Most benefit from tax breaks and they do not want to lose them. Mr Schröder and his allies have exploited the fears by portraying the professor as a threat to the entire German social contract [48].

Voters are, thus, depicted as self-interested economic men, who are not capable of understanding the reasonable logic of reform. The real issues cannot be discussed in the public election debate, as voters would not back them up. Democratic politics are thus caught in the gridlock of the unreasonable voter.

Consequently, in some cases it is made clear that the government has to act despite the 'will of the electorate'. For instance, the analysis story as well as the leading article on the 2002 Czech elections suggest that economic reforms should be implemented even when they are adverse to the election-winning manifestos. As the reforms do not pass in elections, they need to be implemented just after the new government has been elected and well before the next elections.

The Prime Minister Spidla is recommended to immediately go on with an unpopular reform well before the next elections, as the 'main challenge' of the new prime minister is to cut the budget deficit and 'to reform the welfare state, particularly the loss-making state pension system'. The immediate pension reform is urged by a US think tank professor concluding '[t]he only time a new government can do it is one to two years after the election' [49].

The primacy of economic reform thus rolls over democracy. If the voters do not back the reform, it is to be implemented long before new elections take place and the elected politicians are to act against their election promises. In cases where the election results are in discrepancy with the ideas of the economic reform, the former gives way. The perception of voters is formulated by the financial journalistic discourses in ways, which do not hamper the primacy of the economic reform.

Sad truth about politics

The antidemocratic tone of FT's financial journalism is also visible in the ways national politics are described. National politics, which are the primary arena of democracy, are often treated with cautious criticism. At times, it looks like the sceptical discourse of the watchdog journalist and of the market liberalist suspicious of state, find each other and form a particular discourse of political cynicism, which is directed towards anti-reformatory politics. For example, in a post-election story on the German elections, the new prime minister is blamed for flowery language and described sceptically because he might not implement the liberal market reforms the FT supports:

> *While fitting for a morning-after speech, such flowery language gives few answers to the key question hanging over Germany's new government: whether the chancellor will use his renewed mandate to introduce the far-reaching reforms needed to kick-start the weak economy and restructure the country's creaking pension, health and social welfare systems* [50].

Most often the suspicion with politics seems to be linked with the national element of politics. The logics of globalizing capital and weakening of the nation state seem to be reflected in the discourse of the FT and its suspicion towards national politics. Politics often gets a somewhat dubious sound, as a way of dealing with things. There is lots of suspicion with regard to the 'old' national interest groups. This is related to the perspective of the global investor, who favors the new globalizing economy:

> *From the point of view of foreign investors, the crucial point is that economic reform, deregulation, privatization and the opening up of India to the world through lower tariffs and fewer trade barriers are likely to continue* [51].

This point of view seems to contribute to the rather negative tone towards nationally based politics and economies. The post-war national systems are seen in a negative light. The old nationally based politics are often depicted in a negative tone and seen as opposed to economic reform. In the Turkish case, a tough fiscal policy and the 'cleaning up of the banking system' are seen as foundation for a much 'healthier' economy. However it is warned that 'There is a danger that partisan politics might again be allowed to subvert transparency and genuine competition in the marketplace' [52]. In Japan, the pro-market reform, the 'lionheart' Prime Minister Koizumi is seen battling against the 'political machine' [53].

In the coverage of the Mexican elections in 2000, the until-then hegemonic Institutional Revolutionary Party is characterized as 'the world's longest-ruling political dynasty' [54]. Mexican society is hampered by 'oligopolists' and 'special interest groups' [55]. The German interest groups are described as 'antediluvian' [56]. Japan is hampered by 'pork-barrel' politics [57]. Politics, still very much a national activity, is characterized as 'partisan', as an antidote to something unpartisan and neutral. Politics incline towards 'political horse trading' [58] and 'ideological zigzags' [59].

After the German election 2005, the unfortunate election result is seen in terms of an opposition between politics and economic sensibility: 'As of today, the politically most likely and economically least sensible option is a grand coalition of some sort' [60].

Strong leaders wanted

As democracy, voters, elections, and politics pose problems for economic reformers, the solution is often seen in strong leadership. Strong leaders are sought and wanted in order to drive through the necessary liberal reforms and they are praised for their actions – at least as long as they are also economic reformers along the lines of the FT. Japan's Junichiro Koizumi fits the picture. In the case of the Japanese election in 2005 a column starts:

> *Junichiro Koizumi is the type of leader markets love: one with overwhelming public support and a mandate for reform. Japan's stock market yesterday added its vote of approval to his landslide election victory, hitting a four-year high* [61].

In another story, the following comment is made: 'many voters find attractive the idea of a leader standing up for what he believes in and daring to take on the sacred cows of the LDP'. The analysis is enhanced by quoting an informant:

'Koizumi is taking on the ancien régime,' says one person who has worked closely with the prime minister. 'He's the only one with the guts to do it. People like him for that' [62].

As the voters act somewhat irrationally, strong leadership, a semi-antithesis of democracy, is seen as the way to solve the problems of democracy. In the UK elections, the dilemma is summarized by a columnist, who compares the first-past-the-post and the proportional voting systems vice versa economic reforms:

But if we think of democracy as a decision rule, the issue is a little more complicated. At times when radical reform is needed, such as in the Britain of the late 1970s, first-past-the-post enables a government such as Margaret Thatcher's to take unpopular initiatives and allow the electorate to vote subsequently on the results. In Germany today the combination of proportional representation, plus the need on many issues to get a majority of the regional governments as well, puts a brake on needed reform [63].

In a similar tone, the prospect of UK politics is described in 2005 as depending on the capability of leading politicians and warns that a considerable part of the labor MPs are 'hardened rebels' who could pose a threat to reform:

Tony Blair and Gordon Brown forged a powerful alliance in the election campaign in order to put Labour back in power. The central question in British politics now is whether that co-operation will continue – or whether we will soon be back to the old squabbles of the past. If co-operation between the prime minister and the chancellor carries on with the same intensity seen recently, then Labour has a chance of pushing through a third-term reform programme [64].

The idea is not about respecting the views of the elected MPs but rather about hoping that opposing voices are silenced in the face of the 'united front'.

In the case of Mexico, the Mexican president is compared unfavorably with the determinate leadership of President Reagan:

Mr Reagan set an agenda with a limited number of clear priorities and hired effective 'enforcers' to work for him. Mr Fox appointed a politically diverse yet inexperienced cabinet with no clear 'enforcer' and failed to lay out a clear agenda [65].

In the Polish elections in 2001, the result is interpreted as unfortunate as it 'has left the country facing political uncertainty just when it needs strong leadership to prepare for European Union accession' [66]. In Sweden, the referendum on adopting the Euro and joining the EMU is seen as a matter of party leadership. In a pre-referendum story in 2002, where party leaders clearly supported the Euro but voters were divided, the FT sees that 'A strong and united SDP is seen as being best able to persuade sceptical Swedes that joining the single currency is in the country's interest' [67].

Also Germany – the country with voters most stubbornly resisting economic reforms – is suffering from the lack of strong leadership, which is noted in both the elections in 2002 and 2005. A leader concludes in 2002 'Germany and Europe need a chancellor who will be bloody, bold and resolute – and willing to take on vested interests for the greater good' [68].

The German 2005 elections are interpreted as a sign of a wider problem of the European political leaders in a news story entitled 'Spectre of election defeat stalks Europe's reformers'. Despite their constant 'vows' for economic reform, the European leaders have difficulties 'turning the rhetoric [of economic reform] into vote winning strategies'. The FT story infers that – with the notable exception of Margaret Thatcher – it has been not possible to promise a programme of radical economic reform in Europe and win elections. And further on, the same dilemma applies to the 'almost every post-communist government in central Europe' [69].

This emphasis on strong leadership seems to be linked with a rather anti-democratic understanding of democracy. If the outcomes of democracy are not what the FT hopes for, the problem lies with its weak leaders, not in weak ideas loosing in elections. The main task of the political leadership is thus to implement the economic reforms even when they are contradictory to the election results. This rather anti-democratic call for strong leadership can thus be understood as a way of trying to solve the discrepancies between the economic and democratic discourses by framing the unpopularity of the economic problems in terms of leadership rather than of democracy.

Political imaginary of financial journalism
The political imaginary of the early twenty-first century FT is founded on democracy and on market liberalism. However, when the hierarchy between these two discourses is analyzed, it becomes clear that the central element in the political imaginary of financial journalism is its priority for liberal market reforms. When in conflict, democracy, elections, voters, and politics are subservient to them.

The FT strongly promotes democracy both in western and non-western countries, but in cases where the proponents of market liberalism are not on the winning side in elections, the paper gets deeply critical of democracy. When the liberal economic reformers loose in elections, the FT frames the issues in ways, which belittle the democratic principles and practices. Moreover, the FT often takes clear political stances and maintains the need for the implementation of liberal economic reforms notwithstanding their poor performance in elections. The market reforms are seen as unavoidable, despite contradicting election results. In order to maintain the reasonability of its own political stance, the paper labels the voters as emotional or self-interested, national politics as morally questionable and calls for strong leaders.

The political imaginary of the FT can perhaps be understood as an element of the political regime of globalization as an attempt to re-imagine and redefine the national polis at the age of internationalized capital. This global imaginary questions the reasonability of national democracies and sees them as secondary to the primary aims of economic liberalism. The mobile capital has a need for a political language, which reduces the local meanings and co-ordinates them in a standardized way. David Harvey (1989: 284–307; 2001: 121–7) speaks of the time–space compression entailed in capitalism. Capital accumulation has always thrived for the speeding and widening up of action. It thus reduces and brings down temporal and spatial barriers that flexible capitalism does not need and only tolerates localized identities and polities. The early twenty-first century FT seems to be contributing to this globalizing discourse of the liberalized economy by questioning the premises of the nation state, national politics, and elections. The FT seems to carry on the interest of the internationalized investor and finance capital by trying to promote democracy and market economy in order to open up the national economies for international finance.

The practises and discourses of modern journalism have a role to play here. Modern journalism, which includes the financial journalism of the FT, has been characterized by strives for autonomic professionalism, for impartiality, as well as for independence and freedom from external control. The Anglo-Saxon press adopted these ideals of the news paradigm first during the nineteenth century, and their birth has been linked with the historical and economic conditions of news production as well as with attempts to create professional integrity and to legitimize journalistic work (Barnhurst, 2005; Pöttker, 2005a; Schudson, 2005). This tradition of impartial professionalism should however not be understood as the only constitutive element of journalism. In many cases, its importance might even be exaggerated. For instance, Michael Schudson argues that the norm of objectivity was never adopted with such fervour in British journalism as in the case of North American journalism (Schudson, 2001: 165–7). Thus rather than being only a fact-finding mission, journalism is a mixture of various elements (Carpentier, 2005; Deuze, 2005; Pöttker, 2005b), and this indeed also seems to be the case with FT's financial journalism. Covered by the language of impartial journalism, the paper takes strong political stances.

From the point of the democracy, the political imaginary of the FT has a questionable element in its cynicism towards politics, voters, and democracy. The

FT's journalism seems to contribute to the anti-political vein of the trans-national economy, undermining the principles of democracy (Kantola, 2001). The FT seems to have a master plan of politics, a pre-ordained 'black box' of economic reform that must be implemented in any case. The political imaginary of the FT journalism is thus dominated by economism – a strong belief that societal and political issues are economic issues and can be solved by economic solutions. This imaginary is based on an antithetical position towards the democratic polis: the imaginary of the economic machine, which needs to be run according to clear rules and which needs to be controlled by strong leaders; not by politics, a diversity of opinions and heteronomy but rather by a unity of opinions. The paradox is that this system of preordained order is promoted in the name of liberalism, freedom, and democracy. Thus one could say that the political imaginary of FT's financial journalism has a flavour of hypocrisy: democracy hailed in principle but belittled in practice.

At the same time, the FT seems to construct a globalizing deterritorialized elite space in the public sphere. What is left is a deterrorialized language not linked to any specific place. National and local circumstances are transformed into an 'environment' or a home base, which needs to be developed from the point of the view of global capital as sites of production and consumption. Thus democracy, elections and voters become troublesome when representing logics and ideas that might harass the advance of the capital. Globalizing capitalism, or as Marc Augé (1995) says, supermodernity, develops abstract notions, which bypass the local histories and reformulate local spaces as sites of production. There is less special meaning attached to a space. A space can be characterized by more general qualifications, which may be standardized and applicable to other spaces as well. As this unifying and deterritorialized language is loosing its links with everyday reality and local circumstances, it is used primarily for governing spaces with a globalized imaginary of productivism, which belittles the local polities and democracies as nuisances for the inevitable advance of the global economy.

Notes for Chapter Nine

[1] The selection of the research material on the 2-week period might leave out some nuances of the election coverage process. However, the majority of the election reporting is concentrated within the researched period. An explorative check of the other election stories confirmed that they were similar to the actual research material. The main advantage of the 2-week selection period is that the material is more consistent and comparable between countries as the research material concentrates on the main stories surrounding the elections.

[2] World News – Europe: Red faces in ministry over fiasco at the poll booths: High turnout reflected the strong popular interest in the election, but caught the organizers on the hop, Paul Betts, 14 May 2001.

[3]   Leader: Return to the centre, 24 January 2003.

[4]   Leader: Indian vote signals, 3 May 2004.

[5]   Comment and analysis: Fox spurs a revolution: The former Coca-Cola salesman's victory marks Mexico's transition from one-party rule to pluralist democracy, Henry Tricks and Richard Lapper, 4 July 2000.

[6]   Postal vote: Koizumi makes Japan choose between paternalism and the free market, David Pilling, 10 August 2005.

[7]   Leader: Japan in transition, 10 September 2005.

[8]   Europe: Leaders fall on swords as voters rise in rebellion, Leyla Boulton, 5 November 2002.

[9]   Europe: Putin holds political cards after opponents trounced, By Andrew Jack and Arkady Ostrovsky, 9 December 2003.

[10] Leader: Putin power, 9 December 2003.

[11] Europe: Triumph brings Persson closer to euro, Christopher Brown-Humes and Nicholas George in Stockholm; 17 September 2002. Comment and analysis: Germany resists change, but Joschka Fischer looks ahead. Brian Groom and Haig Simonian; 24 September 2002. German elections: Schröder promises to 'push forward with renewal', Hugh Williamson in Berlin; 24 September 2002.

[12] Europe: Czechs' modest new premier faces up to huge reform challenge. Robert Anderson; 19 June 2002.

[13] Comment and analysis: Free trade with the United States and Canada did not spur wider economic reform, and limited progress towards creating prosperity is in danger, John Authers and Sara Silver; 1 July, 2003.

[14] Comment and analysis: Hail Berlusconi: The scale of the centre-right's victory suggests Italy's new premier has a mandate for change but he faces difficulties on at least three fronts, James Blitz, 15 May 2005.

[15] Europe: Portuguese PM faces tough route to 'Nordic' prosperity, Peter Wise in Lisbon; 22 Feb 2005.

[16] Lex column: Enemy of the state, 13 September 2005.

[17] Comment and analysis: A second bite for Gerhard Schröder, Heinrich Von Pierer, 24 September 2002.

[18] Leader: Time for leadership in Germany, 24 September 2002.

[19] Poll deals blow to advocates of EU economic reform, George Parker and James Blitz, 19 September 2005.

[20] Companies International: India emerges as the new star of Asia: Democracy – and growth, Daniel Bogler, 10 May 2004.

[21] Europe: Centre-right poll win boosts Slovakia's EU chances, Robert Anderson in Bratislava, 23 September 2002.

[22] Europe and International Economy: European Union hails centre-right victory in Slovakia, Robert Anderson, 24 September 2002.

[23] Asia-Pacific: Election setback for Indian reformers, Edward Luce in New Delhi, 12 May 2004.

[24] Leader: Indian vote signals, 3 May 2004.

[25] Asia-Pacific: Election setback for Indian reformers, Edward Luce in New Delhi, 12 May 2004. Leader: India's challenge, 19 April 2004.

[26] Asia-Pacific: Voters take revenge on India's leading symbol of reform, Edward Luce, 12 May 2004.

[27] World News: Jubilant Persson increases his vote, Nicholas George and Christopher Brown-Humes in Stockholm, 16 September 2002.

[28] Leader: Same Swedes, 17 September 2002.

[29] Leader: Czech chance, 17 June 2002.

[30] German elections: Business gloomy on growth prospects, By Bertrand Benoit in Berlin, 24 September 2002.

[31] Inside track: Colors of coalition, Daniel Bogler, 27 September 2002.

[32] Leader: Czech chance, 17 June 2002.

[33] Political gridlock in Germany reflects a vote against change, Wolfgang Munchau, 20 September 2005.

[34] Radical reform alarms German voters, 15 September 2005.

[35] Asia-Pacific: Voters take revenge on India's leading symbol of reform, Edward Luce, 12 May 2004.

[36] Leader: Poll Shock, 25 September 2001.

[37] World News – Europe: Norwegian electorate set to abandon party loyalties: There is uncertainty about which will emerge as biggest party, Christopher Brown-Humes and Valeria Criscione, 6 September 2001.

[38] Radical Reform alarms German voters, 15 September 2005.

[39] Comment and Analysis: France goes on sale, Victor Mallet, 18 June 2002.

[40] Leader: French lessons, 18 June 2002.

[41] Centre-left wins majority in Norwegian election, Päivi Munter in Oslo, 12 September 2005.

[42] Leader: Bush gets mandate to be strong abroad, 4 November 2004.

[43] Comment and Analysis: Hail Berlusconi: The scale of the centre-right's victory suggests Italy's new premier has a mandate for change but he faces difficulties on at least three fronts, James Blitz, 15 May 2001. Leader: Rasmussen twins, 22 November 2001. Leader: Same Swedes, 17 September 2002. Europe: Leaders fall on swords as voters rise in rebellion, Leyla Boulton, 5 November 2002. Europe: Prospect of Haider comeback looms over coalition politics, Eric Frey in Vienna, 26 November 2002. Leader: Putin power, 9 December 2003. Leader: Indian vote signals, 3 May 2004.

[44] Politicians fail to connect as voters look to their wallets, Richard Milne in Munich and Bertrand Benoit in Berlin, 19 September 2005. The Americas: Battle for Danforth Avenue could swing Toronto vote, Ken Warn, 25 June 2004.

[45] Comment and analysis: Four more years: but will Putin's desire for a strong state hamper economic reform? Top jobs set an assertive tone; Andrew Jack and Stefan Wagstyl, 17 Mar 2004.

[46] FT Money: The morning after, and a nation beset by debts, Philip Coggan, 6 November 2004.

[47] Radical reform alarms German voters, 15 September 2005.

[48] Radical reform alarms German voters, 15 September 2005.

[49] Europe: Czechs' modest new premier faces up to huge reform challenge, by Robert Anderson, 19 June 2002.

[50] German elections: Schröder promises to 'push forward with renewal', By Hugh Williamson in Berlin, 24 September 2002.

[51] Companies International: India emerges as the new star of Asia: Democracy – and growth, Daniel Bogler, 10 May 2004.

[52] Comment and analysis: Turkey should not abandon Ataturk, Kemal Dervis, 5 November 2002.

[53] Koizumi vindicated: renewal is achieved for his party and is in prospect for Japan, David Pilling, 13 September 2005.

[54] Comment and analysis: Fox spurs a revolution: The former Coca-Cola salesman's victory marks Mexico's transition from one-party rule to pluralist democracy, Henry Tricks and Richard Lapper, 4 July 2000.

[55] Comment and Analysis: Free trade with the United States and Canada did not spur wider economic reform, and limited progress towards creating prosperity is in danger, John Authers and Sara Silver, 1 July 2003.

[56] Inside track: Colors of coalition, Daniel Bogler, 27 September 2002.

[57] Koizumi vindicated: renewal is achieved for his party and is in prospect for Japan, David Pilling, 13 September 2005.

[58] Lex Column: German gridlock, 19 September 2005.

[59] Leader: Germany votes, 20 September 2002.

[60] Political gridlock in Germany reflects a vote against change, Wolfgang Munchau, 20 September 2005.

[61] Lex Column: Enemy of the state, 13 September 2005.

[62] Postal vote: Koizumi makes Japan choose between paternalism and the free market, David Pilling, 10 August 2005.

[63] Samuel Brittan: Democracy alone is not enough, Samuel Brittan, 12 May 2005.

[64] Election 2005. The third term: United front needed to face down rebels, James Blitz, 7 May 2005.

[65] Comment and analysis: Free trade with the United States and Canada did not spur wider economic reform, and limited progress towards creating prosperity is in danger, John Authers and Sara Silver, 1 July 2003.

[66] Leader: Poll shock, 25 September 2001.

[67] World News: Jubilant Persson increases his vote, Nicholas George and Christopher Brown-Humes in Stockholm, 16 September 2002.

[68] Leader: Time for leadership in Germany. 24 September 2002.

[69] Leader: Time for leadership in Germany, 24 September 2002. Spectre of election defeat stalks Europe's reformers, Robert Anderson, Paivi Munter, George Parker and John Thornhill, 22 September 2005.

References for Chapter Nine

Anderson, B. (1983), *Imagined Communities: Reflections on the Origin and Spread of Nationalism*, New York: Verso.

Augé, M. (1995), *Non-Places, Introduction to an Anthropology of Supermodernity*, London: Verso.

Barnhurst, K. (2005), 'News Ideology in the Twentieth Century', in S. Høyer and H. Pöttker (eds.), *Diffusion of the News Paradigm*, Göterborg: Nordicom, pp. 239–62.

Bauman, Z. (1999), *In Search of Politics*, Cambridge: Polity Press.

Blumler, J., Gurevitch, M. (1995), *The Crisis of Public Communication*, London: Routledge.

Cameron, A., Palan, R. (2004), *The Imagined Economies of Globalization*, London: Sage.

Carpentier, N. (2005), 'Identity, Contingency and Rigidity. The (Counter-)Hegemonic Constructions of the Identity of the Media Professional', *Journalism*, 6: 2, pp. 199–219.

Cerny, P. (1990), *The Changing Architecture of Politics. Structure, Agency and the Future of the State*, London: Sage.

Clarke, J. (2004), *Changing Welfare, Changing State. New Directions in Social Policy*, London: Sage.

Dahlgren, P. (2001), 'The Public Sphere and the Net. Structure, Space and Communication', in L. W. Bennett and R. M. Entma (eds.), *Mediated Politics. Communication in the Future of Democracy*, Cambridge: Cambridge University Press, pp. 33–55.

Deuze, M. (2005), 'What is Journalism? Professional Identity and Ideology of Journalists Reconsidered', *Journalism*, 6: 4, pp. 442–64.

Financial Times (2005a), 'European Opinion Leaders Survey 2003'. www.ft.com/mediakit. Downloaded on 19 August 2005.

—— (2005b), 'The FT audience in the UK. The FT Audience in Europe. The FT Audience in Asia.' www.ft.com/toolkit. Downloaded on 19 August 2005.

Franklin, B. (2004), *Packaging Politics. Political Communications in Britain's Media Democracy*, (2nd ed.), London: Arnold.

González-Vélez, M. (2002), 'Assessing the Conceptual Use of Social Imagination in Media Research', *Journal of Communication Inquiry*, 26: 4, pp. 349–53.

Habermas, J. (1999), 'The European Nation-State and the Pressures of Globalization', *New Left Review*, 1: 23, pp. 46–59.

Hardt, M., Negri, A. (2000), *Empire*, Cambridge, Massachusetts: Harvard University Press.

Harvey, D. (1989), *The Condition of Postmodernity*, Oxford: Basil Blackwell.

—— (2001), *Spaces of Capital. Towards a Critical Geography*, Edinburgh: Edinburgh University Press.

Hay, C. (2004), 'The Normalising Role of Rationalist Assumptions in the Institutional Embedding of Neoliberalism', *Economy and Society*, 33: 4, pp. 500–27.

Hirst, P., Thompson, G. (1996), *Globalization in Question: the Iinternational Economy and the Possibilities of Governance*, Cambridge: Polity Press.

Kantola, A. (2001), 'Leaving Public Places: Antipolitical and Antipublic Forces of the Transnational Economy', *Javnost*, 8: 1, pp. 59–74.

Kynaston, D. (1988), *The Financial Times. A Centenary History*, London: Viking.

Louw, E. (2005), *The Media and Political Process*, London: Sage.

McNair, B. (2000), *Journalism and Democracy: An Evaluation of the Political Public Sphere*, London: Routledge.

Pöttker, H. (2005a), 'The News Pyramid and its Origin From the American Journalism in the 19th Century. A Professional Approach and an Empirical Inquiry', in S. Høyer and H. Pöttker (eds.), *Diffusion of the News Paradigm*, Göterborg: Nordicom, pp. 51–64.

—— (2005b), 'Epilogue. Perspectives on the Development of the News Paradigm', in S. Høyer and H. Pöttker (eds.), *Diffusion of the News Paradigm*, Göterborg: Nordicom, pp. 263–72.

Schmidt, V. (1995), 'The New World Order, Incorporated: The Rise of Business and the Decline of the Nation State', *Daedalus*, 124: 2, pp. 75–106.

Schudson, M. (2001), 'The Objectivity Norm in American Journalism', *Journalism*, 2: 2, pp. 149–70.

Schudson, M. (2005), 'The Emergence of the Objectivity Norm in American Journalism', in S. Høyer and H. Pöttker (eds.), *Diffusion of the News Paradigm*, Göterborg: Nordicom, pp. 19–36.

Sklair, L. (2002), 'The Transnational Capitalist Class and Global Politics: Deconstructing the Corporate-State Connection', *International Political Science Review*, 23: 2, pp. 159–74.

Strange, S. (1996), *The Retreat of the State: The Diffusion of Power in the World Economy*, Cambridge: Cambridge University Press.

Taylor, C. (2004), *Modern Social Imaginaries*, Durham: Duke University Press.

Touraine, A. (1990), 'The Idea of Revolution', *Theory, Culture and Society*, 7, pp. 121–41.

Warf, B. (1999), 'The Hypermobility of Capital and the Collapse of the Keynesian State', in R. Martin (ed.), *Money and the Space Economy*, Chichester: John Wiley & Sons, pp. 227–39.

Activism and Media

Bart Cammaerts

Activism is a relatively new term, introduced in the mid-70s and referring to the ability to act and make or change history. 'It reminds us that the world not only is, but is made', as Gitlin (2003: 5) wrote to a young activist. However, what is implied here is theorized at the level of social change theory, social movement theory, or notions such as resistance, advocacy or protest (Kling and Posner, 1990; Tarrow, 1998; Goodwin and Jasper, 2003). In any case, agency and the makeability of society is central to any tentative definition of activism. As Jordan (2002: 23) points out, 'activism is generating the future of societies'. Activism, from this perspective, represents the practice of struggling for change and can be fueled by reactionary tendencies and aims, as well as progressive. The online participatory encyclopedia *Wikipedia* [1] is thus fairly on the spot when it defines activism as an 'intentional action to bring about social or political change'. It is appropriate to use Wikipedia here, as it is in its own right a form of media activism, driven by the copyleft Creative Commons ideals. Other forms of media activism include electronic advocacy, hacktivism, and culture jamming. But it would be reductive to only consider media activism here, excluding the crucial role of media and communication in activist strategies and processes of social change.

Although not the only form of activism, direct action or what Kluge (1982: 212) calls the 'immediate on-the-spot struggle', is nevertheless central to every historic struggle for new rights, as well as those for the extension – or the safeguarding – of existing rights (Mellor, 1920; Wallerstein, 1990). Whether it will be through (sometimes but certainly not always violent) protests and demonstrations, strikes, sit-ins, consumer boycotts, or non-violent civil disobedience, direct action is at the core of processes of social change. This, however, does not mean that activism is synonymous with direct action. There are also practices or forms of activism that are less direct action driven and operate more within the dominant political and judicial system. Examples of this are judicial activism – challenging the state and companies through the court, and lobbying – attempting to influence legislators or governments.

Processes of social change, activism and social movements, which in a sense can be seen as the institutionalization of particular struggles, cannot be viewed without taking into account the notion of revolution (Lenin, 1929; Robert, 1978; Wood, 1992; McLaren, 2001). The American, French, Russian, and Cuban revolutions have all in their own way radically changed society, not only locally, but well beyond the territories where they took place. Disrupting the vested hierarchies within society and other structures, not in the least economic structures, did, however, come at a cost. The coercive and often very violent practices forcing the ruling elite to relinquish power and the bloody repression that usually followed revolutions, would be deemed unacceptable today.

In recent history, a delicate balance between on the one hand public pressure, confrontation, violence at times, and on the other hand the gradual pacification of the social, cultural, and political conflicts by the dominant economic, political, and judicial elites, was established within democratic societies (Harvey, 1989: 129; Rootes and Davis, 1994; Dahl, 1998). In this regard can also be referred to the 'Janus-head strategy' that activism increasingly adopts, 'combining strategic and partial incorporation with continued resistance and independent critique,' (Servaes and Carpentier, 2005: 10). For example, the adoption of ecological policies by most democratic countries or the legislative changes allowing same-sex couples to marry or adopt children, show that long-term struggles, waged by the green movement and the gay-lesbian movement, do ultimately (albeit gradually) result in societal change, at least within most democratic societies.

As these examples show, current struggles for social change relate to a much lesser extent to the dichotomies of labor and capital, of class, then was the case in past struggles (Hall, 2002). Some sociologists also point towards the general contentment of working classes in many Western countries (Galbraith, 1992), which might in turn explain increasing conservatism, exclusionism, xenophobia and fear of change amongst large parts of the working classes (Dahrendorf, 1987).

Issue-oriented struggles, identity politics and lifestyle politics, pose a very different – often moral or ethical – challenge to the dominant order than the classical conflicts between labor and capital did (Beck, 1994; Giddens, 1994). The pacification of these new more ethical conflicts is a complex and slow process, a balancing act of diverging interests, views, and convictions, more consensual then revolutionary. Social and cultural change has become even more so a process that involves changing attitudes, values and behaviors, hearts and minds of citizens (sic), after which the issues ideally permeate into the formal political agenda, leading to changes in the law.

As a result of these developments, and for other socio-economic and cultural reasons, violence has – at least in the West – largely lost much its legitimacy as a tool to resist or promote change. The recent fairly peaceful transitions in Georgia (2003), Ukraine (2004), and Lebanon (2005) are also proof of that, despite exceptions as the bloody disintegration of Yugoslavia. This, however, has not led to a decline of direct action, on the contrary. Empirical research suggests that mobilization and protest by citizens, as well as civil society actors, is on the rise in advanced capitalist countries when compared to other periods in Western history (Meyer and Tarrow, 1998; Norris, 2002). Direct action – civic disobedience, demonstrations, protest-actions – is more than ever an essential tactic for any movement or activist to attract attention in the public sphere for the causes and aims they fight for. Political participation also partly shifted from involvement in political parties and old social movements to engagement in civil society organizations, NGOs, specific campaigns, or a certain direct action (Norris, 2002).

Current social movements and activists no longer strive to achieve change through 'conquering' formal political power, such as the labor movement beginning of twentieth century or the green movement accomplished in 1980s. Subcommandante Marcos, leader of the Zapatista-uprising in Chiapas, stated in 1996:

> *We do not struggle to take power, we struggle for democracy, liberty, and justice. Our political proposal is the most radical in Mexico (perhaps in the world, but it is still too soon to say). It is so radical that all the traditional political spectrum (right, center left and those of one or the other extreme) criticize us and walk away from our delirium.*
>
> *It is not our arms which make us radical; it is the new political practice which we propose and in which we are immersed with thousands of men and women in Mexico and the world: the construction of a political practice which does not seek the taking of power but the organisation of society* (Marcos, 1996).

There is an apparent inconsistency in what Marcos sets out, as deciding on how society is organized, as well as enforcing or implementing those decisions, is very much at the heart of what politics and power is about. In effect, Marcos' argument is a manifestation of the Janus-head strategy, whereby a movement constantly applies outside pressure, while at the same time parts of that movement engage in a political process of dialogue. Both elements of the movement strive for the same goals, but with distinct political strategies. This interaction between dialogue and conflict is, in part, made possible because the movement has no ambitions to gain institutional power, become incorporated by the political system or overthrow its adversary.

This also had to be seen against the backdrop of the so-called end of ideologies or, as one author asserted optimistically, even the end of history (Fukuyama, 1992). While neo-liberal authors proclaimed the victory of capitalism and democratic rule, Giddens (1994b) pleaded for socialism to fully embrace the (corrected) free market and move beyond the left-right dichotomy to regain or retain political power. In a bid for the narrow margin of floating voters, party policies of dominant parties tend to converge towards the political center, thereby obscuring ideology (and power) from the public debate (Faux, 1999). Others argue against this and promote a radically pluralistic public sphere where political differences, tensions and conflicts of interest – still present in every society – are made explicit again (Mouffe, 1999).

Crucial to current 'non-institutional' politics, as Offe (1987: 69) calls it, is the need to strategically essentialize and defragment often disconnected struggles. In this regard, the anti-/alter-globalization movement can be considered as the first clear attempt to provide an ideological framework to structure and connect a 'multitude' of current struggles (Held and McGrew, 2003; Hardt and Negri, 2004) and thus construct an alternative citizen-oriented discourse to the hegemonic neo-liberal recipes.

In recent years, with the Zapatista uprising in Chiapas-México as a catalyst, we have clearly witnessed a new surge in transnational resistance and the transnational organization of civil society actors (Holloway and Peláez, 1998; Guidry *et al.*, 2000; Smith and Johnston, 2002; Clark, 2003; Della Porta and Tarrow, 2004). This is, of course, not a totally new phenomenon (Boli and Thomas, 1997; Keck and Sikkink, 2000). For instance the 'Socialist International' was a more or less successful – albeit fragmented – attempt to internationalize the class struggle. Another example of an early transnational movement was/is the movement for women rights – seeking to extend citizenship rights for women and later fighting for the equal treatment of woman in society. From the 1970s onwards the green movement – also operating at a transnational level – has managed to strike a chord in many countries. The increased ability of civil society to transnationalize its practices and discourses of resistance, aided by information and communication technologies, should not be exaggerated. Even though transnational or international initiatives are increasingly relevant and crucial to counter the dominant neo-liberal paradigm, and to have an impact at the international level of governance, the national, local initiatives and local direct actions are equally important and often also more effective in getting results. Many of the issues being addressed today are, however, often transnational in nature or at least requiring a transnational resolution (Vertovec and Cohen, 2002).

Media, in this context, can be understood both as a medium to communicate, propagate and interact, as well as a battlefield – a 'symbolic arena' – for the struggle to signify, where meanings making sense of the world and ideas of what citizenship entails – from a national, but increasingly also from a regional or global perspective – compete.

In order to grasp the complexity of the panoply of civil society actors, as well as their very different strategies and aims, analytical distinctions such as online/offline, alternative media/mainstream media, new media/old media, need to be overcome. For direct action to be successful, it is important to have own means of communication and self-representation, but it is equally important to use the mainstream media in order to communicate beyond the cosy circle of likeminded sympathizers (Gitlin, 1980; Gamson and Wolfsfeld, 1993).

The Internet and its effect on activism have received a considerable amount of attention in recent years amongst scholars (Hill and Hughes, 1989; Meikle, 2002; van de Donk *et al.* 2004). Many civil society organizations are, however, conscious that the use of the Internet is burdened with many constraints, of which access and fragmentation are the most obvious. As such, they diversify their media strategies to also include more traditional forms of media such as print or radio (Cammaerts, 2005).

Activism can, however, not be confined to the media-realm. Establishing trust amongst activists, collaborative arrangements between organizations and diverse forms of direct action need the offline, as much as the online. As often, it is the interaction between the two binaries of the dichotomy that is most relevant and crucial towards organizing, mobilizing and debating resistance.

Notes for Section Four: Introduction

[1]   See http://en.wikipedia.org/activism.

References for Section Four: Introduction

Beck, U. (1994), 'The Reinvention of Politics: Towards a Theory of Reflexive Modernization', in U. Beck, A. Giddens, and S. Lash (eds.), *Reflexive Modernization: Politics, Tradition and Aesthetics in the Modern Social Order*, Cambridge: Polity Press, pp. 1–55.

Boli, J., Thomas, G. M. (1997), 'World Culture in the World Polity: A Century of International Non-Governmental Organisations', *American Sociological Review*, 62, pp. 171–90.

Cammaerts, B. (2005), 'ICT-Usage Among Transnational Social Movements in the Networked Society – to Organise, to Mobilise and to Debate', in R. Silverstone (ed.), *Media, Technology and Everyday Life in Europe: From Information to Communication*, Aldershot: Ashgate, pp. 53–72.

Clark, J. (ed.) (2003), *Globalizing Civic Engagement: Civil Soicety and Transnational Action*, London: Earthscan.

Cohen, J. L., Arato, A. (1992), *Civil Society and Political Theory*, Cambridge, MA: MIT Press.

Dahl, R. (1998), *On Democracy*, New Haven, London: Yale University Press.

Dahrendorf, R. (1987), 'The Erosion of Citizenship and its Consequences for us all', *New Statesman*, 12 June: p. 13.

della Porta, D., Tarrow, S. G. (eds.) (2004), *Transnational Protest and Global Activism*, Lanham, MD: Rowman & Littlefield.

Faux, J. (1999), 'Lost on the Third Way', *Dissent*, 46: 2, pp. 67–76.

Fukuyama, F. (1992), *The End of History and the Last Man*, London: Pinguin.

Galbraith, J. K. (1992), *The Culture of Contentment*, London: Penguin.

Gamson, W. A., Wolfsfeld, G. (1993), 'Movements and Media as Interacting Systems', *Annals of the American Academy of Political and Social Movements*, 526, pp. 114–27.

Giddens, A. (1994a), *Modernity and Self-Identity: Self and Society in the Late Modern Age*, Cambridge: Polity Press.

—— (1994b), *Beyond Left and Right: The Future of Radical Politics*, Cambridge: Polity Press.

—— (2000), *The Third Way and its Critics*, Cambridge: Polity Press.

Gitlin, T. (1980), *The Whole World is Watching: Mass Media in the Making & Unmaking of the New Left*, Berkeley/London: University of California Press.

—— (2003), *Letters to a Young Activist*, New York: Basic Books.

Goodwin, J., Jasper, J. M. (eds.) (2003), *The Social Movement Reader: Cases and Concepts*, Oxford: Blackwell Publising.

Guidry, J., Kennedy, M. D., Zald, M. (eds.) (2000), *Globalizations and Social Movements: Culture, Power, and the Transnational Public Sphere*, Ann Arbor: University of Michigan Press.

Hall, S. (2002), 'Democracy, Globalization and Difference', in O. Enwezor, C. Basualdo, U. M. Bauer, S. Ghez, S. Maharaj, M. Nash and O. Zaya (eds.), *Democracy Unrealized – Documenta11_Platform1*, Kassel: Hatje Cantz, pp. 21–6.

Hardt, M., Negri, A. (2004), *Multitude: War and Democracy in the Age of Empire*, New York: Penguin.

Harvey, D. (1989), *The Condition of Postmodernity: an Enquiry into the Origins of Cultural Change*, Oxford: Blackwell.

Held, D., McGrew, A. (eds.) (2003), *The Global Transformations Reader*, Cambridge: Polity Press.

Hill, K. A., Hughes, J. E. (1998), *Cyberpolitics: Citizen Activism in the Age of the Internet*, Lanham, MD: Rowman & Littlefield.

Holloway, J., Peláez, E. (eds.) (1998), *Zapatista!: Reinventing Revolution in Mexico*, London: Pluto Press.

Jordan, T. (2002), *Activism! Direct Action, Hacktivism and the Future of Society*, London: Reaktion Books

Keck, M., Sikkink, K. (2000), 'Historical Precursors to Modern Transnational Social Movements and Networks', in J. Guidry, M. D. Kennedy, and M. Zald (eds.), *Globalizations and Social Movements: Culture, Power, and the Transnational Public Sphere*, Ann Arbor: University of Michigan Press, pp. 35–53.

Kling, J. M., Posner, P. S. (1990), *Dilemmas of Activism: Class, Community, and the Politics of Local Mobilization*, Philadelphia: Temple University Press.

Kluge, A. (1982), 'On Film and the Public Sphere', *New German Critique*, 24/25, Fall/Winter, pp. 211–12.

Lenin, V. I. (1929), *Preparing for Revolt*, London: Modern Books.

Marcos (1996), 'What Makes us Different is our Political Proposal', Open Letter of the Zapatista Army of National Liberation Mexico to National and International Civil Society, August 30.

Mclaren, P. (2001), *Che Guevara, Paolo Freire and the Pedagogy of Revolution*, London: Routledge.

Meikle, G. (2002), *Future Active: Media Activism and the Internet*, New York: Routledge.

Mellor, W. (1920), *Direct action*, London: L. Parsons.

Meyer, D. S., Tarrow, S. (1998), *The Social Movement Society: Contentious Politics for a New Century*, Lanham: Rowman & Littlefield.

Mouffe, C. (1999), 'Deliberative Democracy or Agonistic Pluralism?' *Social Research*, 66: 3, pp. 746–58.

Norris, P. (2002), *Democratic Phoenix: Reinventing Political Activism*, Cambridge: Cambrdige University Press.

Offe, C. (1987), 'Challenging the Boundaries of Institutional Politics. Social Movements Since the 1960s', in C. S. Maier (ed.), *Changing Boundaries of the Political. Essays on the Evolving Balance Between the State and Society, Public and Private in Europe*, Cambridge: Cambridge University Press, pp. 63–105.

Roberts, J. M. (1978), *The French Revolution*, Oxford: Oxford University Press.

Rootes, C., Davis, H. (eds.) (1994), *Social Change and Political Transformation*, London: UCL Press.

Servaes, J., Carpentier, N. (2005), 'Introduction: Steps to Achieve a Sustainable Information Society', in J. Servaes and N. Carpentier (eds.), *Deconstructing WSIS: Towards a Sustainable Agenda for the Future Information Society*, Bristol, UK and Portland, OR, USA: Intellect, pp. 5–16.

Smith, J. G., Johnston, H. (eds.) (2002), *Globalization and Resistance: Transnational Dimensions of Social Movements*, Lanham, MD: Rowman & Littlefield.

Tarrow, S. G. (1994), *Power in Movement: Social Movements, Collective Action and Politics*, Cambridge: Cambridge University Press.

—— (1998), *Power in Movement*, (2nd ed.), Cambridge: Cambridge University Press.

van De Donk, W., Loader, B. D., Nixon, P. G., *et al.* (eds.) (2004), *Cyberprotest: New Media, Citizens, and Social Movements*, London: Routledge.

Vertovec, S., Cohen, R. (eds.) (2002), *Conceiving Cosmopolitanism: Theory, Context and Practice*, Oxford: Oxford University Press.

Wallerstein, I. (1990), 'Antisystemic Movements: History and Dilemas', in S. Amin, G. Arrighi, A. G. Frank, *et al.* (eds.), *Transforming the Revolution*, New York: Monthly Review Press, pp. 13–53.

Wood, G. S. (1992), *The Radicalism of the American Revolution: How a Revolution Transformed a Monarchical Society into a Democratic One Unlike Any That Had Ever Existed*, New York: Alfred A. Knopf.

Chapter Ten

Contesting global capital, new media, solidarity, and the role of a social imaginary

Natalie Fenton

Introduction

> *Maybe it is not really possible, at least not in the foreseeable future (…) to undermine the global capitalist system because we cannot imagine any alternative to it.* (Žižek, 1999: 352)

This chapter suggests that the social and political dynamics of protest are changing due to the ways in which economic globalization and technological revolution has reconfigured politics, social institutions and identity formation within societies. The relationship between new media technologies and social/political mobilization is a specifically modern phenomenon, contemporaneous with and responding to dominant capitalist communications. Today the trend towards concentration marches forth, policies of privatization and deregulation of the media reveal a world-wide trend towards the commodification of information, culture and, hence, of democracy. We are witnessing the privatization of access to information and culture with the shrinking of public space in mainstream communications. Alongside this decline in public space is a digital explosion. This chapter begins from the standpoint that we cannot ignore that we still live in deeply unequal capitalist societies, driven by profit and competition operating on a global scale. It is also premised on the belief that we live in a media dominated world with many different ideas and identities in circulation at any one time. Future studies in communication and mediation need to more adeptly understand the former to appreciate the latter – the relationship between individual autonomy, freedom, and rational action on the one hand and the social construction of identity and behavior on the other. This is often expressed in the catch-all categories of structure and agency, the public and the private, and production and consumption. In other words, in the current media landscape within an ever-globalizing economy, the political, cultural, and economic are interconnected and interdependent. As more and more aspects of social life become subject to commercial pressures or become commercial in and of themselves how can we ever conceive of transcending capitalism and progressing a democratic political project?

One way of approaching this task is to consider the role of new media in mobilizing oppositional politics. In the last 5–10 years, protest upsurges have been facilitated by new communication technologies. In a global economy, new social movements are now indelibly connected to new media that affords them the possibility of transnational activism. This is, in part, a factor of the aesthetics and form of new media suggestive of the end of linearity, dissolution of the sequel narrative, a communicative process that is additive, interactive, and always unfinished – a form that suits the dynamic, fluid nature of social movement politics. But it is also in large part both dependent on and a response to the structuring forces of global capitalism. This ever-densening web of micro-activisms that enables transnational alliances between disparate groups and causes to condense against the macro logic of global capital is also localized, fragmented, disaggregated, and divided.

In this chapter, it is argued that new media have the potential to mediate solidarity, but that in order for a political project to emerge from a collective identity, a collaborative and collective understanding of an end point is necessary – the hope of a better tomorrow, however thinly expressed. In promoting an analytical framework that can address both political economic, technological, social, and cultural factors the chapter proposes that one of the key questions for future studies in communication and mediation is to ask ourselves 'What is the role of new media in establishing a social imaginary?'

Contesting global capital: the role of the Internet

Klein (2000) argues that the Internet facilitates international communication between non-governmental organizations (NGOs) thus allowing protesters to respond on an international level to local events while requiring minimal resources and bureaucracy. According to Klein, the Internet is more than an organizing tool. It is also an organizing model for a new form of political protest that is international, decentralized, with diverse interests but common targets. Salter (2003) claims that the Internet is a novel technological asset for democratic communications because of its decentred, textual communications system with content most often provided by users. On this basis it accords with the requisite features of new social movements: non-hierarchical, open protocols, open communication, and self-generating information and identities. Social movements share common characteristics with web-based communication – they lack membership forms, statutes, and other formal means of organizing; they may have phases of visibility and phases of relative invisibility; social movements may have significant overlaps with other movements and are liable to rapid change in form, approach and mission.

As pointed out by van der Donk, *et al.* (2004: 18) the Internet is used by two kinds of movement structures: (1) informal networks with a large geographical reach and (2) big, powerful and more centralized social movement organizations. Furthermore, the ability of new communication technologies to operate globally and so respond to global economic agendas is the key to their contemporary capacity to mobilize against the vagaries of global capital. The Internet plays a crucial role in transnational protest allowing for immediate communication across the globe. This synergy between social movements and the Internet emphasizes the interrelationship between the nature of civil society (in terms of its form and organization) and attempts to explain the social foundations of democracy (or its political and ethical premise). In other words, the link between the specific organization of social and cultural bases (such as the Internet) within civil society for the development of an effective rational–critical discourse or fully functioning public sphere (Habermas, 1989). Calhoun (1993) reminds us that what is at issue is the relationship between patterns of social organization and a certain kind of discourse and political participation, a public sphere in which rational–critical arguments are decisive, rather than the status of actors. It is not helpful to collapse discourse or politics into social organization as if neither culture nor the wills of actors mattered. Neither is it helpful to forget how much democratic life depends on specific kinds of social organization, even though they do not necessarily and deterministically produce it (Downey and Fenton, 2003). Public communications are part of the process of realizing the public sphere, allowing us to analyze how shared democratic values and identification as democratic citizens are achieved and maintained; how political/civic cultures are generated – essentially, to begin to imagine how civil society can potentially organize democratically for politically progressive ends. The democratic potential of the Internet is not dependent on its intrinsic features. It is realized only through the agents who engage in reflexive and democratic activity. It is an enabling device that is as susceptible to the structuring forces of power as any other technology.

It is false to say that individuals possess immediate control; they have control only through assenting to an asymmetrical relationship to various agents who structure the choices in the communicative environment of cyberspace (Bohman, 2004: 142).

The use of the Internet by New Social Movements (NSMs) may be, and is, frequently problematic at the democratic level. Many sites are generated and maintained by individuals or small groups of people with little or no accountability or representativeness.

Taking this integrated theoretical stance extends to a consideration of the relationship between the virtual and the material. The use of the Internet can affect the internal organization of social movement organizations through the manner in which they operate online and the extent to which they forge alliances and coalitions across different movements. Similarly, the protest activity and alliances of social movements on the ground affects the internal organization of the Internet. It is possible, therefore, to argue that the Internet represents a new technology that has the potential to communicate and mobilize political agency and as a consequence reinvent activism.

Being true to the theoretical premise established at the beginning of the chapter means that the earlier optimistic interpretation has to be critically examined in relation to the dominant social context of global neo-liberalism. Can we confidently say that the margin of unpredictability, disjunction, and improvization has increased with the 1980s turn to the post-Fordist economy of cultural diversification resulting in new means of mobilization? Or, is the growing multiplicity of protest rendered irrelevant by the concomitant move towards ever-greater privatization? The tension between the relations of structure and agency are framed within overarching concerns of the nature and role of opposition within contemporary bureaucratic capitalist states that can be usefully examined by recourse to Foucault's concept of the biopolitical:

> *In the postmodernization of the global economy, the creation of wealth tends ever more toward what we call biopolitical production, the production of social life itself, in which the economic, the political, and the cultural increasingly overlap and invest in one another* (Hardt and Negri, 2000: xiii).

Hardt and Negri's re-interpretation of Foucault can be further extended. The economic, political, and cultural feed off each other to the extent that they become entangled in symbiotic relationships. These relationships are neither equally nor mutually beneficial but they are interdependent (as established right at the beginning of this chapter in the discussion of the relationship between mass media and alternative media). Markets and politics become intertwined so that what seems to be political may be no more than market-based activism. Proponents of biopolitics state that new forms of social militancy are allowed to arise within capitalism with no possibility of transcending it. Following on from this, those groups within civil society who strive to contest contemporary capitalism do so from within the very system of governmentality they seek to oppose. This outward sign of protest can project an illusion of civility and democratic practice that ultimately has a civilizing influence on market and state rather than create a genuinely free space where political agency might be articulated and lead to a political project. Biopolitics frames agency within a symbolic system in which both the power to create symbols and access to the channels of their circulation is hierarchically structured and intimately integrated into a system of capitalist economic production and exchange. The symbolic tools we have at our disposal are determined by the system we may be struggling against. The result is that the political mobilization of individuals and organizations in civil society act to normalize and stabilize conditions that threaten the well-being of populations 'but not to alter the structural conditions responsible for those threats and disturbances' (Lipschutz, 2005: 28).

For example, campaigns such as 'No Sweat' that are directed at the likes of the Nike corporation and aim to improve health and safety conditions and provide minimum wages to workers in Nike's plants scattered around the world have gained much attention and resulted in Nike joining the Fair Labor Association, co-establishing the Workers and Communities Association, and improving the terms and conditions of their workers. But, as Lipschutz (2005) notes, we would be hard pressed to claim that these campaigns have changed corporations of capitalism in discursive terms. Nike workers and consumers continue to be part of a regime of consumption that is neo-liberal contemporary globalization. The structures of capitalism remain firmly intact, and one could even argue they are substantially strengthened.

Similarly, for Castells (1996), the globalization of the capitalist system does not open up the possibility of a labor-led emancipatory project. In his view, the network society results in labor becoming localized, disaggregated, fragmented, diversified, and divided in its collective identity:

> *While capitalist relations of production still persist, capital and labor increasingly tend to exist in different spaces and times; the space of flows and the space of places, instant time of computerized networks versus clock time of everyday life. Thus, they live by each other but do not relate to each other as the life of global capital depends less and less on specific labor and more and more on accumulated generic labor, operated by a small brains trust inhabiting the virtual palaces of global networks* (Castells, 1996: 475).

Concluding that:

> *Under the conditions of the network society capital is globally coordinated, labor is individualized. The struggle between diverse capitalists and miscellaneous working classes is subsumed into the more fundamental opposition between the bare logic of capital flows and the cultural values of human experience* (Castells, 1996: 476).

Approached from this perspective, the fragmented nature of new media does limit the capacity of social movements creating coherent strategies. Problems of quantity and chaos of information challenges the way analysis and action are integrated in decision making processes as well as existing configurations of power and collective identity in social movement organizations. Habermas (1992) also notes that the mechanism for counter publicity may 'not' work because of a fragmentation within civil society. He too registers his ambivalence towards new ICTs as a potential source of equal and inclusive communication:

> *Whereas the growth of systems and networks multiplies possible contacts and exchanges of information, it does not lead per se to the expansion of an intersubjectively shared world and to the discursive interweaving of*

conceptions of relevance, themes, and contradictions from which political public spheres arise. The consciousness of planning, communicating and acting subjects seems to have simultaneously expanded and fragmented. The publics produced by the Internet remain closed off from one another like global villages (Habermas, 1992: 120–1).

But the 'fundamental opposition' that Castells refers to earlier stems from the ever more efficient circulation of commodities. Information has also been argued to open up greater potential for strategies of resistance that reside in the conflicts over communication:

With the dominance of communication there is a politics of struggle around not accumulation but <u>circulation</u>. Manufacturing capitalism privileges production and accumulation, the network society privileges communication and circulation (Lash, 2002: 112).

Cleaver (1999) also points out that one of the main means by which anti-capital movements communicate is through the circulation of struggle. This circulation benefits from fragmentation that can be both inclusive and diverse but produces nonetheless a high degree of identification among citizens of the web. The capacity to maximize connectivity and interaction is 'the' political act. Local organizations confined to localized actions realize similar types of activity is taking place in locality after locality and by their participation they can contribute to reshaping these global networks for communication into global zones for interactivity (Sassen, 2005).

These large, decentralized, and leaderless networks facilitated by new communication technologies operate a form of politics that is based on the participation of all citizens rather than the hierarchical model of traditional politics. 'Moreover, the essence of politics is considered the elaboration of 'demands and responses' – constructing identities rather than 'occupying power' (Della Porta, 2005: 201). Participation then can be both online and offline. But the online participation is often about moving people to action offline. It is about building relationships and forging community rather than simply providing information (Surman and Reilly, 2003). In her extensive interviews with and questionnaires to activists Della Porta (2005) also discovers a link between mistrust for parties and representative institutions with very high trust and participation in social movements. The distinction between institutional politics and social movements rests on the former acting as bureaucracies founded on delegation and the latter being founded on participation and direct engagement.

Sassen (2005) notes that for many, cyber space is a more concrete space for social struggles than that of the national political system, which is difficult to access and from which people feel alienated. Cyberspace is inclusive, accommodating a broad range of social struggles thereby facilitating the emergence of new types of political subjects more at home outside formal political systems.

If the global, polycentric, interactive, additive space both feeds from and contributes to the actual shape of political mobilization and organization, it follows that a theoretical stance refusing to separate the virtual from the actual, but recognizing the matter of the virtual and the circulation of the actual may be more productive than approaches that seek to treat them as distinct entities.

If we accept the possibility for resistive, differentiated, individual political identities that are able to resist mass mediated representations of society and create their own political interventions via the Internet, we can then attend to the prospects for emergent political projects. The problem rests in the inevitable multiplicity of competing counter publics, each marked by specific terms of exclusion (class, race, gender, etc.) yet each understanding itself as a nucleus for an alternative organization of society. The 'proliferation of subaltern counter-publics' (Fraser, 1992: 69–70) does not necessarily lead to a multiplication of forces. Unless powerful efforts at alliances are made, the oppositional energy of individual groups and subcultures can sometimes be neutralized in the marketplace of multicultural pluralism or polarized in a reductive competition of victimizations.

The notion of fragmentation in modern life and, in particular of political culture, is fuelled by the rise of identity politics that focuses on consumption not production. Issues that relate to lifestyles are fore-grounded over and above the domain of work. Party allegiances and class alliances are joined by more fluid and informal networks of action. Postmodern theorists celebrate fragmentation because it allows the recognition of diversity in political desires, acknowledges difference between individuals, and debunks the myth of homogenous political units leading ultimately to liberation. Social movements are agglomerations of organizations, events, actions, publications, struggles and individuals. They are never unified or straight forwardly coherent. They are marked by contradiction and complexity and survive on breadth, complexity, and uncertainty. Apart from traditional threats of state repression, social movements, such as the anti-globalization movement, which embraces everything that is not of the neo-liberal global economic order, may run the risk of implosion through uncertainty or internal friction. While uncertainty and friction can create useful political dynamism, feminist theorists have noted (Braidotti, 1991; Spivak, 1992; Fenton 2000) that for political efficacy there must be more than the apparent freedom that comes with embracing difference and diversity, more than just an increase of instances of mediated protest or opposition. If we accept the description of society as fragmented, then solidarity is crucial in order to create a viable political community. Solidarity is the socio-political glue that prevents dissolution through difference (Dean, 1996, 1997).

Contesting global capital: the role of solidarity

So how will a politics of solidarity in difference be realized? Social solidarity can be described as a morality of cooperation, the ability of individuals to identify with each other in a spirit of mutuality and reciprocity without individual advantage or compulsion, leading to a network of individuals or secondary institutions that are bound to a political project involving the creation of social and political bonds. There must be a commitment to the value of difference that goes beyond a simple respect and involves an inclusive politics of voice and representation. It also requires a non-essentialist conceptualization of the political subject as made up of manifold, fluid identities that mirror the multiple differentiations of groups. Chosen identities at any one time can not be taken as given or static – political identities emerge and are expressed through an ongoing social process of individual and collective identity formation. In this manner, social solidarity can be augmented. Diani (2005) insists that it is the networking of collective action that constitutes a social movement. Solidarity also reaffirms the need for political intervention that may be translated and relayed in the symbolic immaterial world of cyberspace but necessarily originates from and solidifies in the material world of the real. The Internet can proffer a cultural politics that resists, transforms, or presents alternatives to the dominant virtual and real worlds.

> *This cybercultural politics can be most effective if it fulfils two conditions: awareness of the dominant worlds that are being created by the same technologies on which the progressive networks rely (including an awareness of how power works in the world of transnational networks and flows); and an ongoing tacking back and forth between cyberpolitics (political activism of the Internet) and what I call place politics, or political activism in the physical locations at which the networker sits and lives* (Escobar, 1999: 32).

Tarrow and Della Porta (2005: 237) refer to the interconnections between online and offline participation as 'rooted cosmopolitans' (people and groups rooted in specific national contexts but involved in transnational networks of contacts and conflicts); 'multiple belongings' (activists with overlapping memberships linked with polycentric networks); and 'flexible identities' (characterized by inclusiveness and a positive emphasis on diversity and cross-fertilization). Participants in these movements are drawn together by common elements in their value systems and political understandings and, hence, by a shared belief in narratives that problematize particular social phenomena (Keck and Sikkink, 1998; Della Porta and Diani, 1999).

In her interviews with activists, Della Porta (2005) notes that common solidarity develops in concrete actions that are immediately gratifying. It is the act of participating itself that creates the collective identification rather than sacrifice for the sake of a distant future as in old style political activism. Mutual trust and shared understandings developed in offline protests and demonstrations have been consistently identified as important facilitators of collective action. Virtual computer-mediated ties will not replace traditional forms of protest, such as rallies and demonstrations, but may complement them in terms of building collective identity and reinforcing solidarity. Social movements that use the Internet must find the balance between the virtual connection and exchange and the actualization or the enacting of that politics. The effectiveness of the Internet as virtual activism lies in its ability to connect with the real world (Terranova, 2001).

Mansbridge (2001: 240–1) argues that oppositional consciousness requires identifying with an unjustly subordinated group, recognizing a group identity of interest in doing so, understanding the injustice as systemic, and accepting the need for and efficacy of collective action. She also states that the formation of an oppositional culture is both an additive and an interactive process (2001: 249), where a variety of motivations are at play within the group. Seen in this way solidarity is no longer about struggles relating to each other like links in a chain but communicating like a virus or a global web (Hardt and Negri, 2000; Klein, 2000) facilitated by new communication and information technology – a techno politics of the information age (Jordan and Taylor, 2004). Tomlinson (1999: 2) refers to this as 'complex connectivity': 'By this I mean that globalization refers to the rapidly developing and ever-densening network of interconnections and interdependences that characterize modern social life'. Solidarity does not need to be linear; it does not need to follow a prescribed narrative:

These initiatives proceed without central focus. They constitute a diffuse coalescence of microactivisms contesting the macrologic of capitalist globalization.... They exist as a sort of fine mist of international activism, composed of innumerable droplets if contact and communication, condensing in greater or lesser densities and accumulations, dispersing again, swirling into unexpected formations and filaments, blowing over and around the barriers dividing global workers (Dyer-Witheford, 1999: 157).

Hardt and Negri (2000: 65) ask 'how can the endeavor to bridge the distance between the formation of the multitude as subject and the constitution of a democratic political apparatus find its prince?' In accord with Lash (2002), they believe that the answer lies in working with the flattened, fragmentary, immanent world of the information order and its relationship to the external, material world:

Any postmodern liberation must be achieved within this world, on the plane of immanence, with no possibility of any even utopian outside. The form in which the political should be expressed as subjectivity today is not clear at all (Hardt and Negri, 2000: 65).

One possible response is that solidarity expressed through new communication technologies can embrace a thousand fragmented subjectivities:

Contemporary movements are prophets of the present. What they possess is not the force of the apparatus but the power of the word.... They force the power out into the open and give it a shape and a face. They speak a language that seems to be entirely their own, but they say something that transcends their particularity and speaks to us all (Melucci, 1996: 1).

Emphasis on the material, visible conflict as the defining attribute of a collective identity reduces collective politics to the moment when struggle is mediated. Refusing to see the material as the crux of identity allows us to escape the traditional logic of politics, acknowledges the non-spectacular and infers a history of identity development. It is useful here to consider the work of Lovink (2002) who refuses to comply with ready-made dichotomies between the real and the virtual. The virtual is not unreal neither does it function to inculcate a de-realization. It does not somehow exist 'out there' untouched by reality rather it is continuous with reality; it is part of our reality. The two spheres of activity shape each other in terms of organizational structures, network stability, and capacity (Bennett, 2004a).

The dialogic and globalizing characteristics of new communication technologies do not eradicate difference but can be said to promote political consciousness, reflexivity, and agency. Breslow (1997) argues that the Internet promotes a sense of sociality, but its anonymity and lack of spatiality and density may be counterproductive to solidarity. Similarly, van der Donk *et al.* (2004) note that the very ease of mobilization may devalue it as a political resource that attracts public attention and respect and be devalued by the activists because it takes the fun and adventure out of some forms of collective protest. The crucial point is that the performative capacity of solidarity, the ability to give power to the word comes from the felt existence of struggles that are situated in the real material world of poverty, inequality, and other social injustices. Furthermore, only through the embodiment of solidarity offline will social movements gain public legitimacy and political force. The immaterial mediated world that embraces fragmented political subjectivities connects with the material world at the site of conflict, bringing together disparate experiences of political reality and finding common ground, though that ground may be uneven, contested, and complex.

Chesters and Welsh (2004: 317) call this an 'ecology of action' defined as:

The systems of relations between differing groups and individuals who are engaged in producing collective action within a context determined by fixed temporal, spatial and material constraints which are themselves a product of contingent social, political and cultural forces.

This is an important reminder of the social constraints all participants are subject to. Issues of cultural and economic capital are ever prevalent. The ability to define and shape the nature of any movement often falls to those with the relevant social and educational resources. Many of the high-profile protests take place at distant locations – only those protestors with funds for travel can get to them. And as these protests are often organized on the Internet, the economic and cultural resources involved in the use of this technology also exclude many potential participants, probably those suffering the most impact of the very thing being protested against (Crossley, 2002).

As noted earlier, the Internet is only as democratic as the agents who use it. New media can become the location for counter reflexive political deliberation and activity – but that activity must be organized and planned to be deliberative and democratic. It remains to be seen whether the likes of the Internet can avoid the way in which state sovereignty organizes public space and time. Its aterritorial character helps this process but the way in which the Internet reproduces inequalities to access to rule making institutions is a major hindrance.

Kavada (2005) notes that the Internet has not led to a greater integration within civil society due to the restrictive policies on external links on web pages adopted by civil society organizations and a lack of trust and solidarity between them. This further highlights the fact that new media technology alone does not lead to a brand new age of political collective radicalism. New forms of mediation have revealed new forms of protest but mediated solidarity is far more than signing an online petition or clicking on protest websites while alone in your own home – this is, however, not techno-determinism. Indeed online activism can be seen as lazy politics – it makes people feel good but does very little. It allows like-minded individuals and organizations to talk to each other unfettered by too many social norms and actually do nothing. It can be criticized for further distancing people from each other and deepening already abstract social relations as well as increasing competition between organizations.

Solidarity is about engaging beyond the click of a mouse and much more than mediation. Solidarity insists on foregrounding the link to the enduring primacy of capitalist relations of production and capitalist imperatives that dominate not only production but also consumption and other domains of society and culture. Workers remain exploited by and struggle against capitalists and capital remains as the hegemonic force. Solidarity also emphasizes that the global reorganization of capital is not a monolithic force of impenetrable power and domination. The powers of mediation are now where the struggles of cultural activism find their home. The use of new communications technology to spread radical social critique and alternative culture is the realm of new social movements marked by fragmentation – a postmodern notion that embraces the possibility of social agency.

Social agency alone, however, does not make a political project. Gerlach (2001) notes that in contemporary social movements, such as the anti-globalization movement, the primary basis of their integration and growth has shifted from ideology to more personal and fluid forms of association well suited to computer-mediated networks. It can be argued (Drache, 2005) that part of the success of Internet dissent is that you can enter and exit easily. Collective identity has always been a central concern of social movement theorists. Melucci (1996) sees collective identity as a continuous, dynamic, and self-reflexive process defined by its multiplicity of interactions, negotiations, and conflicts among fellow participants. The Internet, relying as it does on a network of networks, can assist collective identity and reinforce solidarity. In other words, it partakes in the process of meaning construction. The nature and scope of the technology affects not only the way the movement communicates its aims and objectives but also its geographical scale, organizing structure, and collective identity. The decentralized, non-hierarchical modes of organizing allow for diverse political agendas and identities to exist without conflict.

Conclusions: contesting global solidarity and the role of a social imaginary

Can loose, multi-issue networks progress from a resistance identity to a political project that is sustainable and likely to produce social change? The danger in constructing global solidarity online, as Tarrow (1998) points out, is that the speed at which social movement actors can respond and the short term and rapidly shifting issues that are their focus rather than fully fledged ideologies do not lend themselves to long standing commitments or deeply held loyalties, but a following that is also fleeting and momentary. This sort of issue drift whereby individuals or groups can shift focus from one issue to another or one website to another raises the question of whether global civil society has a memory that can retain a collective political project. The ultimate problem that arises is how to ensure that non-hierarchical, open, and participatory movements are also effective in influencing public policies. Habermas (2001: 126) has argued that solidarity at this level cannot simply be based on shared moral conceptions of human rights but only on a shared political culture. That political culture is constituted not only of social agents who can enable the mediation of dialogue across borders and publics but also institutions that can translate those claims into a reality.

> The issue-and-identity bridging facility of social technologies may explain the organisational capacity of what appears to be a movement with weak collective identity and relatively weak core political agenda. At the same time these defining features of the movement raise questions about other aspects of movement political capacity, from communicating clear messages to larger publics, to developing effective relationships with political targets (Bennett, 2005: 225).

Rosenkrands (2004: 75) notes that although several websites refer to themselves as part of an anti-corporate movement, they do not push alternative epistemologies or political programmes reflecting a 'logic of protest more than a logic of project' (see also van Aelst and Walgrave, 2004). Wright (2004: 91) concurs with this assessment adding that keeping 'action' and 'theory' as separate, while always privileging the first over the second, is part of the current anti-capitalist movements' mindset. This prompts the question that given the fact that networked communication increasingly enables the success of campaigns, can networks without a political project sustain any degree of political coherence? Can, in other words, a networked, polycentric global civil society movement deliver the policies, strategies, ideologies, and plans for socially progressive change? It can be argued that the lack of ideological rigor allows the growth of much broader networks creating a vast web of oppositional politics. It can also be argued to lead to problems of control, decision-making, accountability, and collective identity. Talking about the World Social Forum, Hardt (2002: 113–14) stated:

What kinds of transformations are necessary for the Euro-American globalization movements and the Latin American movements, not to become the same or even unite, but to link together in an expanding common network? The Forum provided an opportunity to recognize such questions and differences for those willing to see them, but it did not provide the conditions for addressing them. In fact the very same dispersive, overflowing quality of the Forum that created the euphoria of commonality also effectively displaced the terrain on which such differences and conflicts could be confronted.

Mouffe (2005: 107–15) criticizes Hardt and Negri's (2004) faith in the multitude as being unable to transfer antagonistic struggle into agonistic politics without which politics cannot function. Waterman and Wills (2001) ask whether – being post-Seattle – it is now time to give the negative name of anti-capitalism a positive face or whether socialism will remain a utopia that dare not speak its name. Has the time come to publicly declare the reinvention of a socialist internationalism? Or does this fix us back in to hierarchical modes of political organizations based on national sovereignty and, therefore, existing legal and social systems rather than borderless networks? The desperate desire to avoid a politics based on binary oppositions and exclusionary meta-narratives may end up with biting our individual noses off to spite our collective face. Building collective solidarity is partly to do with organizational capacity but just as vitally it is about a battle of ideas. A collective movement needs credible mobilizing rhetorics, visions of a better future; it needs utopias – the role of a social imaginary. To sustain a collective oppositional identity requires a vision of a post-capitalist society that can be named or at least recognized.

Bauman (2003: 22) argues that 'the utopian model of a "better future" is out of the question' because of (1) its reliance on fixity both in terms of geographical context and the immobility of the meta-narrative; (2) the tendency to locate the secret of happy life in social reform that is now discredited; and (3) the detachment of trust from the future and faith in progress from the flow of time. This has resulted in a shift from a focus on a better tomorrow to the more tangible, securely within reach, 'today':

> *Happiness and more happiness are desired now as they used to be in bygone times of utopia-writing; but happiness means now a different today rather than a more felicitous tomorrow as it did in the past* (Bauman, 2003: 22).

We are left with an unending sequence of new beginnings. Although this perspective resonates clearly with much of what has been described earlier, others have been rather more optimistic.

Levitas (2000) talks of the necessity of combining a dialogical utopianism with visions of a post-capitalist society. She also warns that an undifferentiated notion of dialogical transformation that ignores the diversity and conflicting interests within contemporary society will take us nowhere. The contestation of global capital needs to move beyond the identification and publicity of injustices to political interventions that may lead to transformation. The Internet with its networked, additive, interactive, and polycentric form can accommodate radically different types of political praxis from different places at different times. Sometimes this may fall into the realms of a traditional politics based on national sovereignty at others it may call for an internationalist approach. Both may be appropriate to the particular circumstances of capital, the potential for mobilization, and the specific processes of transformation available. For a collective consciousness to be maintained and developed in this complex, confusing, and contradictory tangle of global capitalism, nation, states, and everyday life a social imaginary is required that will be flexible, inclusive, and visionary – that will offer us all the hope of a better tomorrow.

References for Chapter Ten

Bauman, Z. (2003), 'Utopia with no Topos', *History of the Human Sciences,* 16: 1, pp. 11–25.

Bennett, W. L. (2004a), 'Communicating Global Activism: Strengths and Vulnerabilities of Networked Politics', in W. Van Der Donk, B. D. Loader, P. G. Nixon *et al.* (eds.), *Cyberprotest: New Media, Citizens and Social Movements,* London: Routledge, pp. 123–146.

—— (2005), 'Social Movements Beyond Borders: Understanding Two Eras of Transnational Activism', in D. Della Porta and S. Tarrow (eds.), *Transnational Protest and Global Activism*, Lanham: Rowman and Littlefield, pp. 203–27.

Bohman, J. (2004), 'Expanding Dialogue: the Internet, the Public Sphere and the Prospects for Transnational Democracy', in N. Crossley and J. M. Roberts (eds.), *After Habermas: New Perspectives on the Public Sphere*, London: Blackwell.

Braidotti, R. (1991), 'The Subject in Feminism', *Hypatia*, 6: 2, pp. 155–72.

Breslow, H. (1997), 'Civil Society, Political Economy and the Internet', in S. Jones (ed.), *Virtual Culture: Identity and Communication in Cybersociety*, Thousand Oaks, CA: Sage, pp. 236–57.

Calhoun, C. (ed.) (1992), *Habermas and the Public Sphere*, Cambridge, MA: The MIT Press.

Castells, M. (1996), *The Rise of the Network Society, The Information Age: Economy, Society and Culture*, Oxford: Blackwell Publishers, vol. 1.

Chesters, G., Welsh, I. (2004), 'Rebel Colors: "Framing" in Global Social Movements', *The Sociological Review*, 52: 3, pp. 336–50.

Cleaver, H. (1999), 'Computer Linked Social Movements and the Global Threat to Capitalism', http://www.eco.utexas.edu/faculty/Cleaver/polnet.html. Consulted 7 February 2006.

Crossley, N. (2002), 'Global Anti-Corporate Struggle: A Preliminary Analysis', *British Journal of Sociology*, 53: 4, pp. 667–91.

Dean, J. (1996), *Solidarity of Strangers; Feminism After Identity Politics*, London: University of California Press.

—— (ed.) (1997), *Feminism and the New Democracy; Re-siting the Political*, London: Sage.

Della Porta, D. (2005), 'Multiple Belongings, Tolerant Identities and the Construction of "Another Politics": Between the European Social Forum and the Local Social Fora', in D. Della Porta and S. Tarrow (eds.), *Transnational Protest and Global Activism*, Lanham: Rowman and Littlefield, pp. 175–203.

Della Porta, D., Diani, M. (1999), *Social Movements, an Introduction*, Oxford: Blackwell Publishers.

Diani, M. (2005), 'Cities in the World: Local Civil Society and Global Issues in Britain', in D. Della Porta and S. Tarrow (eds.), *Transnational Protest and Global Activism*, Lanham: Rowman and Littlefield, pp. 45–71.

Downey, J., Fenton, N. (2003), 'Constructing a Counter-Public Sphere', *New Media and Society*, 2: 5, pp. 185–202.

Drache, D. (2005), *New Geographies of Power and Counter Publics: The Political Economy of Dissent and Battle for Public Space*, Paper presented at

Re:Activism Conference, Budapest, 14–15 October, 2005 http://mokk.bme.hu/centre/conferences/reactivism/submissions/drache. Consulted 7 February 2006.

Dyer-Witheford, N. (1999), *Cyber-Marx: Cycles and Circuits of Struggle in High Technology Capitalism*, Illinois: University of Illinois Press.

Escobar, A. (1999), 'Gender, Place and Networks: A Political Ecology of Cyberculture', in W. Harcourt (ed.), *Women@Internet: Creating New Cultures in Cyberspace*, London: Zed Books, pp. 31–55.

Fenton, N. (2000), 'The Problematics of Postmodernism for Feminist Media Studies', *Media, Culture and Society*, 22: 6, pp. 723–41.

Fillieule, O. (1999), '"Plus ça Change, Moins ça Change" – Demonstrations in France During the Nineteen-Eighties', in D. Rucht, R. Koopmans, and F. Neidhardt (eds.), *Act of Dissent: New Developments in the Study of Protest*, Lanham MD: Rowman and Littlefield.

Fraser, N. (1992), 'Rethinking the Public Sphere. A Contribution to the Critique of Actually Existing Democracy', in C. Calhoun (ed.), *Habermas and the Public Sphere*, Cambridge, MA: The MIT Press, pp. 109–42.

Gerlach, L. P. (2001), 'The Structure of Social Movements: Environmental Activism and its Opponents', in J. Arquilla and D. Ronfeldt (eds.), *Networks and Netwars: The Future of Terror, Crime and Militancy*, Santa Monica: Rand, pp. 289–310.

Habermas, J. (1989), *The Structural Transformation of the Public Sphere*, Cambridge: Polity Press.

—— (1992), 'Further Reflections on the Public Sphere', in C. Calhoun (ed.), *Habermas and the Public Sphere*, Cambridge, MA: The MIT Press, pp. 421–61.

—— (2001), *The Postnational Constellation*, Cambridge: MIT Press.

Hardt, M. (2002), 'Porto Alegre: Today's Bandung?' *New Left Review*, 14, March–April: 114.

Hardt, M., Negri, A. (2000), *Empire*, Cambridge MA: Harvard University Press.

Jordan, T., Taylor, P. (2004), *Hacktivism and Cyberwars: Rebels Without a Cause?* London: Routledge.

Kavada, A. (2005), 'Civil Society Organisations and the Internet: the Case of Amnesty International, Oxfam and the World Development Movement', in W. de Jong, M. Shaw, and N. Stammers (eds.), *Global Activism, Global Media*, London: Pluto Press, pp. 208–23.

Keck, M. E., Sikkink, K. (1998), *Activists Beyond Borders: Advocacy Networks in International Politics*, New York: Cornell University Press.

Klein, N. (2000), *No Logo*, New York: Flamingo.

Lash, S. (2002), *Critique of Information*, London: Sage.

Levitas, R. (2000), 'Discourses of Risk and Utopia', in B. Adam, U. Beck, and J. Van Loon (eds.), *The Risk Society and Beyond: Critical Issues for Social Theory*, London: Sage, pp. 199–210.

Lipschutz, R. D. (2005), 'Networks of Knowledge and Practice: Global Civil Society and Global Communications', in W. De Jong, M. Shaw, and N. Stammers (eds.), *Global Activism, Global Media*, London: Pluto Press, pp. 17–33.

Lovink, G. (2002), *Dark Fiber: Tracking Critical Internet Culture*, Cambridge MA: MIT Press.

Mansbridge, J. (2001), 'Complicating Oppositional Consciousness', in J. Mansbridge and A. Morris (eds.), *Oppositional Consciousness: The Subjective Roots of Social Protest*, Chicago, IL: University of Chicago Press, pp. 238–64.

Melucci, A. (1996), *The Playing Self*, Cambridge: Cambridge University Press.

Mouffe, C. (2005), *On the Political*, London/New York: Routledge.

Rosenkrands, J. (2004), 'Politicising Homo Economicus: Analysing Anti-Corporate Websites', in W. Van Der Donk, B. D. Loader, P. G. Nixon, *et al.* (eds.), *Cyberprotest: New Media, Citizens and Social Movements*, London: Routledge, pp. 57–76.

Salter, L. (2003), 'Democracy, New Social Movements and the Internet: A Habermasian Analysis', in M. McCaughey and M. D. Ayers (eds.), *Cyberactivism: Online Activism in Theory and Practice*, London: Routledge, pp. 117–45.

Sassen, S. (2005), 'Electronic Markets and Activist Networks: The Weight of Social Logics in Digital Formations', in R. Latham and S. Sassen (eds.), *Digital Formations: New Architectures for Global Order*, Princeton, NJ: Princeton University Press, pp. 54–88.

Spivak, G. (1992), 'French Feminism Revisited: Ethics and Politics', in J. Butler and J. Scott (eds.), *Feminists Theorise the Political*, London: Routledge, pp. 54–85.

Surman, M., Reilly, K. (2003), *Appropriating the Internet for Social Change: Towards the Strategic Use of Networked Technologies by Transnational Civil Society Organisations*, New York: Social Sciences Research Council.

Tarrow, S. (1998), *Power in Movement – Social Movements and Contentious Politics*, Cambridge: Cambridge University Press.

Tarrow, S., Della Porta, D. (2005), 'Globalization, Complex Internationalism and Transnational Contention', in D. Della Porta and S. Tarrow (eds.), *Transnational Protest and Global Activism*, Lanham: Rowman and Littlefield, pp. 227–47.

Tomlinson, J. (1999), *Globalization and Culture*, Cambridge: Polity.

Terranova, T. (2001), 'Demonstrating the Globe: Virtual Action in the Network Society', in D. Holmes (ed.), *Virtual Globalization: Virtual Spaces/Tourist Spaces*, London: Routledge, pp. 95–113.

Van Aelst, P., Walgrave, S. (2004), 'New Media, New Movements? The Role of the Internet in Shaping the "Anti-Globalization" Movement', in W. Van Der Donk, B. D. Loader, P.G. Nixon, *et al.* (eds.), *Cyberprotest: New Media, Citizens and Social Movements*, London: Routledge, pp. 97–122.

van der Donk, W., Loader, B. D., Nixon, P. G., *et al.* (eds.) (2004), *Cyberprotest: New Media, Citizens and Social Movements*, London: Routledge.

Waterman, P., Wills, J. (2001), 'Space, Place and the New Labour Internationalists: Beyond the Fragments', *Antipode*, 33: 33, pp. 305–11.

Wright, S. (2004), 'Informing, Communicating and ICTs in Contemporary Anti-capitalist Movements', in W. Van Der Donk, B. D. Loader, P. G. Nixon, *et al.* (eds.), *Cyberprotest: New Media, Citizens and Social Movements*, London: Routledge, pp. 77–94.

Žižek, S. (1999), *The Ticklish Subject: the Absent Centre of Political Ontology*, London: Verso.

Chapter Eleven

Civil Society Media at the WSIS: a new actor in global communication governance?

Arne Hintz

Introduction

Community, alternative, citizens, and other civil society–based media are increasingly recognized in media and communication theory. Even though major mass media systems and organizations still represent the core object of media studies, a growing body of case studies highlights the importance of community radios, activist websites, and alternative news chapters, to name just a few examples [1]. However, often presented as small media, local alternatives, and fringe actors, their connection with global policy and regulation processes has so far been neglected in most research.

With interdependence between states, regions, and social actors increasing, these global policy processes are no longer the exclusive domain of governments. In the age of global governance, channels are opening to include business and civil society in global decision-making. A growing number of civil society–based media actors are recognizing the effects which the global political sphere is having on their work and are starting to make their voices heard on the policy level. Yet, as a deeply fragmented set of actors, ranging from grassroots media activists to professionalized transnational news organizations, and often having little or no policy experience, they face serious challenges. In this chapter, emerging practices by these media of intervening in global communication governance will be highlighted. As such, an attempt will be made to draw links between civil society–based media projects and the global political arena.

The arena that will be discussed here is the World Summit on the Information Society (WSIS) [2]. As a major United Nations conference on information and communication issues, the WSIS provided a prominent platform for civil society actors to discuss proposals for an alternative vision of communication governance and to test their proposals in a global policy forum. It offered a major occasion to participate in global political processes and influence their outcomes. In this chapter, the interventions into, and activities around, the WSIS summit by civil society–based media actors will be analyzed. In doing so, their thematic inputs and objectives, as well as the spaces, particularities, and effects of participating in the WSIS process will be assessed. The perspective will be that of an active participant in the WSIS. For 4 years (2002–2005) I took part in the summit process, including the spaces that will be highlighted in this chapter. The assessment will be based on participatory observation, content analysis of summit documents and mailing list discussions, and interviews with key actors [3].

In defining the 'subject' of this analysis, the umbrella concept of Civil Society Media will be introduced first. An overview of current trends in global communication governance as well as the WSIS itself will follow, to then illustrate the structures and spaces which these media have used to participate and intervene in summit processes, and look at the policy proposals they have submitted to the thematic debates. From that conclusions will be drawn as to the extent, the strategies, the successes and failures, and the future perspectives of the involvement of Civil Society Media in global governance.

Civil Society Media

A synthesis of Civil Society Media

The model of Civil Society (CS) Media proposed here is based on a structural understanding of the term 'civil society', which encompasses the non-state and non-business sector and is typically formed by non-governmental and non-profit initiatives – from neighborhood associations to labor unions, and from eco-activists to consumer lobbies. This definition has increasingly replaced the older tradition of integrating civil society and the private sector into one category (Calabrese, 2004; Hadl, 2004). Most UN processes have adopted a model, which excludes business from the civil society sphere.

Civil society is characterized by a diversity of approaches and objectives. The structural model, which is applied here, embraces actors focusing on stability and service provision, as well as those aiming at radical change. It contains both what Mary Kaldor calls the 'activist'/'Post-Marxist' and the 'neo-liberal' versions of civil society (Kaldor, 2003). However, there is a set of normative aspects common to most of these organizations, associations, and movements. They often share an opposition to the overwhelming power (and power abuses) of large institutions, a tendency towards self-organization, citizen empowerment, horizontality, voluntary association, and a concern for civil and human rights and the 'common goods'. They also tend to agree on the need for participatory social and political organization and for an extension of democracy (Dawkins, 2003). These normative tendencies draw a clear dividing line towards reactionary and right-wing movements which may be formally non-state and non-commercial but advocate for the concentration of power, subordination and exclusion.

The concept of CS Media encompasses media organizations, groups, and projects, which fit into the basic non-state non-commercial model and share the structural and thematic tendencies of civil society. Generally, it comprises all 'third sector' media and, therefore, excludes the two biggest sectors, namely commercial and public service media. There is a fragmented web of concepts to describe the types of media that concern us here. Some of the most widely used examples are community, autonomous, alternative, radical, and tactical media.

'Community Media' are 'developed in response to local needs and under community control' (CMWG, 2003). They focus on issues which are directly relevant to a specific community and involve that community in all aspects of media production. 'Autonomous media' put even more focus on participation and openness, often showing the ability of 'non-professionals' to organize media production themselves (Langlois and Dubois, 2005). 'Alternative-' and 'Radical Media' combine a structural 'alternative', based on collective production and a non-hierarchical organizational model, with 'alternative' content and counter-information. They seek to break hegemonic discourses, uncover and criticize power and domination, as well as highlight social struggles and the activities of social movements (Downing, 2001). 'Tactical Media', in contrast, attempt to transcend the bipolar world of counter-information and create a 'repertoire of dirty little practices' (Garcia and Lovink, 1999), encompassing critical media actions, campaigns and interventions which are temporary, pragmatic and flexible, and which are often initiated by smaller groups or individuals, rather than wider social movements.

Each of these concepts has its specific historical, ideological, geographical, and political contexts. Each category focuses on particular approaches and thus only represents a certain section of the vast range of non-state non-commercial media. The concept of CS Media seeks to combine these different aspects towards a common frame of reference. It embraces a wide range of media actors, from small grassroots media projects to large media organizations, from a photocopied newsletter, to an activist website, to satellite distribution of film material. In a broad concept, there can be vast differences between individual entities, but they all share a distinct set of common features and a commitment towards a similar framework of values.

Characteristics of CS Media

Questions of ownership, control, and organization are at the heart of what constitutes non-governmental and non-commercial media. A basic definition would be 'a media organization owned/controlled by members of civil society' (Hadl, 2004: 10). Control is ultimately in the hands of self-organized and independent citizens' groups, associations, or organizations. CS Media are non-profit or not-for-profit entities, and they are typically designed as small-scale groups or organizations, favoring collective decision-making over hierarchical command structures and relying to a larger extend (or entirely) on voluntary work. Participation, emancipation, and empowerment represent crucial features [4]. Whereas traditional commercial and public service media are operating according to a one-way flow of information from sender to receiver, CS Media try to break the boundaries between active producers and passive consumers. Most of them offer low-level access for media non-professionals to get involved in media production, sharing skills and know-how. The use and development of free and open source software are widespread, and knowledge is understood as a global common good, rather then an 'intellectual property'.

CS Media serve as the main access channels to information for large parts of the world population. For many people in the Global South, community radios offer the only channel to receive news, while for many marginalized communities, CS Media represent the only channel to hear about their culture and to make their voices heard [5]. Criticizing mainstream media content, addressing worrying trends such as poverty, inequality and environmental degradation, while at the same time expressing 'an alternative vision to hegemonic policies, priorities, and perspectives' (Downing, 2001: v), represents a general tendency in CS Media content. Many of them explicitly bring forward subjective accounts of events and thereby break with traditional journalistic values of impartial and objective reporting (Hintz, 2003).

Opening spaces for participatory communication, CS Media create fractures in the domination of, and reclaim public space from, the large mass media. While the latter is operating in increasingly concentrated structures, CS Media are usually organized as decentralized networks of local groups, based on common values of diversity, autonomy, decentralization, and horizontality. They challenge the vision of a single all-inclusive 'global village', suggesting instead a diversity of smaller 'villages' (Dowmunt, 1993). In the rapidly changing global political, economic, and cultural landscape, they, thus, represent a counterpart to forces of centralization and homogenization. Many of them explicitly participate in struggles against the centralization and expansion of authority and influence, for example in the protests against the G8 and the World Bank in recent years, and thereby transform into social movement media (Notes from Nowhere, 2003).

Global communication governance

Global governance
In the state-centred world of the past two centuries, international relations were an intergovernmental affair. Sovereign states represented the basic units in the international system, and 'international governance' was based on inter-state diplomacy. However, from the late 1980s, an accelerating increase in cross-border flows and global integration has changed the global political landscape considerably. The environmental crisis has shown the unavoidable interconnected-ness of the world, as well as the permeability of national borders. In the economic sphere, international division of labor has deepened, and globally integrated production chains have emerged. Symbolic forms, languages, and cultural patterns are equally spreading around the globe, greatly aided by new information technologies, the Internet, and the spread of transnational media corporations. Similar forms of (sub-)cultural expressions in different and previously unconnected parts of the world have emerged, while global migration streams are increasingly overcoming the persistent barriers of national borders [6].

With 'globalization' – as these developments have been termed – the world has experienced a(nother) 'time-space compression' (Held and McGrew, 2003: 3). The constraints of distance and time on social organization and interaction have been eroded, and actions in one locale increasingly have consequences for 'distant others'. In terms of political organization, interconnectedness is restricting the choices made by states. The actual control most states possess over their territory becomes limited, and some authors are already recognizing an end of the Westphalian system of states (Messner, 2003: 3). The question is how to govern the world under the condition of globalization.

The concept of 'global governance' has emerged as a response to this challenge. It differs from a notion of 'government' which implies the direct capacity of political leaders to steer society and focuses instead on systems of rules and interdependent problem solving by a diversity of actors on a diversity of policy levels. It encompasses self-organizing networks and webs of policy-making forums, in which control is dispersed and capacity for decision-making and implementation is widely distributed, and which have thus 'transformed sovereignty into the shared exercise of power' (Held and McGrew, 2003: 11). The specific characteristics of global governance are:

- The participation of new actors, particularly from business and civil society
- The re-distribution of spaces and policy layers between local and global and
- The interaction and cooperation between different actors and layers

Even though the concept is based on a 'global' approach, it does not just transfer policy-making from one level (nation-state) to the next (global), but it involves 'systems of rule at all levels of humanity' (Rosenau, 1995: 13).

Yet a network policy structure is only emerging step-by-step. In 1995, the Commission on Global Governance still regarded states as the main actors and the United Nations as the 'central mechanism' for facing the challenges of the future (Commission on Global Governance, 1995: 8). The world conferences of the past decade, starting with the Rio summit on environment and development in 1992 and representing the most prominent approach to global governance, took place within the UN framework and were, thus, still based on state-organized 'inter-national' multilateralism. For the time being, states are retaining their dominant position in global policy processes, even though their role is changing from a sovereign ruler to an 'interdependency manager' (Messner, 2003: 17). Held and McGrew (2003: 13) argue that nation states are increasingly 'embedded' in webs of global interconnectedness and of new emerging players.

Civil Society participation

One of the main challenges of global governance processes is how to achieve legitimacy. In a confined state-centred world, legitimacy was based on elected national parliaments. However, with global multilateral decision-making structures increasing, the corridors of power are wriggling out of the embrace of democratic accountability. The share of decisions taken externally, beyond the space of democratic legitimization, is increasing, and so the concept of democratic self-determination is seriously compromised.

As traditional representative democracy is put into question, there are calls for an increase in public participation in global decision-making to develop forms of 'global' or 'cosmopolitan democracy' (Held, 2003; Kjaer, 2004). At their centre is the recognition of the crucial role of civil society in developing new forms of accountability. Since the 1992 Rio summit on the Environment and Development, when some fifty thousand activists participated in summit proceedings, civil society has become an integral part of global politics. Its increased involvement can be seen as an attempt to raise transparency and accountability of global decision-making processes, yet its role goes far beyond that of a passive watchdog. By influencing inter-governmental negotiations and setting policy agendas, it is 'altering the norm structure of global governance' (Sikkink, 2002: 302), occasionally instigating fundamental changes in the nature of international debate and international interactions. In some global policy forums, new forms of 'multi-stakeholder' governance are emerging as a collaborative process involving all 'stakeholders' – usually governments, business, and civil society.

However these forms of 'neo-corporatism' (Messner, 2003: 16) only involve certain sections of civil society – usually the large professionalized non-governmental organizations (NGOs). Grassroots groups, social movements, fluid networks, and many other civil society associations without hierarchical structure, legal status, and sufficient funding, are left out of the governance equation [7]. Repeatedly, splits have occurred between those (large NGOs) who engage with global institutions in an effort to trigger reform, and those (grassroots activists) that fundamentally oppose elite-driven policy processes in large unaccountable organizations [8]. Being 'inside' or 'outside' has represented a dividing line for civil society actors and social movements – sometimes only a strategic one, but often one that generates identity and excludes other approaches. This fault line has been the most visible constraint to the efforts to foster a more coordinated and homogenous civil society 'stakeholder'. It thus challenges the development of 'network density', i.e. a high level of connection between actors, which is deemed to be a major precondition for successful interventions in policy arenas (Keck and Sikkink, 1998).

Communication Governance

The distinction in 'old' and 'new' governance models (Kjaer, 2004: 10) also fits the communication sphere. For several decades, UN organizations, such as the International Telecommunication Union (ITU), the World Intellectual Property Organization (WIPO), and the UN Educational, Scientific, and Cultural Organization (UNESCO), played a leading role in regulating cross-border communication flows.

Yet in the past decade, business and, to a lesser extend, civil society have entered the arena, for example as 'sector members' of the ITU and as prime movers in the Internet Corporation for Assigned Names and Numbers (ICANN). With increasing interventions by these actors, communication governance, too, has moved beyond pure inter-governmental processes and towards an interdependent network of multiple actors and venues (Raboy, 2004).

Large civil society networks, such as the Association for Progressive Communications (APC) and the World Association of Community Broadcasters (AMARC), have begun to intervene in global policy processes and to participate in new multi-actor governance. However, many smaller actors, including many CS Media, continue to lack channels of intervention, as they struggle with precarious legal status, funding, organizing, and the day-to-day work of media production. Suspicion towards elite-driven governance processes and a focus on technical bypasses around political challenges add to their exclusion.

This does not mean they are ignored on the policy level. During the UNESCO debate around a New World Information and Communication Order (NWICO), the role of 'group and local media' (MacBride *et al.*, 1980: 55–7), as well as the importance of alternative communications for social movements were recognized. UNESCO and other international organizations have also funded numerous community media projects. Yet the ideological shift of the past two decades towards the neo-liberal trade paradigm, assigning a central policy role to trade-/business-institutions, such as the World Trade Organization (WTO), strengthening a globalizing media industry, and favoring market- and industry-dominated regulatory mechanisms, has brought new challenges (Ó Siochrú and Girard, 2002). In this free-trade environment, global regulation limiting media ownership concentration and ensuring public service and support for community-based media alternatives seems to be beyond realistic expectation.

However, cracks in the neo-liberal paradigm have recently emerged, and one may speculate just how long this paradigm will persist. Economic breakdowns in East Asia and Latin America, the anti-/alter-globalization protests, and calls for robust global commons and global public goods by international organizations all question neo-liberal policies, and have opened spaces for alternative concepts. We may be entering a vacuum in which neo-liberalism has been demystified, while a new paradigm is not yet in reach. In this situation, the global discussion space of a world summit can set discourses, create moral obligations, and set the framework within which future governance can be 'thought'.

World Summit on the Information Society

Structure, discourses, outcomes

The World Summit on the Information Society (WSIS) has been the first UN summit dealing exclusively with information and communication. Its objective has been to develop a common understanding of the information society and a common response to challenges such as the digital divide. The 2-year preparatory process for the first WSIS summit in Geneva 2003 led to the adoption of two official summit documents: the Declaration of Principles (WSIS, 2003a) and the Plan of Action (WSIS, 2003b). The thematic framework ranged from Internet governance to education, from cultural diversity to security aspects. The main conflicts revolved around financial mechanisms to bridge the digital divide, frameworks for and approaches to Internet governance, intellectual property rights (IPR) and free/open source software, human rights, media governance, and information security. The regulatory framework emphasized market-friendly, liberalized environments, with public-private partnerships as a primary strategy, though several sections (e.g. WSIS, 2003a, paragraphs 23 and 26) also argued the importance of public services and the public domain.

The second phase, leading to WSIS2 in Tunis, focused on the two issues unresolved at WSIS1: funding and Internet governance. A 'Task Force on Financial Mechanisms' (TFFM) reviewed financial mechanisms to bridge the digital divide, while a 'Working Group on Internet Governance' (WGIG) developed proposals for enhanced administration and regulation of the Internet. Both debates uncovered deep divides between Northern governments – proposing an intensification of market-led approaches and a central role for the business sector – and Southern governments – favoring stronger state interventions. The Tunis summit nevertheless led to the creation of a voluntary Digital Solidarity Fund and an Internet Governance Forum.

Media debate

Organized by the ITU, a UN specialized organization concerned primarily with technology and infrastructure, the WSIS focused on an 'information society'-discourse, which left little room for traditional media and content aspects. Media appear only towards the end of the Geneva Declaration (Article 55 of 67) and the Plan of Action (Article 24 of 29). Yet the media debate represented one of the major points of conflict during the WSIS negotiations. A prominent emphasis on the right to freedom of expression and the role of media as independent, un-controlled actors were opposed by governments interested in media control – particularly China, but defended by the Swiss delegation and a vocal media and journalistic lobby. Governments with strong ties to national media corporations, led by El Salvador, opposed measures limiting media concentration and refused any mention of community media [9].

The final version of the Declaration reaffirms freedom of the press and information and calls for pluralism and diversity in media. However, it does not support these aims with concrete measures such as limiting ownership concentration or supporting non-commercial media. The control interests of some governments even led to opening backdoors for censorship by calling for 'appropriate measures (…) to combat illegal and harmful content'. Any mention of community and other non-commercial/non-governmental media was deleted at the final stages, except for a vague call to 'give support to media based in local communities' (WSIS, 2003b, Article 23j).

Civil society participation

Based on a declared 'multi-stakeholder' approach, civil society and business were invited to participate fully in summit processes [10]. However the reality of this supposedly 'new kind of summit' looked rather conservative (see also Cammaerts and Carpentier, 2005). Those sections of civil society not formally set up as NGOs (and not generating sufficient funding) had difficulties overcoming even the hurdles of registration, let alone full participation, and those civil society actors that made it to the preparatory conferences were often excluded from the negotiation process and saw themselves relegated to the role of 'observers'.

Yet the civil society actors participating in summit processes initiated a vibrant culture of debates around the WSIS themes, set up administrative and lobbying mechanisms and organized a variety of side-events at the summit itself [11]. Thematic caucuses and working groups were formed and developed input statements for the negotiation process [12]. Shortly before the WSIS1 summit, the civil society network responded to its continued exclusion and to the thematic deficiencies of the summit by withdrawing from the lobbying process and instead drafting the alternative summit declaration *Shaping Information Societies for Human Needs* [13]. This declaration criticizes privatization and monopolization of knowledge and emphasizes the need for community media, the global commons, free software, human rights, privacy, and participatory communication. It thus calls for a people-centred 'communication society' rather than a technology-focused and business-oriented 'information society' (Ó Siochrú, 2004). In a concluding statement, presented after the Tunis summit and appropriately named *'Much more could be achieved'* [14], the civil society caucus welcomes the progress that the WSIS made on internet governance, but expresses disappointment and strong critique the summit's shortcoming to adequately address the financing and development needs of the South, human and civil rights, free software, cultural diversity, the public domain and traditional knowledge, community and civil society–based media.

Within the network of civil society caucuses, the Media Caucus was the main body for advancing media interests. In addition, several CS Media established the Community Media Working Group (CMWG), while others joined different caucuses and working groups. Others, especially those from the more 'activist' and 'autonomous' sections of CS Media, refused to participate in summit processes and, instead, organized events around the summit.

Participation of CS Media

Media Caucus

Established as a follow-up structure to previous collaborations between large broadcasting unions, the Media Caucus went beyond the more narrowly defined understanding of 'civil society' which I used above and which was largely adhered to by other caucuses and the WSIS generally. The Media Caucus was composed of public service broadcasters, commercial TV and radio networks, media associations, such as the World Association of Newspapers, media-related NGOs, such as the Media Institute of Southern Africa, press freedom organizations, such as Article 19 and the World Press Freedom Committee, professional associations, such as the International Federation of Journalists and individual media researchers. Delegates from AMARC brought a community media voice into the caucus debates, complemented by a few activists from Indymedia and other CS Media groups.

Thematically, the caucus highlighted the role of content, attempting to balance the dominant focus on technology and called for a worldwide implementation of Article 19 of the Universal Declaration on Human Rights (UDHR) on freedom of expression. It emphasized the rights and freedoms of media organizations and journalists as the primary producers and distributors of content, and it had some success in strengthening these points in the summit documents. Further objectives included media pluralism, universal and affordable access, cultural diversity, and the protection of the rights of online media workers. Yet criticism of media concentration was vague, failing to advance specific anti-monopoly laws. Community media were recognized in principle, but were confined to the edges and niches of the media sphere, 'serving traditionally disadvantaged groups' and requiring 'legally established (...) non-profit' status [15]. Concrete proposals for supporting community media, as well as other CS Media, were blocked, particularly by the representatives of commercial media.

In light of the human rights violations in the WSIS2 host country Tunisia, community media representatives accepted the narrow agenda of the Media Caucus, opting to participate in a strong alliance to advance freedom of expression and to establish community media as an accepted partner in the international media environment. Others were less prepared to agree to the shortcomings of the caucus. After all, its thematic vision was at odds with the media reform agenda developed by a large network of civil society–based media at the World Social Forum and elsewhere. This vision emphasizes limits to media concentration, opening up traditional media for public participation, making media more responsive to society at large, and advancing interactive communication by everyone. It also opposes the safeguarding of the information monopoly of media organizations and professional journalists (Hintz and Milan, 2006).

Furthermore, the caucus' 'multi-stakeholder' arrangement allowed commercial interests to use designated civil society space to further their interests [16].

Community Media Working Group

With the Media Caucus being dominated by the interests of bigger, mainstream media, and with CS Media being marginalized in numbers and in content, the latter created the Community Media Working Group (CMWG). The group produced separate lobby documents and position papers, yet many of its members continued to engage inside the Media Caucus, positioning the CMWG rather as a sub- than a counter-group.

The concept of 'community media' was used partly because of the relative acceptance of the term in previous policy forums, and partly because of the composition of the group. Initiated and led by AMARC, the CMWG was largely composed of representatives of community radios and of NGOs working with community media. At times, a small, but active, contingent of representatives from radical activist media organizations, such as Indymedia, MediAct, and Deep Dish TV, attended. This diversified the otherwise mostly community-oriented structure and agenda.

Within the ICT-focused policy environment of the WSIS, the CMWG served as a strong advocate for traditional media, such as radio and print, which continue to be the main channels of information for the vast majority of the world population. It had less to say, though, about 'new media' and Internet governance, even though for many CS Media web-based distribution of content increasingly plays a significant role. CMWG statements did reflect further important objectives of CS Media, such as interactive information exchange, non-hierarchical structures, and the participation of non-professionals in media production, but its focus was on highlighting the development-oriented function of community media in giving access to information and communication for the large parts of the world population that continue to live on the 'other side' of the 'digital divide'.

This focus tapped into the predominant discourses of WSIS and, thus, was a strategic choice. Operating within the dynamics and necessities of a UN policy process, the CMWG's main practice was to intervene strategically into the negotiation process to get community media recognized in the WSIS documents. At the summit, the development/access angle with a focus on the digital divide represented the most promising way to achieve result. On the downside, this approach failed to generate a more elaborate policy framework for developing CS Media. Particularly, critique of the mainstream media system was largely absent from CMWG statements so that the latter lacked a deeper connection with the wider media-reform movement.

Just as other civil society working groups seeking to advance human rights and citizen participation and following a potentially oppositional agenda, the

CMWG meetings during the second WSIS phase were heavily attended by Tunisian delegates 'who can be reliably expected to report back (...) to the host country government' [17] and who regularly interrupted discussions. Strategic debates and consensus building were rendered difficult in this obstructive and intimidating environment.

Outside WSIS

For many grassroots activist media, participation in summit processes was neither a practical possibility nor a particularly attractive option. Following the process actively required the time to take part in long preparatory meetings, the financial means (or the support from a large organization) to pay for travel and accommodation, and the patience and particular skills to deal with the complexities of UN diplomacy. Furthermore, many of them reject global summits and other international institutions as illegitimate bodies to regulate (and thus to control, repress, and appropriate) communication processes which have often been developed bottom-up by members of civil society. Participation, according to that view, means to legitimize an otherwise illegitimate process.

Around the WSIS1 summit in Geneva, a number of spaces were set up by civil society actors to discuss WSIS themes and intervene in summit processes from outside. Media activists were at the heart of these efforts. The most distinct space was *'WSIS?WeSeize!'* – a series of events in the city centre of Geneva, including a conference, a video stream, a media laboratory, and protest actions, all organized by a loose network of autonomous media groups, Indymedia activists, hackers, free software developers, and grassroots campaigners, called the 'Geneva03 Collective'. WSIS?WeSeize! served as a space to voice radical critique of neo-liberal global governance and business-led information/communication policies. Participants celebrated a culture of non-hierarchical association, non-commercial creativity, experimenting and skill-sharing. Geneva03 rejected the WSIS' 'rhetoric of inclusion' as a 'smokescreen' to 'mystify the continuing use of information to protect and advance the interests of global capital' [18]. Rather than influencing the official process, they opted for autonomously developing communication concepts 'from below'.

At the edges between inside and outside, further side-events assembled activists and advocates and provided public spaces to discuss their experiences and propagate their views. The 'World Forum on Communication Rights' and the 'Community Media Forum' were organized by civil society groups participating in the summit, yet they served as platforms to criticize the summit's shortcomings and to focus on its blind spots. WSIS?WeSeize! participants interacted through these events with NGO representatives 'inside' the summit process, while some of the 'insiders' came 'out' to, for example, join the media lab, and acted in solidarity with those 'outside' through press releases. The embryonic stages of a multi-level strategy emerged, in which fundamental criticism, public pressure and protest 'outside' linked up with strategic policy interventions 'inside' [19].

The actual degree of exchange was limited, due to organizational problems of WSIS?WeSeize!; the busy schedule of those inside the WSIS compound, and the persistent political and cultural differences between grassroots media activists, on the one hand, and policy advocates, on the other. Representatives of 'community media' and major NGOs largely remained 'inside', while those identifying as 'autonomous', 'alternative', and 'tactical' media remained mostly 'outside'. Activities were not sufficiently linked up so that, for example, the radio stream set-up by community radio activists in the summit building had no connection with the video stream from WSIS?WeSeize!. Many possibilities for cooperation were not seized, but a few first steps towards collaboration were taken.

Tunis saw a further increase in overlaps and underpasses between the different spheres. The media activist delegation from the US organization Third World Majority offered a whole series of events inside the summit compound, while NGO delegates from AMARC and APC were confronted by Tunisian police in the city centre. A 'Citizens Summit', organized in part by the latter organizations, was largely and – in some instances – violently prevented by Tunisian authorities. Yet the Tunisian case was special; a wider range of protest and 'outside' activities was never an option there and caused many media activists to stay away in the first place. Whether the traditional boundaries between 'inside' and 'outside' have suffered sustained damage remains to be seen.

A future policy framework – proposals and approaches

CMWG: interventions in the negotiation process

Despite the pragmatic and strategic approach of the CMWG, it is possible to extract elements that constitute a policy framework from its various statements and lobby documents [20]. An important foundation of such a framework is the right to freedom of expression, enshrined in Article 19 of the UDHR. However, while traditional mainstream media (implicitly or explicitly) apply this right primarily to 'content providers', thus focusing on press freedom (on the producer side) and the right to information access (on the consumer side), many CS Media embed freedom of expression in a wider set of 'communication rights', including participatory production and interactive distribution of content, as well as seeking to prevent a monopolization of information rights by mainstream media and/or global media conglomerates.

Media pluralism has thus been at the heart of CMWG concerns, but again there is a significant difference in interpretation. The Media Caucus' narrow notion of 'pluralism' is extended to include not just a variety of outlets and content providers, but a diversity of actual content, opinions and societal groups represented in the media. Strengthening the role of a third media sector alongside the existing dichotomy between public service and commercial media is advocated as the prime means to add diversity to the media sphere. This third sector is to be participatory, self-organized, and under community control. Typically using traditional technologies, it serves as the main channel for large parts of the world population to access information.

These media, urges the CMWG, need to be supported and promoted by establishing a secure legal basis in both national and international law, by opening broadcast licenses and allocating radio and satellite spectrum to non-commercial media and by offering public funding schemes. A reform of both the allocation and the governance model of communication channels should involve reserving a fixed percentage of radio frequencies and satellite channels for community and non-profit broadcasting. Airwaves and orbital paths should be recognized as a public resource to be allocated in the public interest. Spectrum should be publicly owned, governed in a transparent way, and thereby secured as a global commons.

Regarding possible financing schemes for community/non-profit media, the CMWG called for the establishment of a Community Media Fund 'to support new community radio development and community media content', particularly in the Global South and for disadvantaged communities, as a targeted way to bridge the digital divide. With the theme of finance at the centre of the second WSIS phase, the establishment of such Community Media fund became central to the CMWG interventions during the preparation for WSIS2.

WSIS?WeSeize! and beyond: a different 'information society'

In contrast to the strategic interventions of the CMWG into the ongoing negotiation process, those media activists outside the official summit process cared less about the exact wording of the official documents. They challenged both the structure and the content of the summit. The structural challenge questioned the very approach to governance on which the WSIS was based. The 'information society' is, according to the WSIS?WeSeize! organizers, the result of collaborative experiments by activists, social movements, researchers, and technological experts. The media laboratory and the video stream were to exemplify how committed citizen are continuously developing what those inside the summit compound are merely discussed. From their perspective, the communities generating information societies should be the protagonists of governance debates, rather than government, business, and NGO officials [21].

The second challenge was thematic. WSIS?WeSeize! served as a space for debates on critical issues that were left off the WSIS agenda but that, according to the Geneva03 collective, were crucial to understanding the further development of the information society, namely information wars and propaganda, surveillance and information control, the privatization of ideas through trademarks and copyrights, autonomous media infrastructure, citizen-based peer2peer and wireless networks, openness as strategy and methodology, hacking techniques, and the links between freedom of communication and freedom of movement [22].

In preparation of the second WSIS summit, a loose network of Indymedia activists, led by Indymedia Beirut, discussed a similar list of issues that they thought should be at the heart of any debate about the 'information society'. The list included the issues of censorship and freedom of expression, repression of media activists, precarious working conditions and exploitation of information workers, support for locally appropriate technology, and, again, the inevitable connection between free communication and free cross-border movement of all people. The DVD 'Datafighters', presented by the media group EclécticaDV at the Tunis summit, deals with similar issues, focusing on copy-left culture and knowledge commons, casualized information work, and threats by surveillance and info-war techniques [23]. Meanwhile the 'Third World Majority' delegation presented a variety of grassroots and autonomous media practices.

None of these initiatives seeks a place at the negotiation table in current governance processes, but all of them attempt to influence the discourses around the 'information society'. With a recurring list of themes and debates, CS Media suggested an agenda for an alternative thematic and structural framework of communication governance. For the time being, these agenda proposals are only addressed at other civil society entities. Statements discussed at WSIS?WeSeize! were submitted for inclusion in the civil society alternative declaration [24] but not in the official summit documents. However, the discussion and consensus-building process on policy issues within the wider civil society networks will certainly be influenced by these interventions.

A new actor in global governance?

WSIS represented a laboratory of new modes of governance, struggling between, on the one hand, the promise of a multi-stakeholder environment, in which all actors can participate on equal footing and, on the other hand, the attempts by many governments to retain a dominant role for state actors. It sent mixed signals to civil society – sometimes offering unprecedented levels of participation, but then again pushing it out of the negotiation spaces. Some CS Media organizations used the temporary openings to advance their inclusion in global governance, while others could enter the level of global decision-making for the first time. Civil society groups praised the 'innovative rules and practices of participation' established in some areas of the WSIS process, which they see 'as an experience to be learned from for the overall UN system and related processes' [25]. Yet even the instances of successful implementation of the multi-stakeholder principle uncovered the need to create mechanisms for the less-organized, less-resourced and less policy-fluent parts of civil society, such as activist and grassroots groups, to participate in governance processes, as well as the necessity to transform these processes into an attractive environment for such groups. If legitimacy and accountability are a serious objective, multi-stakeholder governance will have to move far beyond the steps taken at WSIS.

The experiences of CS Media underline these challenges, but also the potentials. Divides between different types of CS Media persisted, with those organized as 'community media' and as NGOs tending to participate in summit processes and those identifying themselves as 'autonomous', 'alternative', 'tactical', and 'activist' media largely choosing to remain outside. While the former were consumed by the 'realpolitik' of UN processes and strategic negotiations, many of the latter refused to see any value or necessity in following the summit process. Yet a significant achievement of these various approaches to the WSIS was that the rather predictable divisions were sometimes crossed and constituencies sometimes overlapped. Indymedia activists participated in the CMWG, small and radical community radio groups appeared at the NGO-led Community Media Forum, while the Venezuelan media organization Aporrea participated in WSIS?WeSeize!. A small but increasing number of participants from both camps understood the differences between, for example, the CMWG and WSIS?WeSeize! not as fundamental dividing lines, but as complementary approaches. Where the CMWG focused on traditional technologies, developed relations with the mainstream media, and drafted specific proposals for influencing the ongoing government-led negotiation process, WSIS?WeSeize! could add expertise on new technologies, serve as a space to develop radical reform agendas, promote a bottom-up governance framework, and organize public pressure to support CS Media interventions.

At WSIS itself, this combination of approaches and expertise did not yet fully develop, and as such it remains a potential rather than a reality. Yet the common use of WSIS as a platform has fostered new coalitions across traditional boundaries, leading, for example, to post-WSIS projects such as the European Forum on Communication Rights in London 2004, which was commonly organized by major media NGOs and by Indymedia activists. Bridging the boundaries between media actors with different strategies and thematic focuses, the WSIS highlighted the potential of a complementary multi-layered strategy connecting 'inside' and 'outside' – and thus of transcending the 'predictable spheres of influence' (Calabrese, 2004: 323).

A common set of proposals, setting out a coherent alternative governance structure, is not quite in reach yet. The CMWG programme was geared towards particular stages of the WSIS negotiations and did not evolve into a clearly defined and systematically developed agenda. Demands changed with the changing composition of the group, the life-span of proposals sometimes lasted only for their use in a particular document, and the proposals of the CMWG rarely fitted the far-reaching media-reform agenda developed at the Social Fora and other civil society networks and spaces. The absence of a generally agreed framework of proposals hampered the continuous and successful work of the group. The connection with the – even more heterogeneous – agenda of the media activists of Geneva03, et al. still has to be developed.

So Civil Society Media are not a singular actor, it is rather a theoretical umbrella covering a diversity of actors with very different approaches and objectives. Yet this fragmented arena of actors is weaving the first ties of a loose network by developing communication channels, testing collaboration, discussing objectives and strategies, and thus approaching a common discourse. Different perspectives on policy issues are slowly converging, forming a basis for future involvement in communication governance. Clusters on specific issues or activities have emerged, with some even developing temporary or issue-based campaigns, yet linkages between those are still weak. To form a sustained network, a deeper coalition, or a proper social movement, CS Media will need to develop denser information exchanges, a greater level of co-ordination, build a sense of shared values, and eventually a collective identity (Khagram *et al.*, 2002). A common conceptual frame of reference, such as CS Media, may be able to offer some of the necessary linkages.

Without those, the internal preconditions for successful policy interventions, as proposed by social movement theory [26], were hardly met at WSIS. External factors were even more worrying. The predominant policy paradigm favored information technology over communication media, and furthermore most states and business-actors were uninterested, at best, or hostile, at worst, towards the grassroots-based bottom-up approach of CS Media, which goes beyond the state-market nexus and challenges prevalent capitalist modes of control by the powerful players. So it may not be surprizing that the results of the interventions by the CMWG and other activist media networks into the WSIS negotiation process were rather limited. Commitments to freedom of expression and media diversity were confirmed both after long struggles with hostile governments, and these represented the only small gains derived from these efforts. Communication rights had been temporarily accepted in the drafts of the WSIS documents, but were later reduced significantly, and the CMWG proposals to enable and promote country-level legislation for community media, a reform of spectrum allocation, and the establishment of a community media fund were all ignored. On the issue of IPRs and free software, the Brazilian government managed to balance the US agenda of expanding IPR, but a fundamental review of IPR, as the media activists at WSIS?WeSeize! had propagated, was beyond reach. Unsurprisingly, support for privacy rights and for citizen-/community-based communication networks was not widespread amongst governments either.

However, the defeat in the official WSIS negotiation process contrasted with the events and public discourses around the summit. Numerous side-events including even the parallel mainstream media summit, the World Electronic Media Forum, celebrated the practices of grassroots/citizens/activist media. 'Create your own media – make your own voice heard' was repeated in many summit-related debates as a prime strategy to bridge the information divide. Other issues, such as IPR and financial mechanisms, were equally discussed widely. So if CS Media failed to leave their mark in the official documents, they raised their profile in the discourses around the summit and influenced the agendas of future debates. These 'indirect' effects, although more elusive, should not be underestimated. The WSIS achieved few binding agreements, instead it could be characterized as a platform to discuss the priorities and guiding principles of communication governance – and as such it structured the discourse on information and communication and set the parameters of future policy processes. Intervening into this policy discourse represents a starting-point for influencing the policy framework within which CS Media operate and for developing a common understanding of that framework, as well as its possible alternatives.

Notes for Chapter Eleven

[1] See, for example, Rodriguez (2001), Downing (2001), Couldry and Curran (2003), Carpentier *et al.*, (2003), Atton (2002). The Civil Society Media model, which I will develop on the following pages, will draw from the work of these and other authors.

[2] The first half of this two-part summit took place 10–12 December 2003 in Geneva, the second half 16–18 November 2005 in Tunis.

[3] Some of the ideas and arguments presented in this chapter have been developed together with my colleagues Stefania Milan (European University Institute, Florence) and Gabriele Hadl (Ritsumeikan University, Kyoto). See, e.g., Hintz and Milan, 2006, and Hadl and Hintz, 2006.

[4] Milan (2004) regards participation as the most central aspect of CS Media.

[5] For an elaboration on the democratic character of CS Media see Sreberny-Mohammadi (1997), Rodriguez (2001).

[6] There has been a wide variety of literature on each of these dimensions. For an overview Held and McGrew (2003) offer a starting-point.

[7] ...even though they may be as fully 'globalized' as, for example, the network People's Global Action which has initiated several global days of action.

[8] See, e.g., Wilkinson (2002), Nelson (2002).

[9] The information presented here about the WSIS negotiation process (and about the civil society processes presented later) is based on my participation in working groups and meetings, and on interviews with key participants, in this case Wolf Ludwig, note-taker in the inter-governmental negotiation group on media issues, and Steve Buckley, President of AMARC.

[10] UN General Resolution 56/183 of December 2001

[11] At the initial stages, the CRIS campaign – an NGO platform on communication rights – served as the main force to mobilize civil society interventions and to facilitate self-organizing; http://www.crisinfo.org.

[12] http://www.wsis-cs.org/caucuses/html.

[13] http://www.worldsummit2003.de/en/web/573.htm.

[14] http://www.worldsummit2003.de/download_en/WSIS-CS-summit-statement-rev1-23-12-2005-en.pdf.

[15] http://www.worldsummit2003.de/en/web/231.htm.

[16] Media giants, such as Time-Warner, Sony and Vivendi, are members of the International Chamber of Commerce (ICC) – the leading actor of the business sector which represented a further separate 'stakeholder' in addition to civil society. Through the separate channels of the Media Caucus and the ICC, commercial media achieved double representation in the summit process.

[17] Report on CMWG meetings by Steve Buckley, 2 October 2005.

[18] http://www.geneva03.org.

[19] Servaes and Carpentier (2005: 10) have termed this the 'Janus-head strategy' of activism, 'combining strategic and partial incorporation with continued resistance and independent critique'.

[20] I refer here to the many statements which have been drafted during the four-year WSIS process but which, in many cases, have not been publicly archived.

[21] This claim was supported by the fact that the only free public wireless network at or around the Geneva summit was set up by media activists at WSIS?WeSeize!, and the latter's use of online methods to support and document activities was generally far advanced compared to those used at the summit.

[22] http://www.geneva03.org.

[23] http://www.eclecticadv.net.

[24] The section on Infowar, particularly, was drafted by members of Geneva03.

[25] See the civil society statement 'Much more could have been achieved', http://www.worldsummit2003.de/download_en/WSIS-CS-summit-statement-rev1-23-12-2005-en.pdf.

[26] See, e.g., Khagram *et al.* (2002); Keck and Sikkink (1998).

References for Chapter Eleven

Atton, C. (2002), *Alternative Media*, London: Sage.

Calabrese, A. (2004), 'The Promise of Civil Society: a Global Movement for Communication Rights', *Continuum: Journal of Media & Cultural Studies*, 18: 3, pp. 317–29.

Cammaerts, B., Carpentier, N. (2005), 'The Unbearable Lightness of Full Participation in a Global Context: WSIS and Civil Society Participation', in J. Servaes and N. Carpentier (eds.), *Towards a Sustainable Information Society. Deconstructing WSIS*, London: Intellect, pp. 17–50.

Carpentier, N., Lie, R., Servaes, J. (2003), 'Making Community Media Work', in J. Servaes (ed.), *Approaches to Development: Studies on Communication for Development*, Paris: UNESCO Communication and Information Sector, pp. Chapter 15-1–Chapter 15-44.

CMWG (2003), 'Contribution by the Community Media Initiative to the Drafting Process', http://www.worldsummit2003.de/en/web/229.htm. Downloaded on 29 August 2005.

Commission on Global Governance (1995), *Our Global Neigbourhood*, Oxford: Oxford University Press.

Couldry, N., Curran, J. (2003), *Contesting Media Power. Alternative Media in a Networked World*, Lanman: Rowman & Littlefield.

Dawkins, K. (2003), *Global Governance: The Battle Over Planetary Power*, New York: Seven Stories Press.

Dowmunt, T. (1993), *Channels of Resistance: Global Television and Local Empowerment*, London: BFI Publishing.

Downing, J. D. H. (2001), *Radical Media: Rebellious Communication and Social Movements*, London: Sage.

Garcia, D., Lovink, G. (1999), 'The ABC of Tactical Media', www.sarai.net/events/tml/tml_pdf/abc_tactical.PDF. Downloaded on 5 October 2005.

Hadl, G. (2004), *Civil Society Media Theory: Tools for Decolonizing the Lifeworld*, Paper for the International Association of Media and Communication Research (IAMCR), Porto Alegre, 28 July 2004.

Hadl, G., Hintz, A. (2006), 'Framing Our Media for Transnational Policy: The World Summit on the Information Society and beyond', in D. Kidd, C. Rodriguez, and L. Stein (eds.), *Making Our Media*, Cresskill, NJ: Hampton Press, Forthcoming.

Held, D., McGrew, A. (2003), 'The Great Globalization Debate: An Introduction', in D. Held and A. McGrew (eds.), *The Global Transformations Reader*, Cambridge: Polity Press, pp. 1–50.

Held, D. (2003), 'Cosmopolitanism: Taming Globalization', in D. Held and A. McGrew (eds.), *The Global Transformations Reader*, Cambridge: Polity Press, pp. 514–29.

Hintz, A. (2003), 'Indymedia Germany: A Local Node of the Global Network', *Media Development*, XLX: 4, pp. 21–5.

Hintz, A., Milan, S. (2006), 'Towards a New Vision for Communication Governance? Civil Society Media at the World Social Forum and the World Summit on the Information Society', *Communication for Development and Social Change: A Global Journal*, Forthcoming.

Kaldor, M. (2003), *Global Civil Society: An Answer to War,* Cambridge: Polity Press.

Keck, M. E., Sikkink, K. (1998), *Activists Beyond Borders. Advocacy Networks in International Politics*, Ithaca: Cornell University Press.

Khagram, S., Riker, J. V., Sikkink, K. (2002), 'From Santiago to Seattle: Transnational Advocacy Groups Restructuring World Politics', in S. Khagram, J. V. Riker, and K. Sikkink (eds.), *Restructuring World Politics: Transnational Social Movements, Networks, and Norm*, Minneapolis: University of Minnesota Press, pp. 3–23.

Kjaer, A. M. (2004), *Governance*, Cambridge: Polity Press.

Langlois, A., Dubois, F. (2005), *Autonomous Media: Activating Resistance and Dissent*, Montréal: Cumulus Press.

MacBride, S., Abel, E., International Commission for the Study of Communication Problems (1980), *Many Voices, One World. Communication and Society Today and Tomorrow. Towards a New More Just and More Efficient Information and Communication order*, Ibandan and Paris: Ibandan University Press and UNESCO Press.

Messner, D., Nuscheler, F. (2003), 'Das Konzept Global Governance: Stand und Perspektiven', *INEF-Report* 67, Duisburg: Institut für Entwicklung und Frieden.

Milan, S. (2004), *Communicating Civil Society: Participation as the Main Benchmark of Civil Society Media. The Case of the Third World Social Forum*, Paper for the International Association of Media and Communication Research (IAMCR), Porto Alegre, 27 July.

Nelson, P. J. (2002), 'Agendas, Accountability, and Legitimacy Among Transnational Networks Lobbying the World Bank', in S. Khagram, J. V. Riker, and K. Sikkink (eds.), *Restructuring World Politics: Transnational Social Movements, Networks, and Norms*, Minneapolis: University of Minnesota Press, pp. 131–54.

Notes from Nowhere (2003), *We Are Everywhere: The Irresistible Rise of Global Anticapitalism*, London/New York: Verso.

Ó Siochrú, S., Girard, B. (2002), *Global Media Governance*, New York/Oxford: Rowman & Littlefield.

Ó Siochrú, S. (2004), 'Will the Real WSIS Please Stand Up? The Historic Encounter of the Information Society and the Communication Society', *Gazette: The International Journal for Communication Studies*, 66: 3–4, pp. 203–24.

Raboy, M. (2004), 'The WSIS as a Political Space in Global Media Governance', *Continuum: Journal of Media & Cultural Studies*, 18: 3, pp. 345–59.

Rodríguez, C. (2001), *Fissures in the Mediascape: An International Study of Citizens' Media*, Cresskill, NJ: Hampton Press.

Rosenau, J. N. (1995), 'Governance in the Twenty-First Century', *Global Governance*, 1: 1, pp. 13–43.

Servaes, J., Carpentier, N. (2005), 'Introduction: Steps to Achieve a Sustainable Information Society', in J. Servaes and N. Carpentier (eds.), *Deconstructing WSIS: Towards a Sustainable Agenda for the Future Information Society*, Bristol, UK and Portland, OR, USA: Intellect, pp. 5–16.

Sikkink, K. (2002), 'Restructuring World Politics: The Limits and Asymmetries of Soft Power', in S. Khagram, J. V. Riker, and K. Sikkink (eds.), *Restructuring World Politics: Transnational Social Movements, Networks, and Norms*, Minneapolis: University of Minnesota Press, pp. 301–17.

Sreberny-Mohammadi, A. (1997), 'Small Media and Revolutionary Change: a New Model', in A. Sreberny-Mohammadi, D. Winseck, J. McKenna, *et al.* (eds.), *Media in Global Context*, London: Arnold, pp. 220–35.

Wilkinson, R. (2002), 'The Contours of Courtship: The WTO and Civil Society', in R. Wilkinson and S. Hughes (eds.), *Global Governance: Critical Perspectives*, London: Routledge, pp. 193–211.

WSIS (2003a), 'Declaration of Principles. Building the Information Society: a Global Challenge in the New Millenium'. http://www.itu.int/dms_pub/itu-s/md/03/wsis/doc/s03-wsis-doc-0004!!msw-e.doc. Downloaded on 5 October 2005.

—— (2003b), 'Plan of Action'.http://www.itu.int/dms_pub/itu-s/md/03/wsis/doc/s03-wsis-doc-0005!!msw-e.doc. Downloaded on 5 October 2005.

Chapter Twelve

Media and communication strategies of glocalized activists: beyond media-centric thinking

Bart Cammaerts

Introduction

The Internet has provided activists new opportunities to build networks (across borders) and exchange alternative information or distribute counter-hegemonic discourses in a more (cost-)efficient way. It also provided activists and civil society organizations more control over the content of their message and the tools to independently inform citizens and sympathizers worldwide. This strength is partly also often perceived as a weakness, since the Internet tends to strengthen the fragmentation of the public sphere into what Gitlin (1998) calls 'public sphericules'.

However, Gitlin, as well as other authors such as Putnam (1995, 2000) or Galston (2003), seem to imply that this fragmentation is to the detriment of democracy and leading to a non-committing 'lazy' politics. This is, however, not necessarily the case. As the World Social Forum and many coordinated actions against international organizations show, fragmentation does not *per se* exclude strategic cooperation between very different civil society associations – from very loose activist networks to structured and professional civil society organizations, labor unions, or even political parties, from revolutionary movements to reformist movements (Held and McGrew, 2002; Tarrow, 2005).

Similarly, coalition building also occurs at a national or local level, where activists can potentially be much more effective and influential then at an international or global level. In this regard, transnationalization and transnational activism should not merely be conceived as coordinated actions at an international level, or as activism embedded in a local/national context, but at the same time also as active at an inter – or transnational level of governance. Transnational activism can also be conceived as the transnational distribution and appropriation of counter-hegemonic discourses and action-strategies to a local setting. As Tarrow (2005: 103) points out when he writes, amongst others, on the worldwide diffusion of Ghandi's strategy of non-violent direct action and civil disobedience, this is not a new phenomenon:

> *Determined activists have always been able to adapt new forms of contention across borders. But with the growth of internationalization and global communication, diffusion has both increased and accelerated.*

It will also be argued that an overemphasis on the Internet and communication as such tends to obscure that social change and achieving political aims has to be fought for beyond the media too. This involves gaining support, changing values, and influencing the political agenda, as much as the media agenda. Offe (1987:69) refers to this when he speaks of 'non-institutional politics'. Beck (1994: 23) also points to this field of politics from below with his notion of sub-politics or 'the non-institutional renaissance of the political':

Sub-politics means shaping society from below. Viewed from above, this results in the loss of implementation power, the shrinkage and minimisation of politics. In the wake of sub-politicization, there are growing opportunities to have a voice and a share in the arrangement of society for groups hitherto uninvolved in the substantive technification and industrialisation process.

In mature democracies a complex interplay and overlap between non-and institutional politics can be observed. As such they cannot be construed as a dichotomy, but oscillate between convergence and contention. The state is not an entity separated from society and neither is there a clear distinction between what is called civil society and institutional and formal politics. Interpenetrations from institutional into non-institutional politics and vice versa occur at different levels and are essential. It is in this permanent organic process that media fulfil, increasingly so, a mediating and facilitating function (Bennett and Entman, 2001; Silverstone, 2005). However, in a democracy the extent and form of social change is not determined by the media, but by citizens – their (in)capacity, willingness, or unwillingness to change behavior, patterns of consumption, ways of life, and by this dynamic organic interaction between society and democratic institutions, deciding to encourage/promote change or resist/discipline it. Although the focus in this chapter is clearly on progressive movements and direct action, reactionary forces in society also transnationalize and adopt similar media strategies, which should not be ignored (Downing, 2001: 88).

Keeping these issues in mind, this chapter will analyze a particular form of localized transnational activism and their communication practices to foster their political aims, namely local activists who appropriate and adapt/adopt transnational discourses and action strategies to apply them in a local context. This 'glocalized' type of transnational activism will be explored by deconstructing the communication strategies of a group of young and radical activists and their sympathizers in their struggle to save a privately owned city forest in North Belgium. In the summer of 2001, activists occupied the Lappersfort forest on the outskirts of Bruges and stayed there for more than a year before being forcefully evicted by the police, executing a court order initiated by the owner Fabricom. This direct action was supported by a large coalition of very diverse civil society organizations, but also by some political parties and by local citizens.

This case [1] will show that the successful adoption and adaptation of trans-national direct action strategies at a local level is not only dependent on a refined communication strategy directed towards core supporters, sympathizers, and the population at large, but as much on broad (local) popular and political support.

Activism and media

Although in mature democracies, violence is discredited as a means to achieve social change, direct actions are still very much a legitimate way of voicing dissent for activists and movements in their struggles. Gamson (1990: 87) argued that movements who do pursue violent revolutionary tactics 'seem to pay the cost of violence without gaining the benefits of employing it. They are both threatening and weak, and their repression becomes a low-cost strategy for those whom they attempt to displace'. However, after 9/11 and the attacks in Madrid, London and other parts of the world, this claim is increasingly untenable, at least at an international level and in terms of the costs of repression and its consequences for civil liberties in mature democracies.

Direct action strategies of progressive movements have undergone consider-able changes in recent years, while at the same time also paying tribute to a historical legacy, such as the civic rights movement in the United States, the student movements of the 1960s, the women's right movement, the green movement and the gay rights movement (Gitlin, 1980; Freeman, 1984; Cruikshank, 1992; McAdam, 1999). Gamson was certainly right that the violent strategies of the Black Power movement were highly destructive for the civic rights movement. Both the green movement and the gay-rights movement illustrate that social change can be achieved through sustained non-violent struggle that involves both changing values and behaviors amongst the population, in youth culture, and through gradual often delayed re-active changes in legislation and regulation, be it regarding the adoption of a more ecological lifestyle, separating waste or a more tolerant and more open attitude towards gay and lesbian life-styles, protection against discrimination and opening up adoption and marriage to gays and lesbians (Feher and Heller, 1983: 37; Offe, 1987; Turner, 2001). As these examples already indicate, these struggles are less class-based than the traditional labor movement was, and their aims are also more geared at changing (certain) values within society. Their struggles concentrate more on the acceptance or normalization of different lifestyles and respect for difference, than on taking over power from the ruling classes. Melucci (1981: 179), from a New Social Movement perspective, points out that processes of social change involve foremost the development of an alternative counter-hegemonic discourse geared at changing values, attitudes, and behavior amongst citizens.

Today's activism and concerns relate more to what Giddens (1991: 214) calls 'life-politics':

Life politics concerns political issues which flow from processes of self-actualisation in post-traditional contexts, where globalising influences intrude deeply into the reflexive project of the self, and conversely where processes of self-realization influence global strategies.

This points to the relevance of the self, as well as its relation with 'the other', also from a global perspective. Others refer to the notion of identity politics (du Preez, 1980; Calhoun, 1994; Bennett, 1998) to indicate changes within society, as well as in politics. It deals with the struggle for self-determination and recognition of cultural, sexual, ethnic differences, and against discrimination on the basis of these differences.

Life- and identity politics, although different, imply that politics is about much more than the stark – but now more latent – ideological divides between labor and capital and that the self, gender, sexuality, race, ethnicity, and religion are also political in their own right.

The advent of life- and identity politics also gives rise to concerns. Fraser (1996: 4) points to a progressive, but also to a fundamentalist form of identity politics. Similarly with life-politics the distinction could be made between a solidarity perspective, focussing on abolishing world poverty for example and an individualistic perspective, as is the case with NIMBY-activism [2]. Life- and identity politics have also given rise to a splinterization in demands, claims, and aims, lacking an overall underpinning ideological framework. This also exposes a key debate and conflict within political theory, namely between those celebrating difference and focussing on recognition, embedded in a culturalist perspective (Taylor, 1994) and those, such as Gitlin (1995), embedded in a more Political Economy paradigm, who reduce identity politics to 'a counterproductive diversion from the real economic issues, one that balkanizes groups and rejects universalist moral norms', as summarized by Fraser (1996: 10). Instead Fraser asserts that culture versus economy, recognition of identity versus a redistributive project are false anti-theses, that social, economic, and political realities cannot be essentialized or reduced to single dimensions. She argues for a more open, flexible, and overlapping conception of these dualisms that does justice

both to the apparent institutional separation of economy and culture in capitalist society and to their interpenetration. It alone can conceptualize the possibility of practical tensions between claims for redistribution and claims for recognition (Fraser, 1996: 66).

What Fraser also implies is that it is impossible to address issues of identity without accounting for economic interests and the mediating role of politics to redress injustices, not only relating to respect and recognition of difference, but as much in terms of socio-economic injustices, local and global.

To frame the diversity and multiplicity, but at the same time the rather loose inter-connectedness of current day struggles, and the role of media and communication in sustaining and supporting them, the 'multitude' - a notion originally developed by Spinoza and re-introduced into political theory by Hardt and Negri (2004) - might also be useful. According to Hardt and Negri (2004: 105), the multitude can be conceived as the 'multiplicity of all these singular differences'. As such it allows 'the social multiplicity to manage to communicate and act in common while remaining internally different' (Hardt and Negri, 2004: xiv). In replying to the criticisms that the multitude puts itself in dialectic opposition to power, Negri (2002, translation by Arianna Bove) defends his interpretation of Foucault's analytics of power as:

> *an analysis of a regional system of institutions of struggles, crossings and confrontations, and these antagonistic struggles open up on omnilateral horizons. This concerns both the surface of the relations of force and the ontology of ourselves.*

Negri also points to the dialectic between two basic forms of power: constituted power that is characterized as re-active, resting with the state and with its role to mediate conflicting interests; and the unmediated constituent – active – power of the multitude. The constituted power of the state is being legitimized and challenged at the same time by the constituent power of the multitude. The social contract, which legitimizes state authority and sovereignty, rests on the pacification of conflicts and antagonisms (Negri, 1999: 29), but cannot be seen as fixed. It is permanently being re-negotiated and challenged, never reaching a perfect ideal solution. This points to the flexible ability of the capitalist paradigm to re-act and transform itself to accommodate demands and pacify conflicts, for the time being, until new demands emerge.

As Urry (1999: 318) rightly states, 'Citizenship has always necessitated symbolic resources distributed through various means of mass communication'. Media thus play a crucial role in the mediation, the convergence of different interests, spheres, and actors, as well as in exposing the tensions and divergences between them. This can be seen in terms of the intrusion of alternative into mainstream public spheres – providing a platform for alternative discourses, in terms of representation – normalizing alternative discourses or lifestyles, but also in terms of being a battleground over meanings and conceptions of what constitutes the public interest and the common good (Mouffe, 1999).

Communication strategies of activists, be they Internet-based, or using pamphlets, stickers, community radio, and even getting attention by the mainstream media, should be seen in a dynamic relationship with each other and not in a dichotomous way.

Most recent empirical studies on activism within Media and Communication Studies focus foremost on the opportunities and constraints the Internet provides in organizing movements, 'networking', mobilizing online, as well as offline, and/or strengthening the public sphere by facilitating discussion and the development of counter-hegemonic discourses (Hill and Hughes, 1998; Dahlberg, 2001; Webster, 2001; Van Aelst and Walgrave, 2002; Van Audenhove *et al.*, 2002; Meikle, 2002; Gibson *et al.*, 2003; McCaughey and Ayers, 2003; van de Donk *et al.*, 2004; Dahlgren, 2005). Alternative information needs alternative channels of distribution and the Internet provides activists with a user-friendly medium for the unbiased and especially the (cost-)efficient distribution of alternative information across the boundaries of time and space. Its viral characteristics are in this regard an important asset (Rushkoff, 1996), whereby individuals pass on information through mailing lists or by forwarding the information to their personal and/or professional networks. As such, alternative information can spread rapidly at a limited cost. Besides this, websites allow activists and social movements to be more in control of their message and self-representation, which can be seen as empowering (Rucht, 2004). In this regard, websites, e-mail, forums, and mailing-lists are used extensively to distribute and share alternative information, to mobilize and organize internally or in coalitions with other organizations, and to a lesser extent also to debate issues and strategies (Cammaerts, 2005).

While the Internet increasingly constitutes an opportunity structure for activists and social movements, in terms of self-representation, mobilizing for (direct) actions, or distributing information, this clearly has to be seen as being embedded in a larger communication strategy, including other media and ways to distribute their aims and goals. In this regard, (positive) attention in the mainstream media, pamphlets or community radios are as important as it relates more to reaching a broader constituency than those already convinced. An example in this regard is the coverage of the protests against the EU summit in Brussels in December 2001, where Indymedia pooled-up with community and university radios as well as an art cinema house to form Radio Bruxxel [3]. During four days, volunteers and activists produced radio programs covering the summit from a critical left-wing perspective. These not only featured on the participating radio stations, all located in Brussels, but were also streamed live through the Internet, allowing other activists-radios worldwide to pick-up the feed and re-transmit it on FM. Besides this, Indymedia also distributed many stickers, brochures, and pamphlets during the demonstrations. This shows that a pre-dominantly Internet-based organization, such as Indymedia, is aware that although penetration rates of the Internet have risen in recent years (at least in the West), the digital divide is still a reality for many people, especially so for disadvantaged groups in society. The Internet is also very much a pull-medium, meaning that citizens need to be already informed and interested to go and seek information about the activists and their aims. As such, activists necessarily need to diversify their media-strategies hence the use of other media such as (community) radio or print.

Finally, studies trying to make sense of the impact of the Internet on activism often point to its capacity to transnationalize struggles and build coalitions beyond the nation state (Della Porta *et al.*, 1999; Florini, 2000; Tarrow, 2001; Cammaerts, 2005). These studies also point out that different types of transnationalization can be observed. The first type could be called 'trans-international' activism, strongly organized and integrated at a transnational level, with staff or members dispersed internationally and aiming to translate local 'grass roots' issues and interests to a global level of governance. Examples of this type are Transparency International (TI), striving for good and open government, or the Association for Progressive Communication (APC), struggling, amongst others, for communication rights. A second type of transnationalization is 'trans-national' activism in that the transnational provides a common frame of reference, but local/national cells have relative independence. At the same time local struggles link-up with an international or regional agenda and vice versa. Examples of this type are Indymedia or ATTAC, but also 'older' organizations, such as Greenpeace or Amnesty International, clearly embedded in a local (offline) context too. However, besides these two, a third – more abstract – type of transnationalization can be identified, which could tentatively be called 'glocal' activism. In local struggles at a national level transnational discourses and action-methods are 'imported' and consequently appropriated and adapted to the local context. This chapter explores this latter 'more localized' type of transnationalization.

This chapter also concurs with Diani's observation, referring to Della Porta (1988) that:

> *Participatory movement organisations – especially the most radical – are more dependent upon direct, face-to-face interactions, for the purpose both of recruiting members and of securing their commitment. Engaging in what are potentially high-risk activities requires a high level of trust and collective identification which is unlikely to develop if not supported by face-to-face interaction* (Diani, 2001: 126).

Although media and communication are increasingly important in different ways, as will be shown later, the offline or the more banal micro-level of having a drink together and building trust, developing a collective identity and framework of reference, and negotiating different identities, is not to be neglected in any account of activism. Besides this, also the formal institutional level of politics and the dynamic relationship between the non-institutional and the institutional remains relevant. In this regard can be referred to what Deleuze and Guattari (1987: 216–17) call the ongoing negotiations between the 'molecular' – the micro level of the political and the 'molar' – the structural segmentations at a macro-political level:

> *Molecular escapes and movements would be nothing if they did not return to the molar organisations to reshuffle their segments, their binary distributions of sexes, classes and parties.*

This relates to the inherent dynamic relationship between the constituent power of the multitude and the constituting powers of the state. From a framing-perspective, McAdam (2005: 119) identifies six strategic challenges for movements that really aim to become 'a force for social change' and also integrates both facets. The first two challenges are inward oriented: recruiting core-activists and sustaining the organization. This has been covered extensively by the dominant literature on social movements (for an overview see Della Porta and Diani, 1999). The four other challenges for activists can be characterized as more outward oriented. They relate to getting attention in the mainstream media, to mobilizing beyond those already convinced, to over-coming social control, as well as possible repression and finally to 'shape public policy and state action' (McAdam, 2000: 119).

Different media impact in different ways on each of these strategic aims. We will return to these strategic aims and their relation to media and communication later. First, an analysis will be presented of the glocalized direct action that was the occupation of the Lappersfort forest. The context of the action will be outlined, the media-strategies assessed, as well as the political implications and strategies to influence state action, without ignoring the economic interests at play.

Communication strategies of glocal activism: occupying the Lappersfort forest

Discourses of forest preservation and the technique of occupation, building tree-cabins and a maze of tunnels is not new. This tactic originated in the United Kingdom where a group of local activists from Norwich, calling themselves the flowerpot tribe, occupied a small forest to stop the building of a bypass in 1993. They belonged to a worldwide movement called Earth First! [4] and were also illustrative of the radicalization of the ecological movement in the United Kingdom (Anonymous, 2003). The transnationalizing strategies and discourses led the radicalization of the ecological movement to spread fairly rapidly to other countries.

Context

Activists occupied the threatened Lappersfort forest on the fringes of the provincial city of Bruges (Belgium) in August 2001, using similar tactics as their

United Kingdom counterparts some years earlier. The aim of this occupation was to save the forest from being chopped down to make way for a road, an industrial terrain and a bus station for which Fabricom, the owner of the forest and part of the multinational Tractebel, had received permission from the local authorities. While the activists were a small radical anarchist group, their action was promptly supported by a larger constituency of civil society organizations, which made that the discourses relating to the aims of the action were amplified exponentially. This coalition of 103 small and larger, mainly environmental, organizations was called the Green Belt Front (Groene Gordel Front). Beyond that, a so-called protection committee was set-up to which some 400 sympathizers of different backgrounds – citizens, artists (...) and celebrities – signed-up. Besides this, there were also a number of befriended civil servants that did not openly support the action, but provided valuable information regarding the forest and planning decisions.

As such, three concentric circles of support around the radical activists occupying the forest could be identified; the Green Belt Front of supporting environmental and other civil society organizations, the so-called protection-committee of citizens sympathizing with the cause and lastly an informal and above all invisible network of contacts within the administration.

In September 2002, after one year of occupation, Fabricom summoned the activists to court. The judge subsequently ordered the activists to leave the forest immediately and to pay an 'occupying fee' of 1 € per person per day for as long as they remained in the forest. As the green party was part of the Government and had self-evidently a lot of sympathy for the action, the Flemish green minister for the environment started negotiations with the owner Fabricom with the intent to buy and thus save the forest.

However, by mid-October 2002, the major of Bruges, who sympathized with Fabricoms' plans for the forest, ran out of patience and he ordered the police to forcefully evict the activists from the forest. A few hours after the police started their action, a spontaneous demonstration of sympathizers was mobilized in the vicinity of the forest, but almost everybody was arrested. The police acted coercively and pro-active, arresting as much activists as possible as well as sympathizers arriving at the train station. In the afternoon some 150 sympathizers assembled in front of the City Hall to hold a noise-demonstration; many of them were arrested too. By the evening on the same day another protest started in the city centre of Bruges, which was attended by some 500 people, with more local citizens joining the activists. No more arrests were made. This showed that the activists had generated considerable support and sympathy from the local population, many of which were also in favor of saving the forest. All this culminated in yet another demonstration the next weekend, which more than 4.000 people attended (Indymedia, 2002a, b). Undisputedly, it was one of the biggest demonstrations the provincial city of Bruges had seen to date. Indymedia reported on Els, a mother of three children, present in the big demonstration:

Yes, I'm a mother of three and that is precisely why I think it is important to be here. It's about the future of our children. This forest has to be saved [...] I think it is very exciting that there are so many people. Now I hope that something is done too. It is very important that we raise our voices, but they have to listen too (Indymedia, 2002h, translation by the author).

Media and communication strategies

The case of the Lappersfort forest is a prime example of how ICTs, such as the Internet, but also mobile communication, can foster and sustain real-life direct action, networking, and mobilization. The activists put up their own website [5] where citizens and sympathizers could find information, a petition, contact-information, new actions, etc. Having a site of their own allowed the activists more control over their own message, their self-representation, and it also served as a means to attract new sympathizers and activists.

The site of Indymedia-Belgium was also used frequently as a platform to communicate independently to a wider 'alternative' public of sympathizers and fellow activists, which was then subsequently also picked up by other Independent Media Centres, amongst others in the United Kingdom and in the Netherlands [6]. Like all independent media centres, Indymedia-Belgium acted as a valuable interface for direct action. As such a lot of information could be found regarding the occupation, the rulings of the judge, the violent eviction from the forest, and the actions that ensued [7]. Indymedia also serves as an alternative source for journalists looking for another perspective, besides the official one, as well as an entrance-point to contact activists.

One of the interesting articles on the Indymedia-site, giving an insight in the strategies of the activists, was an urgent call for research on the owner of the forest, posted in English.

Urgent call from Lappersfront: we want to know our enemy, and we're looking for people that have the time and the knowledge to do this properly. And yes, we're looking for DIRTY business. Fabricom Group is one of the super-lobbying-bastards that are destroying the planet. Lappersfort against Fabricom = David against Goliath (Indymedia, 2002c).

This also resulted, amongst others, in a short occupation of the offices of Fabricom in Gent (Indymedia, 2002d), as well as the posting of e-mail addresses of Fabricom employers 'harvested' through Google (Indymedia, 2002e). The focus on Fabricom also shows that this local struggle of saving the forest was embedded in the wider struggle against neo-liberalism and global capitalism, hence the involvement of organizations such as ATTAC for example, inter-linking different struggles.

The Internet also played an important role in mobilizing activists before and after the evictions started. This real possibility was prepared well in advance.

When the judge ruled that they had to leave the forest, the following message appeared on the site of Indymedia-Belgium:

> *The Lappersfront launches a call to all sympathizers: To those who can make themselves available when the police clears the forest, we ask to leave an email-address or a telephone-number to Pat; CALL or EMAIL: Xx.x@pandora.be, 0497/XX-XX-XX. You will not have to be in the forest yourself, but you can help by forming a buffer* (Indymedia, 2002f, translation by the author).

In this regard, it is also noteworthy to mention the extensive use of mobile cell-phones besides e-mail for internal organizational purposes, as well as for mobilizing at short notice.

When the police actually started their action, almost simultaneously an alert mobilization call was sent out through mobile communication and the Internet.

> *URGENT MOBILIZATION: 16h00 Town Hall Bruges - Emergency protest meeting for the saving of the Lappersfort forest (...) Please forward this message to as many people and post it on as many lists and websites as possible* (Indymedia, 2002g, translation by the author).

A few hours later ATTAC-Flanders distributed a call for a next day's demonstration in front of the offices of Tractebel in Brussels under the heading 'Our world is not for sale'; some 100 people showed-up. In this regard, the economic interests underlying this struggle need to be highlighted. While at first sight this is an environmental struggle, it is at the same time also a conflict between different conceptions of the common good, the limits and rights of private ownership, and the powers/weakness of the state to intervene.

Although the Internet was crucial for initial alert-mobilizations on the day itself, the mobilization for the large demonstration on the weekend following eviction was much wider, tapping into the mobilizing potential of the coalition of organizations and sympathizers, as well as using mainstream media, pamphlets and word of mouth. The uses of the Internet could thus be characterized as foremost being instrumental in facilitating the mobilization of initial support, the recruitment of new activists and the organization of resistance to the eviction and social control.

Luc Vanneste, chairman of the Green Belt Front, also identifies another important – less instrumental, but constitutive – function of the Internet, namely sustaining a network in the long term:

> *The sites, the mailings, the press-releases keep the network going, prevents it from falling asleep. It serves to remain vigilant even if nothing happens... to be prepared for when the enemy re-emerges... to service the machine, oil it, so that it can be started-up again quickly, if need be!* (e-mail Luc Vanneste – 2 January 2006, translation by the author).

Another more elusive potential of the Internet relates to the everyday micro-context of activists. The distance and relative anonymity of the Internet is often deemed to be a negative attribute in terms of the democratic potential of the Internet, but here is shown that this distance can also be seen as a strength, as it allows different identities to co-exist side by side, as an activist, as an employee and/or as a parent and partner. Jozef De Coster, a former chairman of the Green Belt Front, refers to this:

> *Most of the activists and sympathizers in the Lappersfort-case have a full-time job. Being called up during working hours for urgent co-ordination or actions would be considered too intrusive. A few of them, who work for the government or for companies dealing with Fabricom or the city of Bruges also run the danger of being caught 'collaborating' with the Lappersfronters and the Green Belt Front. Sympathizers that are being informed and mobilized through email, can decide themselves when to dedicate time and attention to 'the action'. As such, they can easily adapt their action-rhythm to the highs and lows in their own personal and professional timeframes* (e-mail Jozef De Coster, 6 February 2006, translation by the author).

The importance of the Internet should, however, not be exaggerated. A good relationship with the mainstream press was also one of the strengths of the activists. Inviting journalists into the forest, providing them with a good story and a clear-cut message: 'what is forest, stays forest'. The fact that the action lasted for such a long time and the easy-to-communicate cause made the media construct them as perseverant and likeable. This is by no means self-evident as representations of protest-movements, and direct actions are often biased towards negative representations (Lee and Solomon, 1990). This is why a media-savvy strategy directed at the mainstream media is crucial.

The activists acknowledged 'the forces of the fourth power', thereby refer-ring to the press, and the need for their support to sustain the direct action. On their website, four ethical principles in dealing with the local and national media are presented:

1. *don't hate the media, be the media*
2. *a correct relationship with the press*
3. *we cannot, won't, should not determine the agenda of the fourth power*
4. *transparency in internal governance and action. (For example, the 'subjects' of our press-releases, the city council, the company Fabricom, etc. – always get a copy).*
   (Site GGF: http://www.ggf.be/index.htm, translation by the author.)

This can be framed as a dynamic, open, and basic-democratic communication strategy, combining self-representation with respect for the logic of mainstream media and news-production.

In the beginning of the action, there was only limited attention from the mainstream press for the occupation and the issue of forest-preservation. When the activists managed to sustain their action, the media-logics of an ongoing story started to play. The activists' stubborn struggle, remaining in the forest during the winter, became a story that was covered in all newspapers, in television news broadcasts, and in infotainment programs. The activists were increasingly represented as idealist young people who had given-up everything for a just cause and willing to live in difficult 'cold' circumstances for that cause.

This raised sympathy for the activists and their aims. Moreover, during the summer times, the activists opened-up the forest, which had been closed to the general public for many years. Schools visited the forest and the occupiers and several cultural events were organized, which were again covered by the local and national press. These events also attracted large crowds and gave local citizens the opportunity to visit the forest and the activists a way to get their message across in a positive setting. This can also be related to the introduction of popular and youth sub-cultures into activist strategies. In an e-mail, Luc Vanneste, chairman of the Green Belt Front, also points to the organizational importance of the forest as a location for holding meetings and forging links between activists inside the forest and outside, as well as with civil society organizations:

> *Crucial for that time was that the occupied forest served so to speak as a roundtable/free-place/local pub where everybody met. The good contact with the people of Indymedia West-Flanders also stems from meetings in the forest. That period of intense bonding in an accessible forest with accessible occupiers is of course the motor and energy that keeps us going, up until today* (e-mail Luc Vanneste, 2 January 2006, translation by the author).

The Internet is most useful at the level of internal communication between dispersed activists, although here the importance of face-to-face interaction in building trust should not be ignored. Besides this, the Internet also serves as a way to pull sympathizers from the periphery into the core, but in line with Gamson and Wolfsfeld (1993: 116) social movements also need mainstream media to 'broaden the scope of conflict' and push its message to a mass audience.

In other words, for a direct action to resonate beyond a 'ghettoized' community of like-minded, beyond the fragmented public sphericules of the (spl)Internet, where you need to be already interested or semi-informed in order to actively seek information regarding the aims of the action, activist communication strategies also need to be directed towards the mainstream public sphere. In this regard, a push-strategy is enacted in an attempt to reach a broader constituency and gain public support, which then can potentially transform into political influence.

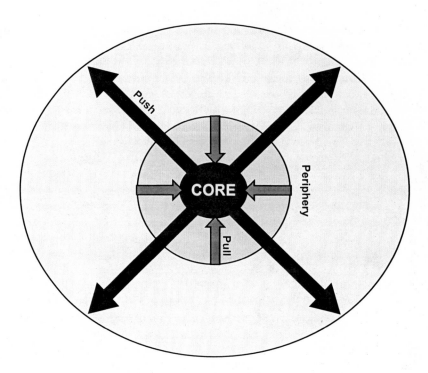

Figure 1: Activist communication strategy model.

The model in Figure 1 attempts to capture these different activist media usages directed at different target groups. Within the core group, face-to-face communication, mobile communication as well as point-to-point Internet communication, is important. The Internet and especially mailing lists are also useful to pull sympathizers situated at the periphery into the core group or sustain the dynamism within the movement. Communication strategies directed at the mainstream media represent a push strategy towards a broader audience, be it local or national.

It can be concluded that this fairly successful direct action adopted a dual communication strategy combining an independent voice through the Internet directed at core supporters and a mediated voice through local and national press directed at the general population. Referring to Ruchts' (2004: 36) quadruple 'A' in activist media strategies – 'abstention, attack, adaptation and alternatives', the Lappersfort case clearly combined adaptation to the logic of mass media with developing alternatives in the form of 'movement controlled media' in order to 'secure autonomy and operational flexibility' (Rucht, 2004: 55).

In this regard our analysis also concurs with Hill and Hughes' (1998: 186) observation that:

The Net is not going to radically change us; we are moulding it to our own ways of thinking and action. It is neither a monstrosity nor a saviour; it is a new venue for the same old human compunction: politics.

Real politik

To have a real impact on society, and also subsequently on the formal democratic process, a direct action or an innovative idea must be able to generate citizen and political support. This in turn requires, amongst others, mobilization, attention in the mainstream media and building coalitions with other civil society organizations. The three concentric circles of support ensured not only that the Lappersfort forest stayed on the political agenda but also that the pressure for finding a solution to save the forest remained present after the activists were forcefully evicted.

This case is also relevant because of the complex inter-relations and tensions between the activists and their aims, the interests of the private owner, and the state, all of which cannot be conceived as singular actors. Within civil society, the labor unions were very reluctant to support the action and reacted at times even fairly aggressively towards the activists, as exemplified by the statement of a labor union representative that their 'attitude is more negative than the Vlaams Blok' [8], associating them with the North Belgian post-fascist party. This also shows that the attempts to link the environment and the non-material to other (more economic) struggles have only partly succeeded, as many, especially in the labor movement, still place ecology in opposition to economy.

Similarly, the state can also be seen as wavering in this regard. While the local authorities supported the owner Fabricom and had issued planning permissions for the forest to be 'used for other purposes', the regional government was much more susceptible to the aims of the activists and their sympathizers. As the action was generating support and sympathy amongst the broader population, catalyzed by the mainstream media, several political parties started to take stances. During the summer of 2002, the North Belgian minister for the environment, Vera Dua (Green Party), visited the activists in the Lappersfort forest. When the eviction started, she also issued a press-release condemning the eviction and at the same time putting more pressure on the owners of the forest to sell:

The Minister would like to point out that an encounter was planned this week between the Minister and Fabricom about the possible purchase of the Lappersfort-forest. The Minister had therefore urged, Fabricom as well as the municipal authorities in Bruges, to wait for the outcome of these negotiations. The Minister is appalled that this did not happen. 'Apparently there are people who don't want a fair solution', the Minister concludes. 'We want to buy the forest and give Bruges a city-forest like no other Flemish city has. We want to do this, but only at a reasonable price' (Cabinet of the Flemish Minister for the Environment, 2002, translation by the author).

Besides the involvement of a minister, individual representatives of the North Belgian socialist party and a leftish liberal party called SPIRIT signed-up to support the action and its aims. Even at the time of writing the Green Belt Front still counts two ministers in its so-called 'protection committee'. In this regard, it is relevant to note that the Green Belt Front decided to keep political parties out of the front itself, but welcomed individual politicians to join a supportive committee. Vanneste confirms this:

Political parties did want to become member of the civil society coalition, but it was a conscious decision to only invite politicians to join the protection committee. It's a matter of safeguarding our own agenda. Of course, behind the scenes there was intense co-operation at times (Mail Luc Vanneste, 2 January 2006, translation by the author).

Nevertheless, this case also shows that there was 'intense co-operation' and that the state cannot be conceptualized as one entity, but constituting of different forces, some resisting change, others promoting or supporting change.

The case of the occupation of the Lappersfort forest illustrates how struggles by a radical group of young activists can raise a high level of passive engagement or sympathy, which can even transform into active civic engagement and policy-influence at a certain moment in time. Not unimportant in this regard is that the long struggle to save the Lappersfront forest was supported by the local population. Opening-up the forest to the public for visits and walks, the organization of cultural activities in the summer and also many positive accounts of the action in the mainstream media all played a positive role.

However, reality is messy, and despite the support from the local population, the mainstream and off-stream media, as well as (some) formal political actors, the forest is still not saved in its entirety. The new minister for the environment, a Christian Democrat who previously headed an employer's organization for medium and small enterprises, delayed reaching a compromise due to corporate pressures of having office-space close to the city centre. As such, 4 years after the occupation, negotiations regarding the future destination of the forest are still ongoing. Vigilance and persistent action by the civil society coalition and the members of the protection committee have, however, prevented the destruction of the forest to date. Some 70% of the forest is now permanently saved and will become a city-forest, while some 30% is still under threat of being cut down to habor offices and a road.

This also shows that in politics in the real world you seldom get everything you want. Diverging and conflicting interests always shape political decisions.

In this specific case, corporate and/or economic interests did not exactly prevail, but neither were they ignored.

Conclusions

Activists are aware that the Internet, although very useful, also has its limits in terms of reaching a broad audience. Indymedia, for example, would never have existed without the Internet, but nevertheless they produce brochures and pamphlets to raise awareness of their existence, but also to distribute part of their content to an audience that has no access to the Internet. In terms of the Lappersfort case, it can be concluded that the Internet did play an important role in terms of initial/alert mobilization and self-representation, in terms of organizing the struggle, but also in sustaining the action and keeping a connection between the activists and their sympathizers. Besides this, it also has to be said that in the end the positive representations in the mainstream media played an important role is terms of mobilizing beyond the activists and sympathizers, much more so than the Internet.

Table 1 relates the communication and media strategy enacted in this case to the different challenges put forward earlier by McAdam (2005: 119).

What Table 1 does not capture, however, is the organic hybrid interplay between the online and the offline that goes on within the civil society coalition, as well as the formal and informal network of sympathizers, combining face-to-face meetings and social/cultural activities with online interaction and exchange. It also does not account for the more tacit impact the Internet has on the practice of activism. Relevant in this regard is that the Internet is a non-intrusive medium that allows citizens to determine and control the degree of their involvement, as well as balancing out their engagement with other roles they have. As such, this also confirms other research suggesting that contrary to what is commonly perceived, the weak ties that the Internet enables, contributes to the ability of citizens to participate and engage and manage the degree of their involvement (Granovetter, 1982; Haythornthwaite, 2005; Kavanaugh et al., 2005). In a way we need to de-essentialize the virtual and the real and respect different identities and different degrees of participation.

However, this case also shows that it is important to transform weak ties into strong ties. In this regard, a too media- or Internet-centric approach to activism and social change should be avoided. Such a reductionist view holds the danger that the offline realm is black-boxed. The importance of the nitty-gritty of lobbying, making your case, formulating a consistent counter-discourse, writing letters/e-mails to newspapers, journalists, and politicians, putting pressure on politicians and other stakeholders, holding meetings to coordinate actions, and indeed also of offline direct actions and social activities, tend to be ignored in popular accounts of hacktivism or media activism. It is, however, in that 'real' messy world that social change has to be argued for the most, winning over the 'hearts and minds' of citizens and political actors. Local citizen support and the

Table 1:

Communication strategies of the Lappersfort activists

	Online	Offline
Recruit:	• Mailing lists • Website • Indymedia	• Face-to-face contacts • Social and cultural activities
Sustain:	• Mailing lists • Point-to-point e-mail • Mobile communication • Indymedia	• Face-to-face meetings • Social and cultural activities
Media coverage:	• E-mails to journalists	• Face-to-face contacts • Specific strategy directed at mainstream media
Mobilize beyond:		• Coverage in the mainstream media • Pamphlets • Social and cultural activities
Constrain control and repression:	• Mobile • E-mail coordination • Website	• Sustained action • Demonstrations • Coverage of police violence
Shape politics:	• Mobile • E-mail	• Face-to-face lobby efforts

involvement of formal political actors has most probably been more important to the success of a direct action or for the introduction of innovative 'alternative' discourses in society than the Internet as such.

Clever communication strategies certainly contributed to the success of this action, but the determination of the activists, the sustained actions and lobby-efforts, as well as their ability to generate support amongst the population and the press for their cause and strategy was at least equally important. In this regard, the Lappersfort case shows how a direct action, persistently organized by radical activists, can nevertheless be very present in the dominant public sphere and influence the political agenda by tapping into transnational strategies and struggles, in this case forest preservation as well as the anti-globalization movement, while at the same time ensuring that they have a local base and support for their direct action.

Finally, this case shows that contrary to the observations of Gitlin (1980) in the 1970s, fragmented oppositional movements composed of groups and organizations with distinct political ideologies and strategies are able to converge much easier at a given moment in time to foster common aims, whereby the

Internet is increasingly becoming a lubricating infrastructure to enable that. As such, the Lappersfort case can also be deconstructed as the multitude in action. It illustrates the mutual hybrid interpenetrations between non-institutional and institutional politics, exposing the complex relationships between the molecular and molar, to use the metaphors of Deleuze and Guatari. In this regard, the state cannot be constructed as a singular actor, but nor can civil society. The labor movement was very reluctant to support the action and parts of the state resisted, while other parts supported the activists. Intersecting this are economic interests and the political debate on how as a society we reconcile economic interests with social and ecological concerns. It is very much democracy at work with media in a supporting and facilitating role.

Notes for Chapter Twelve

[1] The author would like to thank Luc Vanneste and others of the Green Belt Front (Groene Gordel Front) who gave valuable feedback to drafts of this chapter, thereby also increasing the validity of the analysis.

[2] Nevertheless the point that NIMBY-activism is more complex than often thought, raised by Auli Harju in this book, is well taken.

[3] http://www.nova-cinema.com/main.php?page=archives/2001/52/08radiobxxl. en.htm (consulted 1 March 2006). The radios involved were Radio Air Libre, Radio Panik, FM Brussel, and Radio Campus.

[4] http://www.earthfirst.org/.

[5] http://www.lappersfront.tk (not online anymore). Also the external communication of the activists was fairly quickly taken over by the site of the Green Belt Front (Groene Gordel Front – http://www.ggf.be), as well as by using Indymedia to communicate with sympathizers in Belgium and beyond.

[6] http://www.indymedia.nl/nl/2002/09/6262.shtml or http://indymedia.org.uk/en/ 2002/10/44817.html.

[7] For an overview in English, go to http://www.indymedia.be/news/2002/10/ 36569.php. The fact that some effort was put in translating contributions in English is also relevant in itself, in view of transnationalizing this specific struggle and to reach out to a wider (global) constituency of likeminded activists.

[8] Quoted in *Het Nieuwsblad – regio Brugge*, 22 May 2004, translation by the author.

References for Chapter Twelve

Anonymous, (2003), 'Down with the Empire! Up with the Spring!' *Do or Die*, 10, pp. 1–101. http://www.eco-action.org/dod/no10/empire.htm. Consulted on 1 March 2006.

Beck, U. (1994), 'The Reinvention of Politics: Towards a Theory of Reflexive Modernization', in U. Beck, A. Giddens, and S. Lash (eds.), *Reflexive Modernization: Politics, Tradition and Aesthetics in the Modern Social Order*, Cambridge: Polity Press, pp. 1–55.

Bennett, W. L (1998), 'The Uncivic Culture: Communication, Identity and the Rise of Lifestyle Politics', *Political Science & Politics*, 31: 4, pp. 741–61.

Bennett, W. L., Entman, R. M. (eds.) (2001), *Mediated Politics: Communication in the Future of Democracy*, Cambridge: Cambridge University Press.

Cabinet of the Flemish Minister for the Environment (2002), 'Lappersfortbos: Absoluut Fout Signaal Volgens Dua', *Press Release*, 14 October 2002.

Calhoun, C. (ed.) (1994), *Social Theory and the Politics of Identity*, Oxford: Blackwell.

Cammaerts, B. (2005), 'ICT-Usage Among Transnational Social Movements in the Networked Society – to Organise, to Mobilise and to Debate', in R. Silverstone (ed.), *Media, Technology and Everyday Life in Europe: From Information to Communication*, Aldershot: Ashgate, pp. 53–72.

Cruikshank, M. (1992), *The Gay and Lesbian Liberation Movement*, New York: Routledge.

Dahlberg, L. (2001), 'The Internet and Democratic Discourse: Exploring the Prospects of Online Deliberative Forums Extending the Public Sphere', *Information, Communication & Society*, 4: 4, pp. 613–33.

Dahlgren, P. (2005), 'The Internet, Public Spheres, and Political Communication: Dispersion and Deliberation', *Political Communication*, 22: 2, pp. 147–62.

Deleuze, G., Guattari, F. (1987), *A Thousand Plateaux. Capitalism and Schizophrenia*, Minneapolis: University of Minnesota Press.

Della Porta, D. (1988), 'Recruitment Processes in Clandestine Political Organisations. Italian Leftwing Terrorism', in S. Tarrow, B. Klandermans, and H. Kriesi (eds.), *From Structure to Action*, New York: JAI Press, pp. 155–69.

Della Porta, D., Diani, M. (1999), *Social Movements: An Introduction*, Oxford: Blackwell.

Della Porta, D., Kriesi, H., Rucht, D. (eds.) (1999), *Social Movements in a Globalising World*, London: MacMillan.

Diani, M. (2001), 'Social Movement Networks: Virtual and Real', in F. Webster (ed.), *Culture and Politics in the Information Age: A New Politics?* London: Routledge, pp. 117–28.

Downing, J. (2001), *Radical Media: Rebellious Communication and Social Movements*, Thousand Oaks, CA.: Sage Publications.

du Preez, P. (1980), *The Politics of Identity*, New York: St. Martin's Press.

Feher, F., Heller, A. (1983), 'From Red to Green', *Telos*, 59, pp. 34–44.

Florini, A. M. (ed.) (2000), *The Third Force: The Rise of Transnational Civil Society*, Washington: Carnegie Endowment for International Peace.

Fraser, N. (1996), 'Social Justice in the Age of Identity Politics: Redistribution, Recognition, and Participation', Tanner Lectures on Human Values, Delivered at Stanford University, 30 April–2 May. http://www.tannerlectures.utah.edu/lectures/Fraser98.pdf. Consulted on 1 March 2006.

Freeman, J. (1984), 'The Women's Liberation Movement: Its Origins, Structure, Activities, and Ideas', in J. Freeman (ed.), *Women: A Feminist Perspective*, Palo Alto, CA: Mayfield, pp. 543–56.

Galston, W. A. (2003), 'If Political Fragmentation is the Problem, is the Internet the Solution?' in D. M. Anderson and M. Cornfield (eds.), *The Civic Web: Online Politics and Democratic Values*, Lanham, MD: Rowman & Littlefield, pp. 35–44.

Gamson, W. A. (1990), *The Strategy of Social Protest*, (2nd ed.), Belmont, CA: Wadsworth.

Gamson, W. A., Wolfsfeld, G. (1993), 'Movements and Media as Interacting Systems', *Annals of the American Academy of Political and Social Movements*, 526, pp. 114–27.

Gibson, R. K., Römmele, A., Ward, S. (eds.) (2003), *Electronic Democracy: Mobilization, Organisation, and Participation Via New ICTs*, London: Routledge.

Giddens, A. (1991), *Modernity and Self-identity. Self and Society in the Late Modern Age*, Cambridge: Polity Press.

Gitlin, T. (1980), *The Whole World is Watching: Mass Media in the Making and Unmaking of the New Left*, Berkeley, CA: California University Press.

—— (1995), *The Twilight of Common Dreams: Why America Is Wracked by Culture War*, New York: Metropolitan Books.

—— (1998), 'Public Spheres or Public Sphericules', in T. Liebes and J. Curran (eds.), *Media, Ritual and Identity*, London: Routledge, pp. 168–74.

Granovetter, M. (1982), 'The strength of Weak Ties: A Network Theory Revisited', in P. V. Marsden and N. Lin (eds.), *Social Structure and Network Analysis*, Beverly Hills: Sage, pp. 105–30.

Hardt, M., Negri, A. (2004), *Multitude: War and Democracy in the Age of Empire*, New York: Penguin Press.

Haythornthwaite, C. (2005), 'Social Networks and Internet Connectivity Effects', *Information, Communication & Society*, 8: 2, pp. 125–47.

Held, D., McGrew, A. (2002), *Globalisation and Anti-Globalisation*, London: Polity Press.

Hill, K. A., Hughes, J. E. (1998), *Cyberpolitics: Citizen Activism in the Age of the Internet*, Lanham, MD: Rowman & Littlefield.

Indymedia, (2002a), 'Lappersfort: Honderden Betogers in en om Brugge' [Hundreds of Protesters in and Around Bruges], 16 October, http://www.indymedia.be/news/2002/10/34152.php. Consulted on 1 March 2006.

—— (2002b), 'Betoging Behoud Brugs Lappersfortbos' (Demonstration to Save the Lappersfort Forests in Bruges), 20 October, http://www.indymedia.be/news/2002/10/35188.php. Consulted on 1 March 2006.

—— (2002c), 'Lappersfort-Urgent-Know Your Enemy!', 13 September, http://www.indymedia.be/news/2002/09/31238.php. Consulted on 1 March 2006.

—— (2002d), 'Picture Report Occupation Fabricom Gent', 15 November, http://www.indymedia.be/news/2002/11/38765.php. Consulted on 1 March 2006.

—— (2002e), 'Lappersfort: Electronic Defense', 16 September, http://www.indymedia.be/news/2002/09/31422.php. Consulted on 1 March 2006.

—— (2002f), 'Alternatief Ontruimingsplan: Gefaseerde en Vrijwillige Opkuis Lappersfort' (Alternative Disengagement Plan: Fased and Voluntary clean-up), 13 September, http://www.indymedia.be/news/2002/09/31187.php. Consulted on 1 March 2006.

—— (2002g), Lappersfort: Dringende Mobilisatie (Urgent Mobilization), 18 September, http://www.indymedia.be/news/2002/09/31568.php. Consulted on 1 March 2006.

—— (2002h), Betoging Voor Lappersfort: Els, Moeder Van Drie Kinderen (Demostration for Lappersfort: Els, Mother of Three Children), 20 October, http://indymedia.all2all.org/news /2002/10/35156.php. Consulted on 1 March 2006.

Kavanaugh, A. L., Reese, D. D., Caroll, J. M., *et al.* (2005), 'Weak Ties in Networked Communities', *Information Society*, 21, pp. 119–31.

Lee, M. A., Solomon, N. (1990), *Unreliable Sources: A Guide to Detecting Bias in News Media*, New York: Carol Publishing Group.

McAdam, D. (1999), *Political Process and the Development of Black Insurgency, 1930–1970*, (2nd ed.), Chicago, IL: Chicago University Press.

—— (2005), 'Movement Strategy and Dramaturgical Framing in Democratic States: The Case of the Civil Rights Movement', in S. Chambers and A. Costain (eds.), *Deliberation, Democracy and the Media*, Lanham, MD: Rowman & Littlefield, pp. 117–35.

McCaughey, M., Ayers, M. D. (eds.) (2003), *Cyberactivism: Online Activism in Theory and Practice*, New York: Routledge.

Meikle, G. (2002), *Future Active: Media Activism and the Internet*, New York: Routledge.

Melucci, A. (1981), 'Ten Hypotheses for the Analysis of New Social Movements', in D. Pinto (ed.), *Contemporary Italian Sociology*, Cambridge: Cambridge University Press, pp. 173–94.

Mouffe, C. (1999), 'Deliberative Democracy or Agonistic Pluralism?', *Social Research*, 66: 3, pp. 746–58.

Negri, A. (1999), *Insurgencies: Constituent Power and the Modern State*, Minneapolis: University of Minnesota Press.

—— (2002), 'Pour une Definition Ontologique de la Multitude', *Multitudes*, English Translation by Arianna Bove, 9, pp.36–48, http://multitudes. samizdat.net/article.php3?id_article=269. Consulted on 1 March 206.

Offe, C. (1987), 'Challenging the Boundaries of Institutional Politics. Social Movements Since the 1960s', in C. S. Maier (ed.), *Changing Boundaries of the Political. Essays on the Evolving Balance Between the State and Society, Public and Private in Europe*, Cambridge: Cambridge University Press, pp. 63–105.

Putnam, R. D. (1995), 'Bowling Alone: America's Declining Social Capital', *Journal of Democracy*, 6: 1, pp. 65–78.

—— (2000), *Bowling Alone: The Collapse and Revival of American Community*, New York: Simon and Schuster.

Rucht, D. (2004), 'The Quadruple "A": Media Strategies of Protest Movements Since the 1960s', in W. van de Donk, B. D. Loader, P. G. Nixon, *et al.* (eds.), *Cyberprotest: New Media, Citizens and Social Movements*, London: Routledge, pp. 29–56.

Rushkoff, D. (1996), *Media Virus! Hidden Agendas in Popular Culture*, New York: Ballantine Books.

Silverstone, R. (2005), 'The Sociology of Mediation and Communication', in C. Calhoun, C. Rojek, and B. S. Turner (eds.), *The SAGE Handbook of Sociology*, London: Sage, pp. 188–207. http://www.lse.ac.uk/collections/media@lse/pdf/ mediation.pdf. Consulted on 1 March 2006.

Tarrow, S. (2001), 'Transnational Politics: Contention and Institutions in International Politics', *Annual Review of Political Science*, 4, pp. 1–20.

—— (2005), *The New Transnational Activism*, Cambridge: Cambridge University Press.

Taylor, C. (1994), 'The Politics of Recognition', in C. Taylor and A. Guttman (eds.), *Multiculturalism*, Princeton, NJ: Princeton University Press, pp. 25–74.

Turner, W. B. (2001), *A Genealogy of Queer Theory,* Philadelphia, PA: Temple University Press.

Urry, J. (1999), 'Globalisation and Citizenship', *Journal of World-Systems Research*, 5: 2, pp. 311–24.

Van Aelst, P., Walgrave, S. (2002), 'New Media, New Movements: The Role of the Internet in Shaping the "Anti-Globalisation Movement"', *Information, Communication & Society*, 5: 4, pp. 465–93.

Van Audenhove, L., Cammaerts, B., Frissen, V., *et al.* (2002), 'Transnational Civil Society in the Networked Society: A study on the Relation Between ICTs and the Rise of a Transnational Civil Society'. *Study in the Framework of TERRA 2000, EU Project Under IST 2000*. Maastricht: Institute of Infonomics, http://www.ecdc.nl/publications/reports/terra_eindrapport.pdf. Consulted on 1 March 2006.

van de Donk, W., Loader, B. D., Nixon, P., Rucht, D. (eds.) (2004), *Cyberprotest: New Media, Citizens, and Social Movements*, London: Routledge.

Webster, F. (ed.) (2001), *Culture and Politics in the Information Age: A New Politics?*, London: Routledge.

Notes on the Contributors

Margit Böck (Margit.Boeck@sbg.ac.at) is lecturer at the Fachbereich Kommunikationswissenschaft, at the University of Salzburg. She has conducted large-scale studies of reading habits and media-use in Austria. In her recent research, she has increasingly focused on questions of social inequality in the context of the digital media and changes in communication, and their likely effects on individuals, groups, and society. Her recent publications include *Gender und Lesen*, Wien: BMBWK (forthcoming); 'Life worlds and information habitus', *Visual Communication,* 3: 1, pp. 281–293; 'Information, Wissen und medialer Wandel', *Medien Journal,* 27: 1, pp. 51–65.

Bart Cammaerts (B.Cammaerts@lse.ac.uk) is a political scientist and media researcher lecturing on media, citizenship, and democracy at the Media and Communication Department of the London School of Economics and Political Science (LSE), University of London. His research interests include the impact of the Internet on the transnationalization of civil society actors, on direct action, activism, and interactive civic engagement, as well as the use of the Internet by international organizations (UN and EU) in order to involve civil society actors in their decision-making processes and its effects on the ground in terms of networking and attempts to democratize global or regional governance processes. He publishes widely and chairs the Communication and Democracy section of ECREA.

Nico Carpentier (Nico.Carpentier@vub.ac.be) is a media sociologist working at the Communication Studies Departments of the Free University of Brussels (VUB) and the Catholic University of Brussels (KUB). He is co-director of the VUB research Centre for Studies on Media and Culture (CEMESO). His theoretical focus is on discourse theory, his research interests are situated in (media)domains as sexuality, war, and conflict, journalism, (political and cultural) participation, and democracy. In 2004, he co-edited the book *The Ungraspable Audience* and wrote together with Benoît Grevisse *Des Médias qui font Bouger.* In 2005, he co-edited the book *Towards a Sustainable Information Society. Deconstructing WSIS.* Since 2004, he is a member of the Executive Board of the ECCR, now ECREA.

Peter Dahlgren (Peter.Dahlgren@soc.lu.se) is professor of media and communication at Lund University, Sweden. He received his doctorate at City University of New York, and has taught at Fordham University, Queens College, and Stockholm University. He has also been visiting scholar at l'Université de Paris II, Rhodes University, University of Stirling and l'Université de Québec à

Montréal. His research focuses on democracy, the evolution of the media, and contemporary socio-cultural processes. Most recently he is looking at how young citizens make use of new communication technologies for democratic engagement and identity work. His forthcoming book is *Media and Civic Engagement*, from Cambridge University Press.

Natalie Fenton (N.fenton@gold.ac.uk) is a senior lecturer in the Department of Media and Communications, Goldsmiths College, University of London. She has published widely on topics such as the popular presentation of public issues, the voluntary sector and the media, feminist media theory, and alternative media. Her research examines the relationship between the media and resistance – either as a dominant social force which through uniformity of representation encourages digression, or as a means of forging other identities and developing alternative political projects. Her work spans both cultural studies approaches and social scientific approaches to the study of media, culture, and society. Her publications include *Mediating Social Science* (with Alan Bryman, David Deacon, and Peter Birmingham) (Sage, 1998), *Trust and Civil Society* (with Fran Tonkiss, Andrew Passey, and Les Hems) (Macmillan, 2000).

Auli Harju (auli.harju@uta.fi) is a Ph.D. student in Department of Journalism and Mass Communication, University of Tampere, Finland. She studies local cases of civic action and public discussions on the issues that instigated these civic actions. In her research specific attention is paid to the ways local journalism represents citizens and their point of view towards local issues.

Arne Hintz (arne.hintz@uni-hamburg.de) is a media researcher/activist based at the Research Centre Media and Politics at the University of Hamburg. He studied economics, political science, and international political economy at the Universities of Hamburg, Germany, and Warwick, United Kingdom. His main research interests are the political economy of the media, the theory and practice of community/alternative/activist media, social movements, and participatory approaches to global governance. As a media activist, he has worked with Indymedia, community radio, communication-related campaigns, such as the CRIS campaign, and he was thus an active participant in civil society action platforms within and outside the World Summit on the Information Society (WSIS).

Anu Kantola (anu.kantola@helsinki.fi) is a senior lecturer in mass communication at the Department of Communication in the University of Helsinki. Her research interests have been on political communication, journalism, and globalization. Currently, she is a research fellow in the Finnish Academy of Sciences on a project on the transformation of political imaginaries under the market regime.

Kari Karppinen (kari.karppinen@helsinki.fi) is currently a doctoral candidate and a researcher at the Department of Communication at the University of Helsinki. His research interests include theories of the public sphere, media and democracy, and media policy, and his prospective doctoral dissertation deals with freedom and pluralism as contested concepts in European media policy debates. He is currently participating in two research projects funded by the Academy of Finland, European Public Sphere(s), Uniting and Dividing; and Social and Juridical Constituents of Communication Law.

Giorgia Nesti (giorgia.nesti@unipd.it) holds a Ph.D. in European and comparative politics and is researcher in political science at the Department of Historical and Political Studies at the University of Padova, Italy. Her research interests focus on European policies for telecommunication and information society, Europeanization and public administration.

Hannu Niemienen (hannie@utu.fi) is professor of communication at the University of Turku, Finland. He received his Ph.D. in 1996 in the University of Westminster, London. In 2003–2005, he worked as the director of the Communication Research Centre, University of Helsinki. His research interests include media and democracy and theories of public sphere, on which themes he has published several books and articles. Currently he is leading the research project European Public Sphere(s), Uniting and Dividing (2005–2007), funded by the Academy of Finland. His publications include *Democracy and Communication: Habermas, Williams, and the British Case* (1997), *Hegemony and the Public Sphere* (2000), and *People Stood Apart: the Constitution of the National Public Sphere in Finland 1809–1917* (2006, in Finnish).

Claudia Padovani (claupad@libero.it) is researcher of political science and international relations at the Department of Historical and Political Studies at the University of Padova, Italy. She teaches international communication and institutions and governance of communication, while conducting research in the fields of the global and European governance of the information and knowledge society. She is particularly interested in the role of civil society organizations and transnational social movements as stakeholders in global decision-making processes. From this perspective, she has followed closely the WSIS process and has written extensively on the experience. She is a member of the International Association for Media and Communication Research (IAMCR) and international campaign Communication Rights in the Information Society (CRIS).

Egil G. Skogseth (egil.skogseth@infomedia.uib.no) is media researcher at the Department of Information Science and Media Studies of the University of Bergen and the Institute for Educational Research of the University of Oslo. He is interested in research areas such as social movements, new (digital) media, the network society, democracy, the public sphere, and journalism.

Arjuna Tuzzi (arjuna.tuzzi@unipd.it) is associated professor of statistics for the social sciences at the Department of Sociology (University of Padova, Italy). She has a Ph.D. in applied statistics for economics and social sciences and teaches methods for the social research and statistics for the social sciences. Her main research interests concern content analysis and statistical analysis of texts; closed-ended questionnaires, open-ended interviews, and the problem in comparing different stimuli-answers data collecting tools; statistical methods in evaluation; electoral data analysis and Italian electoral abstensionism; multimedia, long-life learning and on-line education.

Tamara Witschge (T.A.C.Witschge@uva.nl) is currently finalizing her Ph.D. thesis at the Amsterdam School of Communications Research, University of Amsterdam. Her research focuses on online discussions of contested issues. By studying the online discourse on the issue of immigration in the Netherlands, she aims to gain insight into the process of online discussions, specifically regarding the openness of the debates towards alternative discourses. She teaches at the Department of Communication Science and the International School of Humanities and Social Sciences at the University of Amsterdam.